CITY ON A HILL

CITY
ON A HILL

A History of American Exceptionalism

ABRAM C. VAN ENGEN

Yale

UNIVERSITY PRESS

New Haven and London

Published with assistance from the foundation established in memory of James Wesley Cooper of the Class of 1865, Yale College, and from the Ronald and Betty Miller Turner Publication Fund.

Yale University Press books may be purchased in quantity for educational, business, or promotional use. For information, please e-mail sales.press@yale.edu (U.S. office) or sales@yaleup.co.uk (U.K. office).

Set in Janson type by IDS Infotech Ltd., Chandigarh, India.
Printed in the United States of America.

Library of Congress Control Number: 2019945887
ISBN 978-0-300-22975-2 (hardcover : alk. paper)

A catalogue record for this book is available from the British Library.

This paper meets the requirements of ANSI/NISO Z39.48-1992 (Permanence of Paper).

10 9 8 7 6 5 4 3 2 1

For Simon and Grace,
who have lived almost the whole of their lives with the
making of this book,

and for Hendrik,
just born, who can live life free of it.

You have blessed me more than you could ever know,
or I could ever tell.

Contents

Note on the Text

Early modern spelling and grammar have been modernized throughout the book.

Introduction

The Birth of a Story

W HAT IS THE ORIGIN of America?
Pose that question to over two thousand people and a wide variety of answers will arise. Most
focus on the founding era of the United States:
the Declaration of Independence, the American Revolution, and
the Constitution. Others turn to the colonial days, observing that
"America" existed long before the nation. Some answers dwell on
the originating presence of Native Americans—the first people on
the soil of the Americas. Others focus more on the arrival of Europeans. Amerigo Vespucci gets mentioned. The coming of Columbus. Jamestown, Captain Smith, Pocahontas. So many possible
answers, so many different times and places to begin. And always,
in the midst of these responses, one answer will emerge among the
rest: Pilgrim Landing, Plymouth Rock, and the Puritans.[1]

The question of American origins, of course, has no real answer. People can argue for their particular choices, but such debates tell us much more about how they view America today than
how "America" actually began. In that sense, historical origin stories function primarily as present-day descriptions. Each answer
defines what a person *means* by America. Beginning with Native
Americans, for example, suggests a story of chronological priority
untethered to modern political boundaries: "America" is all the

territory from the Bering Strait to the bottom of Argentina, including all the people who have ever lived and moved and had their being here. It is a long story, a tale teeming with diversity. Rather than beginning something new, Europeans stumbled onto well-established nations and civilizations, disrupting cultures and forms of life, adding to the mix, changing and reshaping an "America" that existed long before them.

Answers that emphasize the Revolutionary era, meanwhile, define America much more narrowly. They focus on one particular nation that came into being at one particular time. Even here, however, the distinctions can be quite telling. Does "America" start with a fundamental statement of principles (the Declaration of Independence), a bloody war (the American Revolution), or the eventual establishment of a mostly stable government (the Constitution)? No doubt, most people see these answers as related, but the specific responses embed quite different accounts of what makes America *America* after all.

When respondents point to Jamestown, a separate element enters the picture. Jamestown is the first permanent English settlement in what would later become the United States. As a result, it defines "America" as a nation that blossoms forth from English roots. Jamestown outweighs and overshadows all other potential nationalities, ethnicities, races, immigrants, and colonial experiments, along with all their consequences and contributions. Very few ever know that the Spanish established St. Augustine in Florida in 1565, more than four decades before the English came to Jamestown. More broadly, the Spanish had been living in the Americas for a full century before the English and had already pushed into Florida and the territory of what is now New Mexico. The French also arrived earlier than the English, beginning explorations in the sixteenth century and establishing Quebec in 1608, then encroaching into what is now the Midwest and down the Mississippi. Around the same time, the Dutch headed up the Hudson. And in 1619 another Dutch ship brought enslaved Africans to Virginia. As often as I ask the question, however, no one ever mentions Spanish, French, Dutch, African, or any other national, ethnic, or racial roots.

And then, of course, there are the Pilgrims. On the face of it, their appearance as an origin makes no sense. They were not the first people here, nor the first Europeans here, nor the first English here, nor did they establish a new and separate nation. What possible claim can they have to beginning the story of America? Here, the answer focuses specifically on ideas and beliefs. Pilgrims surface as an origin because, we are told, they were the first ones—the *only* ones—who came in search of something better, something nobler, something *different*. They sailed for civil and religious liberty. They came to worship God. They established democracy on distant shores. However one defines it, the Pilgrims arrived with a *principle*, and that principle, we are led to believe, is what has defined "America" ever since. If origin stories are present-day definitions cast back onto history, then the Pilgrims and Puritans have historically enabled Americans to define their nation not as the outcome of events but as the fruition of exceptional ideals.

For many years now, this story of America has been supported by one particular, powerful phrase: the declaration that we are a "city on a hill." When scholars and politicians first began calling the United States a "city on a hill," they pointed to the place of these words in a Puritan sermon, *A Model of Christian Charity*, preached in 1630 by John Winthrop, the first governor of Massachusetts Bay, just before he and his followers arrived. In that moment, in that sermon (we have been told), Winthrop opened the story of America. He called on us to serve as a beacon of liberty, chosen by God to spread the benefits of self-government, toleration, and free enterprise to the entire watching world. Invoking the Sermon on the Mount, in which Jesus uses the metaphor to describe his followers (Matthew 5:14), Winthrop declared to his fellow Puritans, "For we must consider that we shall be as a city upon a hill. The eyes of all people are upon us." Ignoring the scriptural basis for this proclamation, President Ronald Reagan explained in his "Farewell Address to the Nation" (1989) that "the phrase comes from John Winthrop, who wrote it to describe the America he imagined. What he imagined was important because he was an early Pilgrim, an early freedom man."[2] The significance of Winthrop's statement, in other words, has everything to do with its *timing*—with the "fact" that Winthrop made this statement at the very beginning of America, defining its identity and purpose ever since.

Because Winthrop's sermon has so often been said to open the story of America, pundits, politicians, commentators, and scholars have often found that they cannot avoid it. *A Model of Christian Charity* has become fundamental to the meaning of America. The significance of Winthrop's sermon has been bolstered by republishing it in anthologies, teaching it in classrooms, and pronouncing it from lecterns and pulpits. Beginning in the 1970s, for example, *A Model of Christian Charity* opened the influential *Norton Anthology of American Literature* as the foundational statement of American literary history. In 1989, when David Hollinger and Charles Capper put together a sourcebook on the American intellectual tradition, they started with Winthrop's sermon. Textbooks, anthologies, syllabi, speeches, blogs, articles—the examples go on and on. *A Model of Christian Charity* has become so central to American traditions that one scholar has pronounced it the "Ur-text of American literature," another has declared it the "cultural key text" of the nation, and still another called it "the best sermon of the millennium."[3]

Yet Winthrop's sermon came to fame only recently. It is, in many respects, a product of the Cold War. In the 1950s, a widespread and worried search for the meaning of America turned increasingly to *A Model of Christian Charity* as the answer, the *origin*, that could best define the ideals and principles America has always stood for. Definitions of the nation loop back onto origins. New accounts of the nation's exceptional character require new narratives of the nation's exceptional beginnings. And in the middle of the twentieth century, in the process of one such redefinition, Winthrop's sermon came to serve as a starting point for the new true meaning of America—the origin of American exceptionalism. Before the Cold War began, no politician and hardly any scholar had ever bothered with it at all.

Not only did most scholars and politicians ignore Winthrop's text, but so did the Puritans themselves. Someone should have told them they were listening to "the best sermon of the millennium": maybe then they would have listened. As it stands, hardly anyone in the seventeenth century gave Winthrop's sermon a second thought. It was never printed or published in either England or America. No one noted in a diary the day Winthrop delivered *A Model of Christian Charity*. Even Winthrop, who kept a diary from the day he left England, never mentions having given it. Perhaps the settlers had other concerns. Maybe it failed to strike a chord. Perhaps the sermon seemed too commonplace. Maybe it was never delivered at all. Whatever the reason, it seems clear that the existence of *A Model of Christian Charity* in the seventeenth century went almost completely unknown. In one letter, written in the 1640s, one man requests a copy of "the Model of Charity."[4] That man seemed to know about Winthrop's sermon, but he was in rather slim company. From the writing of this letter in the 1640s until the printing of Winthrop's sermon in 1838—for almost two hundred years, through all the histories of Puritanism that were written and all the biographies of Winthrop that appeared—no one ever mentions *A Model of Christian Charity* again. The supposed foundation of the nation, the document fundamental to the meaning of America, the best sermon of the millennium, and the cultural key text of American society was nothing special in its day.

What is more, it did not suddenly become a foundational document when it finally appeared. Perhaps even more surprising than the lack of attention paid to Winthrop's sermon in the seventeenth century is the repeated neglect of it in the nineteenth. Published and proclaimed a "prophetic vision" of America in 1838, *A Model of Christian Charity* once again disappeared. Through the rest of the nineteenth century, hardly any soul managed to care that John Winthrop—on the eve of his arrival in America—had proclaimed that "we shall be as a city upon a hill."

I am not the first to notice this ringing silence. The historian Richard Gamble, in his own account of this sermon, remarks on the surprising absence of *Christian Charity* in nineteenth-century culture. So, too, does the historian Daniel T. Rodgers. Both demonstrate that in the usual places where one might expect to find Winthrop's *Model of Christian Charity* no mention can be found. In the first two decades after it was published, for example, Winthrop's sermon never graced the pages of the nineteenth century's most important and influential account of America, George Bancroft's *History of the United States*. When Bancroft did finally include a section of this sermon, he failed to cite his source. Explaining that the Puritans knew "they would be as a city set upon a hill, and that the eyes of all people were upon them," Bancroft alerted no reader to where such words could be found. But even in this use, Bancroft did more than his peers. Most never bothered to quote *any* part of Winthrop's text, and when a few did turn to *A Model of Christian Charity*, they seemed to think that other lines—not the proclamation "that we shall be as a city upon a hill"—mattered more.[5]

We can track the lack of attention paid to Winthrop's "city on a hill" sermon through multiple methods. First, like Gamble and Rodgers, we can simply search for it in the major anthologies, histories, textbooks, and materials most commonly used for the teaching of American history and literature. American literary history, for example, saw virtually no use for this sermon until 1979. From 1838 to 1938, its utter absence from the major sources gives us a solid glimpse of the sermon's total neglect. To be sure, it does appear briefly now and then in a rare collection. Yet even when the sermon shows up, it never gets touted as the origin of America. Mentioning it in *American Literature: 1607–1885* (1910), for example, Charles F. Richardson explains that the treatise "need not long detain the literary student. It was one of the many religious tracts produced during the Puritan revival in England and America, and it surpassed some of its fellows in spirit and execution."[6]

Beyond a nominal list of anthologies and editions, however, digital methods allow us to see something even more significant. It was not just *A Model of Christian Charity* that went missing from the nineteenth and early twentieth centuries; it was also the phrase "city on a hill"—at least insofar as that line applied to America. The magnitude of the Google Books collection, with its millions of scanned items, offers a good way to glimpse how frequently the most famous phrase of Winthrop's sermon occurs from 1800 to the present day. With the Humanities Digital Workshop at Washington University in St. Louis, I worked with graduate and undergraduate students over the past six years to search, read, tag, categorize, and graph every finding of "city on a hill," "city upon a hill," "city set on a hill," and "city set upon a hill" that appears.[7]

What we found was rather startling (see figure 1). First, *A Model of Christian Charity*—at least as it came to be summarized by the phrase "city on a hill"—did not become canonical until the 1960s. If the sermon appeared before that time, its proclamation that "we shall be as a city on a hill" did not matter and was not

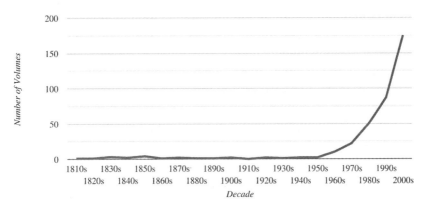

Figure 1: Volumes referring to the United States or America as a "city on a hill" or a variant of the phrase, by decade. Courtesy Humanities Digital Workshop, Washington University in St. Louis.

cited. But just as importantly, the phrase "city on a hill" had almost no relation to the United States until after World War II. The concept of "American exceptionalism"—the idea that the United States has a unique history giving it a distinctive identity and purpose in the world—does not in itself depend on the phrase "city on a hill." American exceptionalism can express itself through any number of words and terms, as we shall see. But the fact that this ideology adopted the phrase "city on a hill" in the 1960s raises an important question about what those four simple words did for Americans during the Cold War era. Why did the phrase "city on a hill" become so popular in the 1960s and 1970s? Why has its usage continued to expand? What idea does this phrase capture in a way that no other expression had captured before? Most importantly, how did the emerging rhetoric of America as a "city on a hill" *change* the meaning of America, even as it offered yet another, new way to express the ideology of American exceptionalism?

The answer to that last question has everything to do with origin stories, for that is how the phrase "city on a hill" entered American politics. "City on a hill" became a shorthand way to assert what America means based in how America *began*. All by themselves, these four words told a whole story of the nation, offering a continuous history of unfolding principles and purpose from John

Winthrop's first sermon before his arrival in New England to Ronald Reagan's "Farewell Address" on the eve of his exit from office—as though America was founded as a "city on a hill" and has been so ever since. And yet the story of the sermon itself—the history of the manuscript, its meaning, and its eventual rise to fame—differs radically from the tale it promotes. For the "city on a hill" line and the text from which it emerges have appeared only recently on the American scene.

We can begin to see how this phrase changes the meaning of America by examining what these words indicated *before* they became a national slogan. Though "America" was rarely called a city on a hill, plenty of people still used such language before the twentieth century. Because it comes from Jesus's Sermon on the Mount, "city on a hill" remained most relevant to Christians within their various religious organizations. Throughout the nineteenth century and into the twentieth, the phrase "city on a hill" primarily described disciples, apostles, churches, preachers, Christians, missionaries, and so forth. Only in the past few decades have political referents for the phrase (cities, countries, states, and elected officials) begun to take precedence. In other words, for most of American history, when people heard the words "city on a hill," they were discussing discipleship, not citizenship. It took the cultural work of scholars and politicians, dedicated to diverse projects over many years, to turn a phrase of the church into the definition of a nation.

Much of that cultural work was carried out by a host of relatively unknown figures, many of whom played an unrecognized role in shaping our modern political rhetoric. It was not just Daniel Webster, a powerful politician and orator, who nationalized Pilgrims as the origin of America, or George Bancroft, the influential historian, who published the nineteenth century's best-selling history of America. The dominant story of the nation, as it developed, also relied on the sudden boom and spread of textbooks in the 1820s and 1830s, most of which were written by far less famous authors, such as Emma Willard. And it wasn't just politicians, historians, and textbook writers who created the conditions for an eventual celebration of Winthrop's sermon. The text itself could only become famous after it was found, and it could be found only because a portly Boston minister named Jeremy Belknap, a Pennsylvania postal worker named Ebenezer Hazard, and a New York merchant named John Pintard started a system of historical societies to collect, preserve, and pass on the nation's texts. The first introduction, edition, and publication of Winthrop's sermon, meanwhile, came from the pen of the antiquarian James Savage—another person and another culture (antiquarianism) that have been almost completely forgotten. When John F. Kennedy, Ronald Reagan, Michael Dukakis, Bill Clinton, Barack Obama, Mitt Romney, Elizabeth Warren, and countless others cite Winthrop's sermon and use it to explain what America means, they depend on the work of these largely unknown figures from America's past—people who quietly built historical societies, published textbooks, preserved documents, copied manuscripts, printed collections, and pursued their research in time stolen from work and often at considerable private expense, creating the conditions in which American history would be studied, written, and eventually proclaimed.

In many ways, the story created and communicated about the Pilgrims and Puritans culminated in the career of Ronald Reagan. And the role of Winthrop's sermon in his political rhetoric was best captured in his last speech, that "Farewell Address to the Nation" on January 11, 1989. Coming before Americans one final time, the "Great Communicator" told his loyal followers that it was time for him to go. But before he left, Reagan wanted to clarify one thing: "I've spoken of the shining city all my political life," he explained, "but I don't know if I ever quite communicated what I saw when I said it." For one last time, now with added detail and a nostalgic touch, Reagan sketched his image of "a tall, proud city" rising from the Puritan past, then signed off and said good-bye.[8]

That last farewell of Ronald Reagan, that final speech of his career, encapsulated so many of the ideas that lie behind the full story of Winthrop's sermon and its rise in American history. Reagan opened his address with "a small story about a big ship, and a refugee, and a sailor." This was not the story of Winthrop in the 1630s; it was a tale, instead, of a South Asian migrant in the 1980s. When an American serviceman saw "a leaky little boat" in the South China Sea, he responded by sending aid. "As the refugees made their way through the choppy seas," Reagan continued, "one spied the sailor on deck, and stood up, and called out to him. He yelled, 'Hello, American sailor. Hello freedom man.'" This was, in other words, the *modern* story—the image from the 1980s—that Reagan would use to tie America all the way back to its *beginning*. He closed his speech by returning to John Winthrop, "an early Pilgrim, an early freedom man." Like the later refugee in the South China Sea, Winthrop "journeyed here on what today we'd call a little wooden boat" in search of "a home that would be free." From America's origin all the way through to its present day, Reagan was proclaiming, America has always been the land of liberty—"a magnet for all who must have freedom, for all the pilgrims from all the lost places who are hurtling through the darkness, toward home."[9]

In turning back to Winthrop, moreover, Reagan insisted that all Americans do the same—that we turn to the past and relearn the history that makes us great. "If we forget what we did," he declared, "we won't know who we are." And so he ended his presidency by calling for "more attention to American history and a greater emphasis on civic ritual." As he explained, "An informed patriotism is what we want. And are we doing a good enough job teaching our children what America is and what she represents in the long history of the world?" America, for Reagan, has a unique place in human history, and the study of American history, he believed—at least, a study of its *true* history—would bear him out. That's why, he argued, "we've got to teach history based not on what's in fashion but what's important." With such a line, Reagan opened the contest he could not ignore. He recognized that competing interpretations of the American past have always existed and that new understandings constantly arise. Yet he insisted that only one version, *his* version, was true.[10]

And what was Reagan's version of the past? He gives only two examples of events that all Americans should know: first, "why the Pilgrims came here" and, second, "who Jimmy Doolittle was." For his most telling examples of the nation's true history, Reagan does not turn to the Native Americans or to the coming of Columbus and the Spanish or to the arrival of the Dutch and the French or to the establishment of Jamestown or to the start of slavery. Like so many Americans then and since, Reagan turns to Plymouth. In particular, he turns to their motive: we must know "*why* the Pilgrims came." In the case of Jimmy Doolittle, the deed (the long-range bombing mission over Japan in response to Pearl Harbor) speaks for itself. But in the case of the Pilgrims, their mere arrival is not the point. Reagan focuses rather on the *purpose* of their migration, the underlying system of values that drove them—*that* is what represents the true beginning of America. And so, in calling John Winthrop "an early Pilgrim, a freedom man," President Reagan ended his address by finally answering for himself why the Pilgrims came. John Winthrop, he said, sailed in search of liberty, and in doing so, Winthrop established America ever since as a "city on a hill."[11]

On January 11, 1989, when the screen flickered off, Reagan's political career came to an end, but the "city on a hill" did not go with him. Instead, it has remained a signature element in American nationalism and the unofficial motto of American exceptionalism—the line that still summarizes America's character and purpose for a whole host of citizens and politicians. Set apart as a beacon of liberty; called to be an example of democracy; given the task to spread free enterprise and any number of other virtues abroad—all this and more has been ascribed to the "city on a hill" and placed at the opening of America, marked by that precise moment of origin, the proclamation by the first Puritan governor of Massachusetts Bay, on the eve of his arrival, that "we shall be as a city upon a hill"—a sermon and a statement that, for over three centuries, went entirely ignored.

Who were these Pilgrims and Puritans, and what motivations actually drove them to the American shores? The story of Winthrop's sermon critically turns on understanding the difference between these two groups of people and their separate comings to New England. For Governor John Winthrop was not in fact "an early Pilgrim" at all. The Pilgrims, as we call them, sailed on the *Mayflower* and came ashore in 1620. They were a poor lot, and they came at a poor time, just as winter set in. During those first cold months, half of the 102 who managed to make it here died, and at one point, only seven Pilgrims were healthy enough to serve the rest. It was a brutal time, a period of suffering they inflicted on others and endured themselves, constituting—like so many other colonial settlements and their consequences elsewhere—a long season of misery.[12]

These Pilgrims had come to America not from England but from Holland, and they had been living in Holland because *that* is where religious toleration could be found. The Pilgrims needed such conditions. Unlike Winthrop and later Puritans, they officially separated from the Church of England, and in doing so they became known, appropriately, as Separatists. The problem with separating, however, was that it simply was not allowed. The king was officially the head of the Church of England, and to condemn the Church of England was to reject the monarch's authority. It amounted to an act of treason. For several years, the Separatists were harried through England until, in 1608, they managed to escape to a place where they could practice what they believed. That place was Holland.

Unfortunately, Holland did not provide Pilgrims with sustenance. As unskilled immigrants, these Pilgrims had to find a new way to make a living, and for as long as they stayed in the Netherlands, most remained in poverty. They worried about their children in particular—first, for their physical health, since they labored under such harsh conditions, and second, for their spiritual health, since poverty could drive the next generation into the clutches of the ungodly Dutch. And so twelve years after landing in Holland, a fifth of the congregation decided to leave, hoping to prepare a way for others. Desperately poor, cheated by a merchant, taking out loans they could never repay, the Pilgrims did their best with what they had. In the end, they came to America because they saw no other way. We know all this and more largely through the written history of William Bradford in a book called *Of Plymouth Plantation*, another manuscript that was lost, found, and published only in the nineteenth century.

But William Bradford was not John Winthrop, and their followers were not the same. John Winthrop and his Puritan entourage came a full decade later. Born in 1588, raised on a wealthy estate, trained as a lawyer, and appointed governor of the new Massachusetts Bay enterprise in 1629, Winthrop arrived in America at the head of a miniature fleet.[13] These Puritans, several hundred strong, arrived at the right time, in spring, and began building and planting immediately. Hardships certainly arose, but they also had far more resources on which to rely. Several of these colonists, like Winthrop himself, came with sizable endowments. And many had elite connections. Boston, unlike Plymouth, was not dreadfully poor, and those who settled in Boston, Salem, and the surrounding areas had not signed away the first fruits of their labors, as the Pilgrims had done.

In addition, these Puritans came with the king's permission in the form of a royal charter. Unlike the Pilgrims, who landed on territory where they had no patent and no right to be, the Puritans sailed to America in possession of a document that—in their minds anyway—gave them full title to the land. Puritans argued that recent plagues had left the land vacant, and so long as they gave the few remaining Indians enough ground on which to live, they could take the rest for themselves. In the end, Puritans felt they had the blessing of God and the authority of the king, and when it came to claiming the territory, those were their primary concerns.

They had the king's permission but not exactly his admiration. When Charles I ascended to the throne in 1625, he sought to limit the influence of the Puritans and bolster conformity to the Church of England. The Archbishop of Canterbury, William Laud, took to this task with fierce determination, silencing the most vocal Puritan ministers and revoking their licenses. Without a license to preach, these ministers could not find jobs, and without a job, they had no way to support their families. Meanwhile, those Puritans who were not ministers, like the lawyer John Winthrop, felt constrained by the policies and attitudes of what they considered a broadening ungodly culture. They watched in horror as their beloved nation descended into unrighteousness, and they worried aloud whether God's wrath would soon break out.

Most Puritans responded to this dire state of affairs by staying right where they were. Pushing for greater reform in the Church of England, a diverse group of people—who called themselves "the godly" and whom others called "Puritans"—understood religious duty as a requirement to remain in place. Abandoning England, they argued, would amount to Separatism, an act of condemnation and despair. And if the righteous left England, then the numbers of the unrighteous would rise so rapidly that God's doom would surely descend. For such reasons, most of the godly called on their godly peers to stay put, to pray for God's strength, to wait on the Lord, and to fight the good fight.

Winthrop, however, left. And in the next two decades, many others did too. In leaving England, Puritan settlers had to explain and justify their decision, defending themselves against accusations of desertion. With other leaders of this so-called Great Migration, Winthrop asserted again and again that the departing English were *not* separating from the Church of England. They were *not Pilgrims*. They were reformers—those who hoped to save the church by changing it. In sailing for a new land, they argued, they were merely extending the reach of the Church of England, not attempting to break its grasp.

The king in many ways agreed. Believing the Puritans would discover gold and other precious metals in New England, he granted a charter in return for a portion of the riches. Charles I envisioned a business deal, a trading organization. The "government" established by the charter would, in effect, be a corporate board operating a colonial settlement from a London seat, answerable to stockholders and the king. The charter, however, never specified that the company's board had to meet in London. Puritans, seeing their chance, sneaked this legal document to New England, where the king would be unable to review or revoke it, and they used it to establish a new government centered in Boston. When the king got wind of it, he demanded that the Puritans return the charter and go about business in the proper way. Puritans, however, stalled. They promised to return the charter soon, but somehow they never got around to it. Finally the king's other concerns overwhelmed him, culminating in a devastating civil war, and Massachusetts Bay held its charter for another sixty years.

In taking this charter to New England, the Puritans claimed they had legitimate reasons for seeking a new place to live and a new way to live there. In a series of documents, including John Winthrop's "city on a hill" sermon, they spelled out exactly why they were leaving and what they hoped to achieve. Some reasons were religious: Winthrop argued that unrighteousness in England threatened the nation, that a true church planted anywhere supported the church everywhere, and that the planting of a new reformed Protestant church in America could serve as both a refuge to true believers and a bulwark against the Jesuits. But there were also practical considerations: England, Winthrop explained, was overrun. Its economy had reached capacity. The place had become so crowded, he argued, that no godly person could make a decent living without deceitful competition. In short, both the religious and the economic conditions of England justified expansion across the sea. These and other reasons Winthrop spelled out in several surviving texts.

But for whom did Winthrop speak? Certainly his voice resonated with some Puritans in power, and certainly it fit with the mind-set and mold of many ministers. But what about the population itself? Just how "Puritan" were the migrants who came? When later Americans began to cast Pilgrims and Puritans as the origin of America, they not only blended together two separate groups of people but also formed in American cultural memory a homogeneous mass of like-minded religious zealots all declaring allegiance to the same written protocols, all backing the same sermons and laws. Some did. Others didn't. Many worshipped diligently, kept diaries, respected leaders, and spent their days trying to draw ever closer to God. Others thought little of God, went to church because they had to, and spent their lives in pursuit of land, money, power, and fame. More than ten thousand people migrated in the first decade, twenty thousand by the second decade. That many people can never be the same. For an origin story to emerge from this mass migration, many in that mass would have to be ignored.[14]

Even more to the point, in order to create a coherent story of national origins, the mixed motivations, lives, conditions, and cultures—the goals and strivings of all sorts of people spread all across the Americas—would all have to be flattened, neglected, or erased, so that the motives of the "Pilgrims" alone could explain the opening and identity of America ever since. How did that happen? How did Pilgrims and Puritans come to be the foundation of the entire United States? When and where did such cultural work occur? Who did the labor of making this story stick? And why did one particular sermon—delivered in 1630 and promptly forgotten, printed in 1838 and immediately ignored—come to stand as the fundamental document of American history and literature, the origin of American exceptionalism?

These are the questions I set out to answer. When I started several years ago, I thought it would be a fairly straightforward task to follow the life story of a single text. But it turns out the full biography of Winthrop's sermon involves two stories, not one, and both involve a much larger history of American exceptionalism. The first story focuses on the sermon itself: when it was delivered, what it meant in its own day, how it was copied, why it was lost, and what enabled it to be discovered, printed, publicized, and eventually politicized in our modern day. The second follows the Pilgrims and Puritans into and through American culture, asking how they have been remembered and commemorated from one generation to the next. Neither tale stands without the other. For it required the creation and assertion of Pilgrim and Puritan origins in the earliest days of the nation to make Winthrop's sermon wield political might a full century later. Twentieth-century American exceptionalism takes shape from the intertwining of these two tales—a cultural history of collective remembering and a rags-to-riches biography of one now-significant text, John Winthrop's 1630 sermon *A Model of Christian Charity*.

PART I

Message

CHAPTER ONE

The Mystery of Winthrop's Manuscript

WHEN JOHN WINTHROP ENVISIONED a good and godly society, what did he see? To begin at the beginning of what has become Winthrop's place in American politics, we have to understand what his "city on a hill" sermon actually says. But that is a harder task than it might seem. Winthrop starts his sermon with a statement about social hierarchy, then follows that seeming "doctrine" with several paragraphs about financial regulations—how to give aid, lend money, and forgive loans. From there, he pivots to what seems like an entirely new conversation, talking about the community as a body united by ligaments of love. He discusses the necessity of sympathy. He runs through several biblical illustrations of love and affection. He invokes a covenant with God. He tells his listeners not to forget that "we shall be as a city upon a hill." And then he ends by calling his audience to absolute obedience, telling them to choose "life and good" rather than "death and evil." Because he does so much in such a relatively short amount of time, readings of this sermon have diverged wildly over the years. What is Winthrop's message? Whom is he delivering it to? And why does he think it matters?

A great deal rides on how people answer these questions. Whenever politicians quote Winthrop today, they end up either explicitly or implicitly interpreting his message, its audience, and its lasting significance. Many commentators and politicians focus on Winthrop's moving language of mutual affection—the idea, as Winthrop says, that we "must delight in each other; make others' conditions our own; rejoice together, mourn together, labor and suffer together." For those who quote such lines, Winthrop's sermon stands as the first and most fundamental call to civic *community*. Others, however, emphasize Winthrop's covenantal language—the calling, commands, and promises of God. "Thus stands the cause between God and us," Winthrop declares, "we are entered into a covenant with him for this work." In the next paragraph, he adds, "For we must consider that we shall be as a city upon a hill, the eyes of all people are upon us." For many Americans today, these words make Winthrop's sermon the first and most fundamental statement of their God-given responsibility on the world stage. Already, then, we have two very different meanings of Winthrop's sermon and its relation to the nation. Is this text about community or covenant? Mutual affections or godly commissions? The only way to answer such questions is to read the sermon as a whole. For this text, like all texts, has not just an ending (often quoted) but also a beginning (always ignored). And though that beginning never appears on the national stage, it raises perplexing issues about how to understand the meaning of Winthrop's sermon as a whole.

Here, then, is how the "best sermon of the millennium" begins: "God Almighty in His most holy and wise providence, hath so disposed of the condition of mankind, as in all times some must be rich, some poor, some high and eminent in power and dignity; others mean and in subjection." When my students stumble across this sentence, they often wonder what could possibly be so "American" about this text—or why Reagan and others would want to quote from it so frequently. Winthrop, it seems, posits an unchanging hierarchical order with a total absence of social mobility. God puts some in charge, and others obey; he makes some rich and others poor. And because God has structured the world this way, no one can object. In the surviving manuscript, this first line is set apart from the rest of the sermon as though it functions as the central principle, or "doctrine," of the entire text. But if this sentence is Winthrop's message, then all those stirring citations in modern political speeches miss the point. Instead of a communitarian and egalitarian utopia standing in a special covenantal relationship with God, Winthrop's sermon is nothing more than a defense of unchanging power structures—with himself placed squarely at the top.[1] How do we hold together the visionary language at the end of the sermon with this odd opening line?

The problem gets worse before it gets better, for the paragraphs that follow this opening statement offer a complicated theological explanation of economic exchange. "What rule shall a man observe in giving in respect of the measure?" he asks. Winthrop offers several answers, each depending on the precise situation of the one giving and the one receiving, all of it backed by scriptural passages. "What rule must we observe in lending?" he inquires next, and, having answered that, he asks, "What rule must we observe in forgiving?" Winthrop does not mean forgiving *sins* but forgiving *debts*. For the first half of his sermon, he seems obsessed with financial concerns and commercial exchange—so much so, in fact, that some scholars think of his sermon as "one long manifesto for a godly economy." Clearly, Winthrop had an economic vision in mind. But just as clearly, the tangled language of hierarchy and finance sits uneasily with the inspiring rhetoric of love and affection that comes later, creating a divide in this sermon that runs right down its middle. Although it has become one of the most important texts of American history and literature, and although it often gets presented as a founding text of American exceptionalism, *A Model of Christian Charity* still does not make sense to most of those who actually start in the beginning and read through it to the end. How, in short, does this whole thing hang together?[2]

The solution to this puzzle turns on the mystery of the manuscript itself, for the "cultural key text" of American history has come down through American history incomplete. Only one copy of this fundamental sermon exists. It survives in the New-York Historical Society, and if you request to see it, the librarian will bring you a small box containing a bound set of pages with neat handwriting that supposedly lays out Winthrop's complete vision of a good and godly society. That manuscript cannot be trusted.

Consider, for example, the cover (figure 2). Though nineteenth-century antiquarians had never seen this sermon before, someone before them certainly had—and that person provided Winthrop's text with an influential title page of sorts. In the manuscript passed to posterity, a cover note calls what follows "A Modell of Christian Charity," and it proclaims that Winthrop wrote it "On Boarde the Arrabella, On the Attlantick Ocean." It further situates this moment of origin in a broader context of beginnings, explaining that Winthrop composed the sermon "In His passage, (with the great Company of Religious people, of which Christian Tribes he was the Brave Leader and famous Governor;) from the Island of Great Brittaine, to New-England in the North America. Anno 1630." This descriptive title page overlays the entire Puritan migration with a story about the sermon's significance. It renders the text, in effect, *the* statement of *the* leader delivered at *the* moment of origin—precisely how it would eventually be read.

Yet much about this title page remains dubious. First, it is a mess. Parts of it have been crammed between previously existing lines, including two important insertions squeezed in with carets. Judging by the script of this note, it would seem that the title originally read: "A / Modell of Xtian Charity. / By the Honrbl John Winthrop. Esq;. / Anno 1630." Placing this sermon on board the *Arbella* seems like an overexcited addition (complete with what seems like exclamation marks), and the whole narrative of the "passage" is shoved yet again between other already-existing lines. Finally, "Xtian Tribes" and the phrase "Brave Leader and famous" have been added even later, possibly by yet another hand. It is highly unlikely that this sort of cover note—describing Winthrop as the "brave leader and famous Governor" of the "Christian tribes" who sailed to America in 1630—would have been written while Winthrop was still alive. And certainly it could not have been composed in 1630, since Winthrop was not yet famous and had no success to tout. The cover note, clearly, has been added later.

Even more important, however, is the simple fact of handwriting. Turning the page, we find the sermon itself, which is now called "Christian Charitie: A Modell hereof" (figure 3). The title page and the text that follow are in different hands. And neither of these hands belong to Winthrop. Winthrop had remarkably miser-

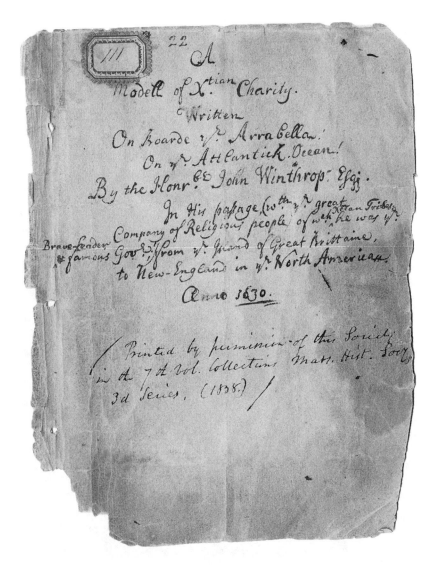

Figure 2: Cover, "A modell of [Chris]tian charity: Written on board [the] Arrabella, on [the] Atlantic Ocean," John Winthrop, 1630. BV Winthrop, John; nyhs_jwmcc_v-01_01, New-York Historical Society. Photography © New-York Historical Society.

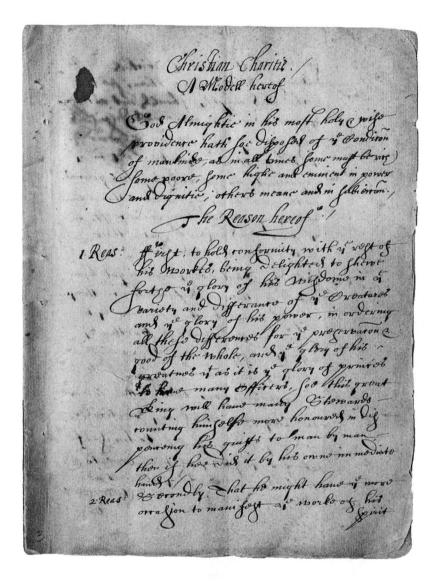

Figure 3: First page of text, "A modell of [Chris]tian charity: Written on board [the] Arrabella, on [the] Atlantic Ocean," John Winthrop, 1630. BV Winthrop, John; nyhs_jwmcc_v-01_03, New-York Historical Society. Photography © New-York Historical Society.

able handwriting that only trained experts can read, but almost anyone with a basic knowledge of cursive can begin to work out the words in our sole surviving manuscript. In short, the one and only manuscript we have of Winthrop's now-famous "city on a hill" sermon has not been written by Winthrop himself. Because this sermon was so obscure, because so many people ignored it, because no one published or preserved the original (not even Winthrop), the text that survives is nothing but a copy—and possibly just a copy of a copy. And that copy is corrupt.

How do we know this manuscript contains errors? For starters, take the obvious mistakes in scriptural citations. The sermon speaks of the Macedonians from "Cor: 2. 6" when it should read "2 Cor. 8." Later, it cites 1 John 3:10 for 1 John 3:16. Several passages are identified only broadly (simply Matthew or 1 John) with no specific chapter or verse, and oftentimes the writer leaves a blank space, as if intending to return later and complete a reference. The copyist has made mistakes—which is not unusual when dealing with long manuscripts. Try to copy out any long text by hand and compare your production to the original. Errors will occur. And we can confirm that the copyist made mistakes through a few scribbled notes in the back of Winthrop's journal. Most scholars still believe this sermon to have been delivered by Winthrop (even though his version does not survive) because, in part, his journal lists a series of verses that seem related to the writing of *Christian Charity*, including the *correct* citation "2 Cor. 8." When Winthrop gave this sermon, he got his scripture right. It was the scribe who erred.[3]

Such mistakes are a rather minor concern and easy to correct. But a more serious error also seems to have afflicted the manuscript: it has lost its beginning. The content of Winthrop's sermon looks very much like a normal Puritan sermon, except for the way it opens. Puritan sermons had six basic parts, all following the same basic order: (1) a citation of scripture; (2) an explanation of that scripture; (3) a "doctrine" derived from scripture; (4) reasons for the doctrine; (5) an application of the doctrine; and (6) an exhortation to move listeners into accepting the sermon's message. The last four of these elements can all be found in *A Model of Christian Charity*, and all in the proper order. The scripture and its explanation cannot. In other words, Winthrop's first sentence—his statement about hierarchy—is dramatically out of place. This would appear to be the sermon's "doctrine," its guiding premise or principle. But doctrines do not stand alone. They can never, by themselves, start a sermon. Instead, doctrines derive first and *only* from scripture. As one of the most influential Puritan preaching manuals of the seventeenth century explained, the first step in preparing a sermon is "the unfolding of the [scriptural] passage into its various doctrines, like the untwisting and loosening of a weaver's web."[4] Puritans fought with the Church of England because they felt it too often and too heavily relied on human invention, not the sound truths of scripture. They would never start preaching without opening the Bible first. Puritan sermons begin with scripture. Winthrop's sermon does not.

But why believe this text is a "sermon" at all? Winthrop himself was not a minister. He was a lawyer and a statesman, who gave many different kinds of speeches throughout his life. Perhaps this is one of those: a treatise or a discourse or some other kind of tract? That is possible. But it must be remembered that lay "prophesying"—that is, the delivery of sermons by laypersons like Winthrop—was not unusual. The historian Francis Bremer has found many examples of Puritans doing just this sort of thing in both England and New England. In the early migration of Pilgrim Separatists to Plymouth, for example, a grocer and wool carder named Robert Cushman delivered a lay sermon in 1621 aimed against self-love and self-seeking that has striking parallels to *A Model of Christian Charity*. Moreover, we know that Winthrop was specifically empowered (with two others) to preach in Boston for a time. We do not have to believe Winthrop delivered this sermon on the *Arbella*, as the title page claims, for us to believe that he could have preached it somewhere at some time. Most scholars now believe that Winthrop delivered this sermon in England, before the departure, which would make far more sense than preaching to the few Puritans who happened to be on his own particular ship.[5]

Even so, why believe that this text is a corrupt and incomplete sermon rather than a full and finished treatise? A simple reason is that it's structured like a sermon. Texts never enter the world in a void. They take shape in relation to other writings and speeches a person has read and heard, and those texts sort themselves into genres. Each genre has a certain feel and form, a way of proceeding that prepares the anticipations of readers. If you know what genre you have entered, you know where the pieces will fit: you know what should come first and what should come next, and you can follow the sense of the whole. Genres communicate meaning through structure. Their purpose is to raise expectations and then meet them.

Puritan sermons were a genre. They had a way of proceeding. They had a structure, form, and feel that listeners could follow. And that way of proceeding is present in Winthrop's text. In other words, most scholars have called *Christian Charity* a "sermon" simply because it looks and reads so much like one. Even if we wanted to believe that Winthrop wrote a "treatise" or gave a "discourse," it remains unclear why he used *most* of the classic Puritan sermon genre without using all of it—especially since the two parts he left out were the most important of all: the scripture and its explanation. It is far more likely that *Christian Charity* is incomplete. The opening, the origin, has disappeared.[6]

Knowing that something has gone missing, it becomes possible to imagine how the sermon once began. As two missing puzzle pieces can be visualized through the rest of what remains, so in the case of *Christian Charity* we can begin to figure out the scripture behind this sermon through what else the sermon says. There are many reasons to believe that Winthrop initially began this sermon with Galatians 5:13–14 from the Geneva Bible: "For brethren, ye have been called unto liberty: only use not *your* liberty as an occasion unto the flesh, but by love serve one another. For all the Law is fulfilled in one word, which is this, Thou shalt love thy neighbor as thyself." These verses suggest, first and foremost, a casting off, a new beginning. The gloss on Galatians 5:13 in the Geneva is instructive here. According to that commentary, this verse shows "that the right use of Christian liberty consisteth in this, that being delivered from the slavery of sin and the flesh, and being obedient to the Spirit, we should serve unto one another's salvation through love."[7] That sounds very much like the entirety of Winthrop's sermon. It aligns a converted individual heart with the corporate community of Christians: those who are liberated are called upon to "serve one another." In other words, just as Winthrop's sermon in several places links communal prosperity to private spiritual regeneration, so does Galatians 5.[8]

Even more clearly, Galatians 5:13–14 provides a kind of road map for the whole of Winthrop's sermon. These verses explain how the two seemingly divided halves of *Christian Charity* fit together: first Winthrop talks of social stations and money, then he turns to mutual affections and love. The sermon has those parts in that order because that is exactly what happens in the scriptural passage that stands behind it. The Bible that Winthrop knew would have contained commentary linking Galatians 5:13–14 to other verses where the Apostle Paul again moves from talk of debt and obligation to a language of love. Consider, for example, Romans 13:8: "Owe nothing to any man, but to love one another: for he that loveth another, hath fulfilled the Law." This tidy verse, linked to Galatians 5:13–14, reads like an equally tidy summary of Winthrop's sermon, explaining how Winthrop could move from obligations and the regulation of exchange to an account of the absolute necessity of love. The question we begin with is simple: *What do we owe each other?* And Winthrop's answer is the same as Paul's: whatever love requires.

Moreover, in the key transition when Winthrop moves from the first half of his sermon to the second—in the precise moment when he turns from his talk of commerce to his language of love— he refers specifically to these passages from Paul. About halfway through the surviving sermon, Winthrop signals to listeners that he is making his transition *according to the dictates of scripture*: "Having already set forth the practice of mercy according to the rule of God's law," he preaches, "it will be useful to lay open the grounds of it also *being the other part of the Commandment*." As he goes on to explain, the practice of mercy depends on the presence of the love that gives it rise, for "the Apostle tells us that this love is the fulfilling of the law." Following scripture closely, Winthrop echoes exactly the language of the Apostle Paul in Galatians 5:13–14 and in Romans 13:8–10. Galatians 5:14 claims that "all the Law is fulfilled" in loving one's neighbor as oneself; Romans 13:8 adds, "He that loveth another, hath fulfilled the Law"; and Romans 13:10 proclaims that love is "the fulfilling of the Law."⁹ The turn in Winthrop's sermon, in other words, follows the pivot in these passages.

Given such evidence, it would seem that the Pauline theology expressed in Galatians 5 and Romans 12–13 launches Winthrop's sermon and holds it all together. Winthrop is not trying to be creative or mysterious in *A Model of Christian Charity*. Instead, he is trying to be faithful to scripture. His sermon outlines a model society based on the models he has found in the Bible. Once we discover the passages that guided Winthrop, we can begin to see that the two halves of his text are not divided at all. Talk of debt, loans, and financial exchange in a godly society *necessarily* leads to a language of love and affection, for as Paul repeatedly declared, only love could cover all disputes and nourish all exchange.[10]

As a result, sympathy—defined as the God-given, grace-enabled mutual exchange of love within a godly community—becomes central to *Christian Charity*. If viewed properly and practiced well, Winthrop believed, both hierarchy and exchange would actually *further* the bonds of mutual affection. For this reason, Winthrop cites several biblical passages that Puritans often invoked to demonstrate the necessity of sympathy to a godly society (such as 1 Corinthians 12:26 and Romans 12:15). Using such passages, Winthrop explains that a "sensibleness and sympathy of each other's conditions will necessarily infuse into each part a native desire and endeavor to strengthen, defend, preserve and comfort the other." Christ and the Apostles, Winthrop asserts, offer the first and best example. "From the like sympathy of parts," he explains, "did the Apostles and many thousands of the saints lay down their lives for Christ." And that model of mutual affection becomes the example for the body of Christ, which is held together by "ligaments of love" and animated by a reciprocal, unifying sympathetic exchange. The sermon in effect begins with a *seeming* problem—how we stand unequally in relation to one another and how we should act in our dealings with one another—but then posits the ultimate solution. However God has arranged our various stations in society, the call is always the same: we must love each other as Christ loved us, which he did by putting himself in our place, sympathizing with us, and giving of his very life to save ours—what the apostles and the martyrs and the best of all the church have always been inspired to imitate. For Winthrop, Christian charity in a model society both leads to and flows from a "sweet sympathy of affections."[11]

It is a vision as inspiring as it is limited. For this sweet sympathy of affections, Winthrop believed, could only arise among those who were converted and regenerated by the power of the Holy Spirit. Every person, he explains, "is born with this principle in him to love and seek himself only." Selfishness defines a person until "Christ comes and takes possession of the soul and infuses another principle, love to God and our brother." It all depends, therefore, on God. Community hangs on grace. The society that Winthrop envisions— the model of Christian charity he lays out—hinges on something he cannot make happen: spiritual regeneration. According to Winthrop, any "body" of persons will be disproportionate and disordered until "Christ comes, and by his spirit and love knits all these parts to himself and each to other." His audience, in other words, is clear: as Winthrop says near the end of his sermon, "First, for the persons. We are a company professing ourselves fellow members of Christ." The truth of that profession is what this new society will test: Will they live for one another out of their membership in Christ's body, or will they live for themselves alone? Will the "sweet sympathy of affections" abound, or will the Puritans devolve into selfish pursuits?[12]

It is clear, then, that the lures of private self-interest deeply worried John Winthrop. And, as we shall see, self-interest would become a recurring motif among scholars, pundits, and public figures who returned to Winthrop's sermon much later. The markets of New England could be especially tempting to those who came in search of riches, which explains why Winthrop spent so much time in his sermon discussing proper economic exchange and financial aid for the poor. In an "ordinary time," he preached, a person "is to give out of his abundance. Let him lay aside as God hath blessed him." But when it comes to an "extraordinary time"—when it comes to a "community in peril" such as a new colony in a distant land—"then a man cannot likely do too much." Winthrop told his listeners to keep just enough for themselves and give all the rest away. Throughout his sermon, he urged a broad-based "liberality." In his talk of financial exchange, he foregrounds above all the needs of the community. Regular commerce has its place, he admitted, but when the ruin of another seems imminent, that person's need must prevail.

For this reason, Winthrop preached his sermon not primarily to the *poor* (telling them to accept their position and refrain from rising up against the rich) but to the *rich* (telling them they must reach out to the poor and help them in their deepest need). Moreover, he defined the "rich" broadly: not the 1 percent or the top 10 or 20 percent but rather "all such as are able to live comfortably by their own means duly improved." According to Winthrop, if you can meet your basic needs, you are rich. And if you are rich, you have a duty to care for the poor. What Winthrop hoped to see established in New England was a community where those who had enough would support those who did not and where those who found themselves supported would demonstrate their gratitude in return, together building up bonds of mutual affection. God made some rich and others poor, Winthrop explained, so that all might love each other more.[13]

It is right, then, to claim that Winthrop was deeply concerned about the economic arrangements of society and that he argued for a certain economic liberty and liberality, but his account of a godly society has very little to do with modern visions of free enterprise and social mobility. The point and purpose of Winthrop's ideal society is not to create private wealth or to get ahead but to establish community—an ethic of mutual affection and care sustained by the love of Christ and supported by an abundance of goods that have been acquired without greed. Winthrop did not believe all wealth could or should be equally distributed, nor that all people could or should be considered equal. The world has its stations. It has order and hierarchy. Winthrop did not dispute that arrangement or attempt to overthrow it. At the same time, he never celebrated the rich for being rich or embraced an unregulated free-market economic order that would encourage people to seek gain for themselves at another's expense. Such arrangements, Winthrop believed, operated on corrupt principles of selfish competition. It was precisely what he feared had taken hold in England—one of the many things he fled. Instead of competition and self-seeking, Winthrop advocated community. He was trying to give accumulation a purpose. The point of wealth, he preached, is to share it with others.

Just as politicians might invoke Winthrop today in order to further an economic vision that Winthrop himself would never recognize or endorse, so they also turn to the Pilgrims, the Puritans, and the "city on a hill" in order to claim an American foundation in freedom that John Winthrop would certainly reject. Popular and political culture are oddly divided about early New England. In novels, movies, and television shows, we often find Puritans portrayed as evil theocratic authoritarians. Dressing characters in Puritan-style clothes signals to viewers that we have entered a repressive, religious regime (consider *The Handmaid's Tale*). Politicians, in contrast, have historically gone too far the opposite way, describing John Winthrop, for instance, as "an early freedom man" who came "looking for a home that would be free." In textbooks and speeches, American culture has repeatedly rehearsed a story in which Pilgrims and Puritans flee persecution and cross the Atlantic Ocean in search of religious liberty, then immediately deny that liberty to others.[14]

It is not exactly wrong to link Puritans to a language of liberty. Such talk can be found throughout their writing. Yet this language of liberty, especially in a religious context, had little to do with the idea of freedom that many people have since embraced. For Puritans, "freedom" was not primarily a matter of "free choice." They certainly never equated it with practicing whatever religious beliefs one pleased. If we want to understand the language of liberty among Puritans and the way it informs Winthrop's sermon, we must instead consider their presiding concern for order and authority. For according to the Puritans, liberty could not exist without a proper social order, and a proper social order could not be maintained without due subjection to authority. In that sense, Puritans defended and restrained both freedom and authority equally. The ideal society found a balance between two extremes: unrestrained liberty (or "licentiousness") and arbitrary rule (or "tyranny"). Both of these extremes they ardently abhorred.[15]

The line between such extremes threads all the way through Winthrop's sermon. After the citation of Galatians 5:13 ("For brethren, ye have been called unto liberty"), Winthrop's explanation of this verse would have carefully traced a path from the scriptural language of liberty to the sermon's stated principle of rank-ordered social stations. Strange as it may sound to modern ears, the relation between those concepts would not have seemed odd to Winthrop. Years later, in fact, Winthrop made that exact connection again. In a small talk that came to be known as his "little speech on liberty"—an address that was for many years far more famous than *A Model of Christian Charity*—Winthrop defined "liberty" in such a way that it defended social order and the God-given authority of magistrates. He distinguished "natural liberty" (a kind of unrestrained free will, or just doing whatever you want) from "civil liberty" (a freedom to pursue the right and the good in a properly ordered society), explaining that real liberty lay only in the latter. According to Winthrop, liberty comes to be realized, exercised, and achieved only through the maintenance of hierarchy and authority. If Winthrop did open his sermon with Galatians 5:13, as I believe he did, his next move would be to emphasize—exactly as the rest of his sermon *does* emphasize—that liberty was never to be used "as an occasion unto the flesh" (the second half of Galatians 5:13). "Liberty" was not a license to do as one pleased. Rather, liberty entailed and required a kind of self-control, or self-mastery, brought about by God's love and enabled to flourish only in a truly godly society. It meant being freed from evil ways and evil desires in order to want, seek, and pursue what pleases God. That was the message of liberty Winthrop integrated into *A Model of Christian Charity*—a message consistent with his and other Puritans' understanding of Galatians 5:13.[16]

This point cannot be stressed too much. After all, Winthrop and his fellow Puritans *did* envision New England as a place where the godly were "called unto liberty," but their definition of liberty is not what most people today would understand. Theirs was not a call to civil and religious liberty in some open form of a tolerant and pluralistic society where all may do as they please. Winthrop and other Puritan leaders never intended to create such a place. What they hoped to establish, instead, was a place where the "godly" would no longer be *prevented* from worshipping God as they ought. Thus, Puritans frequently paired "liberty" with "purity." As the leading minister John Cotton explained in his farewell sermon to departing Puritans, the people of God would be able to discern God's blessing when they found in their dwelling place "the liberty and purity of his ordinances." Liberty *and* purity. As Cotton wrote in a 1634 letter, "It hath been no small inducement to us to choose rather to remove hither [to New England] than to stay

there [in England], that we might enjoy the liberty, not of some ordinances of God, but of all, *and all in purity.*" In another dispatch,
two years later, Cotton specifically rejected the idea of democracy,
for "if the people be governors, who shall be governed?" Instead, he
said, three things mutually support one another: "authority in magistrates, liberty in people, purity in the church." As he explained,
"Purity, preserved in the church, will preserve well-ordered liberty
in the people, and both of them establish well-balanced authority in
the magistrates."[17] Winthrop agreed. For the Puritans, freedom did
not establish religious pluralism but something much closer to its
opposite. As they understood it, liberty was nothing less than a removal of corruption and constraint so as to enable people to flourish within a pure church and a well-ordered commonwealth. No
longer *forced* to worship God falsely, Puritans would be *free*—in a
better society—to worship him in spirit and in truth.

Understanding this pairing of liberty and purity allows us to see
how and why the Puritans acted as they did in New England. On the
one hand, fearing arbitrary rule, they established a system of church
and state that was remarkably reformed and progressive for their day
and age. On the other hand, fearing licentiousness and hoping to experience the pure ordinances of God, they cracked down on religious
dissent. The Puritans had a powerful sense of right and wrong, and
they did not understand why anyone would allow the wrong to per-
sist. When they spoke of their longing for liberty, they wanted
true godliness, as they understood it, to be set free from an ungodly
culture. But they never intended to allow erroneous religion to
take root. In fact, that is precisely why so many of them left
England—because false religion, or "men's inventions," had so
deeply informed the Church of England. The Puritans wanted to set
it right. In moving from England to New England, therefore, these
Puritans remained consistently intolerant of religious practices they
considered untrue, pernicious, and wrong.[18]

And so, in the coming years, as new forms of devotion took
shape among Antinomians, Baptists, and Quakers, Puritans expelled
them from their midst. Banished Quakers who returned to Massachusetts Bay were whipped, and those who refused to stay away
were hanged. The Puritans had gone to New England not for an
abstract ideal of "civil and religious freedom" but for the removal of

all obstacles to proper godliness and order. The word "liberty" frequently occurs in Puritan documents, but we have to understand what that word meant: for Puritans it meant a new *ability* to do what was right, not a broadening of *choice* to do as one pleased. It was the same term we use today, but it had a very different meaning.

Liberty, liberality, new beginnings, social stations, a well-ordered society, financial exchange governed by a law of love—above all, the mutual affections of a godly community generated first and foremost by the love of God—*these* are the dominant themes of John Winthrop's *Christian Charity*. All of them fit together and flow out of Galatians 5:13–14: "For brethren, ye have been called unto liberty: only use not your liberty as an occasion unto the flesh, but by love serve one another. For all the Law is fulfilled in one word, which is this, Thou shalt love thy neighbor as thyself." When Winthrop preached, he tried to sketch a model of Christian charity that he found first modeled in his Bible.

But not just any Bible. Winthrop specifically wrote his sermon in the light of the Geneva Bible, which was an English translation of scripture first published in 1560. When the King James Version appeared five decades later, these two translations began vying for preeminence in England, and by the time Winthrop delivered his sermon in 1630, it was clear that the King James Version was winning. But when Winthrop preached *Christian Charity*, he ignored the King's Bible and instead shaped his sermon around the old Geneva masterpiece. Such a seemingly slight decision carried a great weight of meaning. For the way the Geneva Bible was structured not only influenced what Winthrop had to say but also taught him how to say it.

CHAPTER TWO

The Significance of Winthrop's Bible

THE IMPORTANCE OF IDENTIFYING Winthrop's Bible becomes clear when we see how long, and in how many ways, it has been either misidentified or ignored. Every semester, for example, students in American history and literature courses dutifully plow through John Winthrop's 1630 "city on a hill" sermon, *A Model of Christian Charity*. If they make it to the end, they find the governor closing his sermon "with that exhortation of Moses, that faithful servant of the Lord, in his last farewell to Israel, Deuteronomy 30." Since Winthrop directed his listeners exactly where to look (Deuteronomy 30), it may seem a bit too obvious to note. But until recently, every edition of both the Norton and Heath anthologies of American literature have gotten it wrong. A footnote for students quotes the first three verses of Deuteronomy 30, which have nothing to do with Winthrop's sermon. Stalwart students who read this footnote will figure that the governor has made a passing reference to Moses and moved on. But in fact, Winthrop does no such thing. Instead, he ends his sermon by quoting almost directly from Deuteronomy 30:*15–20* (fifteen verses later), and that *almost* is important. For Winthrop both utters and alters Moses's "last farewell." If the proper reference were actually identified, the last paragraph of Winthrop's sermon would offer a complex and richly layered climax summarizing all that has come before and gesturing toward all that he hopes will follow.[1]

We can see that relation, however, only if we know which Bible Winthrop used. For when the Norton and Heath anthologies quote Deuteronomy 30:1–3, they not only turn to the wrong passage, but also use the wrong Bible. Winthrop's sermon relies solely on the Geneva Bible, not the King James Version (KJV), which we can determine by tracking various verse translations throughout. To give just one example, in quoting Proverbs 3:9, Winthrop writes, "honor the Lord with thy riches," as the Geneva has it, whereas the KJV tells readers to "honour the Lord with thy substance." In those few cases where Winthrop does not follow the Geneva exactly, he actually provides his own loose translation or paraphrase. For example, Winthrop quotes Galatians 6:10, "Do good to all especially to the household of faith." But neither the Geneva nor the KJV nor any other Bible translates the verse precisely this way. In every instance, then, Winthrop offers his own translation or quotes the Geneva exactly—and most often it is the latter.[2] Matching one text to another from beginning to end reveals the Geneva, not the KJV, behind *A Model of Christian Charity*.

To understand why that matters, we have to know something of the seventeenth-century Bible wars that surged across England. Beginning in 1611, two English translations of scripture vied for authority: the King James Version, authorized by King James I (1603–1625), and the Geneva, produced by Calvinist scholars in Switzerland fifty years earlier. Before the KJV appeared, the Geneva was the most widely read Bible in English, running through 140 editions between 1560 and 1644. It had emerged from a context of persecution and exile. During the reign of the Catholic monarch Mary I (1553–1558), many Protestants fled England and ended up in Geneva, the center of John Calvin's authority. These exiled Protestants collaborated on a new translation of scripture, and their edition soon became enormously popular—in part because it was so much smaller and more affordable than any alternative. The way a book is built tells us a great deal about how it gets used and by whom. And the Geneva Bible, we know, was built for all.[3]

In trying to reach the masses, the Geneva also tried to guide them. What the population found in this Bible was far more than a translation of scripture. They also discovered a whole world of helpful notes. The Geneva divided chapters into verses for the first time in English, and it annotated those verses with moral explanations and theological glosses—an immense Calvinist commentary of over three hundred thousand words crowding every single page. In addition, the Geneva Bible cross-referenced passages, so that someone reading Romans 13:9 ("Thou shalt love thy neighbor as thyself") would also be directed to Leviticus 19:11, Matthew 21:39, Mark 12:31, Galatians 5:14, and James 2:8. In other words, the Geneva Bible conceived of scripture as a vast system of unified meaning, a web of scriptural passages interlinking, paralleling, and supporting one another. Whenever Winthrop quoted from one passage in the Geneva, its implications rippled out to others, verse flowing into verse. Such was the power and importance of the Geneva. It was, in effect, the first "study Bible" in English—prepared and annotated for all.[4]

Beyond the Geneva's network of passages and its guiding moral theology, however, its notes also provided a biblical rationale for resisting ungodly rule. These notes are what made the Bible potentially dangerous—and why it would later take on so much significance. Emanating from Geneva in the time of John Calvin, the text embraced his core principle that God alone is sovereign. That belief did not necessarily distinguish Reformed thinkers from anyone else in this period, but its wholehearted acceptance could sometimes pose a challenge to the authorities in place. In various passages—especially in the Old Testament—the Geneva Bible identified wicked kings as "tyrants" and explained that godly subjects should respond to their ungodly demands by exercising a limited form of civil disobedience. The monarch was not the final word. Loyalty to God could require resistance to the king.

Though the Geneva supported such a view, this sense of godly, civil disobedience should not be carried too far. After all, the Geneva Bible also instructed readers to honor their magistrates, and it upheld the God-given authority of superiors. The notes supporting civil resistance were few and far between, scattered about in the Old and New Testaments, never prominent. At the same time, they existed. They stood in the notes of the Bible itself, printed on the same page as sacred scripture, and they could be used if one had a mind to use them. While the vast majority of commentary in the Geneva Bible had nothing to do with resisting earthly rulers, the parts that did packed power.[5]

That power did not go unnoticed. King James insisted that the Geneva Bible was the worst of all translations, and when he gave permission for a new translation of scripture, he included a caveat: "that no marginal notes should be added, having found in them, which are annexed to the Geneva translation ... some notes very partial, untrue, seditious, and savoring, too much, of dangerous, and traitorous conceits."[6] In fact, not only were the Geneva's notes removed from the new Bible, but specific words disappeared as well. Where the term "tyrant" had appeared here and there throughout the Geneva Bible, it was consciously and carefully cut from the KJV.

To be sure, King James did not set out from the start of his reign to silence and supplant the Geneva Bible. The idea for a new translation was not even his own. Puritans suggested it. In 1604, at the start of James's reign, English bishops and Puritan leaders met together at Hampton Court Palace to address calls for reform within the Church of England. Most ideas that the Puritans put forth were promptly ignored. But when John Reynolds, a Puritan and president of Corpus Christi College, called for a new translation of scripture, King James gleefully accepted his request. It was the only appeal he endorsed, and in the coming years King James used the project of a new translation to further his desire for a unified and reconciled church—one expressly subordinate to the monarch. James wanted a clear church hierarchy organized around a system of bishops leading all the way up a chain of command to the king. The need for a strict hierarchy and the strong sense of due subordination spelled an end to Geneva's commentary. In the KJV, notes would be limited to just a few linguistic clarifications.[7]

As a result, even though the Geneva and KJV translations share much in common (including many similar translations of individual passages), the ways they were conceived, and conceived of, differ radically. The Geneva Bible had never been constructed as a spur to civil disobedience; it was not designed from the beginning to be a Bible one would wield against kings. But when King James interpreted it that way—and when he then attempted to replace it—the older Bible took on a new resonance of godly resistance. In other words, the making of the KJV remade the Geneva as well. The older Bible became a book that one had to hide from authorities, a translation that embodied the drive of many Protestants for greater purity and reform.

We can see that growing significance by simply looking at who remained faithful to the Geneva and who switched to the KJV. The Pilgrim Separatists of Plymouth, who left the Church of England entirely, carried the Geneva aboard the *Mayflower* and used it exclusively. The Puritans, meanwhile, who never claimed to have separated from the Church of England, brought *both* the Geneva and the KJV to Boston. The suppression of the Geneva Bible is equally telling. Shortly after the KJV appeared, it became illegal to print the Geneva in England, and in 1632, two years after Winthrop used this Bible for his sermon, another man went to prison for importing it from Holland. Such laws were enforced by William Laud, the Archbishop of Canterbury under Charles I (1625–1649) and a primary nemesis of the Puritans. When the Puritans later put him on trial (eventually beheading him), Laud admitted that he had suppressed the Geneva not only to buttress the commercial interests of royal printers but also to dispense with its marginal notes.[8]

Identifying the Geneva translation as the Bible behind *A Model of Christian Charity* thus raises three important points. First, Winthrop's audience would have understood his allusions to the Geneva's notes, glosses, and commentary. As the historian Harry S. Stout explains, "Aside from the Bible itself, the Genevan commentary was the only literary product all people shared in common." Second, the web of biblical citations, quotations, and annotations that make up Winthrop's sermon engaged a much wider network of sacred scripture already created by the Geneva Bible. To quote from one verse was to invoke many others as well. Those connections would have been obvious to listeners either through their past study of scripture or through the text at hand. Sermon-goers often flipped through their Bibles and consulted the verses being used, cited, and illustrated while the minister preached.[9] Third, that network of scripture and commentary included a few notes (especially from Romans 12–13) that explicitly endorsed civil disobedience out of a higher obedience to God. Whatever status such passages had among the godly when they were originally conceived, they had since taken on a new significance with King James's rationale for an *authorized* translation. In other words, it matters which physical Bible Winthrop held and read when he composed *Christian Charity*, and it is no accident that the Geneva, not the KJV, stands behind his text.

The full story of Winthrop's sermon, therefore, necessarily passes through what has come to be called "book history"—that is, what a book actually looks like, how it comes into print, the establishment of presses and licensing, the trade and market, the feel of a volume in one's hands, its heft and binding and images, its structure and commentary, its political resonance and significance. As scholars have been emphasizing for a long time now, the material artifact of a text (the physical object itself) powerfully affects not just the extent of its readership but also the meaning of the words on the page. How a book is made shapes the way readers receive the text. In the nineteenth century, as we shall see, the strange remnant of Winthrop's recovered manuscript—especially its odd cover note in a separate hand—powerfully influenced its history and reception. So too, in Winthrop's day, the elaborate structure and apparatus of the Bible he used had an enormous impact on the sermon he came to write.

We can best see the influence of the Geneva Bible in the climax of Winthrop's sermon: the closing paragraph that both quotes and alters Moses's "last farewell" from Deuteronomy 30. To understand what Winthrop is doing here, it helps to see a page of the Geneva Bible (figure 4). Offering as it does a tapestry of interpretation and annotation, the Geneva commentary at times seems to overwhelm sacred scripture. Notes press in from the margins, defining the words of sacred scripture, explaining terms, pointing readers to the proper understanding of every verse.

What the Geneva Bible does with its marginal commentary is exactly what Winthrop does in the closing paragraph of his sermon. Having seen scripture hemmed in with annotations that constantly interpret and make sense of it, he ends his own sermon with a set of notes and glosses making sense of Moses's "last farewell." Yet in translating the Geneva's blend of text and interpretation into an oral sermon, Winthrop moves seamlessly between scripture and commentary, so that what could be stubbornly held apart on the *c* Looke how the case standeth betwixt Agar and her children, euen so standeth it betweene Ierusalem and hers. *d* That is, Sina. *e* Which is excellent, and of great accompt. *7* He sheweth that in this allegorie, he hath followed the steps of Cap. who foretold that the Church should be made and consist of the children of barren Sara, that is to say, of them which onely spiritually should be made Abrahams children by faith, rather then of fruitfull Agar, euen then representing the casting off of the Iewes, and calling of the Gentiles. *Esa.54.1. f* She that is destroied and wasted. *Rom.8.9. g* After the maner of Isaac, who is the first begotten of the heauenly Hierusalem, as Ismael is of the slauish Synagogue. *h* That seed vnto which the promise belongeth. *i* By the common course of nature, *k* By the vertue of Gods promise and after a spirituall maner. *Gen.21,10. 8* The conclusion of the former allegorie, that we by no means procure and cast backe againe the Slauerie of the Lawe, seeing that the children of the bondmaid shall not be heires.

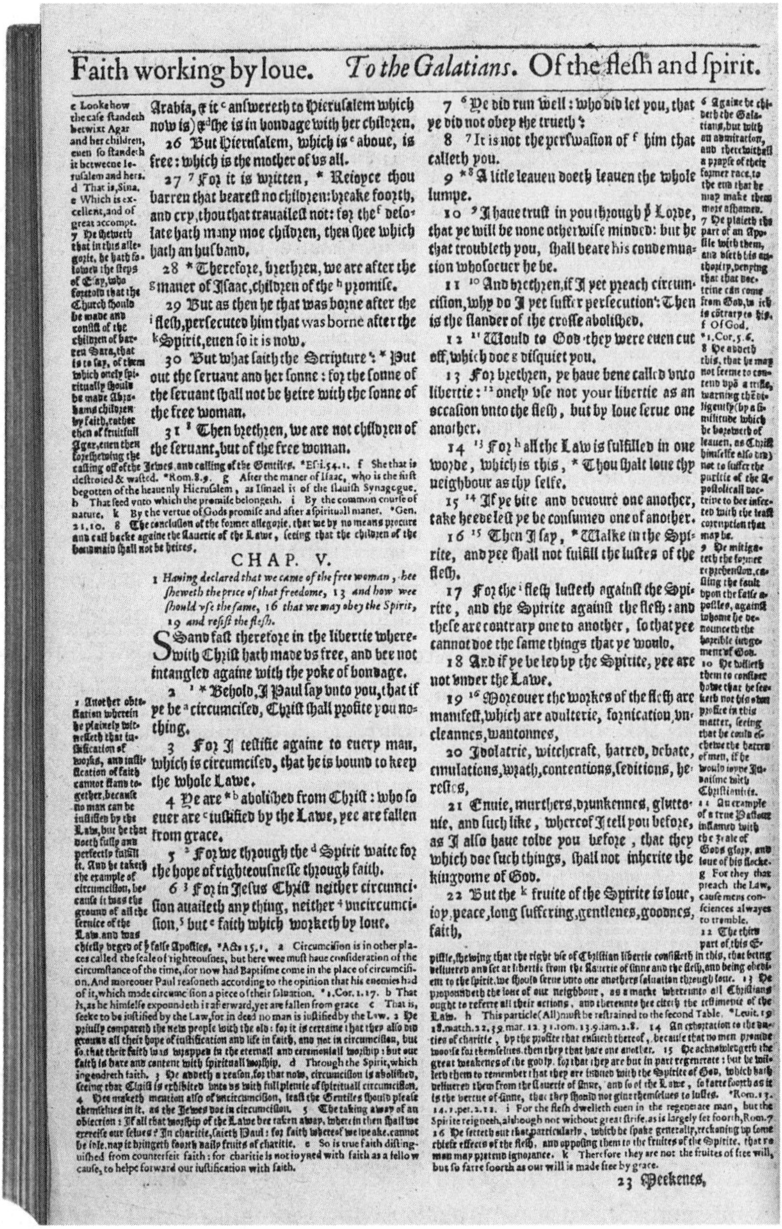

Arabia, & it answereth to Hierusalem which now is, & she is in bondage with her children.

26 But Hierusalem, which is aboue, is free: which is the mother of vs all.

27 For it is written, Reioyce thou barren that bearest no children: breake foorth, and cry, thou that trauailest not: for the desolate hath many moe children, then shee which hath an husband.

28 Therefore, brethren, we are after the maner of Isaac, children of the promise.

29 But as then he that was borne after the flesh, persecuted him that was borne after the Spirit, euen so it is now.

30 But what saith the Scripture? Put out the seruant and her sonne: for the sonne of the seruant shall not be heire with the sonne of the free woman.

31 Then brethren, we are not children of the seruant, but of the free woman.

CHAP. V.

1 Hauing declared that we came of the free woman, hee sheweth the price of that freedome, 13 and how wee should vse the same, 16 that we may obey the Spirit, 19 and resist the flesh.

*1 Another obtestation wherein he plainely witnesseth that iustification of workes, and iustification of faith cannot stand together, because no man can be iustified by the Law, but he that doeth fully and perfectly fulfill it. And he taketh the example of circumcision, because it was the ground of all the seruice of the Law, and was chiefly begun of false Apostles. *Acts 15.1. a* Circumcision is in other places called the seale of righteousnes, but here wee must haue consideration of the circumstance of the time, for now had Baptisme come in the place of circumcision. And moreouer Paul reasoneth according to the opinion that his enemies had of it, which made circumcision a piece of their saluation. *1.Cor.1.17. b* That is, as he himselfe expoundeth it afterward, yet are fallen from grace. *c* That is, seeke to be iustified by the Law, for in deed no man is iustified by the Law. 2 He plainly compareth the new people with the old: for it is certaine that they also did grounde all their hope of iustification and life in faith, and not in circumcision, but so that their faith was wrapped in the externall and ceremoniall worship: but our faith is bare and content with spirituall worship. *d* Through the Spirit, which ingendreth faith. 3 He addeth a reason, for that now, circumcision is abolished, seeing that Christ is exhibited vnto vs with full plentie of spirituall circumcision. 4 He maketh mention also of vncircumcision, least the Gentiles should please themselues in it, as the Iewes doe in circumcision. 5 The taking away of an obiection: If all that worship of the Law bee taken away, where in then shall we expresse our selues? In charitie, saith Paul: for faith whereof we speake, cannot be idle, nay it bringeth foorth daily fruits of charitie. *e* So is true faith distinguished from counterfeit faith: for charitie is not ioyned with faith as a fellow cause, to helpe forward our iustification with faith.*

Stand fast therefore in the libertie wherewith Christ hath made vs free, and bee not intangled againe with the yoke of bondage.

2 Behold, I Paul say vnto you, that if ye be circumcised, Christ shall profite you nothing.

3 For I testifie againe to euery man, which is circumcised, that he is bound to doe the whole Lawe.

4 Ye are abolished from Christ: who so euer are iustified by the Lawe, yee are fallen from grace.

5 For we through the Spirit waite for the hope of righteousnesse through faith.

6 For in Iesus Christ neither circumcision auaileth any thing, neither vncircumcision, but faith which worketh by loue.

7 Ye did run well: who did let you, that ye did not obey the truth?

8 It is not the perswasion of him that calleth you.

9 A litle leauen doeth leauen the whole lumpe.

10 I haue trust in you through the Lord, that ye wil be none otherwise minded: but he that troubleth you, shall beare his condemnation whosoeuer he be.

11 And brethren, if I yet preach circumcision, why do I yet suffer persecution? Then is the slander of the crosse abolished.

12 Would to God they were euen cut off, which doe disquiet you.

13 For brethren, ye haue bene called vnto libertie: onely vse not your libertie as an occasion vnto the flesh, but by loue serue one another.

14 For all the Law is fulfilled in one worde, which is this, Thou shalt loue thy neighbour as thy selfe.

15 If ye bite and deuoure one another, take heede lest ye be consumed one of another.

16 Then I say, Walke in the Spirite, and yee shall not fulfill the lustes of the flesh.

17 For the flesh lusteth against the Spirite, and the Spirite against the flesh: and these are contrary one to another, so that yee cannot doe the same things that ye would.

18 And if ye be led by the Spirite, yee are not vnder the Lawe.

19 Moreouer the workes of the flesh are manifest, which are adulterie, fornication, vncleannes, wantonnes,

20 Idolatrie, witchcraft, hatred, debate, emulations, wrath, contentions, seditions, heresies,

21 Enuie, murthers, drunkennes, gluttonie, and such like, whereof I tell you before, as I also haue tolde you before, that they which doe such things, shall not inherite the kingdome of God.

22 But the fruite of the Spirite is loue, ioy, peace, long suffering, gentlenes, goodnes, faith,

*6 Againe he chideth the Galatians, but with an admiration, and therewithall a pange of their former race, to the end that he may make them more ashamed. 7 He plainely the part of an Apostle with them, and with his owne, that he is, by denying that they doe... trine can come from God, in it is contrary to his, f of God. *1.Cor.5.6. 8* He sheweth this, that he may not seeme to condemn vpon a trifle, warning them diligently to put a mistrust which be bewitched of leauen, as Christ himselfe also teacheth, not to suffer the particle of the old leuen of purpose to bee infected with the least corruption that may be. 9 He mitigateth the former reprehension, casting the fault vpon the false apostles, against whome he denounceth the horrible iudgement of God. 10 He willeth them to consider by the feare they ought to... of men, if he would serue Iudaisme with Christianitie. 11 An example of a true Pastour, inflamed with the zeale of Gods glory, and loue of his flocke. g For they that preach the Law, cause mens consciences alwayes to tremble. 12 The other part of this Epistle, shewing that the right vse of Christian libertie consisteth in this, that being deliuered and set at libertie from the Rauerie of sinne and the flesh, and being obedient to the Spirit, we should serue vnto one another by saluation through loue. 13 He propoundeth the loue of our neighbour, as a marke whereunto all Christians ought to referre all their actions, and therevnto hee citeth the testimonie of the Law. h This particle (All) must be restrained to the second Table. *Leuit.19.18. match.22.39. mar.12.31. rom.13.9. iam.2.8. 14* An exhortation to the duties of charitie, by the profite that ensueth thereof, because that no man procureth more for themselues, then they that hate one another. 15 He admonisheth the great weakenesse of the godly, for that they are but in part regenerate: but he willeth them to remember that they are indued with the Spirite of God, which hath deliuered them from the slauerie of sinne, and so of the Law, so farre foorth as it is the vertue of sinne, that they should not giue themselues to lusts. *Rom.27. 1.4.1.pet.2.11. 15* For the flesh dwelleth euen in the regenerate man, but the Spirit reigneth, although not without great strife, as is largely set foorth, Rom.7. 16 He setteth out that particularly, which he spake generally, reckoning vp some chiefe effects of the flesh, and opposing them to the fruites of the Spirite, that no man may pretend ignorance. k Therefore they are not the fruites of free will, but so farre foorth as our will is made free by grace.*

23 Meekenes,

Figure 4: Galatians 5:13–14 in the Geneva Bible, surrounded by Calvinist commentary. The Bible, that is, the holy Scriptures contained in the Old and New Testament *(London, 1610), RB 97047. The Huntington Library, San Marino, California.*

printed page becomes unified in his sermon. In such ways, the very structure of the Geneva Bible served as license not just to invoke scripture but also to intervene in its language—to quote from the Bible and interpret it at the same time, moving back and forth without pause and without markers, never indicating when he was using his own voice or when he was turning to the voice of Moses.[10]

To illustrate the workings of this process, I have set Deuteronomy 30:15–20 next to its counterpart in *Christian Charity* and put in bold all of Winthrop's alterations and additions (table 1). In this side-by-side comparison, we can see Winthrop doing to Moses what the Geneva Bible does throughout: he interprets and applies as he proceeds.[11] "Beloved" replaces "Behold" to begin the exhortation with a new form of address. Then Winthrop changes his position in relation to listeners. Moses led the Israelites through the wilderness, but he never entered the Promised Land himself; he delivered his commands and instructions to a people who would be setting off without him. Winthrop, however, goes along. Thus, he shifts all the personal pronouns of Moses's last farewell: where Moses spoke with "I" and "thee," Winthrop speaks of "us" and "our" and "we." That shift highlights an important feature of this finale. Divided between the rich and the poor, Winthrop's envisioned community nonetheless stands equal before God: "Beloved, there is now set before *us*," he begins. Spiritual unity cuts across the sermon's opening "doctrine" of social divide. Rulers receive the same instructions and the same commands as those whom they oversee. To disobey such commands is to threaten their God-given authority to rule.

The next major change to Moses's speech highlights the central concern of Winthrop's sermon: that in any financial exchange, the primary factor must be love. God has commanded his followers not only to "love the Lord our God" and to "walk in his ways" (as Moses preached) but also to "love one another" (Winthrop's addition). In the New Testament, Paul uses that command in Galatians 5:13–14 and Romans 12:8–10 to summarize the law and the prophets. As Winthrop had already preached, "love is the fulfilling of the law." Such love, if embodied, would build a community opposed to greedy, self-centered profit-seeking. Winthrop makes his point clear when he *defines* Moses's language of "other gods" as "our pleasures and profits" (another of Winthrop's additions to scripture).

Table 1. Deuteronomy 30:15–20 set side by side with the last
paragraph of *Christian Charity*

Deuteronomy 30:15–20	*A Model of Christian Charity*, final paragraph (differences in boldface)
[15] Behold, I have set before thee this day life and good, death and evil, [16] In that I command thee this day, to love the LORD thy God, to walk in his ways, and to keep his commandments, and his ordinances, and his laws, that thou mayest live, and be multiplied, and that the LORD thy God may bless thee in the land, whither thou goest to possess it. [17] But if thy heart turn away, so that thou wilt not obey, but shalt be seduced and worship other gods, and serve them, [18] I pronounce unto you this day, that ye shall surely perish, ye shall not prolong your days in the land, whither thou passest over Jordan to possess it. [19] I call heaven and earth to record this day against you, *that* I have set before you life and death, blessing and cursing; therefore choose life, that *both* thou and thy seed may live, [20] By loving the LORD thy God, by obeying his voice, and by cleaving unto him, for he is thy life, and the length of thy days; that thou mayest dwell in the land which the LORD sware unto thy fathers, Abraham, Isaac, and Jacob, to give them.	**Beloved there is now** sett before **us** life, and good, deathe and evill in that **wee are** Commaunded this day to love the Lord **our** God, **and to love one another** to walke in his wayes and to keepe his Commaundements and his Ordinance, and his lawes, **and the Articles of our Covenant with him** that **wee** may live and be multiplyed, and that the Lord **our** God may blesse **us** in the land wh[i]ther **wee** goe to possesse it: But if **our** heartes shall turne away soe that **wee** will not obey, but shall be seduced and worshipp other Gods **our pleasures, and proffitts**, and serve them; **it is** propounded unto **us** this day, **wee** shall surely perishe out of the good Land wh[i]ther **wee** passe over **this vast Sea** to possesse it; Therefore **lett us** choose life, that **wee**, and **our** Seede, may live, by obeyeing his voyce, and cleaveing to him, for hee is **our** life, **and our prosperity**.

Winthrop speaks here the way the Geneva commentary reads. The Geneva Bible took a statement of scripture and offered a clear definition, explanation, and application in the margins. In the same way, when Winthrop comes to Moses's "other gods," he clarifies that "pleasures and profits" are the idols they must all avoid. God alone must serve as the source of "our prosperity," Winthrop declares.

Throughout his sermon, and in his other writings as well, it is clear that the worship of riches caused Winthrop to quake with fear. It is what he had already seen ruin other settlements, and he knew that if this drive were not restrained in New England, it would corrupt his entire community.

For all that Winthrop alters Moses's speech, the mere fact that he invokes Moses to send his Puritan followers forward has come to matter most in larger histories of American exceptionalism. In using Moses's last farewell to close out his sermon, Winthrop relates New England to Israel. Transforming the waters of the Jordan into the waves of the Atlantic, he draws clear parallels between his future settlement and the ancient chosen people of God. With such a move, Winthrop seems to open a powerful form of American exceptionalism—a sense that the Puritans had been selected and set apart by God, uniquely blessed and divinely tasked with a special purpose in the world. And that self-conception, the story goes, planted the seeds of American exceptionalism still sprouting up today.[12]

Given the narrative of American exceptionalism that this story supports, it is important to note a small but significant detail: Winthrop and other Puritans also frequently compared *England* to Israel. They used the language of "Jerusalem" and "Israel" to talk as much about the land they were leaving behind as the land they were headed toward. But if England was Israel and New England was Israel, who then was chosen? The answer to that question has everything to do with what it meant to be called. In our attempt to understand Puritan language and its use of scripture, we have to distinguish between what later generations would claim about the Puritans and what the Puritans claimed about themselves. Winthrop, along with his colleagues, certainly *did* believe they were called—but no differently than other Protestants in other places. For those who were "chosen," those who were "called out" (*ecclesia*), were always understood to be the *whole church*—all the saints, all the godly, all the gatherings of the faithful in all the parts of the world wherever the Lord had appointed them to dwell, whether in England, New England, the Netherlands, or elsewhere. Winthrop and his followers never believed that God had set them apart single-handedly to save the world.

Since Puritans understood the whole worldwide church to be the New Israel, they also understood themselves to be just one small part of that much broader communion. From the very beginning of their colonial settlement, New England Puritans conceived of their society in relation to an international community of Reformed Christianity, which they hoped to join and bolster through their example in America. The case of Israel served them, therefore, as a model—just as it did for *any* people who were called by God. Talk of Israel, then, did not necessarily mean that a particular people had been specially chosen or set apart. Instead, "Israel" could mean many things to many people, demonstrating anything from faithfulness to fallenness. This was just how Reformed Christians thought and talked. No matter where they lived or where they might be headed next, they looked to the Bible to guide them. The example of Israel functioned for them as a continuing point of comparison. For Puritans, the reformation of the true church and the coming of the Kingdom of God had nothing to do with New England or America in particular; it had everything to do with constructing models of Christian charity wherever the godly happened to gather.[13]

This broader context helps us understand Winthrop's proclamation that "the eyes of all people are upon us." Such a declaration, again, is not a claim to American exceptionalism. Instead, it is a repetition of the call made to the Church of England, as found—once again—in the Geneva Bible. From 1560 until at least 1576, each edition of the Geneva included an open letter to Queen Elizabeth. Focused on her role as England's reigning sovereign of both church and state, the letter congratulated her for the triumph of Protestantism in her country and proclaimed, "What enterprise can there be of greater importance, and more acceptable unto God, or more worthy of singular commendation, than the building of the Lords Temple, the house of God, the Church of Christ, whereof the Son of God is the head and perfection?" After exhorting her to further reforms of the church, it warned that failure would discourage the godly worldwide, for, as the translators explained, "the eyes of all that fear God in all places behold your country as an example to all that believe."[14]

In Winthrop's charge to the emigrating Puritans—between his "Reasons to Be Considered" and *A Model of Christian Charity*—he deploys the same strategy of celebration, exhortation, and warning that we find in the Geneva's open letter to Queen Elizabeth. "What can be a better work and more honorable and worthy a Christian," he invites readers to ponder, "than to help raise and support, a particular Church while it is in the Infancy." To ensure success, he urges his followers to redouble their efforts toward reform: "Whatsoever we did or ought to have done when we lived in England, the same must we do and more also where we go." Finally, he tempers optimism with a warning against failure: "for we must consider that we shall be as a city upon a hill, the eyes of all people are upon us; so that if we shall deal falsely with our God in this work we have undertaken and so cause him to withdraw his present help from us, we shall be made a story and a by-word through the world."[15] Paralleling the structure of the Geneva translators' open letter to Queen Elizabeth (and using some of the same phrasing), Winthrop balances hope with fear. The Puritans should live so as to be an example of godliness and good community—knowing that if they fail, others will see.

Winthrop, in other words, bases his model of Christian charity on models available to him in the Geneva Bible. With an imagination shaped through the combination of Paul, Moses, and the Geneva commentary, Winthrop issues into the world another vision of godly community. The last paragraph, the climax and exhortation reciting and paraphrasing Deuteronomy 30:15–20, brings together scripture, sacred time, political history, and future hopes to plant a new, additional model of Christian charity on a distant shore. And it all begins with that opening word: "Beloved." It has been suggested that the copyist misread the text and inscribed "Beloved" where he ought to have written "Behold." But the mistake is just too perfect to be mistaken. "Beloved," as a term of address, draws out the sense of Winthrop's entire sermon. Paul frequently called his followers "dearly beloved" and explained that love fulfilled the law of Moses. In this one word, Winthrop weaves Paul into Moses and Moses into Paul while highlighting his primary concern: godly communities, formed under the auspices of the gospel, fulfill Old Testament law only if they live according to love—only if they become, by God's grace, a community of the "beloved."

Winthrop's last words, chosen to motivate his followers, offer them the same decision Moses once set before the Israelites: either "life and good" or "death and evil." Winthrop hoped that his community would choose wisely and so become a model of Christian charity. But if so, the application of his address was still quite limited. Such modeling did not involve a specific form of church-state polity (all of that would be worked out later), nor did it entail a solitary mission to save the world (that would be invented in due time). Rather it was the humbler claim—and insistent hope—that this group of godly emigrants could, along with all other such communities spread throughout the world, demonstrate what a flourishing community of love actually looks like. Winthrop cites within his sermon other famous models of Christian charity, such as the Macedonians and Waldensians, and he calls on his listeners to join in their renown. In doing so, Winthrop sets out to accomplish in his own small way what the Geneva translators—*his* fathers in the faith—had long ago demanded of England's queen, knowing all the while that he, too, might fail.

The Geneva Bible, therefore, is the key to uncovering the meaning of *A Model of Christian Charity*. In the Geneva-inspired alterations and additions to Deuteronomy 30:15–20, we can see how Winthrop ties together all his many hopes and fears. It has been claimed, quite rightly, that the famous "city upon a hill" words "do not stand as climax or conclusion to Winthrop's principal arguments. They occur, instead, in passing, in the midst of a paragraph that commences with and proceeds to other and thematically more central matters."[16] That is true. Winthrop does not bring his sermon to its highest pitch through Matthew 5:14 but rather through Deuteronomy 30:15–20. This closing paragraph is the grand finale—the "last farewell" that attempts to initiate what had been illuminated all along: a model of Christian charity.

As for that phrase of Winthrop's that has become most famous today—his declaration that "we shall be as a city upon a hill"—an even broader seventeenth-century context helps us understand what this verse actually meant to him, and what has become of it ever since.

CHAPTER THREE

The Meaning of Winthrop's City on a Hill

WHATEVER ELSE WINTHROP'S SERMON might have said—however strange its manuscript history, however intricate its structure, however dependent on the Geneva Bible—one enduring phrase has stood above the rest: "For we must consider," Winthrop declares, "that we shall be as a city upon a hill." In the twentieth century, those words would become a kind of tagline for the entire United States, another way to link the "first" American sermon forward to the continuing vision of the nation. But it could become a modern slogan only because of the way it operated in a seventeenth-century theological debate between Protestants and Catholics. On both sides in the debate, this phrase had little to do with exceptional nations. Instead, Catholics and Protestants believed that Jesus's "city on a hill" referred to the true church, the communion of saints and the gathering of the godly in particular places (Protestants) or as one universal institution (Catholics). As they argued over the proper meaning of this phrase, "city on a hill" came to serve as a powerful weapon not for Protestants or Puritans like John Winthrop but for Catholics. Matthew 5:14 became one of the strongest bludgeons in their arsenal, and they frequently hauled it out to pummel their Protestant foes. The way Protestants responded to that assault shaped and enabled the adoption of this line by later American politicians. In other words, to get to Ronald Reagan, Mitt Romney, and many others who have cited Winthrop to define the United States, we have to begin with a Protestant-Catholic struggle over scriptural interpretation and the nature of the true church. That is how "city on a hill" first enters American literature.

The phrase "city on a hill," as we know, comes from Jesus's Sermon on the Mount. "Ye are the light of the world," Jesus proclaims in Matthew 5:14–16: "A city that is set on an hill, cannot be hid. Neither do men light a candle, and put it under a bushel, but on a candlestick, and it giveth light unto all that are in the house. Let your light so shine before men, that they may see your good works, and glorify your father which is in heaven." These biblical words were open and available to any Christian on either side in a dispute. Yet in the seventeenth century, Protestants and Catholics took very different meanings from Jesus's simple declaration. For Catholics, Matthew 5:14 defined the true church as a permanent, visible, universal institution: Jesus's true followers were "set on a hill" to be seen by all. Since Protestants first appeared in the 1500s—since they had been effectively nonexistent, invisible, unknown, or unseen for over a millennium—how could they argue that they were descended from the life and teachings of Christ? How could they claim that they were preserving and passing on the gospel? It was far more likely, Catholics claimed, that these newfangled Protestants were heretics creating false doctrine rather than conserving sacred truth. As such a line of thinking illustrates, Catholics defined the true church through a clear line of descent leading from one pope to the next, from Christ through Peter to the present day. That line of descent is what made the church public and visible. Jesus's declaration suggested that Christians ought to be seen. And if *being seen* is an essential feature of the true church, Catholics argued, then the true church *had* to be Catholic. Theirs, after all, was the only public and visible church from the time of Christ to now.

Moreover, Catholics added, Jesus made the reason for his declaration abundantly clear. The church had to be public and visible—it had to be the "city on a hill" of the Roman Catholic Church—so that all Christians would know where to turn for guidance. In every age, Christians were admonished to obey the teachings of the church, and Catholics wondered how anyone could have done so for the past millennium and more if they had not actually known which church was true or where it could be found. James Sharpe, a Jesuit who worked to convert Protestants in England, used this line of reasoning in 1630, the same year as Winthrop's sermon. Protestants, he argued, can give no reason for believing one thing rather than another. Their church does not have the "visibility of being *as a tabernacle in the Sun, . . . a city upon a hill: a mountain in the top of mountains elevated above the little hills*, that it may be seen, and known of all the world. All which yet are agreeable to the Catholic Church." Catholics thus scoffed at the Protestant notion of an "invisible church"— the idea that the godly might be hidden and unknown to the world. The true church, Catholics proclaimed, was "hid from no man's eyes." It was "as a City on a hill." In Matthew 5:14, Jesus promised *perpetual visibility* to his true followers, Catholics proclaimed. And the only church perpetually visible since the time of Christ was theirs.[1]

This claim persisted throughout the seventeenth century and beyond. In a publication from 1700, for example, the Protestant biblical scholar John Lightfoot could still be found writing about it, still trying to wrest the phrase "city on a hill" from Catholic hands. "The Papists," Lightfoot said, "indeed brag of the Visibility of their Church. They will have it a City on a Hill; a Candle on a Candlestick, . . . and make a puff at the Protestant Church, because it was not visible Two Hundred Years ago." Lightfoot rejected such thinking, of course, but his rejection only proved its persistence. Matthew 5:14 kept requiring a Protestant answer, in part because its Catholic interpretation seemed so strong. So much was this verse identified with Catholicism that when the philosopher Alexander Ross put together an account of all the world's religions in 1655, he explained the Catholic "Doctrine concerning the Church" with reference to Matthew 5:14: Catholics, he wrote, believe "the true Catholic Church is always visible; for it is compared to a Mountain, to a Candle, to a City on a Hill."[2] In the seventeenth century, Catholics owned "city on a hill." It served as a Roman Catholic proof text, a verse from scripture that proved Protestantism false and

Catholicism true. How that phrase came to be identified with a certain form of Christian nationalism and American exceptionalism in the United States depends on how Protestants came to answer Catholic interpretations of Matthew 5:14.

At first, Protestants responded by simply ignoring this verse altogether. In the face of Catholic claims for the "city on a hill," Protestants pointed instead to Luke 12:32 and Revelations 12, both of which seemed to indicate that the true church *could* be invisible or that it *might* be hidden for a great long while—perhaps for the entire duration of the Middle Ages. In Luke 12:32, Jesus proclaims, "Fear not, little flock: for it is your Father's pleasure to give you the kingdom." If seventeenth-century Catholics claimed possession of the phrase "city on a hill," Protestants owned the line "little flock." It was one of their favorite verses. At about the same time as Winthrop's migration, for example, one of the most popular seventeenth-century defenders of Protestantism, Sir Humphrey Lynde, cited this phrase repeatedly. The sheer size and multitude of the Catholic Church stands against it, he argued, "for our Savior Christ doth especially note the members of his body by the name of a *Little flock*." The true church would always be *small*. Protestants "account not universality of nations and people, a mark of our Church, but we say it is a *little flock, and the number of Gods Elect are but few*." Truth is not measured by size. Orthodoxy cannot be claimed by pointing to the power of one's institution or by counting the people in one's pews—as though the bigger the church, the closer one stands to God. If anything, these Protestants said, the reverse is true. According to many Protestants, scripture indicated that the faithful church of God would often be nothing more than a little band of devout believers, inconspicuous in the wider world.[3]

When not calling the true church "a little flock," Protestants often identified it with the woman of Revelations 12 who flees into the wilderness. In an anti-Catholic poem from 1604, the Puritan Samuel Hieron explained in rhyming couplets,

> The Woman, which to Desert fled,
> From Satan's rage to hide her head,
> By all the Learned's full consent,
> The Church on earth doth represent.

All agreed, in other words, that this woman symbolized the church, and as such, Revelations 12 became the perfect biblical proof text for Protestants. "Do you look for *A City upon a Hill* in the dark night of error and ignorance?" Lynde thundered. "I appeal to your own consciences; to what purpose were the prophecies of Christ and his Apostles, that the Church *should fly into the wilderness, and lie hid there?*" Thomas Taylor, in his anti-Catholic treatise, likewise declared that the "Papists" were confuted in "denying that ever their Church fled into the wilderness," for "if their doctrine be true, that the Church must ever be as a City on a hill; the spirit must be false, and the Scriptures, which affirm she must fly into the wilderness from the fury of Antichrist." Far from being mighty and conspicuous, the true church was often small and hidden, a "little flock," a woman fleeing into the wilderness, a band of believers unseen by the world but nourished by God.⁴ When Winthrop used the phrase "city on a hill," therefore, he constituted a bit of an outlier. That verse was most often used by Catholics; Protestants preferred to speak of themselves in other terms.

Even so, Protestants could not leave Matthew 5:14 alone; they could not cede a verse of scripture to the other side. To unpack and reinterpret that verse, therefore, they began by arguing that Christ never promised perpetual visibility to anyone. As John Calvin argued in the early days of the Reformation, "We, on the contrary, affirm that the church can exist without any visible appearance, and that its appearance is not contained within that outward magnificence which they [Catholics] foolishly admire." John Prime, a powerful English Protestant scholar, explained, "The highest hills may be sometimes hid with mists." Lights go out. Hills can disappear. Cities shining in the night can descend into utter darkness—just as the greatness of the early church gave way to the false doctrines and perversions marking the Roman Catholic Middle Ages. For Protestants, the image of a "city on a hill" guaranteed nothing. Years later, the famous Puritan writer John Owen phrased this Protestant position well: "When a Church professeth the Truth, it is the *ground and pillar* of it, a City on a hill; that is visible though no man see it."⁵ *Visible though no man see it*—that line best summarizes how Protestants could reclaim Matthew 5:14. The "perpetual visibility" of the true church was theoretically and theologically always possible, but its actual flourishing varied from age to age. Ideally, these Protestants admitted, the true church should shine forth in all its glory, like a city on a hill. Yet merely being seen was itself no mark of truth.

Instead of guaranteeing visibility, Protestants argued, Jesus was actually warning against falling away. The "cannot" of "cannot be hidden," Prime clarified, "is here taken for *Cannot* in duty, . . . not for an absolute impossibility." Rather than a pledge, Jesus was offering a caution. He was saying that true Christians, wherever they happened to live, had better behave as though the whole world could see. The words "a City set upon a Hill cannot be hid" were "spoken by way of instruction," one writer explained: Christ taught his followers "to be careful and accurate in the ordering of their life, as being to be seen of all." For Protestants, the visibility of true godliness became a duty, not a promise. And as a result, although the true church remained forever *present* in the world, its actual *appearance* could come and go.[6]

The idea that the true church always existed somewhere, even if it went unseen, meant that Protestants had to go about rewriting church history in order to refute Catholic charges about lineal descent. Starting in the sixteenth century and continuing ever since, the phrase "city on a hill" has summoned forth new histories. As American exceptionalism in the twentieth century would rely on narratives of the nation for support—finding an origin point, explaining the glory of the founders, and defining who had remained "true" to them—so Protestant citations of "city on a hill" required a whole new account of the church's true past, something that led straight from Christ to the light of Martin Luther. Puritans, after all, claimed to be getting *rid* of "men's inventions," not inventing something new. But in order to tie themselves back to Christ, they had to argue that they and their ancestors held to the gospel through a millennium of Catholic abuse.

As a result, Protestants penned histories of dissent. They pointed to supposed heretics of previous centuries and reinterpreted them as true believers, reformers, and saints. According to the usual Protestant church histories, Catholicism and its rise had turned the party of protest into the party of truth: dissent marked the descent of true religion. In this way, Protestants could reclaim antiquity and visibility *against* Catholicism, even if, as they admitted, that visibility was seldom seen. The popular Protestant defender Sir Humphrey Lynde explained that he began his voluminous writings because a Jesuit challenged him to "prove out of some good Authors, that the Protestant Church was in all ages visible, especially in the ages before Luther." In response to this challenge, Lynde tried to show that protesters and reformers—the true believers of ages past—had existed and been known from the time of Christ to the present day. Similarly, George Abbot, the Archbishop of Canterbury, claimed that Protestants alone "retained the purity of the Apostles doctrine." He then spent the majority of his treatise (over seventy pages) offering a detailed history of dissenters and reformers before Luther, a long line of protest and true belief.[7]

Again, there is a simple and important point embedded in this complicated, broader debate. Whenever people claim to be a "city on a hill," they imply that they are upholding some foundational truth. They write history. They offer an interpretation of the past that defines who counts as a "hero" or a "heretic." In the seventeenth century, choosing which figures to venerate as founders and followers of the true church depended on how and where one took the "city on a hill" to shine. Moreover, explaining what counted as the actual "city on a hill" in the present day depended on church histories that could spell out its founders and citizens in ages past. What was true in the seventeenth-century debate about the church remains true in modern debates about the nation. Three and four centuries ago, the question concerned who had remained faithful to Christ. In twentieth-century America, the question became who had remained faithful to the founders of the nation. In either case, the invocation of "city on a hill" summons forth an account of history that traces one's own side back to the beginning, a succession of true saints upholding the original revelation against all heretics, however powerful.

When Governor John Winthrop, in 1630, declared to fellow emigrants that "we shall be as a city upon a hill," he entered this broader international debate. Several scholars have argued that Winthrop's sermon does not announce the establishment of an exemplary model or a grand mission for Christendom. According to the rather extreme view of the literary scholar Andrew Delbanco, for example, Winthrop "expresses a desire for anonymity." What he hoped to create, these critics agree, was something like a refuge, a safe haven where the godly could live quietly in the purity of the ordinances of God. Winthrop did not want attention; he wanted to be left alone. But if Winthrop really wanted to make that his message, he had the means and the verses to do it. He could have proclaimed, as many Protestants did, that the true church was a "little flock." Or he could have claimed that true believers would have to bide their time in the wilderness, like the woman of Revelations 12. In fact, that is precisely what several other Puritan colonists did say. In other words, if scholars are right that Winthrop's sermon expresses a hope for a hidden and invisible refuge of true belief, it seems rather strange for him to have skipped the usual Protestant verses cited to make just that point—ones he clearly knew quite well.[8]

At the same time, given the broader Protestant treatment of the phrase "city on a hill"—that it served primarily as a warning and a hope, not a promise or a guarantee—we should note the caution that surrounds Winthrop's use of it. He knew that the "city" could easily fall apart, and if it failed, it would become a notorious "byword to the nations." In the seventeenth century, the Protestant interpretation of "city on a hill" typically distrusted the most prominent visible institution claiming to have the truth and calling itself a "city on a hill." Still, Protestants always *hoped* to gain the higher ground. They did not want to be forever in dissent. With the right sort of people at the helm, they believed, the truth would shine again.

This is the way it went for Protestants. They hoped to create places where the true church would flourish, but whenever it came into power, the sheer visibility of that power made the church institution suspect. In the same year as Winthrop's sermon, for example, Lynde in London was proclaiming against Catholics, "Your *Church* of *Rome* is too too visible in this Kingdom." And within the first decade of settlement in New England, protestors led by Anne Hutchinson and John Wheelwright would make the same claims again, this time dissenting not from Catholics abroad nor from the Church of England but from the Puritan institutions of John Winthrop and his peers. For Hutchinson and Wheelwright, it was the ministers and magistrates of Puritan New England who had become "too too visible," using their power to abuse the faithful. Quite predictably, these New England dissenters defined themselves as a "little flock."[9]

Winthrop's use of "city on a hill," therefore, is much more surprising and significant than we have previously assumed. The striking part is not so much that the line occurs in passing but that it occurs at all. Lynde's words ("too too visible") reveal a tension present already in England and soon to face New England as well: in the midst of defending a worldwide *invisible* communion of saints, how could they hope to establish a local, *visible* "city on a hill"? That question helps explain an important shift in the meaning of Matthew 5:14. For while Catholics saw the verse as applying to one universal church, Protestants much more often aligned the phrase with *particular* instantiations of the church in specific times and places. When Winthrop used the line, for example, he likened *the people of Massachusetts*, not the universal church or the worldwide Protestant cause, to a "city upon a hill." The historian Francis Bremer has demonstrated well how Puritans sometimes used Matthew 5:14 as a call to exemplarity—a call to serve as a *model* to others.[10] But the important point is that those models, those "lights" and "cities," refer only to specific communities and towns, the people of particular places—not Protestantism in general or any other broader institution. When a Protestant like William Wilkinson used the phrase, for example, he claimed that the English town of Colchester, "for the earnest profession of the gospel, became like unto the city upon a hill."[11]

For Protestants, therefore, "city on a hill" identified any gathering of godly Christians, wherever the light of Christ might shine. There was not *one* "city on a hill" (the Catholic Church) but *many* (the gatherings of good Protestants in numerous times and places). Different groups of Christians in far-flung places were each called to be like a city on a hill (a hope, a goal); and all Christians in all places were told to behave as though they lived in the sight of all (an admonition, a warning). In that way, Protestants made the "city on a hill" far more *local* and *particular*. There were many cities on many hills, never just one.

Such usage points us to one other important factor in how "city on a hill" has been deployed both then and now: so much depends on the difference between a metaphor and a simile. Again, this seemingly small detail has surprisingly significant effects on how we understand Winthrop and the rhetoric of American exceptionalism today. Catholics often used Matthew 5:14 as a metaphor. They claimed that their church simply *is* the city on a hill that Christ proclaimed. Protestants, in contrast, used Matthew 5:14 more often as a simile. They made comparisons. William Wilkinson, for example, did not call Colchester *a* or *the* city upon a hill; instead, he said it was "*like* unto the city on a hill." He used a simile. And a simile, as much as it asserts likeness, acknowledges difference. If one thing is *like* another thing, then the two things are not identical. When "city on a hill" is used as a simile, it is not a statement of essential identity but instead the offering of a model, an example. Protestants often suggested that this church or that town, this people or that place, had become—for the time being—"like unto" a city upon a hill.

These differences—the local versus the universal, the simile against the metaphor—entailed wide cultural ramifications. Forced to respond to Catholic interpretations of Matthew 5:14, Protestants emphasized particular places as similar to a city upon a hill, embracing an interpretation of Matthew 5:14 that might, in time, slip from an identification of individual churches into towns and territories, regions and colonies, and then, one day, perhaps a nation, maybe America itself. In fact, we can see such slippage in the very manuscript of Winthrop's sermon. In the text as it was originally copied, just before Winthrop reminds his listeners that "we shall be as a city upon a hill," he expresses his hope "that men shall say of succeeding plantations, 'the Lord make it like that of Massachusetts.'" At least, that is what the text initially said. Someone in the meantime scratched out the word "Massachusetts," tried to erase the ink, and wrote over top of it "New England."[12] In all printed editions of this sermon, Winthrop hopes that others will say, "the Lord make it like that of *New England*." Within the sole surviving manuscript, the "city on a hill" has already expanded, from one colony to several, from "Massachusetts Bay" to the region of "New England." Later generations would expand the scope still further, so that "New England" would be reimagined as the seed and sum of the entire nation.

Thus, as this phrase shifted in geographical scale—from a scattered set of communities across the Atlantic and the European continent to Massachusetts alone and then to New England and finally to the whole United States—the localized Protestant usage of Matthew 5:14 has gradually transformed into the more Catholic universal meaning of a singular and exceptional truth, now applied to a nation, not a church. In the rhetoric of President Reagan, the United States simply *is* the solitary "city" standing "strong and true on the granite ridge" as "a magnet for all who must have freedom, for all the pilgrims from all the lost places who are hurtling through the darkness, toward home."[13] Surprising as it may seem, it takes a seventeenth-century Protestant-Catholic theological debate about the marks of the true church to make possible that twentieth-century claim about a country.

Even more surprising, however, has been the rise of Winthrop's sermon in the rhetoric of American exceptionalism. If the language of "city on a hill" always requires an original revelation, by the end of the twentieth century Winthrop's sermon itself had become that point of origin. Yet at the supposed moment of origin itself, on the day when Winthrop delivered *A Model of Christian Charity*, few people heard it, no one recorded it, and everyone forgot it. The declaration that "we shall be as a city upon a hill" was not, in its own day, foundational at all. For over two centuries—from the time of early English colonialism through the creation of a new nation—Winthrop's sermon was so thoroughly unknown that no one even knew it was lost.

PART II

Materials

CHAPTER FOUR

A True History of America

O NCE WINTHROP'S SERMON WAS lost, it might never again have been found. It came back into the world—collected in the early 1800s and first published in 1838—through the work of historical societies, and those societies existed because texts like *A Model of Christian Charity* were constantly being lost. On January 24, 1764, for example, Harvard Hall burned. Smallpox had been plaguing Boston, so the Massachusetts General Court decided to meet in Cambridge while students were away. After the meeting, a smoldering hearth cast a spark that caught a beam. It was a windy night, and the fire spread quickly. Local residents rushed to the building and managed to put out the fire, but not before the entire hall collapsed. The destruction was enormous. The building housed the library of Harvard College, and every book not checked out on the night of January 24 was lost—almost five thousand volumes. It was, at the time, one of the largest collections in America. The president of Harvard described the blaze and its aftermath as "the most ruinous loss [Harvard College] ever met with since its foundations."[1]

It was not the first "ruinous loss" New England would see, nor its last. The lieutenant governor of Massachusetts Thomas Hutchinson (1711–1780) loved American history, and he studied it by collecting and preserving books and manuscripts throughout his mansion. But Hutchinson was accused of being a Loyalist, and no matter how hard he tried to moderate the rising tensions between taxed Americans and a taxing Parliament, his moves were repeatedly seen as steps in support of the hated Stamp Act. So in 1765, a year after Harvard burned, a mob formed at the lieutenant governor's mansion, burst through the doors and windows, smashed the furniture, stole the silver, and—unfortunately—destroyed the documents of American history that Thomas Hutchinson had so carefully collected.

The destruction was not one-sided. Like Hutchinson, the venerable minister of the Old South Church in Boston, Thomas Prince (1687–1758), had developed a deep devotion to history, and for many years he amassed old books and manuscripts in his church. He used these records to write *A Chronological History of New England, in the Form of Annals* (1736), a large tome that took readers copiously and laboriously through a long list of dates and events from Creation to 1630. It was not a smashing success. Nonetheless, the *Chronological History* was a landmark of its kind, for Prince had carefully verified every entry with a source. He wanted to be accurate. And that accuracy depended on the materials he stored around him, in boxes and barrels stuffed into the church's steeple. Two decades after Prince died, this collection of historical material mattered little to British soldiers stationed in the church. Like the rebels at Hutchinson's mansion, they scattered Prince's books, pamphlets, and papers across the street.

One man, Jeremy Belknap, looked on all this destruction with horror. The ransacking of Prince's church he called an "irretrievable loss" and a "sacrifice to British barbarity." The soldiers of the king had destroyed the very thing they ought to revere: the records and writings of British colonial history, New England's storied past. Yet as much as he feared mobs, mayhem, and fires, there was one source of danger Belknap considered subtler and more dangerous than all the rest: negligence. Papers held in private hands could be lost without ever being found. "As every person of observation must know," he once remarked, "there are in the Libraries and Custody of Gentlemen of the present age many materials which are now neglected and which may soon be scattered, the loss of which posterity may regret as much as we do now the carelessness of former times."[2] Belknap spent his days combating this carelessness, searching out books and manuscripts from the custody of New England gentlemen, traveling great distances, inspecting papers, copying manuscripts, taking notes, and compiling records. Eventually, he founded an institution that would house all he could get his hands on, and that institution was responsible, years later, for printing *A Model of Christian Charity*.

As Belknap toiled through the woods of New Hampshire seeking letters and manuscripts, another man—equally important to the eventual saving of Winthrop's sermon—worked his way across bumpy, muddy roads farther south, gathering and copying all the historical material he could find. Ebenezer Hazard began collecting papers in 1765, preserving the political pamphlets of the Stamp Act crisis that most people threw out. In 1772, he set to work gathering naval laws and their alterations, thinking such a collection would be valuable to overseas traders and perhaps profitable to himself. Yet within a year of beginning, his eyes grew wide at the deplorable state of American archives, and his plans magnified. He would not stop at naval laws; instead, he would collect *all* state papers. In the same year that Belknap began contemplating a repository farther north, Hazard proclaimed, "I wish to be the means of saving from oblivion many important papers which without something like this collection will infallibly be lost."[3]

Crucially, however, these men exercised radically different notions of preservation. Whereas Belknap wanted a central, safe house to hold all his stuff, Hazard proposed the publication and duplication of whatever he might find. His plan was to *make copies*—handwritten at first but eventually printed. Once the sources had been copied and distributed, they could never be threatened, for the loss of any one copy would never lose them all. Years later, when Hazard had finally pulled his collections together and was about to publish the first of his two-volume *Historical Collections*, Thomas Jefferson endorsed this basic idea: "Time and accident are committing daily havoc on the originals deposited in our public offices," Jefferson wrote. "The late war has done the work of centuries in this business. The lost cannot be recovered; but let us save what remains: not by vaults and locks which fence them from the public eye and use . . . but by such a multiplication of copies, as shall place them beyond the reach of accident." What Hazard brought to the business of preservation, in other words, was the importance of publication—an idea that Belknap quickly embraced. In order to preserve and make available the material of America's past, that material would have to be gathered, stored, and printed.[4]

Such ideas came together when the two men finally met. Belknap and Hazard were the same age, though their lives had taken rather different courses. Born in 1744, in Boston and Philadelphia, respectively, they had each graduated from college in 1762: Hazard went to Princeton, and Belknap went to Harvard. After graduation, Hazard entered printing and eventually joined the postal service, rising to become postmaster general in 1782. Belknap, meanwhile, tried teaching, thought of becoming a missionary, and ended up a Congregational minister in Dover, New Hampshire. He stayed with his congregation in Dover for almost twenty years before moving back to Boston as the minister of Long Lane Church in 1787. Belknap and Hazard met in 1778 and instantly formed a strong bond, sharing not just religious sensibilities but also a deep and abiding interest in American history. Through a correspondence of over twenty years (amounting to over one thousand pages of letters, most of which are now in print), these men detailed their various discoveries, requested information from each other, copied manuscripts for each other, and worked out intellectual puzzles in theology, politics, literature, and science—all the while collecting the records of a nation that had just been born.

Throughout the many years of correspondence, Belknap and Hazard talked frequently about the necessity of saving texts, and when Belknap returned to Boston, they raised this possibility with Harvard. They wanted the college to provide money and space for such a project. Harvard at first seemed interested, but ultimately its trustees failed to act. That seemed to be the way of things with them. Years earlier, another history-minded man, named William Gordon, "proposed to the College that a committee should be appointed to collect all sorts of written and printed materials, for the use of some future historian, and deposit them in the library." Then, too, Harvard was intrigued; then, too, it did not act. Instead, Harvard handed the idea back to Gordon and told him to do something about it. But those who generate ideas are not always the best ones to execute them, and Gordon did nothing. When Belknap approached Harvard years later, the college hemmed and hawed but finally offered no encouragement. "From the very great indifference which reigns among our gentlemen to *exert* themselves," Belknap complained, "I imagine it would be a long-winded, and perhaps ineffectual business, to set on foot a collection of dead materials for the use of a future historian. They acknowledge the utility of such a thing, and that is all."[5]

The idea might never have gotten off the ground but for one other influential man, a wealthy merchant from New York named John Pintard. Raised by his uncle and handed a large financial legacy, Pintard rapidly increased his wealth through trade in the East Indies. By the time he was thirty-two, Pintard had been a trader, an insurance man, a commissioner, a politician, and a philanthropist, but he was above all, as Aaron Burr eventually wrote in a recommendation letter for him, "a merchant & man of business." Like Thomas Hutchinson and Thomas Prince, like Jeremy Belknap and Ebenezer Hazard, this man of business loved American history, and in 1790 he organized an institution called the American Museum "to collect and preserve whatever relates to our Country in art or nature, as well as every material which may serve to perpetuate the Memorial of national events and history." Two years after founding it, however, Pintard went bust. Lured into the deceitful financial dealings of his friend William Duer, Pintard invested heavily in a debt securities scheme. When a bank run ensued, Duer lost his bets, and Pintard ended up broke. He fled to Newark but was found there and put in jail for over a year (Duer spent the rest of his life in prison). With Pintard out of the picture, the American Museum showed little interest in historical manuscripts and instead collected a strange assortment of "curiosities and oddments" that it eventually sold, appropriately, to the circus man P. T. Barnum.[6]

Despite Pintard's checkered past, he may have had more to do with finally establishing historical societies in America than any other person—not because he had the idea (Belknap had the idea years earlier) or because he did the work (he visited Boston only briefly) but because he provided the enthusiasm, encouragement, inspiration, and competition that finally prompted others to act. "This day a Mr. Pintard called to see me," Belknap wrote Hazard on August 10, 1789. "He says he is an acquaintance of yours, and wants to form a Society of Antiquaries, etc., etc. He seems to have a literary taste, is very loquacious and unreserved. Do give me his character." Hazard provided his character—a hesitant endorsement—and wrote, "Mr. Pintard has mentioned to me his thoughts about an American Antiquarian Society. The idea pleases me much. We shall have the plan upon paper one of these days, and you will doubtless be made acquainted with it."[7] Before Hazard and Pintard could begin their project, however, Belknap was back at work himself, gathering his own group of history-minded gentlemen into an elite collectors club of Boston. In other words, it took the pushing of Pintard to get Belknap to act, especially when it seemed like Hazard and Pintard might act first.

On January 24, 1791, exactly twenty-seven years to the day after Harvard Hall had burned, Belknap and nine others founded the Massachusetts Historical Society (MHS). Once the institution was up and running, Belknap immediately began petitioning and begging and bugging and searching out his friends and neighbors to build up his collection of books and manuscripts. "We intend to be an *active*, not a *passive*, literary body," he proclaimed: "not to lie waiting, like a bed of oysters, for the tide (of communication) to flow in upon us, but to *seek* and *find*, to *preserve* and *communicate* literary intelligence, especially in the historical way." That preservation and communication would involve the distinct strategies of both Belknap and Hazard. In Belknap's first address to the public, he listed the devastating losses of Prince's library (1775), the British plundering of the court of common pleas (1776), Thomas Hutchinson's mansion (1765), the burning of the Boston Court House (1747), and finally the "old college at Cambridge" (Harvard Hall, 1764). "From these instances which have occurred during our own memory," he wrote, "it is evident that *Repositories* of every kind, however desirable, are exposed to such accidents, from the hand of time; from the power of the elements, and from the ravages of unprincipled men, as to render them unsafe." He concluded, "There is no sure way of preserving historical records and materials, but by *multiplying the copies*." And so began a massive publication effort eventually called the *Collections of the Massachusetts Historical Society*—hefty tomes whose primary purpose was to copy, print, and distribute American historical material. This is the series in which John Winthrop's "city on a hill" sermon first appeared.[8]

Although Winthrop's sermon was eventually printed at the MHS, it was not actually found there. Instead, *A Model of Christian Charity* was first discovered and still remains in the holdings of the New-York Historical Society (NYHS), which John Pintard established in 1804. After his year in prison, where he spent his time reading books and laying plans, Pintard emerged from debt, rebuilt his wealth, and restored his reputation in New York. With new cultural capital came new cultural campaigns. He pursued his interest in American history by drawing together the wealthy and the elite, seeking again to save the materials he feared would otherwise be lost and leaning on his connections to create the New-York Historical Society. In doing so, Pintard made explicit his indebtedness to Belknap and the MHS. "We feel encouraged to follow this path by the honorable example of the Massachusetts Society," Pintard explained, "whose labors will abridge those of the future historian, and furnish a thousand lights to guide him through the dubious track of unrecorded time."[9] Coming alongside the MHS, Pintard and his coterie of New York gentlemen hoped, like Belknap and Hazard, to collect, preserve, and communicate all the records they could find.

These two historical societies were the first of their kind in America, but they would not be the last. The American Antiquarian Society came next in 1812, and then a few years later the movement exploded. Historical societies tripled in the 1820s, quickly expanding beyond New England. By the time of the Civil War, there were seventy-two historical societies spread across the United States. Three decades later, when the American Historical Association held its first annual meeting, two hundred societies had been founded (though some had since folded), and together they had published *several hundred volumes* of historical material. In 1905 it took more than a thousand pages of small type just to *list* all the material that American historical societies had printed and preserved.[10]

Jeremy Belknap, John Pintard, and Ebenezer Hazard: these men began an immense movement designed to save, copy, and distribute American texts. Yet few people have heard their names.[11] Even scholars of American history frequently pass them by with little notice, though the sources historians use often depend on the collections these men either initiated or inspired. The power of these people, however, should not be underestimated. These relatively unknown figures, along with many others like them in American history—the curators, librarians, collectors, archivists, antiquarians, and often-anonymous initiators and organizers of archives, repositories, and libraries—have shaped not only what we *do* say about America's past but what we *can* say. Their choices have fashioned from an early age the data and details that survive, the stories that others would be able to tell. In that sense, Belknap, Hazard, and Pintard were some of the earliest keepers and most formative makers of the American past.

What Belknap, Hazard, and Pintard kept and created was a version of American history that best appealed to their sense of the nation's high destiny and purpose. At the first meeting of the first historical society in America, those who were gathered under Belknap's direction issued a constitution that outlined their mission. The preservation of American materials, they argued, "conduces to mark the genius, delineate the manners, and trace the progress of society in the United States, and must always have a useful tendency to rescue the true history of this country from the ravages of time and the effects of ignorance and neglect." To "trace the progress" and "rescue the true history": that was their goal. As the public address of the NYHS similarly explained, "Without the aid of original records and authentic documents, history will be nothing more than a well-combined series of ingenious conjectures and amusing fables."[12] These men wanted to get history right, and they knew they could get it right only if they collected and preserved the actual records of the past.

At the same time, getting history right meant finding a way to tell a "true history" they already presumed to know. For Belknap and his peers, the story of America was fairly simple. As he frequently explained, "Our virtuous ancestors fled from the impositions and persecutions to which they were subjected in England, and found in this wilderness an asylum from tyranny. Their example was followed by others, and in North America, the oppressed of Europe have always found safety and relief."[13] Across multiple letters, sermons, lectures, and writings, Belknap kept repeating this same basic tale: America was founded by those who were seeking freedom, and it served now, after the Revolution, as a refuge of liberty for all—or, at least, all the oppressed of Europe. In other words, a certain view of the nation's history guided and inspired these men as they set out to preserve historical material; and the historical materials they preserved—like *A Model of Christian Charity*—in turn bolstered a certain view of the nation's history.

The full biography of *Christian Charity*, therefore, necessarily involves the life stories of Jeremy Belknap, Ebenezer Hazard, and John Pintard, three men who ultimately made possible the finding and printing of Winthrop's sermon. Learning how and why they devoted so much energy to the preservation of American history reveals the reciprocal relationship between story and archive. For when the New-York Historical Society and the Massachusetts Historical Society found, printed, and distributed Winthrop's sermon in 1838, they embedded more firmly in American culture the very narrative they had been created to discover and preserve.

The story of Belknap, Hazard, and Pintard begins with delight. These men studied history because they loved it. It was, to them, a rich adventure, and they longed to "be fellow travellers in quest of knowledge." Early in Belknap's ministry, for example, he wrote to a friend, "You cannot help having observed in me an inquisitive disposition in historical matters. I find it so strong and powerful, and withal so increasing with my opportunities for gratifying it, that it has become a question with me, whether I might not freely indulge it."[14]

Yet that question—that worry about *indulging* in history—reveals deeper drives at work. If history were nothing more than mere "amusement," Belknap explained, then it belonged only to his "leisure hours." If he were to pursue it much further, then history would have to serve his ministry or the public good in some clear and evident way. For those who continue in historical work—for those who devote their time, money, and careers to it—something more than pleasure must pull or push them along, some higher calling or greater cause. In Belknap's case, history had to be useful, or it had to be dropped.[15]

This desire to serve the common good appears all over the letters of Belknap and Hazard. As Belknap aged, he mused, "I have an ambition only to be useful in the world, and the thing which I most dread is to live so long as to be past doing any good." Hazard similarly hoped "that some door of usefulness will be opened to me soon; for it is dreadful to be a cipher in creation." The same feeling can be found in the letters of Pintard. For all three, the idea of service framed their historical labors. They saw their work as part and parcel of the "public good," and they pressed on through a "conviction of the utility of it alone." Early in Belknap's ministry, he worried about indulging too much in history. By 1780, he had no concerns about its practical utility and public good.[16]

Today, the practical utility of history might strike some people as rather strange. Yet in the days of Belknap and Hazard, many extolled history as above all *useful*. John Pintard, the merchant, told others that such studies "add greatly to my stock of useful information." Thomas Jefferson praised Hazard's proposal to collect, copy, and preserve American history as "an undertaking of great utility to the continent in general." Even the state legislature of Massachusetts seemed to agree. When the MHS was chartered in 1794, it was proclaimed a "public utility" by the state and given space in a city building. Speaking to the New-York Historical Society twenty years later, its second president, a Founding Father named Gouverneur Morris, began by pointing out that everyone already knew the immense worth and utility of history: "We live in a Period so enlightened that to display the Use of History would be superfluous labor," he explained. And then he repeated what so many others had already professed: "History is the Science of human nature, Philosophy teaching by Example, the School of Princes." Preachers, politicians, lawyers, merchants—all sorts concluded that the work of history constituted a national good and a public benefit, a *useful* subject that all should know.[17]

These various leaders thought so highly of history in part because it fit a wider emphasis that linked learning to liberty. John Adams, for example, believed that ignorance was the source of all ruin, and his *Dissertation on the Canon and Feudal Law* (1765) urged education as vitally important. His sometime friend and eventual archrival, Thomas Jefferson, agreed. From those who would govern to those who would be governed, these men and others believed that a free and flourishing society would depend on an *informed citizenry*. It is no accident, therefore, that Belknap's commonplace books (the notes and quotes he took on whatever he happened to be reading) include many passages devoted to the importance of education—and specifically its significance for the freedom of citizens in a republic. That was why he believed *all* people needed a good education, male and female, rich and poor.[18]

Many people at the time endorsed the basic necessity and importance of education, and as a result, a variety of learned societies were founded (such as the American Academy for Arts and Sciences in 1780). But none of those societies were focused on saving texts. For Belknap, Hazard, and Pintard, that was deeply disturbing. First, they believed that if a little effort were expended, all the texts of American history could be found, stored, saved, and studied. American history, they thought, did not begin until Europeans arrived—it started in the era of modern writing. As a result, the complete record lay all around, in private homes and public offices. All that was needed was a little willpower to gather it up. Once the records were collected, the "true history" of America could be known and told. Second, and just as important, these men believed that the "true history," once found, would tell a singular story of liberty's advance. When Hazard petitioned Congress for support of his project in 1788, he explained that the country's progress had been so rapid that people could still "recur to the first step taken upon the Continent, and clearly point out different advances from persecution to comparative liberty, and from thence to independent empire." Saving, spreading, and rehearsing that story would produce a distinct cultural identity, a self-image replete with national pride. "We are a people *per se*," Belknap's friend wrote to him in 1785, and for that reason Americans ought not to "imitate any nation in Europe." Instead, he insisted, "We ought to be original . . . in our manners, & independent of other nations, of their follies and vices, as of anything else." Many people agreed, and together they began the work of building a new culture with a unique history and destiny. That project has come to be known as cultural nationalism, and cultural nationalism played a huge role in the saving—and eventually the exalting—of Winthrop's text.[19]

Given the patriotic fervor infusing the historical work of Belknap, Hazard, and Pintard, it might seem that public officials would have eagerly supported it. They did, and they didn't. The backing for historical societies and collections can be measured in

two distinct ways: by words offered or cash given. In declared
support, Belknap, Hazard, and Pintard seldom lacked. Many high-
ranking public officials endorsed Belknap's *History of New Hampshire*
and helped him find or copy sources. John and Abigail Adams both
pushed him forward and praised his projects. And Hazard found enthusiastic backing in none less than Thomas Jefferson. Meanwhile,
top officials in New York publicly lent their support to the New-
York Historical Society.[20]

But were any of these people or others willing to pay for the
work of history? In this matter, Hazard fared best. On July 11,
1778, he wrote the Continental Congress, proposing to preserve a
collection of American historical material for the sake of posterity.
Congress read the letter and sent it to a special committee composed of Richard Henry Lee, William Duer (the same man who
later bankrupted Pintard), and Samuel Adams. These three determined "that Mr. Hazard's undertaking is laudable, and deserves the
public patronage and encouragement, as being productive of public
utility." They told state governments to assist Hazard by furnishing
him copies of whatever papers he deemed valuable, free of charge;
and they resolved to advance Hazard $1,000 for his research and
expenses.[21] This is fairly astounding. In the midst of the Revolutionary War—with plenty of other things to think about—leaders
and legislators in the newly formed United States awarded the first-
ever federal grant for historical research to Ebenezer Hazard.

Then again, it is not clear whether the government ever followed through. Certainly, the various states that were urged to
help Hazard never did. If they had, far more historical material
would have been saved. Nonetheless, as one scholar notes, "The
value of the resolution of Congress lay, of course, in the recognition by the national government of its responsibility and duty in
making archives and historical manuscripts safe and available and
in financing their publication." When Hazard later created a subscription in 1791 for the publishing of his collections, it was signed
by the most notable figures of his day, beginning with President
George Washington and including "the Vice-President, members
of the Cabinet, Senators, Representatives, and civil servants."[22]

Perhaps someone should have mentioned all this support to the
officials in New Hampshire or New York, because Belknap and

Pintard had far more trouble. In 1778, the same year Hazard wrote to the Continental Congress, a friend of Belknap's recommended that he approach the General Court of New Hampshire and ask for money to fund his research and writing, assuring him that the legislature would "make the grant without any difficulty." Belknap pleaded his case, but nothing came of it. In 1785, after the first volume of his *History of New Hampshire* had appeared, he again made a formal petition to the General Court. Describing his narrative of "the struggles and sufferings of our ancestors in the cause of liberty," Belknap asked, "with the utmost respect, to present two copies of the said work to this Honorable Court" and then requested financial assistance. Nothing happened. The request hung around until eventually, years later, a small sum appeared. On February 25, 1791, the governor of New Hampshire, Josiah Bartlett, informed Belknap that for his services to the state, he would receive £50. In granting this award, Bartlett himself conceded, "Myself and some others could have wished the sum greater," but he admitted that not all members of the New Hampshire General Court had "a proper sense of the usefulness & importance of such a work, nor of the labor and expense of compiling it." They might not have known, for example, that the first volume of his New Hampshire history cost Belknap roughly £250 to print—more than twice his annual salary—and the second volume cost nearly £130 more. He appreciated £50 from the General Court, but he thought history was worth far more.[23]

It was an argument that Belknap, Hazard, and Pintard had a tough time making to the public. Pintard's historical society could boast the support of Governor DeWitt Clinton, one of its first members. But even Clinton could not move New Yorkers to pay for it. In 1810, he tried to pass a bill that would endow the Historical Society while incentivizing the killing of wolves and panthers in upstate New York. Surely everyone in the state could get behind one or the other of these two wildly different initiatives. As Pintard put it, "Fortunate shall we deem ourselves ... should the extirpation of Wolves and Panthers lead to the cultivation of Science as well as the fruits of the earth." The Senate passed the bill, but it died in the House. In 1810, the New-York Historical Society would have to go it alone.[24]

All the way through the early 1800s, no matter what political and religious leaders felt about the importance of history and education, few people put their finances behind it. Belknap and Hazard produced multiple books, but none of their publications sold. Because authors paid in advance for their works to be printed, Belknap remained in debt for many years to the man who published volume 1 of his *History of New Hampshire*. After volumes 2 and 3 appeared, they still made no money. "I am sorry that so many remain unsold here," Hazard apologized from Philadelphia. "It must be charged to want of taste in the age, I believe." But it wasn't just Belknap's *History of New Hampshire*; the first attempt at publishing the MHS's papers also failed. In 1794, Belknap began the *American Apollo*, a weekly magazine of archival reproductions and historical reports. It died within a year. When Belknap tried to print all thirty-nine issues together, bundling them into the first volume of the *Collections*, the *Collections* also proved unsuccessful. Soon the MHS suspended its publications. "At present, the *sale* of copies does not pay the expense of printing," Belknap complained in 1795; "and it is hard that the Society should work for the public and get themselves in debt, which is, in fact, the case." Belknap appealed to the public directly, warning that it would give the MHS "extreme pain to record this as one of the characteristics of the American people, that they are backward to encourage the publication of materials for the history of their own country." The warning did nothing. In 1796 and 1797, there were not enough funds to publish any collections at all. Nor did Hazard's work fare better. In issuing the first volume of his *Historical Collections*, he hoped to make a little profit; in issuing the second, he hoped to recoup his expenses; he never made enough from either to issue a third.[25] Public support for American historical material still had not arrived. If the prudent means of preservation demanded publication—the *making of copies*—someone other than the public would have to pay.

And someone other than the public did pay. Belknap and Hazard put their own money into writing, collecting, and publishing American history and historical material. Pintard bought so much for the NYHS that years later the institution still owed him $1,400—a debt it never paid. These three, in other words, put down hard cash for history. When the Massachusetts Historical

Society suspended its collections, Hazard sent some new material he had found along with a little money to help publish it. Belknap thanked him for the gift, explaining, "the receipt of this money, has stimulated several other members of the Society to do something handsome in the way of presents; and one gentleman in particular has put some money into my hands, to be laid out according to my discretion."[26] It was as though no one had yet thought to give privately for the preservation of history. In 1798, three years after these gifts appeared, the Massachusetts Historical Society published its fifth volume of *Collections*. Through private donations, the series lived on, eventually printing Winthrop's sermon.

Yet as much as private money financed most historical preservation in its early days, it still took state money to make possible the finding and printing of John Winthrop's sermon. In 1825, the New-York Historical Society discovered itself deep in debt. When the directors met, they tallied up the total to $10,000 and decided that the only way to raise such funds would be to sell off the library and its collections. For Pintard, the library *was* the society. From its first days forward, its collection of papers, manuscripts, and books had been the whole point. He raged at the decision and never attended another meeting, soon abandoning the New-York Historical Society altogether. Those who proposed to sell the books and manuscripts did not think highly of the decision either. They pleaded with the public to save the texts. "We really hope that something will be done, and that speedily," they explained. "For, as New-Yorkers, we should feel deeply humiliated to have the Historical Society's Collection, which many of our most distinguished literary gentlemen have been twenty years in collecting, scattered to the winds under the hammer of the auctioneer." The situation grew dire. Finally, Governor DeWitt Clinton intervened. Turning to the state legislature, he declared the collections "very valuable" and argued that they "ought to be preserved for the public benefit." The worth of the library's holdings became a matter of public debate, and when the time came to vote, all but three of the New York state legislators agreed that the library had to be saved. New York taxpayers footed the bill and paid the society's debt. As a result, the "city on a hill" sermon that no one really knew they possessed would not be lost before it could ever be found.[27]

Profit, then, never served as a sustaining motive for Jeremy Belknap, Ebenezer Hazard, and John Pintard. In their work saving and printing American history, in their efforts to create societies that would house, copy, and communicate the records of America's past, all three men consistently lost money. Cultural nationalism explains far more of what drove them, but even this motivation does not fully illuminate the energy these men devoted to their endeavors. To understand what made these three commit so much of their time, energy, and money to American history, we also have to grasp how the work of history related to their worship of God. For it was a strongly religious form of American exceptionalism that took shape in the years following the American Revolution, and that form of exceptionalism ultimately enabled the rise of historical societies and the saving of Winthrop's sermon.

CHAPTER FIVE

A Providential History of America

FOR JEREMY BELKNAP, EBENEZER HAZARD, and John Pintard, history served piety, and piety spurred history. Religious conviction lay behind their historical endeavors, including their extensive efforts to establish historical societies in America. The few scholars who have studied these figures and the rise of historical societies often miss this fundamental point. They frequently separate Belknap, Hazard, and Pintard from religious beliefs in order to describe a turning point in the writing of history, a movement from something more religious and centered on the doings of God to something more modern and centered on the actions of humans. Yet there is no mistaking the powerful role that religion played in the lives of these men and their pursuit of American history. The Massachusetts Historical Society and the New-York Historical Society—the two societies that preserved, discovered, and printed *A Model of Christian Charity* in 1838—would not exist today without the religious beliefs of Pintard, Hazard, and Belknap.[1]

Those religious beliefs originated in Calvinism. Pintard, for example, came from French Huguenot descent (a Calvinist form of Protestantism in France), and all his life he held to the piety of his

ancestors, though not their specific doctrines. He read the whole
Bible every year and the entire New Testament in Greek over
twenty times, and his collection of books was dominated by history
and theology. Hazard, meanwhile, grew up Presbyterian in Pennsylvania, and Belknap was raised a Congregationalist in New England, a direct heir of the Puritans.[2] Like Pintard, both Belknap and
Hazard came to reject many specific doctrines of Calvinism as they
aged. Nonetheless, all three were shaped by its basic practices and
beliefs. And that early Calvinism ended up playing a surprisingly
large role in their later pursuit of history.

When accounting for the foundation of America's first two historical societies, therefore, we have to understand how these faith
lives functioned—what impact these men's religious beliefs had on
their ideas and pursuits. For example, thinking about how and why
Belknap and Hazard became universalists tells us a good deal about
how and why they went about studying history. For what tied their
beliefs together were two basic convictions—God's benevolence
and human responsibility—which they arrived at through two
basic authorities: scripture and reason. Hazard and Belknap spent
many letters working out the puzzles of universalism, granting the
need for Christ's atonement (as scripture attested), while insisting
that a loving and benevolent God would never condemn anyone to
eternal hell (as their reason assured them). When Hazard approved
of another minister's new book on universalism, therefore, he
wrote excitedly, "I cannot help thinking his system not only rational, but Scriptural, and that it reflects more honour on the divine
character than I have yet met with." In that formulation we find a
way to explain the development of these men's faiths. Wherever
they would go with reason, they would get there with scripture.
And in the end, they went a long way from traditional Calvinism.
By the 1780s, they opposed original sin, election, predestination,
prodigies, superstitions, and enforced doctrinal confessions.[3]

Yet the method of arriving at these new positions shows the
continuous influence of a Calvinist framework on these men's labor
and thinking, including their work saving texts and making history.
For in asserting the authority of reason and scripture, Hazard and
Belknap assumed that God speaks to human beings with many different voices at once—in nature, history, science, and scripture—

without ever contradicting himself. The Word and the world must harmonize. Each form of revelation offered its own kind of witness, and all witnesses were welcome. As Belknap preached in 1785, "The divine counsels are opened to us by the events of time." All of history, in other words, offered an understanding of God's ways. It taught how he had designed the world to work in tandem with the truths of scripture. Both the structure of the world (including "the events of time") and the words of scripture, therefore, could and *should* be equally explored in order to know, worship, and glorify God. For Belknap, Hazard, and Pintard, God exercised his sovereign authority over every square inch of creation.[4]

Such a view represented not a new development in their theology but a long continuation of old Calvinist beliefs. God's sovereignty—a crucial component of Calvinism—meant that his providential hand directed and oversaw all happenings in human history. When Hazard and Belknap tried to understand their own personal miseries and misfortunes, therefore, they looked to the lessons of God. As Belknap's son lay tragically dying of disease, for example, Hazard sent his friend multiple reminders that God controls everything—that *all* events (including the death of a child) have purpose. Afflictions, he said, are even "proofs of a Father's love. They should lead us nearer to him; and, if they do, the time will come when even the remembrance of them will be sweet." Such words would seem harsh to send to a grieving father, but they echoed the same language Belknap sent to another father who sat in mourning ten years earlier. These sentiments were expressions of faith in the sovereignty of God. But they were also views that could have been lifted straight from a Puritan sermon more than a century before, demonstrating just how much unchanging continuity underlies theological transformation. All of their lives, Belknap and Hazard mixed their upbringing in Calvinism with new, emergent, post-Calvinist forms of theology. The constant, throughout, was the sovereignty of God. That belief would never go away. From personal afflictions to public events, Belknap, Hazard, and Pintard all sought to discover the hand of God at work in the unfolding of the world.[5]

As a result of such religious beliefs, these figures tended to approach history as a kind of science. Because the events of time contained the divine counsels of God, historical study could examine the variety of human societies scattered across the world and discover in them divine principles through a kind of experimental and comparative method. Lecturing on Christopher Columbus in 1792, for example, Belknap explained that "the discovery of America has also opened an important page in the *history of man.*" Here, he said, "we see mankind in their several varieties of colour, form and habit, and we learn to consider ourselves as one great family, sent into the world to make various experiments for happiness." That is what history offered, why it seemed so *useful* after all. Historical study, for Belknap and others, was nothing less than a survey of "experiments for happiness," which could help determine the fundamental laws of success—the principles that God had designed into the world and that he intended to be found. As another historian explained at roughly the same time, history was intended to be "subservient to the cause of virtue & human happiness." It served those ends by accumulating social and political arrangements across time and space, then testing the results. Cultures, societies, and governments, Belknap believed, all constituted "experiments for happiness" from which the laws of progress must emerge. The errors of the past, therefore, all held lessons for the present day. Such errors could teach what had failed to work, while offering hints at how human liberty could best be achieved.[6]

And now, Belknap proclaimed, liberty *had* been achieved. "One of the grandest of these experiments has been made in our own part of this continent," he proclaimed. "Freedom, that noble gift of heaven, has here fixed her standard, and invited the distressed of all countries to take refuge under it." Belknap insisted that the progress of liberty in America revealed the "great end" of God's design: that America "might prove an asylum for the oppressed and distressed in other parts of the world." Just as science moved steadily forward with each new discovery, Belknap argued, so history was finally closing in on the right sort of governance and the best form of freedom, guided by the providence of God and protected by the right sort of liberal Protestant religion. As Belknap proclaimed, "The nation of Israel had sufficient means of knowing, worshipping and serving this God, so have we; and when we are sensible of our obligations to him, and disposed to fulfil them, we shall be a truly happy people." For Belknap and many others, cultural nationalism—the building of a unique country distinctly advanced—was a function of religion, and history had a role to play in getting that religion right.[7]

As Belknap, Hazard, and Pintard searched the records of the past, therefore, they believed they would discover the way God's providence had particularly set apart and blessed the United States of America. They would find, they thought, clear signs of God's direction underlying their new nation's creation and development. For these men, God not only planned the unveiling of the continent for a general study of human social experiments but also guided its progress up to and through the American Revolution. When Benedict Arnold's betrayal came to light, for example, Hazard wrote, "We have now another striking proof of the interposition of Heaven in favour of our just cause,—and I am sorry to add, of human depravity too." Usually, though, the "proof" of God's action came indirectly. Toward the end of Belknap's life, for example, he preached, "This separation and the establishment of our independence, were the result of causes, foreseen and foretold by Him, to whom all his works, and all the operations of inferior agents, are perfectly known from the beginning of the world." The work of studying such operations and making them known to fellow human beings never ceased. In 1792, Belknap lectured, "Though we have learned more of the works of creation and providence than was known to preceding ages, yet we find that there is still more behind the curtain." History pulled back the curtain. Although he seldom cited God to explain human events, Belknap believed that every human event pointed back to God. As his friend and relative Andrew Eliot said to him during the American Revolution, "God grant we may never forget his works." That was, for Belknap, the primary call to history. For each of these figures, the records of the past revealed nothing less than the plans and counsels of God.[8]

Such a view of history and providence fit neatly with the politics of Belknap, Hazard, and Pintard. These men were all Federalists—an early political party invested in a strong, central, national administration. For Federalists of their time and type, religion and politics went hand in hand. A proper view of religion unified the country while advancing its good; and therefore, while no religion should ever be nationally established, many Federalists expected that all national figures would be religious. Belknap, for example, supported religious liberty in the United States while simultaneously declaring that all leaders should take a religious oath. In his mind, there was no contradiction. A national religion, he believed, demanded nothing more (but nothing less) than "an acknowledgement of the being, perfections and providence of one supreme God; a sense of his moral government both in this and a future State; and a careful observance of the eternal laws of justice, truth and mercy in all our public conduct"—principles, he believed, that all Americans could accept.[9] Such a society would lead to virtue and order through proper deference to ministers and magistrates. For Belknap, Hazard, and Pintard, religious belief and religious practice of a liberal Protestant variety were fundamental to America's success. That was the lesson of history. It was a principle presumed in advance and then eagerly pursued in the records of America's past.

So useful did these men find history, so much did they see it directed at a deeper knowledge of God, that it could actually produce in them powerful religious responses. Increasingly, Belknap approached his historical work as a form of devotion. Preaching on Job 11:7 in the 1790s, Belknap declared, "We cannot open our eyes but we see the most evident numerous demonstrations of the being, perfections and providence of God, who made, and who upholds all things." Hazard concurred: "the Christian scheme" and "the plan of Divine government," he reflected, were both "sufficient to fill the soul with admiration of the wisdom and benevolence of God; but a more accurate examination of them cannot fail of producing rapturous adoration." According to both Belknap and Hazard, the more one studied, the more one praised. As one scholar has aptly summarized, "Writing history was an act of worship."[10]

For all these reasons—because history functioned as a witness and revelation of God, because it could make a nation embrace right religion, because it could serve as its own way to worship God—Belknap finally had no trouble reconciling his version of America's "true history" with his work in the church. As he explained to a friend, "If I did not think it might be so managed as not only to be a detail of facts, but also a conveyance of reflections tending to the advancement of religion and morality, I would entirely lay it aside as unbecoming my profession."[11] History did not compete with his role as a minister; instead, it became its own form of ministry. The Massachusetts History Society, the turn to "modern" history, the saving of texts, and the eventual printing of Winthrop's sermon—all of this came about *because of* his religious sensibilities, not despite them.

Perhaps the best way to see how faith and history came together in the making of the MHS is to look at Jeremy Belknap's own "city on a hill" sermon, delivered on a Day of Thanksgiving in February 1795. These sermons often described the United States as God's chosen nation—something that began to happen with regular frequency in Federalist pulpits following the American Revolution. These sermons were, in that sense, far more important to the development of American exceptionalism than were the writings of the Puritans. Belknap was no exception to the general rule, and he avidly took his part in the ritual. Fusing American history with biblical stories, he recited a standard Exodus narrative: the United States was founded, he declared, by Puritans in flight for religious freedom, and it has flourished ever since—by God's design—as a model of liberty and freedom for all. "We are as a City Set on a hill which cannot be hid," he preached. "We have already made a distinguished figure in the world and America has become an object of inquiry, and of curiosity among very distant Nations."[12]

With such a statement, we can see once again the general rationale for pursuing American historical material. Believing that the Revolutionary War had achieved for the United States a unique step in the history of humankind, Belknap and his peers assumed that Americans had forced the world to take note. The eyes of all people were upon them. In the first volume of his *Historical Collections*, for example, Hazard claimed that Americans had once been ignored by other nations of the world: "But when they dared to assert their Claims to Freedom . . . they were then thought worthy of more respectful Attention, and an Acquaintance with their History was sought for with Avidity."[13] In other words, Belknap, Hazard, and others thought that non-Americans desperately wanted to know how the American experiment in freedom had come about. And the records of history, they thought, would tell them.

But those records were never opened without an eye toward the providence of God. Belknap saw in history the divine counsels linking the people of scripture to the newly covenanted nation of the United States. Moreover, he believed that as others looked to America and attempted a similar "experiment" on their own, they too could become members of God's expanding kingdom. "We are taught to believe that Christianity is designed to lead not only individuals but nations to the greatest happiness of which they are capable," Belknap continued. "When Nations are governed by the Laws of wisdom, justice, truth, benevolence, sobriety and moderation; when their Laws and the example of their rulers tend to form the people to virtuous habits, then it may be said that the reign of Christ is begun among them." The reign of Christ, in other words, depends on certain forms of social and political arrangements, enabled by—and in turn *enabling*—the embrace of right religion. That is precisely what a study of history (a survey of "experiments for happiness") could reveal. As the proper forms were discovered, the reign of Christ would spread. "As far as [nations] act from these principles and seek the peace and happiness of mankind as the great end of Government," Belknap preached, "so far they become the kingdoms of our Lord and Saviour." In his mind, the more others became like the United States, the more they would extend the Kingdom of God.[14]

But Belknap's own "city on a hill" sermon reveals a curious twist to the tale of Winthrop's text. It shows that linking America to Matthew 5:14 did not necessarily require the finding of Winthrop's sermon. Belknap made that claim without ever knowing *A Model of Christian Charity* existed. John Adams would do the same.[15] In making such a move, both men would prove exceptions to the general rule, for hardly any ministers or politicians over the next 150 years would use Matthew 5:14 to describe America or the United States. Most who quoted that verse still understood it as a description of the church. But the possibility always remained present that this old statement by Jesus Christ could be pulled out of the Sermon on the Mount and applied to a new nation. A particular view of scripture, history, and the United States might designate America as a "city on a hill"—and it could do so without any need to cite or summon a Puritan sermon from 1630.

Even so, when historical societies discovered and printed John Winthrop's *Christian Charity* sermon in 1838, they added a powerful new dimension to the story. One reason why few people called the United States a "city on a hill" in the nineteenth century is because it had no attachment to an *origin*. It had nothing to do, so far as anyone could tell, with how America began. When antiquarians later found the "fact" that Winthrop used this phrase at the supposed start of the American experiment, historians and politicians could begin to make links and assertions that Belknap never could. Finding and printing Winthrop's sermon in the mid-nineteenth century, in other words, solidified and extended a story that was already well along in the making. Thus, the "true history" that Belknap hoped to preserve eventually took shape around *A Model of Christian Charity*—a text that Belknap's historical society brought to print.

CHAPTER SIX

A White History of America

A S WE HAVE SEEN, the founders of American historical societies—Jeremy Belknap, Ebenezer Hazard, and John Pintard—believed that history had to record a continuous trek of human progress. That was what providence and God's sovereignty entailed. American civilization, they assumed, had to be headed somewhere—building one discovery upon another in an ever-ongoing revelation of God's divine counsels. But what could such progress mean if American history recorded instead a *loss* of life, land, and liberty? What could be the trajectory of God's plan if it involved relentless heartache, bloodshed, and death? That was the question posed by Native Americans. Belknap in particular spent a lifetime studying this difficult problem, but in the end, he never found a way to fit Indians into the unfolding and unfailing tale of American progress that he hoped to tell.

Since the beginning of the United States, the continuing presence of Native Americans has been a constant threat to tales of American exceptionalism—a never-ending reminder that American history extends back far longer, that others came and lived and dwelt here first, that origin stories rooted in a flight from persecution in Europe run up uncomfortably against the colonial terror these same people so often inflicted on others. We see that in the work of Belknap, for the more he celebrated the history of America as the rise of liberty, the less tolerance he had for Indians. They became problems, not participants, in the grand American drama. To deal with their losses, Belknap and others reimagined Native Americans not as a people with a history but instead as the setting or backdrop against which the "true history" of America has taken place. They were imagined as part and parcel of the wilderness, the stage for the story that began when Europeans set foot on a savage and silent shore. For American history to cohere—for Belknap's narrative of America to work—Native Americans had to be removed.

Understanding how Indians appear in the work of Jeremy Belknap thus highlights an important dimension in the story of Winthrop's sermon. When *A Model of Christian Charity* entered American political rhetoric in the twentieth century, it did so as an origin tale—a text that could explain the opening moment in American history and proclaim its identity ever since. But starting the history of America with Winthrop, or with the Pilgrims and Puritans more generally, could only be done if other human beings were recast, reimagined, or erased. Indians have repeatedly received such treatment in textbooks and tales of America, and the creation of the Massachusetts Historical Society in 1791 demonstrates the process already at work in the earliest days of the nation.

Jeremy Belknap did not begin his career by seeking to reduce, erase, or ignore Native Americans. Instead, his diaries, commonplace books, and writings reveal a man constantly taking notes on Native Americans, attempting to figure out their nature, their past, their destiny, and the most "benevolent" way to deal with them. At a young age, he read a book by Eleazar Wheelock, who had started a school for Indians, and he became convicted that he ought to serve Indians with the gospel. Inspired by Wheelock's endeavors, he wrote a friend, "I am sensible that a great load of guilt lies heavy on this land in neglecting the means which may be used for the conversion of our Indian neighbors and countrymen to Christianity; and that it is the duty of every person, who professes a regard to the kingdom and interest of Jesus Christ, to contribute his part for this glorious purpose."[1] Notably, at this point in his life, Belknap considered Native Americans as "neighbors and countrymen." For a while, he thought of becoming a missionary. Friends, mentors, and parents all urged him against it, and soon he found a different path. After finally having a religious experience—one he had long sought but always lacked—he decided to give Indians to others and become a minister instead.

Even so, Belknap's interest in Native Americans never flagged. A few years after starting his job in Dover, New Hampshire, Belknap visited Wheelock at Dartmouth. His reaction shows an increasing skepticism of the missionary's efforts. While admiring the buildings that seemed to spring up in the midst of the "wilderness," he found Wheelock himself off-putting—a self-righteous man convinced he had the blessing of God and certain that enemies opposed him. The more Belknap got to know Wheelock, the less he liked him. Soon, Belknap and Hazard were openly mocking Wheelock and scorning his Indian pupils as well. They threw up their hands at the situation: "What the designs of Heaven respecting those poor creatures may be, none can tell," Hazard wrote; "but their present mode of living and their education are much against their conversion, and past experience has too plainly shewn the futility of attempting to alter either."[2] Hazard's reference to "past experience" shows that history was at stake in the status and future of the Indians. For these men, figuring out what to make of Native Americans necessarily involved a study of their past.

Belknap and Hazard in their own historical writings could often be fairly evenhanded about white colonists and their encounters with Indigenous populations. It came with their effort to be "faithful and impartial," and it went a long way in establishing Belknap's reputation as a legitimate scholar of American Indians.[3] In *The History of New Hampshire*, for example, Belknap often blamed greedy white colonists for the conflicts that ensued. But his interest in Indians went much deeper than determining whom to blame for any given tragedy. Belknap most wanted to know whether Native Americans could be "civilized," and the answer for him depended on a careful study of their history. Civilization, Belknap believed, was the achievement of ages, and it was not clear to him how old Native Americans actually were.

This tortured question emerges most clearly in Belknap's belabored attempt to determine the age of America, by which he meant the length of time it had actually been inhabited. In that effort, we can see again how Indians represented a basic problem for Belknap and his pursuit of American history. If America's "true history" did not begin until Europeans arrived, then what was a person to do with Native Americans, who had been living here so long? The solution, for Belknap, involved three strategies: First, he claimed that Indians had not been around nearly as long as others thought. Second, he suggested that they would not be around much longer. And third, he dehistoricized Native Americans altogether by depicting them not as human beings with their own particular pasts but as wilderness creatures forming the setting for the "true history" of America. All of these strategies buttressed an American exceptionalism based in a story that had to begin with the first footsteps of Europeans on the American strand.

First, then, Belknap decided on the basis of scripture that Native Americans had not actually lived in the land since time immemorial. According to the Bible, he believed, the apostles had propagated the gospel to the entire, populated world. Some of Belknap's peers at the time were making elaborate arguments that Indians had in fact descended from the ten lost tribes of Israel or that they showed signs of early religious knowledge now lost. Belknap disagreed. According to him, no trace of the gospel existed in America, and as a result, no one could have been living here when the apostles first went out to preach. It was "a *young* country," Hazard summarized.[4] Just *how* young was it? Belknap again thought he could determine its age by examining the level of "improvement" among Native Americans. In effect, Belknap believed that the longer a civilization had been around, the more it would look like his own. And America, by this reckoning, was not very old: Belknap concluded that the Indians arrived sometime in the twelfth century.

To bring Indians up to speed, therefore, would require skipping centuries of historical change, and Belknap came to believe over the course of his career that speeding up the historical clock would not be possible. In a report to the Society for the Propagation of the Gospel published in 1798, Belknap explained, "The difference between the savage and civilized modes of life is so great, that it is impossible for either the body or the mind to accommodate itself to the change with any great degree of rapidity. If, therefore, expectations of a sudden change have been excited, they must necessarily have been disappointed."[5] In other words, part of Belknap's historical work aimed to determine whether and how Indians could actually be "civilized" and converted, joining themselves to the American tale. Near the end of his life, he concluded that all attempts would fail. The *historical* gap was just too great.

Thus, Belknap concluded that the Indians, who had appeared on the historical scene relatively recently, already had to go. On January 24, 1795, Belknap wrote in the *Columbian Centinel*, "Husbandmen and Hunters, civilized and uncivilized people, cannot generally, live within the same limits; or if there be an attempt to incorporate them into the same society, the former will always rise superior, and the latter will sink into a state of dependence." As a result, those Indians who wished "to retain their original manners and habits, will retire to the uncultivated wilderness," receding from the ever-advancing front of Anglo-American civilization. For Belknap, as for many others at the time, American history would not be a story that included or incorporated the Indians.[6]

Even as Belknap saw Native Americans receding, however, he further removed them from history by presenting them as the setting for a better tale—the story of liberty's rise. Such views appeared most prominently in *The Foresters* (1792), Belknap's most popular book, which narrated American history by turning each colony into a person (Peregrine Pickle was Plymouth, John Codline was Massachusetts, Roger Carrier was Rhode Island, and so on). The book situated these characters in a distant land owned by John Bull (England) and populated that land with "bears and wolves"—that is, the Indians. Clearly, such a view left Indians as less than human. In fact, Belknap scoffed at John Bull's "whimsical" notion of "taming" the wild beasts, induced by "an idea, that these animals [the Indians] were a degenerated part of the human species." Unimpressed, Belknap let his late views of Wheelock surface, deriding not just the missionary but also his most famous student, the influential Mohegan convert and preacher Samson Occom. According to Belknap, Occom "dressed in the habit of a *clergyman*, having been previously taught to lift his paw and roll his eyes as if in the act of devotion." By the end of Belknap's life, that represented the extent of his hopes for Indians: they might be taught some tricks, but they could only don the clothes and ape the manners of true Christians. As Belknap went about establishing and organizing the Massachusetts Historical Society—collecting, preserving, and communicating the raw materials of American history—he felt compelled to denigrate and eliminate Native Americans. Only in that way could his story of America be saved.[7]

As Belknap became increasingly hostile to Native Americans, his early missionary zeal changed focus. Dedicated as a young man to what he then called his Native American "neighbors and countrymen," Belknap gradually turned his attention to a different sort of neighbor and countryman: rural white settlers, whom he variously mocked, ridiculed, scorned, lamented, hoped for, preached to, and prayed over for many years. Being a minister in Dover, New Hampshire, gave Belknap a rather dour view of culture outside the urbane centers of Boston, Philadelphia, and New York. He told Hazard in 1783, "I have long thought, and do still think it one of the greatest misfortunes of my life to be obliged to rear a family of children in a place and among a people where insensibility to the interests of the rising generation, and an inveterate antipathy to literature, are to be reckoned among the prevailing vices." Ranting at the lack of a schoolhouse, Belknap complained that Dover citizens "let their children grow up uncultivated as weeds in the highway." These people had no sentiments "favourable to education." When another subscription for building a schoolhouse started, Belknap predicted that "it would prove abortive." It did. Belknap bewailed his stay in "the semi-barbarous region of the North"—that is, New Hampshire—while his appalled friend Hazard could hardly believe that a man of Belknap's "genius and education should be doomed to drag out a miserable existence among such savages." Hazard's language of "savages" and Belknap's of the "semi-barbarous region of the North" show that these men did not always distinguish between Native Americans and backwoods whites. For Belknap, living in Dover meant cohabiting with the uncultivated.[8]

That experience helps explain Belknap's hopes for the MHS and the effort he put into establishing it. Cultivation was a keyword at the heart of missionary efforts in early America. It had been an assumption since the earliest days of Puritan settlement that "civilization" preceded "conversion," a view that continued into the eighteenth century. But for Belknap, it was not just Indians who lacked "civilization": so did his rural neighbors. Gradually, then, Belknap refocused his missionary zeal toward white settlers, uneducated Anglo-Americans. Like many within his circle, he downplayed the power of sudden conversion and committed himself to the goal of gradual improvement over a long stretch of time. An array of educational institutions, he believed, was the best way to accomplish such an all-important task. "Do you think it your duty to clear the woods and cultivate the wilderness?" he asked his Dover audience in 1785, "and will you not think it your duty to cultivate that nobler soil, the human mind, and clear it of those incumbrances of ignorance and error, with which it is now overspread?" Such a line reveals just how much he and his friends invested in educational institutions. All such institutions dispelled darkness, illumined minds, and prepared people to accept the truth.[9] In endeavoring to create societies of learning, Belknap, Hazard, Pintard, and their peers hoped to do nothing less than advance the progress of "civilization," cultivating hearts and minds.

But gradual cultivation was not the only goal. Beyond advancing a certain form of civilization, Belknap also hoped to track its rise and spread its reach. He was mesmerized by the westward movement of Anglo-American society. On his trip to Dartmouth in 1774, for example, he carefully observed the extension of towns and roads through New Hampshire. Pembroke was "a very pleasant well settled town on Merrimack River." Boscawen was "a good town, well improved." Plymouth "has been settled about eight years and is well improved, the land very good, and the people of reputable characters." Headed home by a different route, he recorded the same observations again. "Clarement is a fine town," he enthused. "Charlestown a pretty place.... There is a wide, strait street here with some good houses." Years later, on a trip to western New York, he noted again how "agreeable" it was "to observe the number of new meetinghouses and schoolhouses, as well as dwelling houses, along the road, and the show of elegance in ornament and painting which appears in them." Towns, buildings, streets, schoolhouses— the general transformation of "a rude wilderness to a well-cultivated and productive country"—these were the things that Belknap looked for as he traveled through New England. His allegorical history of America, *The Foresters*, took its very form and narrative from this sense of American "progress." From the opening pages, Belknap promised to give readers "such an account of this, once forest, but now cultivated and pleasant country."[10] Throughout his historical studies, Belknap attempted to record the growth, progress, and spread of "civilization," by which he meant a way of life best exemplified by Boston.

All of these factors went into the making of the MHS, without which we would not have Winthrop's "city on a hill" sermon or a host of other historical materials. It wasn't just a particular sense of prudence, patriotism, or piety that spurred Belknap; it was also his understanding of education as a way of life, a cultivation of citizens that would not only bring them into the "true history" of America but ensure that the history would continue. Venerating the past out of a pious worship of the sovereign God and a strong sense of cultural nationalism, Belknap, Hazard, and Pintard sought the most prudent way to collect and disseminate a specific kind of historical material that would preserve and communicate the story they most wanted to tell—the tale of liberty's rise tied to the growth and progress of Anglo-American civilization as it cultivated the wilderness, pushed out the Indians, and created a refuge of freedom for "all."

That kind of thinking, in turn, had a dramatic impact on the papers, manuscripts, and books these men actually sought and preserved. The papers of Jonathan Trumbull—the governor of Connecticut who served before, during, and after the Revolutionary War—mattered a great deal to Belknap and Hazard. They sang songs of delight when his letters and manuscripts arrived at the MHS. But the papers of Samson Occom—the Mohegan preacher educated by Wheelock who became a Christian, traveled internationally, wrote an autobiography, preached sermons, ministered to multiple communities, and served as a powerful voice for Native Americans throughout his life—mattered not at all. In fact, these men might never have imagined that Occom had any papers to collect. At the founding of historical societies, then, they emphasized in subtle and overt ways (such as their constitution) that history was not just a matter of accuracy. Records are necessary for the writing of "true history," but which records get saved and which get lost involves a careful process of selection, a definition in advance of what counts. It would take another archive at a different time to save the papers of Samson Occom, recognizing years later that this man, too, played a huge role in the true history of America. The history of historical societies in America, therefore, is not just a tale of preservation. It is also a tale of erasure, a story of removal. To select is to hold onto some things while letting other things go. It means looking hard for the letters of one man, while overlooking entirely the papers of another. In that sense, American historical societies are vast institutions of loss.

But historical societies are also vast institutions of gain. When discussing Belknap's more reprehensible views of Indians, it can be easy to criticize and dismiss this man and his work. Thinking through the ways he committed himself to a story of America while preaching the values of faithfulness and impartiality, we might be tempted to do little more than scorn the blindness that beset his labor. Yet there is more to the story than blindness, and more consequences flow from the MHS than Belknap's initial desire to preserve and pass on one particular story of the nation. Belknap, Hazard, and Pintard represent an important turning point in the new nation's ability to keep and write history. For the movement they began in the late 1700s has inspired, in turn, not just one view of America's past but many—including many new narratives of Native Americans. While working on the Belknap Papers at the MHS, for example, I noticed three books prominently displayed on the shelves around me, all of which offer new understandings of American Indians in New England and all of which utilized resources that Belknap's institution helped preserve—though Belknap himself could hardly have imagined writing them.[11]

The display of those books reveals just how complicated it is to view the failures and achievements of these figures from the past. For all their flaws, Belknap, Hazard, and Pintard began the institutional work of collecting, preserving, and communicating historical material, often at their own expense and often in time stolen from paid labors. Preservation requires selection; but if nothing is ever selected, nothing will be preserved. In the end, Belknap, to his credit, began an institution that has collected, preserved, and printed a plethora of material, still available today, so that a multitude of new stories and voices could be recovered and heard. Belknap, Hazard, and Pintard made this work possible because they believed that history matters. And as they worked to preserve it, they brought their passion and their pleas before the public. Mostly they would get by on private funds, but at the beginning of their labors, the Continental Congress endorsed Hazard's efforts with a $1,000 grant, and in 1825 it took a state legislature and $10,000 of taxpayer money to spare the New-York Historical Society and all the manuscripts it had saved. Among the papers preserved by all this effort and money was one that would eventually change the shape of American political rhetoric, John Winthrop's "city on a hill" sermon, *A Model of Christian Charity*.

PART III
Myths

CHAPTER SEVEN

The Rise of National History

I N THE WAKE OF the American and French Revolutions, the word "nationalism" entered the English language. Its first usage came in 1798, the year Jeremy Belknap died, and over the course of the next several decades, whether people had a word for it or not, the spirit of nationalism gained considerable strength. In 1837, one year before *A Model of Christian Charity* was first published, Ralph Waldo Emerson took the lectern at Harvard and called for the cultural independence of the United States. "Our day of dependence, our long apprenticeship to the learning of other lands, draws to a close," he announced. Demanding that Americans develop their own literature, Emerson thundered, "We have listened too long to the courtly muses of Europe."[1] If the United States was to be its own nation, it would need its own culture, its own character. Emerson echoed and amplified the voice of many Americans at the time, all of whom desired to set their nation apart.

That desire found a powerful advocate in a new journal founded in 1837, John O'Sullivan's *United States Magazine and Democratic Review*. In one of its earliest issues, O'Sullivan declared that the "propensity to imitate foreign nations is absurd and injurious." As Emerson had done, he too lamented the lack of a distinct culture and literature. "When will it assert *its* national independence," he asked, "and speak the soul—the heart of the American

people?" That heart and soul had to do with America's unique republican institutions, its exceptional embrace of freedom. And such
a belief soon led O'Sullivan to coin the phrase "manifest destiny,"
describing America's purpose "to overspread and to possess the
whole of the continent which Providence has given for the development of the great experiment of liberty and federative self-
government entrusted to us." American principles had established
American destiny, and now its destiny lay west.[2]

An expansive mood gripped many Americans as they sought to
establish a unique identity and purpose for the United States. It
was a mood defined not just by massive migrations and Indian Removal but also by a need to control and make sense of the moving
populations and new territories coming under Anglo-American
control. Around the same time that O'Sullivan founded the *Democratic Review* and Emerson spoke at Harvard, the preeminent Calvinist preacher Lyman Beecher published a *Plea for the West* (1835),
calling on his listeners to spread right religion to uncivilized territories. "But if this nation is, in the providence of God, destined to
lead the way in the moral and political emancipation of the world,
it is time she understood her high calling, and were harnessed for
the work." The West was rising, he explained, and if it rose with no
guidance, it would end in "a dark minded, vicious populace—a
poor, uneducated reckless mass of infuriated animalism." What the
West really needed, Beecher insisted, was *schools*—"permanent,
powerful, literary and moral institutions" that could train teachers
and ministers to lead settlers into civil and religious liberty.[3] As Jeremy Belknap had once seen educational institutions as missionary
hubs, so Beecher saw them now—except on a much, much larger
scale.

The desire for a unique, purposive American identity found
perhaps its most influential expression at this moment in the writings of a Frenchman. In 1831, at the age of twenty-five, Alexis de
Tocqueville arrived with Gustave de Beaumont in New York to
begin a study of America's prisons. That, at any rate, is what he told
the French government. In reality, he envisioned a much bolder
and broader enterprise. During the next nine months, Tocqueville
and Beaumont traveled over seven thousand miles through seventeen of the country's twenty-four states. As they trekked their way

north, south, east, and west, they took extensive notes on every aspect of American culture, intending to offer a full portrait of this relatively new country. Tocqueville had come to believe, for good and for ill, that the future of the West could be found in this nation across the sea. Returning to France, he spent the next several years turning his notes into a full-fledged account of the United States. When it finally appeared, *Democracy in America* was greeted with enormous fanfare—receiving one of its first, fullest, and most flattering reviews in O'Sullivan's magazine. So much praise and adulation did Tocqueville receive that it surprised even him: "I am at present therefore on the crest of the tide," he wrote, "much bewildered by what is happening to me and altogether stupefied by the praises which buzz in my ears."[4] Soon a new edition appeared for use in schools, working its way into the culture and echoing down through the decades to become one of the most cited and most famous books on American politics and society.

In chapter 2 of that influential tome, Tocqueville offers "the germ of all that is to follow . . . and the key to almost the whole work." That "germ," that "key," is the location of America's origin. "If we carefully examine the social and political state of America after having studied its history, we shall remain perfectly convinced that not an opinion, not a custom, not a law, I may even say not an event, is upon record which the origin of that people will not explain." For Tocqueville, origins illumine everything. He compared nations to individuals, and he assumed that individuals are formed in their infancy: "The entire man is, so to speak, to be seen in the cradle of the child." For both nations and people, there was no getting away from the point and place of birth.[5]

And where was America born? For Tocqueville the answer was obvious: Puritan New England. As many others then and since would do, he acknowledged the primacy of Jamestown only to dismiss it. In Virginia, said Tocqueville, "No lofty conceptions, no intellectual system directed the foundation of these new settlements." It was left to New England to initiate America, for "the foundation of New England was a novel spectacle, and all the circumstances attending it were singular and original." The principles established in New England, Tocqueville insisted, "spread at first to the neighboring states; they then passed successively to the more distant ones; and at length they imbued the whole confederation." Those principles now "extend their influence beyond its limits over the whole American world. The civilization of New England has been like a beacon lit upon a hill, which, after it has diffused its warmth around, tinges the distant horizon with its glow."[6] This is a powerful image and perhaps a veiled citation of Matthew 5:14. It is *not*, however, a reference to *A Model of Christian Charity*. After all, *Democracy in America* was published in English just a few months before Winthrop's sermon first appeared.

So where did Tocqueville get this idea, this origin story centered on Puritan New England? Most immediately, he got it from Jared Sparks, a Harvard professor and popular historian who had achieved a modest degree of fame for his series of American biographies. When Tocqueville arrived in Boston, Sparks welcomed him, met with him frequently, and conveyed to him the unshakable idea that New England had laid the foundation of America. But Tocqueville did not rely on Sparks alone. As he traveled across America, he could hardly miss this insistence on Puritan origins. Textbooks told the story; children and families imbibed and repeated it; historians were well on their way to inscribing it officially as *the* narrative of America. There was a new sort of piety toward Puritan roots at work, and it rose rapidly in the two decades leading up to Winthrop's sermon.[7]

Tocqueville, Sparks, Beecher, O'Sullivan, Emerson, and many others saw the United States as a new empire, born, bred, and burdened with a unique history and a higher purpose spreading forth from the cradle of New England. Unlike previous republics or empires, these writers claimed, America's continued expansion would bring liberty, democracy, equality, and civilization to all it took beneath its wing. It could accomplish this mission because of what it had become; and it had become what it was because of its unparalleled origin in the Puritans. The rise of nationalism entailed new histories of America, and in the early decades of the new nation those histories focused on New England.[8]

Nationalism depends on many factors, of course. The coherence of citizens—the sense of shared concerns and a common identity—comes about in multiple ways: through an accepted set of general

laws, for example, or by practicing and imagining a shared culture
or by accepting and internalizing a common sense of national borders or by rehearsing the same sorts of rites and rituals all throughout the country. It is a fully embodied experience constantly
mediated by culture. Which is just to say that people have many
identities they cherish, including their religion, family, ethnicity,
town, state, and so forth. Elevating a *national* identity to a place of
central importance and getting people to share and affirm that
identity requires immense cultural labor. In the early 1800s, many
Americans in the new country believed that defining and embracing a national identity was absolutely essential. And as a result, a
wide array of cultural practices lent their strength and bent their
audiences to this project.[9]

In the early decades of this project, certain approaches were
more salient and prevalent than others. Immediately following the
American Revolution, two particular methods focused on common
rites and common maps. Celebrating the Fourth of July, for instance, enabled many Americans to feel bound to one another, rehearsing in solidarity the same victory across each colony. In
addition, new maps repeatedly laid out the shape of the unified nation, so that citizens could easily picture and visually imagine a single country with clear political boundaries incorporating all thirteen
colonies. Americans imbibed that image again and again everywhere
they went—in their schoolbooks, in their homes, hanging on tavern
walls, and painted on tavern mugs. In the 1780s and 1790s especially, national identity was something that could be practiced and
something that could be seen.[10]

Following the War of 1812, national identity increasingly became something that could be heard, something that could be read.
During the war, English forces had humiliated the United States
by burning Washington, DC. But three years later, fortunes took
an unexpected turn with the signing of the Treaty of Ghent. Suddenly, it seemed as though Americans had bested a mighty foe. A
"euphoria of nationalism" followed, and whereas Americans had
first attempted to bind themselves together with rites and maps,
now a burst of historical writing began. Having a unique national
story, many believed, would unite citizens from disparate states,
and knowing that story—learning it, participating in it, and passing

it on—would enable Americans to identify *as American*. History would tell Americans what they stood for on the world stage.[11]

Such a feature of nationalism has been called "temporal depth," which refers to culturally shared memories of the nation (whether actual or imagined) that bind individuals together. A shared story of the country's past, it has been argued, is an essential feature of national identity. And following the War of 1812, many Americans seemed to agree. Yet the acts of remembrance that create a national story also entail a process of selective forgetting, an erasure of all that endangers the prospect of coherence or cohesion. As writers began in earnest to compose a national history, they shunted aside a great many people and events that did not fit the tale. What they wanted was not a narrative of flaws but a story of progress—a tale of liberty that could bind them together in celebration and give them a purpose to push them forward.[12]

We know about history's rise in this period through the staggering numbers it left behind. From 1790 to 1830, historical works climbed in sales until they eventually accounted for more than 85 percent of America's best-sellers in the 1820s. Poor Jeremy Belknap and Ebenezer Hazard were simply ahead of their time. They lost money on almost all of their books and projects. In the earliest days of the nation, the *Collections of Massachusetts Historical Society* had to be suspended for lack of sales. Yet as Americans began to define and tout a unique sense of national identity, citizens swarmed to historical material. The *Collections of the Massachusetts Historical Society* became a source of pride, avidly sought by students of American history. The first two volumes went through three new editions. By 1811, the first ten volumes had become internationally recognized sources on American history, and by 1860, twenty-three volumes had been reprinted to meet demand.[13]

The difference between the two generations can be seen in the success of Samuel Hazard, Ebenezer's son. Ebenezer put together two volumes of *Historical Collections* that never sold well enough to produce a third, while Belknap attempted a magazine of historical material called the *American Apollo* that folded shortly after it opened. Samuel Hazard, one generation later, started a very similar journal in Pennsylvania. Yet Samuel did not fail. From 1828 to 1836, he ran a weekly publication, called *The Register of Pennsylva-*

nia, which would be "devoted to the Preservation of Facts and Documents, and Every other Kind of Useful Information Respecting the State of Pennsylvania."[14] It was the same kind of project, using the same kind of language, that had defined the work of Ebenezer Hazard and Jeremy Belknap a generation before. But now it had a market. Times had changed. Americans wanted to know who they were and what made their nation distinct. And to answer those questions, they turned to history.

Backing that newfound interest in history were new-made laws governing education. In 1813, Connecticut mandated that factory owners provide instruction in reading, writing, and arithmetic to their child laborers, becoming in effect the nation's first compulsory education law. Fourteen years later, Massachusetts established a free public school system. Other states soon followed. These laws, combined with massive population growth, meant an enormous influx of schoolchildren, and the writing, teaching, and reading of American history rose with this expanding system of education. Moreover, state laws started requiring that history be taught. By the 1820s, for example, five states had laws requiring history instruction in any school supported by taxpayer dollars.[15] Demand for history increased, then, because of a swelling population, a general rise in nationalism, an increase in public interest, and an abiding and pervasive sense of history's necessity for citizenship—all reinforced by state law.

Unsurprisingly, the market for textbooks boomed. A few American history schoolbooks had floated around since the mid-1790s but not many, and none sold well before the 1820s. In 1823, for example, one of the nation's earliest textbook authors started his *History of the United States* by explaining how dreadful it was not to have a good textbook for the nation. "To me it has long appeared singular," Salma Hale wrote, "that, while our schools abound with a variety of reading books for children and youth, there has never yet appeared a compendious History of the United States fitted for our common schools." Hale won a prize for his publication, but he soon faced stiff competition. Of U.S. history textbooks alone, less than ten editions appeared between 1775 and 1820. But in each of the next three decades, twenty-three more editions appeared, and in the 1850s, thirty-five new editions of American history textbooks hit the market. So many textbooks came into print that two literary magazines devoted the vast bulk of their reviews to sorting through new textbooks and advising teachers which ones to use. The power, reach, and influence of these books can be seen not just by the number produced but also by the amount they sold. Beginning in the 1820s, history textbooks became best-sellers and continued a steady rise in sales through the succeeding decades, "out-performing the nearest genre of book by over five to one." During this period, four textbook writers in particular emerged as the most successful and influential in antebellum America: Samuel Goodrich, Charles Goodrich, Salma Hale, and Emma Willard.[16]

The textbooks that these writers produced do not bear a simple or straightforward relationship to American culture. On the one hand, textbooks emerge from common sentiments spread broadly across the country. They reproduce a story of the nation that is already in circulation or that readers have already been prepared to accept. On the other hand, textbooks take specific sentiments about the nation and embed them in a new narrative, spreading that story to schoolchildren all across the country. They can be understood as the *effects* of widely shared cultural beliefs and as their *causes*. Textbooks, in other words, both consolidate and create.[17]

In consolidating and creating a national narrative, the new textbooks of the 1820s and 1830s served as the primary venue for American history. Authors understood that their stories would travel beyond the confines of a school, and they designed their works to reach students and families—even, or especially, when schools seemed unable to accomplish the job. Schools, after all, were in a very bad way. Classrooms were chaotic and confused. Teachers faced poor conditions, and they seldom lasted long. Agricultural work called students to the fields, and few could be counted on for attendance. These and other poor conditions paradoxically made textbooks all the more important. Even when schools failed, the written materials could be taken home and passed around, read and discussed by multiple members of a family. In fact, when most Americans sought out the history of their nation, they turned to their family schoolbooks, which were kept in the home for long periods of time. For the two decades leading up to the printing of Winthrop's sermon, as one scholar reports, "these books were very nearly the sole source of information on American history."[18] Their influence is hard to overstate. Beginning in the 1820s, these books would make and communicate the story of America for thousands and thousands of readers.

The story of America these textbooks told came rooted in Puritan New England. There is a simple reason for this: most of those who wrote the nation's textbooks came from New England. Fed by a long tradition extending back to the Puritans themselves, New Englanders were far more prone to write and read history. By 1860, New England comprised only 10 percent of the U.S. population, yet the region produced half of the nation's historians.[19] That edge in numbers gave these writers and their region a key role in shaping and developing the national story. Those who tell the tale decide the plot, and the first and most influential people to tell the story of America primarily hailed from New England.

Still, among the many writers who set out to plot an American tale centered on New England, certain differences arose. One clear battle concerned how exactly to remember the Puritans. Consider the difference, for example, between William Grimshaw's *History of the United States* (1822) and Frederick Butler's *A Complete History of the United States of America* (1821). Grimshaw approached history as a set of ironies and inconsistencies holding lessons for the future direction of the nation. He could acknowledge high-minded goals or actions in the past, but then he would quickly pivot to demonstrate how such noble goals were often followed by narrow-minded intolerance, bigotry, and persecution. By pointing out these errors, one scholar has aptly summarized, Grimshaw aimed to "encourage children to heed and learn from the mistakes and hypocrisies of their inherited past and work to resolve those incongruities in American society."[20]

The Puritans offered Grimshaw a perfect case study. In his textbook, he grants that New Englanders came for "a higher principle" and viewed themselves "as a chosen people of God." Yet, Grimshaw adds, "Much as we respect that noble spirit, which enabled them to part with their native soil, ... we must condemn the proceedings which ensued. In the first moments when they began to taste of

Christian liberty themselves, they forgot that others had a right to the same enjoyment." The "fanatical spirit" of Puritanism "continued to increase," he explained, so that New England outpaced old England in "bigotry, superstition, intolerance, and cruelty." Puritans even required church membership for full citizenship, which effectively "cast out of society" anyone "whose mind was not of a peculiar structure, or accidentally impressed with peculiar ideas." In the end, Grimshaw had little love for the Pilgrims, the Puritans, or their legacy. They served as a warning, not a foundation, demonstrating just how twisted higher principles might become. The point of Grimshaw's history was not to venerate these founders or transmit their values to the next generation but instead "to guard against a repetition."[21]

In complete contrast to William Grimshaw, Frederick Butler viewed the Puritans with unhesitating admiration. Butler aimed in his history textbook to demonstrate "the power, wisdom, and government of God, in planting his church in this wilderness of the west, and thus laying the foundation of a great nation." To that end, he began with New England, excluding from the first volume of his textbook all other people present in colonial North America. Describing his purpose as "an unbiased enquiry after truth, and a faithful narrative of facts," he set out to show that "those principles of civil and religious liberty, which formed the basis of the wise and virtuous institutions of our fathers, and laid the foundation of the United States of America, originated in the Puritan Church." All else and all others were secondary. God so loved his chosen ones that he sent his only begotten Puritans into the wilderness to build up a nation that would prepare the way for Christ. Butler was explicit about this belief. The modern story of the Puritans, he explained, paralleled the calling of Abraham and the exodus of the Israelites out of Egypt—except that where the exodus had prepared the way for the "Jewish Church," now the Puritans, by giving us the United States, had prepared the way for the Second Coming.[22]

Most who wrote about Puritanism in the 1820s and 1830s found themselves somewhere in between. Divisions ran along several lines—Unitarians and Trinitarians read the Puritans differently, for example—but one line divided novelists from textbook authors. Writers of textbooks were more prone to praise than to condemn. Novelists, however, frequently dwelt on the rigidity and confines of the past, the need to resist and escape those stern and awful ancestors in order to trace the progress of America out of darkness and into a better age. Nathaniel Hawthorne, the most famous novelist to write about the Puritans, took a deeply ambivalent position on his Calvinist forebears. In an oft-quoted remark, he said, "Let us thank God for having given us such ancestors; and let each successive generation thank him, not less fervently, for being one step further from them in the march of ages."[23] Even so, novelists like Hawthorne—who often came from New England—still operated on the principle that Pilgrims and Puritans had established the origins of America.

Starting the true story of America with Pilgrims and Puritans, as many novelists and most textbook writers did, was not, however, the easiest position to defend. Consider the significant chronological problems that immediately arise: the Pilgrims, put simply, weren't first. Even apart from the obvious ancient history of Native Americans—which very few textbook authors took seriously and no one considered an actual origin—the first European settlements lay elsewhere. The Spanish had been in America far longer than the English, and the French came before the Pilgrims. The Dutch arrived in New Amsterdam (later New York) in 1609, but its claim to American origins never made it far beyond the walls of the New-York Historical Society.[24] The real problem, the real conundrum, lay farther south. Jamestown was established in 1607, thirteen years before Plymouth. And Jamestown had a really good story in Pocahontas and Captain Smith.

So how did it come to pass that the earlier story could be supplanted by the later as the *true* origin of the nation? Butler offers an extreme example by simply ignoring Virginia altogether in the first volume of his history. Most writers, however, felt compelled by the requirements of historical narrative to proceed chronologically—which meant talking about Jamestown *before* discussing Plymouth. Even as they followed this time line, however, they still found ways to set New England apart. An origin story, it turns out, can come at any time. So long as something is called the "first" of its kind, all that comes before can be ignored, dismissed, or explained away.[25] And that is how Virginia came to be treated in the nation's earliest

crop of textbooks. According to many different writers, colonization until the Pilgrims had been a standard, unexceptional affair of
seeking gold and gain; the Pilgrims, however, sailed in search of
God—the *first* to do so in the whole history of humankind—and in
setting out on such a noble quest, they gave the world something
new. That was the developing context in which Winthrop's sermon
first appeared—a history of America centered on New England that
proliferated through the deliberate cultivation and distribution of
certain cultural memories, not others. And this whole process of
nationalizing the Pilgrims took shape through the influence of one
particular man, Daniel Webster.

CHAPTER EIGHT

The Spread of National Pilgrims

BEFORE 1820, PILGRIMS AND PURITANS were mostly a regional affair. Their history and legacy mattered a great
deal to New Englanders, but citizens elsewhere knew little about them and cared even less. Then, just at the cusp
of the boom in national history textbooks, the Pilgrims suddenly
became a national symbol. Their importance took shape in the
1820s through a series of anniversary commemorations. In 1825,
Americans gathered to lay the cornerstone for a new monument to
remember Bunker Hill. The next year, further celebrations marked
the fiftieth anniversary of the signing of the Declaration of
Independence—an event made all the more poignant by the simul-
taneous deaths, on July 4, 1826, of John Adams and Thomas Jefferson. Yet the decade began with a collective remembering centered
not on the American Revolution but instead on Pilgrim Landing.
The year 1820 marked two hundred years since Pilgrims first set
foot on American shores, and the commemoration of that event
generated an explosion of festivities and events.

The main event, of course, occurred in Plymouth, and the man
chosen to speak at that celebration was a rising lawyer and statesman named Daniel Webster. Born in Salisbury, New Hampshire, in
1782, Webster graduated from Dartmouth and practiced law for
several years in the very world that Jeremy Belknap once ridiculed

as the semi-barbarous backwoods of the North. After Webster spent four years representing his home state in Congress, he decided that his powerful voice needed a larger stage. At first, he considered moving to New York, telling his brother, "Our New England prosperity and importance are passing away.... If any great scenes are to be acted in this country within the next twenty years New York is the place in which those scenes are to be viewed." But when he considered his contacts, Webster, like Belknap, chose Boston. There he quickly became one of the most widely recognized voices in New England, serving multiple roles while winning several significant cases before the Supreme Court. In 1820, amid all his many tasks, Webster took a break to prosecute a very different sort of argument—a celebration of Pilgrim Landing as the origin of America.[1]

To make this case, Webster littered his speech with the language of beginnings. He greeted his audience by explaining, "we have come hither to celebrate the great event with which that history commenced"—a history "of our native land." Here in Plymouth, he declared, could be found "the first footsteps of civilized man!" That claim echoed through Webster's address: the "first," the "commencement," the "origin," a "new society," the place where "civilization and an English race" were finally "introduced."[2] Such words and terms are almost impossible to count in this two-hour-long speech. The point of the anniversary was to celebrate the founding of Plymouth, and Webster left no doubt that the Pilgrims at Plymouth had indeed founded something new.

But what exactly had they begun, and for whom? When Webster announced that the Pilgrims commenced the "history of our native land," he left unclear whether he was talking about New England or the United States, a region or a nation. At various points, he limited himself to a local interpretation. Yet he also kept drifting from New England into a broader sense of national beginnings. Reminding listeners that the Revolution began in Massachusetts, Webster traced a detailed history leading from liberty-loving Pilgrims to the thirteen colonies and their fight for independence. The *our* in "our history" kept expanding. Pilgrims, considered closely, turn out to be the origin of the entire United States.

In order to support such a bold pronouncement, Webster not only offered a history lesson leading from Plymouth to Lexington but also argued that the posterity and legacy of the Pilgrims had spread throughout the land. New England "overflowed" its boundaries, Webster proclaimed, and "the waves of emigration have pressed, farther and farther, toward the West." Describing this widening influence, Webster closed his oration by imagining that the "voice of acclamation and gratitude, commencing on the Rock of Plymouth" would be "transmitted through millions of the sons of the Pilgrims, till it lose itself in the murmurs of the Pacific seas." This was indeed an expansive New England—a New England that made way for a United States stretching from sea to sea.[3]

Of course, in order to reach all that way, a good many Native Americans would need to be removed, assimilated, or annihilated. In this speech, at this particular moment, such thoughts did not bother Daniel Webster any more than they had bothered Jeremy Belknap. By ascribing to Pilgrims the "first" civilized footsteps in America, Webster was already well on his way to erasing others, offering a strict contrast between the savage and the civilized. He pictured Pilgrims and their progeny as creating order out of chaos, a town square where once the wilderness had yawned. The feet of these European colonists brought "farms, houses, villages, and churches"—all language very similar to Belknap's in *The Foresters* and elsewhere. Webster imagined a Pilgrim founder peering into the future and seeing a civilization "extend over a thousand hills" and "along a thousand valleys" that "never yet, since the creation," had been "reclaimed to the use of civilized man." It is almost precisely what Belknap had also trained himself to see as he traveled through New Hampshire.[4]

In Webster's case, however, such language did not necessarily fit well with his politics. Webster was a Whig. And Whigs were not necessarily enthusiastic about American expansion. They resisted the Indian Removal policies of Andrew Jackson, along with the annexation of Texas and the Mexican-American War (which they protested as immoral), worrying especially about the extension of slavery and the brutality of Americans intent on spreading west. Manifest Destiny encapsulated the language and policies of Webster's *opponents*, the party of O'Sullivan's *Democratic Review*. Yet when the story of America turned to Pilgrim and Puritan origins, the narrative seemed to know no other outcome than expansion.

Whigs endorsed a sense of *moral* expansion (the spreading of civil and religious liberty, for example), and the story of Pilgrim Landing offered the perfect seed for the sprouting of such a tale. It was as if Daniel Webster, even as he invented and disseminated this rhetoric, could not resist its force and end. Glorifying Pilgrim Landing at Plymouth Rock, he imagined the Pilgrims' heirs setting up towns on the shores of the Pacific. That was how America would shine its light. This was how civilization, in all its glory, would spread.[5]

But why did all this supposed civilizing work depend on the Pilgrims? Why couldn't Virginia planters be responsible for the spread of civilization, the creation of America? The answer had to do in part with the ceremony itself: Webster had come to celebrate Plymouth, not Jamestown. But in celebrating Plymouth, Webster also wanted to draw a strong contrast between the Pilgrims and all other settlements, migrations, or colonial ventures. And he really meant *all* others. Webster contrasted the Pilgrims to "Grecian emigrations," "Roman colonization," "the Asiatic establishments of the modern European Nations," "the European settlements in the West India Islands," and any other emigration, colonization, establishment, or settlement—including, of course, Virginia. The Pilgrims, Webster asserted, were exceptional. "Different, indeed, most widely different, from all these instances of emigration and plantation, were the condition, the purposes, and the prospects of our Fathers, when they established their infant colony upon this spot." In particular, what made the Pilgrims the origin of America, for Webster and for many others after him, was the exceptional motive that led them on. Whereas others had come for profit, the Pilgrims sought nothing but the freedom to worship God.[6]

That freedom, according to Webster, entailed more than religious liberty. The Pilgrims were republicans, he explained, and they brought to America a coherent set of principles for both civil and religious life. "At the moment of their landing," he declared, "they possessed institutions of government, and institutions of religion: and friends and families, and social and religious institutions, established by consent, founded on choice and preference, how nearly do these fill up our whole idea of country!" As a result, "The morning that beamed on the first night of their repose, saw the Pilgrims already established in their country. There were political institutions, and civil liberty, and religious worship."[7] The Pilgrims came fully formed, the seed of all that was to follow. This is the story that Tocqueville would later learn, the tale he would powerfully retell.

As such a speech makes clear, origins require strong contrasts and a clear sense of self-conscious *form*. It would not do to have the Pilgrims straggle ashore and work things out gradually, piecing together step by step and year by year a way of governing both church and state. Of course, that is exactly what *did* happen: principles of church and state took many years to harden into shape, and even then they kept shifting in response to each new challenge. But such a messy reality will not make for a very good tale. Mythic beginnings cannot develop over time. And so, as Webster's Pilgrims leave their small ship and step across Plymouth Rock, they take into the wilderness a clear sense of purpose, a set of principles that could never change but only grow and spread. Rhapsodizing on this origin, Webster declared, "Poetry has fancied nothing, in the wanderings of heroes, so distinct and characteristic."[8] Set apart from all other settlements, the Pilgrims initiated something the world had never seen.

In doing so, moreover, these Pilgrims of Webster's speech imposed an obligation on all future generations to follow in their footsteps. The job of posterity was not to *create* or *invent* or *begin*, as it had been for the Pilgrims. Rather, the job of future generations was merely to *transmit*. All who follow must leave "some proof, that we have endeavored to transmit the great inheritance unimpaired" and so become "not altogether unworthy of our origin." The descendants of the Pilgrims—both New Englanders and Americans writ large—must accept "the responsibility and duty which they impose on us. We hold these institutions of government, religion, and learning, to be transmitted, as well as enjoyed." "We are in the line of conveyance," Webster emphasized, "through which whatever has been obtained by the spirit and efforts of our ancestors, is to be communicated to our children."[9] The job was not to begin but to pass on.

Daniel Webster's speech, "The Landing of the Pilgrims," lived up to its wildest expectations. For Webster, it solidified his reputation as the greatest orator of the North. George Ticknor, a Harvard professor traveling with him, described the experience in godlike terms: "I was never so excited by public speaking before in my life," he wrote. "Three or four times I thought my temples would burst with the gush of blood. . . . When I came out, I was almost afraid to come near him. It seemed to me as if he was like the mount that might not be touched and that burned with fire. I was beside myself, and am so still." The address was soon printed, and Webster distributed it widely. John Adams, upon receiving and reading the speech, was utterly ecstatic. He proclaimed Webster "the most consummate orator of modern times" and announced, "This Oration will be read five hundred years hence with as much rapture, as it was heard; it ought to be read at the end of every Century, and indeed at the end of every year, for ever and ever."[10] Webster went on from this speech to a celebrated career in the Senate until his disastrous compromise of 1850, when he approved the Fugitive Slave Law in a failed attempt to keep the nation united. He fell from favor more rapidly than he rose, and two years later, in 1852, he died.

Webster's life and career left an enormous impact on many different aspects of American culture and history, from the cases he won before the Supreme Court to the Fugitive Slave Law he signed thirty years later. But for the purposes of understanding the history of American exceptionalism—and, in particular, how twentieth-century Americans could come to embrace a Puritan sermon as their essential starting point—one act of his stands out: his 1820 commemoration of Pilgrim Landing. Webster's speech nationalized the Pilgrims. He moved them from a local legend to the starting point of the entire United States. And that origin story soon spread through the nation's schools.

Of all the schoolbooks and schoolbook writers in America competing for attention, there was one particular author whom Daniel Webster especially loved: Emma Willard (figure 5). Wherever he went, he took with him a copy of Willard's *History of the United States, or Republic of America*, and he urged others—including his protégé, Robert C. Winthrop (a direct descendant of John Winthrop)—to find and read this text.[11] Though Willard is mostly forgotten now, she enjoyed a powerful and extensive reputation in antebellum America. In 1870, when she died, obituaries appeared

*Figure 5: Portrait of Emma Willard. Emma Willard School Archives, Troy,
New York. Michael Furgang Photography.*

in Baltimore, Brooklyn, Boston, Charleston, Chicago, New York,
Philadelphia, San Francisco, and several other cities and towns,
while national magazines like *Harper's Weekly* and *Godey's Ladies
Book* ran tributes. The fame and renown of Emma Willard rested
on two particular innovations: her system of women's education
and her new style of textbooks, both of which spread throughout
the country.

None of Willard's accomplishments would have come about,
however, had not the Vermont State Bank been robbed in 1812. In
the same year that the nation went to war with Britain and Daniel
Webster first entered the House of Representatives, state investi-
gators found the bank missing a hefty sum of money. This minor
event had major consequences—mostly for women's education but
also for the rising rhetoric of American exceptionalism tied to a

Puritan past. At the time, no one could figure out where the money had gone. The three directors of the bank insisted that a thief had managed to sneak off with the funds, but no report of a robbery had been made and no signs of breaking or entering emerged. Few in Vermont believed the directors. Instead, suspicion soon turned against them. Outraged citizens demanded that the bank's directors repay the funds, and the state supreme court agreed, punishing the directors with a massive fine. One of those bank directors was John Willard, who found himself suddenly facing not just the loss of his reputation and employment but also a new and enormous debt. He quickly cut his expenses, mortgaged his lands, and—when all other options failed—turned to his wife.

Emma Hart married John Willard in 1809. She was twenty-two years old and already a teacher so well respected that she had previously entertained multiple job offers throughout New England. Marriage ended that. She left teaching and settled into a domestic life with her wealthy husband, bearing a son in 1810. So it might have gone for her—marriage, domesticity, wealth—had not her husband's career and finances suddenly collapsed. In the aftermath of that event, Emma asked John if she could open a boarding school in their large home on Main Street. Though he would later support his wife's career, John initially refused. He planned to solve these problems himself. But pride and stubbornness could not repay his debts, and as hardships grew, John accepted Emma's plan. In 1814, Emma Hart Willard opened a school. Soon, she would spark a broad movement for female education.[12]

When Emma Willard opened a school, her sense of a vocation came flooding back. She had never taken the task of teaching lightly, and now that she was once again running a school, she had every ambition to excel. She wanted to make it the best of its kind, so distinguished that others would seek to replicate its model elsewhere.[13] Willard believed there was no reason for assuming that female education should focus only on the performance of proper conduct and genteel arts. At her school in Middlebury, Vermont, that curriculum disappeared. In its place, Willard introduced what she herself studied: higher-level mathematics, science, philosophy, history, and geography. Her students thrived, and their abilities demonstrated the power of this new approach.

As Willard's school grew, her reputation expanded—exactly as she had wished—and within five years she began to push her methods more broadly. In 1819, Willard published *An Address to the Public: Particularly to the Members of the Legislature of New-York, Proposing a Plan for Improving Female Education,* which has been called the "magna carta" of female education. The *Plan* offered a new approach to educating women. It took for granted, as so many people in that period did, that an informed citizenry was absolutely vital to any liberty-loving republic. Education was important not just individually and socially—bringing subjects "to the perfection of their moral, intellectual and physical nature" and so making them "of the greatest possible use to themselves and others"—but also nationally. And the nation needed more than just educated *men*, Willard argued. Prosperity and well-being depend on the character of a nation's citizens, she explained, and that character comes chiefly from mothers, who guide the development of children. As Willard noted, many were worried about America's eventual decline: after all, prior republics had all failed, and why should America be any different? But if *all* were educated, including women, such learning could prolong the life of the nation and prevent its eventual collapse. Female education would not only make the nation great; it would make the nation last. And so Willard ended by calling on "patriotic countrymen" to follow her advice and establish a broad system of women's education in "the consideration of national glory."[14]

Willard's *Plan* attracted a great deal of attention. It was first backed by Thomas Jefferson and John Adams, and soon President James Monroe wrote her a note of support as well. In New York, Governor DeWitt Clinton—the same man who would push citizens into bailing out the New-York Historical Society—took up Willard's cause and set it before the legislature. "The *very fact* of such a production from a female pen," he wrote her, "must dissipate all doubts on the subject."[15] At Clinton's invitation, Willard traveled to Albany and lobbied for her ideas, approaching several state legislators. With assurances of support, she opened a school in Waterford, New York. John Willard, the man initially reluctant about his wife going back to work, now became her biggest supporter. Together they moved to New York, where he died five years later.

Unfortunately, the New York legislature did not act as planned or promised. Serious female education still lacked broad appeal. Willard saw for herself the stiff resistance of state legislators: "I never expect that complete justice will be done to our sex until this old set are chiefly with their fathers," she lamented. "But I am confident that our cause is a righteous one, and I believe that from year to year it is growing."[16] Meanwhile, with her school in Waterford facing bills it could not pay, the city of Troy suddenly came to the rescue. A booming manufacturing town about to expand with the Erie Canal, Troy hoped to boost its cultural offerings and establish its reputation more broadly. In 1821, the Common Council of Troy raised $4,000 for a new building and brought Emma Willard to town. There, at the age of thirty-four, she opened the Troy Female Seminary.

Beginning with 90 pupils from leading families in several states, the school succeeded immediately and enrollment rapidly climbed. In the second year, 214 pupils registered, hailing from New York, Vermont, Connecticut, Massachusetts, New Hampshire, Ohio, Louisiana, North Carolina, and Georgia. By the end of the decade, Willard had students as well from Michigan, Alabama, Mississippi, South Carolina, Pennsylvania, Maryland, Rhode Island, New Jersey, and Washington, DC.[17] The draw of her school reciprocally affected Willard's influence, for after training so many women from so many states, her pupils took with them what they had learned—including the New England–centered textbooks they had used—and fanned out across the nation to build their own schools, teaching as Willard taught.

The immense influence of Emma Willard could thus be felt and gauged in distinct ways: first, through the spread of her educational model and, second, through the spread of her textbooks. Her school directly touched the lives of thousands of students, who helped build a system of women's education all across the country. Students of hers could be found teaching in almost every state, many establishing or running their own academies. A decade after founding the Troy Female Seminary, Willard took a trip to Detroit and stayed almost every night with a different graduate from her school. In 1838, she wrote a circular to the students of hers who had become teachers "throughout the extent of the Union, from

Maine to Georgia, from Boston to Natchitoches beyond the Mississippi." Nor did her influence stop at the borders of the nation. Emma Willard sent her *Plan* to Simón Bolívar in Colombia, and soon the new republic there established and endowed a college for females at Santa Fe de Bogotá. In 1834, with Willard's support, Greece also established a seminary for women on the model of Troy, and that academy sent teachers to adjacent islands, as well as to Constantinople and other parts of Turkey. Meanwhile, in 1837, a man named George Combe wrote to Willard from Scotland praising her success. "Your school is so extensive," he said, "and the influence of women on the state of society is, in my opinion, so important that I regard you as the most powerful individual at present acting on the condition of the American people of the next generation." He went on to report that while in Berlin, he met a member of the Prussian Council of Public Instruction who "hailed the little work on education [the *Plan*] with its appendix, which I gave him, with much pleasure, and said that it would strengthen his hands in doing good."[18] From Mississippi to Maine, from Colombia to Prussia, the work of Willard spread.

Yet as important as the *Plan* and Willard's own personal touch were, she soon became even more influential through her textbooks. As her school grew, Willard quickly expanded the subjects offered and hired teachers to specialize in particular fields. She focused on the study of higher-level mathematics and the absolute necessity of knowing history: math enhanced women's reasoning and rationality, she argued, while history made them good citizens. As one scholar has noted, "Willard was convinced by her intense nationalism that history should occupy the center of the curriculum. She even conceptualized her intellectual contribution as a nationalistic one, recalling that there was no better way for her to serve her country than 'by awakening a taste for history.'"[19] But the teaching of history, Willard felt, needed better methods and materials. She wanted to find some way to improve the presentation of ideas, a way that would be better suited to quick learning and easy comprehension. Soon she began inventing a new approach to the writing and study of history, and her approach proved so successful that it would eventually make its way through the entire educational system.

The basic concept Willard introduced remains in use today. Starting with geography, Willard innovated schoolbooks by emphasizing maps and charts. For her, the visual came before the verbal.[20] She collaborated with William C. Woodbridge on *A System of Universal Geography on the Principles of Comparison and Classification* (1822), then wrote her own *Geography for Beginners* (1826). Soon, she brought maps and charts to American history. Rather than asking students to memorize and regurgitate a series of dates, she offered visual cues that divided history into key turning points. She then built a series of chronological maps so that students could see the development of the United States from the first explorations to the present day. Such innovations enabled students to grasp quickly and easily a vast series of events, organized now into plots of liberty's progress culminating in the creation of the nation. In 1828, using this approach, she produced *A History of the United States, or Republic of America* (1828), which she followed seven years later with *A System of Universal History in Perspective* (1835).

As Willard recognized the power and reach of her schoolbooks—including the generous royalties they generated—she gradually devoted more and more of her time to writing and revising them. In the 1830s, she gave over the school's day-to-day operations and budget management to her son, John Hart Willard, and his wife, Sarah Lucretia Hudson, finally resigning as principal in 1838. She left Troy, married poorly, divorced quickly, and in 1844 returned to Troy, where she settled permanently into working on her textbooks. In calling her back to Troy, her son persuaded her to come by offering her space and time to write. "Your writing here could go on without interruption and you would be able to accomplish more in one month than you would do there in three," he wrote. "And after all it seems to me that that is the profession in which you are destined to gain more for yourself and for others than in any other." John Hart saw what plenty of others could perceive as well: that Emma Willard's writing would do more to further her career and shape impressions in the young nation than any other activity. And they were right. Her history textbooks sold over a million copies. *A History of the United States* was reprinted fifty-three times over forty-five years and translated into German and Spanish as well. Different versions aimed at the full range of the reading public. And because of Willard's many students, her textbooks were read all throughout the nation. Wherever her pupils went, in state after state both North and South, they took her textbooks with them. Through the success of her schoolbooks, Emma Willard became one of the foremost voices in the country shaping the public's conception of an exceptional nation rooted in Puritan New England.[21]

Willard's influential schoolbooks began with a single image depicting all of American history. For Willard, history could best be understood through its turning points, and those turning points could best be remembered by seeing them all at once. To that end, she pictured all of American history as a single tree (figure 6). Students who moved from one side of the tree to the other would progress chronologically through the decades and centuries, from the colonial period to the present. The image of that tree reveals how Willard saw and taught American history. While not every branch relates to New England, many do—especially the early ones. Willard marks the 1620 Pilgrim Landing, the 1643 confederacy of New England colonies, and the 1692 Massachusetts charter. More importantly, what does *not* appear is Jamestown. There is no branch, no twig, no beginning or turning point in Virginia. Meanwhile, beneath the shade of this tree, Willard would soon add a visual depiction of the first European landing on the left and the European-style "civilized" town on the right replacing the former "wilderness." It is a cue taken straight from the Plymouth Society membership certificate first issued in 1820 and then reproduced for all future members of the society who gathered to commemorate the Pilgrims (figure 7).

The tree Willard drew was her attempt to put her book's table of contents into a single image. In both cases, Willard focused her teaching on the absolute importance of a comprehensive plan dividing history into distinct "epochs," each with its own theme and meaning. Organizing American history in such a way enabled Willard to offer multiple potential origin points for the story of her nation. And when we look at the table of contents, what we find is rather striking, if not surprising: Willard followed a chronological narrative of America while deftly exploiting the breaks between epochs to assert the fundamental significance of Plymouth.

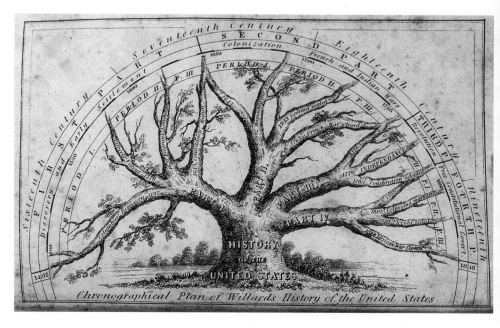

Figure 6: Emma Willard's tree of American history, frequently reused and reprinted, beginning here with A Series of Maps to Willard's History of the United States, or Republic of America; Designed for Schools and Private Libraries *(New York, 1828). Emma Willard Archives, Troy, New York. Michael Furgang Photography.*

Consider the table of contents from her first history textbook, published in 1828. Christopher Columbus is a section unto himself, but after Columbus, the textbook turns to the "first patent granted by an English sovereign, to lands in the territory of the United States, given by Queen Elizabeth to Sir Humphrey Gilbert." This "First Epocha" covers the years 1578–1619, and it tracks "Portuguese, English, Spanish, and French Discoveries." By locating Jamestown, New Amsterdam, and other colonial settlements in the era of "discovery," Willard can effectively move them out of the era of true beginnings. They might find America, but they do not found it. That comes in the "Second Epocha," beginning with the "Landing of Mr. Robinson's congregation at Plymouth" and covering the years 1620–1642.[22]

Contemplating this New England origin, Willard launches into a paean of praise: "On no part of the history of the United

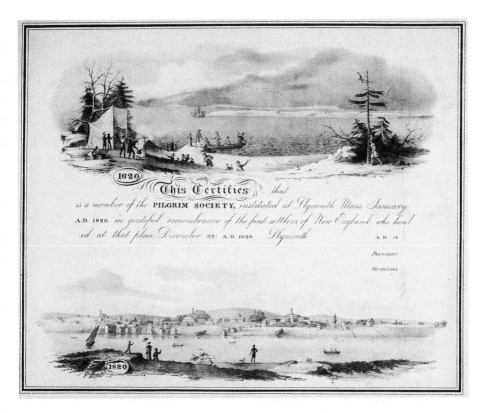

Figure 7: The Pilgrim Society membership certificate, with the same depiction of a "wilderness" turned into a town that would eventually appear under the two sides of Emma Willard's tree of American history. "This certifies that [blank] is a member of the Pilgrim Society, instituted at Plymouth, Mass." 1825, Catalog Record #15247. Courtesy of American Antiquarian Society.

States, perhaps we may say of the world, does the eye of the philanthropist rest with more interest, than on the account of the little devoted band now commonly spoken of under the touching appellation of the PILGRIMS." These Pilgrims, Willard continued, "possessed a much higher cast of moral elevation, than any who had before sought the new world as a residence. The hope of gain was the motive of former settlers,—the love of God was theirs." As a result, she continued, "In their character and in their institutions, we behold the germ of that love of liberty, and those correct views of the natural equality of man, which are now fully developed in the American constitution." It was the language of Webster—the same rhetoric Tocqueville would replicate and redistribute a few years later. Where does America begin? It begins here, she said, with the Pilgrims. They brought the principles that have since sprung into the magnificence of the United States. They sailed for God, not gain. They came for liberty, and what they left was a legacy that all true Americans have since embraced. America thus begins in Plymouth in order to offer an exceptional origin devoted to something nobler, something better, something pure.[23]

That sentiment appeared everywhere. As Salma Hale wrote in his textbook, "New England might have long remained the abode of wild beasts and savages only, had not motives, more powerful than the love of gain or of perilous adventures, impelled men, differing from all others who had been the founders of colonies, to select it as the place of their residence." John Howard Hinton's *History and Topography of the United States of North America* broke into new heights of exaltation when it came to the story of Massachusetts: "The world presents no parallel to the history on which we now enter," he wrote. "The love of glory or of gold has been the impelling cause of the commencement of other colonies, and the foundation of other empires; but in this instance religion, and that of no ordinary kind, either as to its purity or its intensity, was the grand principle of colonization." So extraordinary was this settling of New England, so unparalleled and consequential, that the American editor of Hinton's history—a man named Samuel Knapp—added a long footnote elevating the Pilgrims even further. For six hundred years, he claimed, God had been preparing the way for the discovery and settlement of America, which was "the greatest event in the history of man, saving and excepting the introduction of our holy religion." Because of the Pilgrims, Knapp added, "the moral, intellectual, religious, and political seed sown on these northern shores, was as pure and as full of life as any ever sown on any soil in any age of the world."[24]

No parallel, no peers; a new beginning; something the world had never yet seen; the start of right religion allied with self-government controlled by proper morality and a commitment to the intellectual foundations of an educated citizenry; the proper seed that came to sprout the United States of America—the Pilgrims constituted the origin of America because all this and more could be mythically ascribed to them, however lowly their settlement and however little they actually achieved. And what so many people hoped to say about the Pilgrims, only Emma Willard found a way to show.

CHAPTER NINE

The Creation of an Exceptional
New England

As THE LOVE OF the Pilgrims makes clear, American exceptionalism was tied early on to a conception of New England exceptionalism. The elevated state of the country depended on its origin—as infants mature into adulthood or as seeds sprout into trees. Whichever image one preferred, the point was always the same: all potential exists at the moment of birth and comes to fruition through natural growth. That investment in origins helps clarify why textbook authors so carefully separated Pilgrims from all who had come before. Spanish colonies were a prime example. Theirs was a rapacious, money-hungry origin, said these writers, and the results followed predictably: an unfolding of greed, aristocracy, and improper government that extended vice, wretchedness, and slavery down through the generations. Virginia fared little better. According to prominent historians, it was "planted in discord, and grew up in misery." In fact, many authors explained American slavery primarily through the impure motives of Virginia's first settlers—those whom Willard called simply "bad settlers."[1] The seed grows into the tree; avarice and indolence leads to slavery.

In contrast, these same writers claimed, New England was the land of the free. "The retreat of the pilgrims was never designed to become the nursery of slavery," Frederick Butler proclaimed. The Reverend J. L. Blake, praising New England, exclaimed in direct contradiction to actual fact: "No slave is here—our unchain'd feet / Walk freely, as the waves that beat / Our coast." The long effect of these early histories can still be seen in how few Americans today know that New England ever had slaves. Slavery is considered an institution of the South. In actuality, New Englanders carried enslaved Africans over not long after they were brought to Virginia, and Native Americans were sold and enslaved by Puritans for many years. The buying, selling, and owning of human bodies was not confined to the South. This is not exactly news. It was known in early America and could have been reported in the 1820s and 1830s. In fact, a few textbook authors—mainly those few who took a more critical stance toward the Puritans—actually *did* point out that slavery existed in New England from very near the Puritans' first days.[2] But by and large, the celebratory accounts of a purer and freer New England won out.

One powerful indicator of the willed belief in New England's absolute difference lies in the way textbook authors talked about suffering and self-denial. The "brink of ruin" faced colonists both North and South. In Virginia, however, it indicated the natural result of "transporting vicious and profligate people to that colony, as a place of punishment and disgrace." Ill fortune resulted from bad motives. For New England, in contrast, suffering bolstered celebration. Not just anyone could make it through hardship; only those who came for a higher cause. "This field of distress," Butler wrote, "became to them a field of delight; in the midst of their sufferings, their hearts were unappalled, they trusted in God, and he was their deliverer." Presumably, even if inspired only by greed, the early Virginian settlers were willing to "encounter the dangers and privations which might meet them in the wilderness"; yet this was a quality of courage that Charles Goodrich assigned only to the Pilgrims. Both Virginian and New England settlers suffered setbacks and defeats, but only the Pilgrims and the Puritans could be commemorated for their courage and endurance. The fortitude, the "degree of firmness, which we cannot fail to admire," flowed from the idea that such endurance was fitted to a higher cause. Where the desperate died in the South, martyrs were made in the North.[3]

When martyrs die, they leave a legacy behind. According to many textbook authors of the period, the thought of this future legacy guided the Pilgrims and Puritans from the very beginning of their settlement. As Samuel Knapp explained, "They were anxious for their offspring; and not for their immediate descendants alone, but for more remote posterity." They came with "a hope of laying a foundation for an extensive empire, that should be purged from all religious impurities." Textbook writers often concluded that the Pilgrims and the Puritans knew exactly what they were about. And just what exactly were they about? Almost anything. Trinitarian Congregationalists loved them for planting right religion—by which they meant Calvinism and its various doctrines. Unitarian Congregationalists loved Pilgrims for sowing the *principles* of right religion—by which they meant an ever-evolving revelation progressing toward ever more light and reason. Others, meanwhile, described the Puritans and Pilgrims as essential sources for important reform movements. Abolitionists, in particular—both white and black—linked their cause to the Puritans and inspired followers by insisting that America should remain faithful to the first settlers of New England. Many celebrated Pilgrims and Puritans as founders of religious liberty—which they then defined in any number of ways. Still others honored them as the original proponents of self-government and civil liberty. According to many, the Constitution came about as a natural outgrowth of the Mayflower Compact. All these themes and more could be played together or separated out. The legacy of New England was flexible, and it could be made to bend toward any end, whatever the cause or case required.[4]

No matter the cause, however, all used origins in the same way—in the way origin stories still function wherever the language of American exceptionalism appears. American exceptionalism locates a beginning that is distinct from any other, and it claims that the present day depends on that unique point of origin. We are the unfolding of principles that arrived at one precise moment, like a flash of revelation, and in one place only (New England, not Virginia). Purer purposes and higher principles produce descendants committed to purer purposes and higher principles. American exceptionalism, in other words, requires an unbroken lineage of commitment to God and liberty that cannot be sullied by others who happen to have lived and settled and sought their own ends in America.

Several consequences result from this way of thinking and re-surface still today. First, those who employ this rhetoric repeatedly call on listeners and followers to *stay true*. Since the Founding was a moment of pure principle, an almost-divine revelation, citizens of the United States must further the good of the country by remembering it and remaining faithful. As Knapp explained in introducing Hinton's *History and Topography of the United States*, all citizens of the United States "should know the value of the heritage they enjoy, in order to transmit it unimpaired to posterity"—the same language that Daniel Webster deployed in 1820. Changes might come, of course. In fact, they *must* come. As John O'Sullivan wrote in 1839, "We are the nation of human progress, and who will, what can, set limits to our onward march?" But for most people that "onward march" could succeed only when it represented the natural growth and procession of the origin—a maturation of the potential already present in the seed. There is no further revelation. There is no new idea. There is only the unfolding of an old, sacred idea—the meaning of America—present from the first.[5]

To mark the natural "progress" of the nation, textbooks and histories loved to begin with a "wilderness" scene and then contrast it to the present order. In doing so, they layered American history onto Christian ideas of Creation. Like the beginning of Genesis, this wilderness marked for writers a darkness over which God hovered, a place of mere potential before the beginning of America. America was without form and void; and darkness was upon the face of the deep. And the Spirit of God moved upon the face of the waters. God said, Let there be light! And Pilgrims landed at Plymouth Rock. "Never were any civilized people placed more completely in a state of nature than this little band of pilgrims, as they have justly been called," Hinton wrote. "They had, indeed, literally, a world before them; but that world was a wilderness, and Providence was their only guide." Emma Willard conformed her story to the same trajectory: "We behold in the first place a wilderness inhabited by tribes of savage and independent men," she wrote. When Europeans arrive, the story begins.[6]

As with Willard's other innovations, she became the first to illustrate that creation story through an influential series of maps.
The initial map, depicting the "locations and wanderings of aboriginal tribes," reveals a seeming chaos in the land of America before Europeans arrive (figure 8). Here we can see constant
movement, a lack of settlement—the wild void over which God's
hand in history hovers. Not only did this map attempt to capture a
sense of wilderness, but it greeted readers as merely "introductory,"
not even the "first." The "first" map of America would depict European discovery. The "introductory" map showed only the timeless and primordial void waiting for order and creation.[7]

After the "introductory" map, Native Americans disappear and
emerge again only intermittently in the series. In their place, we meet
an almost equally chaotic depiction of paths illustrating the travels of
the first European discoverers as they begin to explore this "wilderness." While certainly presented as a turning point and a beginning of
sorts, Willard's "first" map still displays a lack of order and does not
demonstrate a stable beginning (figure 9). It is more like the European counterpoint to the movements of the "aboriginal tribes." As a
result, the map that establishes a sense of stasis, a sense of *settlement* in
the New World, comes in 1620. On this map, Willard's third (called
her "second"), settlement appears not in the continued, constant
movements of ships, nor the gradual coloring of the shores, but in the
image at the upper left (figure 10). To explain why this counts as a
new epoch, Willard illustrates Plymouth Rock and writes beneath it,
"THE PILGRIMS LAND AT PLYMOUTH ON THE 22ND OF DEC. 1620." As
for Virginia, Willard skips it entirely. No ship heads to Jamestown in
the 1578 map (that would be too soon), and the only ship headed
there in 1620 (the next map) is "A Dutch Ship with negroes from Africa. Purchased by the Colony at J.Town" (figure 11). Once again,
Jamestown gets cut from the origin and meaning of America. To
focus on Virginia would be to associate America with slavery, not liberty. The South represented for Willard a false beginning, a settlement that could never serve as the nation's true foundation. Instead of
Jamestown, it is Plymouth that marks the new beginning, and from
1620 forward Willard's maps increasingly impose order on chaos.[8]

As the series of Willard's maps demonstrates, progress seldom
accepts limitations. By the time we get to 1789, we have a Constitu-

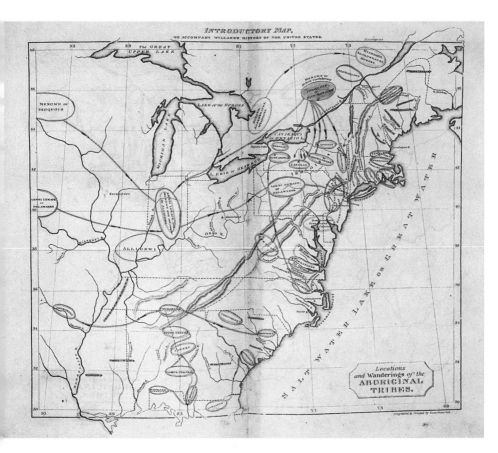

Figure 8: Emma Willard's "Introductory Map" of Native Americans. Willard, A
Series of Maps to Willard's History of the United States, or Republic of
America; Designed for Schools and Private Libraries *(New York, 1828).
Emma Willard School Archives, Troy, New York. Michael Furgang Photography.*

tion (inset on the map), stable state boundaries and a fairly clear
outline of the nation (figure 12). But the westward borders of the
nation remain unclosed. All political boundaries creep west. Printed
just two years before Congress passed the Indian Removal Act,
Willard's map is deeply ominous. In 1830, President Andrew Jackson would announce the unstated principle illustrated here with all
the power of the United States government at his back: "What
good man," he said, "would prefer a country covered with forests
and ranged by a few thousand savages to our extensive Republic,

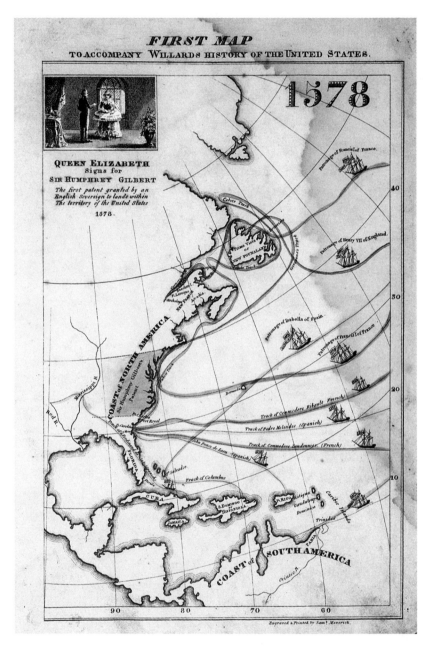

Figure 9: Emma Willard's "First Map" of 1578. Willard, A Series of Maps to Willard's History of the United States, or Republic of America; Designed for Schools and Private Libraries *(New York, 1828). Emma Willard School Archives, Troy, New York. Michael Furgang Photography.*

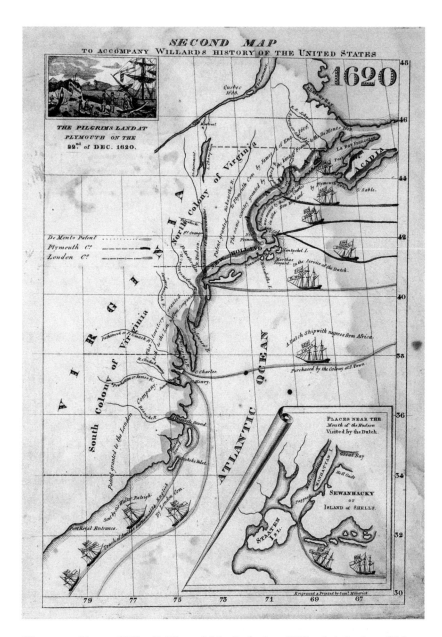

Figure 10: Emma Willard's "Second Map" of 1620. Willard, A Series of Maps to Willard's History of the United States, or Republic of America; Designed for Schools and Private Libraries *(New York, 1828). Emma Willard School Archives, Troy, New York. Michael Furgang Photography.*

Figure 11: Detail from Willard's "Second Map" of 1620: the Dutch ship headed to Jamestown with enslaved Africans. Willard, A Series of Maps to Willard's History of the United States, or Republic of America; Designed for Schools and Private Libraries *(New York, 1828). Emma Willard School Archives, Troy, New York. Michael Furgang Photography.*

studded with cities, towns, and prosperous farms, embellished with all the improvements which art can devise or industry execute?"[9] Jeremy Belknap had once believed that Anglo-Americans and Native Americans were incapable of dwelling side by side and that as white civilization expanded in the progress of liberty, Indians would recede into a shrinking wilderness. It was a story that his historical society was designed to gather, preserve, and communicate. Years later, Emma Willard would illustrate that story with her maps, and Andrew Jackson would enforce it with the might of arms.

Thus, Emma Willard, Jeremy Belknap, Andrew Jackson, and many others—in their speeches, histories, institutions, textbooks, and illustrations—all accepted a central principle at the core of New England exceptionalism: as the origin of America unfolds, it must *expand*. Willard's maps, as one historian observes, include an "empire-building lesson." The revelation at the moment of creation is not for current citizens of America alone. It is for all. And so it becomes the job and duty and responsibility of Americans to spread the light of this revelation across the globe, beginning with

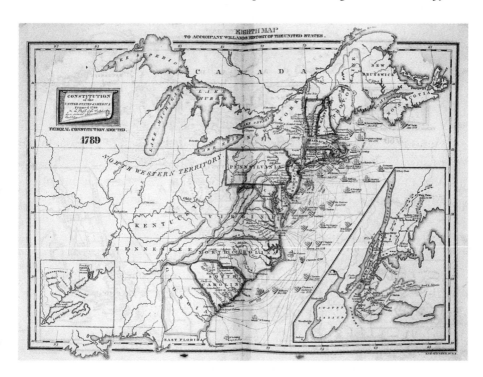

Figure 12: Emma Willard's "Eighth Map" of 1789. Willard, A Series of Maps
to Willard's History of the United States, or Republic of America;
Designed for Schools and Private Libraries *(New York, 1828). Emma
Willard School Archives, Troy, New York. Michael Furgang Photography.*

the West. As Salma Hale expressed it in his textbook, "It is . . . de-
lightful to anticipate the continuance of the Union for centuries;
and to contemplate three or four hundred millions of our fellow
creatures, enjoying climates profuse in every variety of good, bask-
ing in the sunshine of temperate liberty, and bound by the benefi-
cent laws of one government and one constitution; extending, not
over the present dominions of the United States only, but stretching their limits to the shores of the Arctic Sea and Western Pacific." Eventually, many Americans believed, this revelation would
save the world.[10]

All of these themes came to fruition in George Bancroft's *History of
the United States.* Until Bancroft published his history in 1834,

schoolbooks often relied on Abiel Holmes's *American Annals* from 1805 along with a few other resources. When Bancroft's *History of the United States* appeared in 1834, the game suddenly changed. His work consolidated all that the textbooks had been trying to say and became the basis for many new schoolbooks yet to come. Bancroft succeeded, in other words, because he enunciated "with conviction, elegance, and learning what nearly everyone already believed." Moreover, he gave his history the sheen of impartiality and the weight of scholarly learning. In doing so, his account of America—which was continuously written, revised, and republished in ten volumes for almost forty years—became the standard authority on the history of the United States.[11]

For George Bancroft, nothing mattered more to American history than American origins. "I have dwelt at considerable length on this first period," he explained, "because it contains the germ of our Institutions. The maturity of the nation is but a continuation of its youth. The spirit of the colonies demanded freedom from the beginning." Here, in a nutshell, was Bancroft's entire *History of the United States*. It all began, he argued, when Pilgrims first set foot on Plymouth Rock. As Bancroft wrote, "The consequences of that day are constantly unfolding themselves, as time advances."[12] All that we see around us, he explained, is just the growth of that principle of freedom first planted by a small band of Separatists in December 1620.

In order to get to this all-important origin, Bancroft, like many textbook authors, had to pass through Virginia. Unlike others, he did his best to incorporate Virginia into the story. In the preface, he tells readers that this history will detail "the early love of liberty in Virginia." And when he gets to the telling of the tale, he emphasizes that the "spirit of liberty had planted itself deeply among the Virginians. It had been easier to root out the staple produce of their plantations, than to wrest from them their established franchises." Still, that love of liberty was difficult to square with the way Virginia plantations actually produced their staple products, the system of slavery that defined their entire way of life. Bancroft seemed to recognize the tension by simply, quietly moving on. As others did, he acknowledged Virginia, then erased it. If America is the unfolding of an origin, then the proper origin must lie elsewhere. When Pilgrims arrive, Virginians get moved aside.[13]

For Bancroft, those 102 *Mayflower* passengers embodied all that would lead to the rise of the United States. This faithful band of voluntary exiles, he explains, *self-consciously* set out to found an empire: "They were restless from the consciousness of ability to act a more important part on the theatre of the world." When they left for America, they were moved by "the honorable ambition of becoming the founders of a state." In an absolutely incorrect yet incredibly powerful statement, Bancroft proclaimed, "As the Pilgrims landed, their institutions were already perfected. Democratic liberty and independent Christian worship at once existed in America."[14] The exceptionalism of America came rooted in an exceptional origin—the first English settlers of New England.

When it came to summarizing the contributions of the Pilgrims, therefore, Bancroft penned a paragraph that perfectly brings together all the various elements of Puritan origins and American exceptionalism. Pilgrims "showed the way to an asylum for those, who would go to the wilderness for the purity of religion or the liberty of conscience." They endured "every hardship" for the sake of "succeeding generations." And as a result, all citizens should "cherish the memory of those, who founded a state on the basis of democratic liberty; the fathers of the country; the men, who, as they first trod the soil of the New World, scattered the seminal principles of republican freedom and national independence." It would be difficult to come up with a clearer statement of the role of origins in the rhetoric of American exceptionalism.[15]

Yet that context is incomplete without considering how this origin story was recognized and resisted even as it was being created. Not all Americans embraced a tale of heroic Pilgrims. Many saw in this mythic origin story a threat to their very survival. The year 1838 marked not just the appearance of Winthrop's sermon but also the removal of the Cherokees on the Trail of Tears. Everywhere, Native Americans faced danger. And so, in 1836, one of the most vocal and gifted public intellectuals in New England—a Methodist minister and Pequot Indian named William Apess—took the lectern in the best Boston auditorium and rewrote the legend of Plymouth Rock, including all the stories that it had spawned.

The life and career of William Apess spanned the creation and dissemination of the Puritan origin story in America. He was born in 1798, the year Belknap died. He wrote his first book in 1829, published his last book in 1836, and gave his final lectures—under an assumed name—shortly before he died of appendicitis in 1839.[16] Apess's decade of activity as a public intellectual and activist coincides almost exactly with the first history textbook of Emma Willard (1828), the first volume of George Bancroft's *History of the United States* (1834), and the first printing of John Winthrop's sermon (1838). His career also coincides, not coincidentally, with the U.S. policy of Indian Removal, from the first passage of the Indian Removal Act in 1830 until the forced march of Cherokees on the Trail of Tears in 1838. For Apess these were intertwined events, causally related: the celebration of the Pilgrims furthered the removal of Indians.

Growing up in New England, Apess could not have escaped the steadily rising celebration of the Pilgrims and the rhetoric of Puritan origins. Born and raised in Connecticut, he spent most of his life in the Northeast. He would have known about Webster. And he would have been familiar with Willard as well, since in the mid-1820s he moved his family to Troy, New York. An avid student of history, Apess thoroughly understood the New England history of America. This work of national history, he knew, was erasing his people from the map, turning them into little more than an "introductory" setting before the "first" settlers arrived. In his last and best work, therefore, Apess reasserted the long history and continuing presence of Native Americans in New England. There was always a beginning before the beginning. There were Indigenous people here not just prior to but also during and after the Pilgrims' arrival. And those people have always constituted more than a mere backdrop, more than a wilderness setting for the dawn of a new nation. They are a civilization unto themselves, a multitude of nations with towns and territories, communities, families, farms, and ways of life—a whole diverse crowd of cultures, each having a history of its own.[17]

To say all this and to be heard in New England, William Apess had to be careful, talented, intelligent, and dedicated. He acquired the standing to speak in part through his conversion to Christianity and eventual ordination as a Methodist minister. But that position came about slowly and only after a long history of hardship and poverty. Apess's first publication, *A Son of the Forest* (1829), recounted the difficulties of his life through a spiritual autobiography—a common genre and standard literary entry point for many authors of color. That autobiography foregrounds his conversion, but it also never loses sight of the integral way his racial identity shaped his entire life. As his career developed, the specifics of racial discrimination and injustice would become an increasingly prominent part of his work. Soon, Apess found himself actively defending the rights of the Mashpee tribe on Cape Cod, while speaking more forcefully to broader audiences about the need to honor and protect Native American rights. Through such labors, William Apess became one of the most prominent Native American intellectuals and activists in antebellum America—and certainly the most prolific.[18]

The culmination of William Apess's career came in 1836. Speaking to a packed house in Boston on January 8, Apess eulogized a Native American leader named King Philip. King Philip, or Metacom, had waged one of the bloodiest wars of New England's history in an effort to resist the encroachments of the English, and 1836 commemorated 160 years since his death. But January 8 marked in particular the anniversary of Andrew Jackson's victory in the Battle of New Orleans—the victory that had launched not only his political career but also the burgeoning project of American exceptionalism tied to the writing of a new national history and, in Andrew Jackson's case, the removal of Native Americans. When William Apess rose to speak, he could assume that his audience was familiar with both Jackson's policies and Metacom's life. By 1836, prominent writers like Washington Irving had eulogized King Philip extensively, and popular plays, such as John Augustus Stone's *Metamora; or, The Last of the Wampanoags*, ran for many years to huge acclaim and applause.[19] These productions all took a similar approach: they ennobled King Philip and lamented his death as both tragic and necessary. In such accounts, especially in the historical fiction of the period, a critique of Puritanism could often find full-throated expression. But in turning to Metacom, the story always came out the same. King Philip became the glorious representative of a vanished race—a view of Native Americans that actually helped further the efforts of President Jackson and others to make them vanish. The very presence of William Apess, speaking to his audience as a Pequot Indian, undermined the usual narratives of Native Americans and their inevitable disappearance.

But what really distinguished Apess's production from all other accounts of King Philip was his new presentation of Pilgrim history and its relevance for the present. At stake in his address was how to think about progress—how to make the nation a place of freedom not just for some but for all. The only way to do that, Apess insisted, was to think properly about the past.[20] His address centered on one question: what is required of the present generation in relation to remembering and commemorating history? Belknap, Webster, Willard, Bancroft, and many others all had a definite answer to that question: they insisted that Americans in the present must remain faithful to the foundation established by "our fathers." What the Pilgrims and Puritans began must now be "transmitted unimpaired" to our children. Apess thoroughly disagreed. In a complete reversal of the usual logic, he called on his listeners to *break* from the past, to *escape* its legacy so as to bring into existence a new possibility—a reconciliation and extension of equal rights to all.

In making this case, Apess demonstrated a deep knowledge not just of Puritan historical sources but also of contemporary cultural discourses. He saw that the developing story of the nation—the New England history of America—depended on two essential distinctions. First, it separated English "settlers" from Spanish "conquistadors." Second, it differentiated the northern English (New England) from the southern (Virginia). These distinctions were vital not just to New England exceptionalism but to the entire story of America's exceptionalism on the global stage. Everything that made America distinct—its unique identity and purpose— depended on a story about New England settlement that presented it as a purer, nobler, more religious, and more liberty-loving enterprise than any other that had ever occurred. That was the distinction Apess identified in the histories taking shape around him. And that was the story he set out to destroy.[21]

Given this context, two words in Apess's *Eulogy on King Philip* would have rung out loudly to the gathered crowd: "conquest" and "priests." Taken together, these words indicated a narrative of the way evil Spanish conquistadors had come to America. Because Indigenous empires had already established powerful civilizations in Central and South America, the Spanish had to "rob and plunder" their way to wealth and land. They were "ruffians and assassins" who took possession "only by the right of conquest," and they did so—worst of all—in the name of religion. The Spanish would tell "Indians that their God was a going to speak to them" and then place them before a cannon, put "the match to it and kill thousands of them." Only "those who pretend to be Christians" could pull off such savage acts of cruelty, deploying "carnal" weapons for spiritual ends. Conquistadors cursed Indians "according to the order of their priests," praying "bullets through people's hearts" while invoking the words "of their Master, whom they pretended to follow." As a Methodist minister, William Apess concluded, "I cannot, for one moment, look back upon what is past and call it religion. No, it has not the least appearance like it."[22]

All of this would have made perfect sense if William Apess had in fact been talking about the Spanish. But he wasn't. This language, these accusations—the robbing and plundering, the ruffians and assassins, the "conquest" of the land through "carnal" weapons directed by the order of "priests"—all of it, Apess said, applied to the Pilgrims. In his revisionist account of history, the Pilgrims end up looking no different from their Spanish counterparts. King Philip had his own "country," which he ruled from his own "throne" when he "came into office," and the only way the Pilgrims could take it from him was by overthrow, not settlement. When William Apess took the lectern in New England, he therefore began by addressing "those who are in the possession of [King Philip's] soil, and only by the right of conquest."[23] The distinction that was so crucial to American exceptionalism—the idea of a unique origin so radically different from any other—suddenly collapsed.

Just as importantly, William Apess collapsed the distinction between the North and the South, New England and Virginia. He appealed "to the lovers of liberty" in his audience and called on them to rebuke the Pilgrims for never respecting the freedom of others. "December 1620, the Pilgrims landed at Plymouth," Apess declared, "and without asking liberty from anyone they possessed themselves of a portion of the country, and built themselves houses, and then made a treaty, and commanded them to accede to it." But worse even than the possession of soil without "liberty" was the possession of *bodies*. Apess resituated the beginning of slavery in New England. Pilgrims "took a part of my tribe and sold them to the Spaniards in Bermuda, and many others," he explained. Such practice was not an aberration but part and parcel of the English conquest of New England. Apess thundered, "How they could go to work to enslave a free people and call it religion is beyond the power of my imagination and outstrips the revelation of God's word." Speaking to an audience in 1836 that was largely antislavery—and that liked to congratulate itself for Puritan ancestors who had introduced liberty to America—Apess relentlessly brought home the horrors of slavery. "Through the prayers, preaching, and examples of those pretended pious," he proclaimed, "has been the foundation of all the slavery and degradation in the American colonies toward colored people."[24] The sin could no longer be set apart. The purity of the Pilgrims could no longer be distinguished from conquistadors and slavers, from Spain and Virginia, for the Pilgrims were just as impure, just as "carnal," as everyone else. There is no distinction. And without a distinction, there is no New England exception—no high-minded origin to the story of American exceptionalism. Insofar as the present is a continuation of the past, that continuity is wholly bad.

In fact, for Apess to make his point the perfect counter to Webster, Willard, Bancroft, and others, he actually employed the same language of a "seed" maturing into the nation of the present day— except that for Apess, the seed was a deeply problematic weed. The fact that people honor and praise the Pilgrims, he argues, shows that they approve of the Pilgrims' deeds. "And as the seed of iniquity and prejudice was sown in that day, so it still remains." Most unfortunately, "the doctrines of the Pilgrims has grown up with the people." A legacy *has* been transmitted unimpaired, Apess declares, but it is not one of civil and religious liberty; rather, it is an unimpaired legacy of slavery, avarice, and racism that still continues, defining so much of the American character.[25]

The solution, Apess declares, is not to remember and celebrate the past but to mourn and break from it altogether. Speaking immediately to the Webster-induced mania over the Pilgrims, Apess says, "Let the children of the Pilgrims blush, . . . let the day be dark, the 22nd day of December 1620; let it be forgotten in your celebration, in your speeches, and by the burying of the rock that your fathers first put their foot upon." The way to move forward is not through faithfulness to such founders but through *un*faithfulness— a forgetting of Plymouth Rock that would make possible the forging of a new and broader unity. "For be it remembered," Apess reminds his listeners, "although the Gospel is said to be glad tidings to all people, yet we poor Indians never have found those who brought it as messengers of mercy, but contrawise." At the end of his speech, therefore, Apess calls on all people to "bury the hatchet and those unjust laws and Plymouth Rock together and become friends." He reassures his audience that "we have not to answer for our fathers' crimes," but we do have to acknowledge what they did, "regret it, and flee from it." The way forward is through a new account of the past that buries and mourns, rather than elevates and honors. We must have a break, Apess proclaims, a new beginning. And, he adds—appealing to his audience's sense of their own exceptionalism—"this work must begin here first, in New England."[26]

Apess's rewriting of Pilgrim and Puritan history relied on an overwhelming amount of detail. He versed himself in the writings of the Puritans, and he used those writings against them. "It appears from history," he says again and again, and then he proceeds "to show another inhuman act," adding in paragraph after paragraph, "But there is still more." The facts are there. Yet in Apess's telling, these facts serve solely to invert the usual narratives. His villainous Pilgrims become the mirrored opposite of Webster's heroes. In the history of writing about Pilgrims and Puritans, it has often been difficult to find them depicted as full-fledged human beings—creatures both good and bad, both generous and treacherous, neither wholly sinner nor wholly saint.[27]

The battle over how best to remember the Pilgrims would flare up again far later—and Apess's view would find a surprising array of proponents—but in the decade when Winthrop's sermon first came to print, the dominant position ran from Webster to Bancroft. In speeches, histories, and textbooks, heroic Pilgrims fled persecution to plant the seeds of liberty in a new land. Those

English settlers of New England did for Bancroft, Willard, and countless others what the Virginians never could: they stood for something greater than themselves, setting the story of America on a higher plane. In the 1820s and 1830s, Americans learned that the true history of their nation originated with Pilgrims and Puritans—no matter who had lived or landed here first. It was, in many ways, the ideal context for discovering that the first Puritan governor of Massachusetts Bay, just prior to landing, had proclaimed that "we shall be as a city upon a hill."

PART IV

Methods

CHAPTER TEN

Antiquarian America

J OHN WINTHROP'S "CITY ON A HILL" sermon came to print for
the first time ever in August 1838. When the Massachusetts
Historical Society included the sermon in its *Collections*, it
chose James Savage to compose the first public interpretation
of the sermon's meaning and significance. James Savage, a cur-
mudgeonly man devoted to archives, manuscripts, and records, was
fast becoming the most important and renowned authority on
seventeenth-century Puritanism. In 1825, he had carefully edited
and published John Winthrop's important journal, *The History of
New England*. Now, thirteen years later, he introduced the sermon
that would eventually come to summarize, in the twentieth century, both the origin and meaning of America.

When James Savage composed his official introduction, he
spoke in full the feelings of his age. Lifting up the glories of the sermon, Savage praised the Puritan fathers' "devotion to the general
good" and sketched the hardships that the "noble company of pilgrims" endured. His loving account of New England's founders—so
consistent with the histories and textbooks of the period—quickly
progressed to a robust affirmation of American patriotism. What
most stunned Savage was the self-sacrifice of these Puritan fathers
in establishing such an extraordinary "empire." Though they might
have expected "future advancement at home," these "accomplished

gentlemen" instead chose "a spirit of stern patriotism and equal self denial in founding deeply and broadly the edifice of SUCH an empire, whose whole and true glory was all within their prophetic vision." Winthrop and his sermon embodied for Savage a story of intense courage dedicated to the pursuit of a higher cause. The villains in his tale were those who failed to hack it in America, those who "yielded to temptation in returning to their native land, or in emigrating to happier fields and more benignant skies." Without hesitation, the MHS assumed that the sermon had been written by the "Brave Leader" of the Puritans and issued (according to a questionable cover note) at the precise moment of passage. Coming as if out of nowhere, *A Model of Christian Charity* was suddenly handed to the nineteenth century as the westward origin of an American empire still expanding west.[1]

Such an interpretation would have surprised the New-York Historical Society, where the copy of Winthrop's manuscript actually lay. Savage had the privilege of introducing Winthrop's sermon only because the NYHS turned it down. As historical societies cooperated and aided one another in the common cause of recovering, preserving, and communicating the past, they also competed to elevate the importance of their own region's role. In general, the New-York Historical Society committed itself to explaining the importance of Manhattan and the early Dutch settlers of America. When the NYHS hosted its first big gala, therefore, it chose to commemorate the two hundredth anniversary of Henry Hudson's voyage in 1609, and the vast majority of the official toasts offered on that occasion concerned New York, not New England. Whatever region the historical societies happened to highlight, however, each still sought out the help of others in the ultimate, shared cause of rescuing records from oblivion. These societies, which kept popping up across the country, assumed a national heritage, even as they approached that heritage from their own particular point of view.[2]

The tension between competition and cooperation helps explain how Winthrop's "city on a hill" sermon ended up in Savage's hands. In 1837, the MHS reached out to George Folsom, who worked at the NYHS, and made him a corresponding member. One year later, Folsom returned the favor with this news: "our Society has caused a copy to be made of a MSS of Govr Winthrop, not in your Library, never published, which will be soon forwarded."[3] From Folsom's perspective, this document clearly mattered to the MHS, but not very much to himself. If it represented any kind of original vision of America, that idea never occurred to him. Nor would it. New Amsterdam had been around for several years before Winthrop declared that "we shall be as a city upon a hill." And others had been in America far longer. In fact, the correspondence about Winthrop's sermon arose while discussing a recently published book called *Antiquitates Americanæ* (1837) by Carl Christian Rafn of Copenhagen. Rafn's book demonstrated with considerable evidence that the Vikings had arrived in North America many centuries before any other Europeans. Folsom and the MHS librarian, Thaddeus Harris, were writing to confirm that copies of Rafn's work had been received and to check whether all the bills had been paid. In the context of that conversation, Folsom mentioned Winthrop's manuscript.

When Harris received news of Folsom's discovery, he responded with great excitement. "As Chairman of the publishing committee of the Massachusetts Historical Society," he wrote on February 15, "I am highly gratified with the expectation of receiving a copy of the manuscript of Governor Winthrop, and beg you to accompany it with some prefatory account of the original."[4] A new volume of the MHS's *Collections* was in progress, and Harris wanted to print Winthrop's sermon right away. But Folsom's copy did not come. Harris waited. He wrote a letter. He waited some more. The communications reveal a growing impatience as Harris repeatedly delayed the printer in order to include Winthrop's manuscript. Finally, in May, the sermon came.

When Folsom sent his copy, he tried to determine how the NYHS came to have this sermon, but he had little information to convey. In 1809, Francis Bayard Winthrop donated twenty-two historical books and manuscripts to the NYHS, including "A Modell of Christian Charity. Written on Board the Ship Arrabella by John Winthrop." F. B. Winthrop, a direct descendant of John Winthrop, represents the perfect case for understanding how these historical societies actually worked. On the one hand, Francis Winthrop was a New Yorker and justly proud of the new historical institution in his hometown, donating his books and manuscripts to the growing collection in order to bolster the NYHS. On the other hand, since the books and manuscripts were mostly concerned with New England, no one at the NYHS seemed to notice or care. A list of manuscripts in the 1820s once again mentions Winthrop's sermon, but again no one paid it any mind.[5] For almost thirty years, the New-York Historical Society knew it had this manuscript, and for all that time it never displayed any excitement about the fact: it did not pass the information to others, copy the sermon out, or print it in its collections. It was just one manuscript among many. Even Folsom's delay in finally sending off a copy to Harris suggests that Winthrop's sermon registered rather low on his list of priorities. No one in New York ever thought that a cultural key text of American history and literature had been found.

But NYHS members *did* eventually discover it in their collections. They did copy it out. They did send it to the MHS. And eventually, the MHS did print it in its *Collections*. What this simple interaction reveals is the crucial role of a broad, thriving, nineteenth-century interconnected culture of antiquarianism—a community of laborers devoted to recovering old texts, printing them, and pinpointing the precise facts of the past. In the first printing of Winthrop's sermon, what comes to the surface, once again, are the long-term methods and effects of little-known figures. Jeremy Belknap, Ebenezer Hazard, and John Pintard have all slipped from historical memory, but they each played a big part in making it possible to find and publish *Christian Charity*. Emma Willard and other textbook authors are not remembered today, but they built and broadly communicated a story of the nation rooted in Puritan New England. James Savage, the most renowned antiquarian and genealogist in antebellum America, has likewise disappeared from American memory—probably more so than all the rest. Yet his work represented the apex of a broad movement pushing to recover the minutest details of the past. In order to tell the story of Winthrop's sermon, we have to understand this antiquarian culture and how it flourished in antebellum America. For without that culture, Winthrop's "city on a hill" sermon would never have been printed. And the best way to understand antiquarians in America is to study "the

Figure 13: James Savage, miniature portrait, watercolor on ivory by Richard Morrell Staigg, 1849. Artwork 03.238. Collection of the Massachusetts Historical Society.

New England Antiquary by way of eminence"—James Savage himself (figure 13).[6]

Born in 1784, one year after the Revolutionary War ended, James Savage's eighty-nine years of life spanned the dawn of a new nation all the way through its near eclipse in the Civil War. Throughout his long life, Savage had multiple different jobs—a lawyer, a part-time politician in the Massachusetts state legislature, a successful banker—but his sustaining passion (as with Belknap, Willard, and others) lay in history. Perhaps that passion had something to do with his childhood. At the age of four, James became an orphan. "No memory remains with me of my mother, who died before I had finished my fourth year," he later explained to his daughter.

When his mother passed away, his father lost his mind. Previous bouts of mental instability gave way to a complete loss of reason, and James was removed from the home. Older siblings stayed near the house to help out, but "I was not one of those," he recounted, "and can hardly dare to say my memory runs to partaking of his smile more than two or three times in my life." The funeral sermon for his mother took as its verse Psalm 27:10: "When my father and my mother forsake me, then the Lord will take me up." While the boy was eventually taken in by Mary Otis Lincoln, the daughter of the celebrated orator James Otis, Savage lived with this lack of parents for many years. When Mary Lincoln died in 1818, Savage described himself as "doubly an orphan."[7] Perhaps it is only coincidence, not psychology, but the orphan James Savage spent his entire life looking for ancestors.

In pursuing the past, Savage spared no effort and wasted no energy. Even as a young man, Savage committed himself to ceaseless labor. While a student at Harvard, for example, he recorded a dream that defined in many ways the work ethic required of an antiquarian. "I saw an exceeding high hill, on which was erected the temple of science," he began; "it had an hundred doors ever open, but the number of worshippers in the temple was small." Over every door was written the same set of words: "Be not weary of well-doing, without assiduous attention no one can enter here." Inside the temple grew the tree of knowledge, and around the tree sat the world's great thinkers: "poets, orators, and historians of all ages." None had reached this temple easily. The dream began with the motto "Nil magnum sine labore," or "nothing great without labor," and it went on to record the struggle of ascent. Two "frightful monsters" threatened along the way: "Idleness and Pleasure." But for those who were able to follow Prudence, the tree of knowledge lay beckoning ahead. "I awoke pleased with my dream," Savage wrote, "and hope that I may not, like Moses from the top of Pisgah, have a view of that land I am destined never to possess."[8]

While still at Harvard, Savage devoted his energy and labor to venerating the Pilgrim and Puritan past. Such reverence, he felt, was simply required for the common good. In a college essay called "Reverence for Antiquity"—copied in neat handwriting, carefully prepared, and saved for his entire life—he explains that a proper respect for the past preserves "a uniformity of manners and a stability of opinions, which ensures the happiness of society." In an image he would repeat across several different writings, Savage compared a reverence for antiquity to "the fertilizing moisture beneath the surface of the ground," which "winds its secret way through every avenue, penetrates every recess, and nourishes the germ of every sentiment in the mind."[9] Venerating the past mattered a great deal to young Savage, and it would remain important throughout his life.

Yet the context for that particular college essay concerned a specific moment of sectional strife. It came when John Adams, the nation's second president, fell from office, and many New Englanders feared Thomas Jefferson's rise. Jefferson looked, to them, like an infidel with an ear for foreign influence who was bent on destroying all that they held dear. And so Savage, in his student essay, turned to the Pilgrims for aid. "Let us consider ourselves, as heirs of the glorious inheritance of the pilgrims," he proclaimed to his classmates, "and resolve to transmit it with honor to posterity." In 1820, Daniel Webster would broadcast such sentiments from Plymouth Rock, but Savage felt and spoke this way already in 1801. "While the principles of civil and religious liberty have any supporters, while the glory of our ancestors excites emulation in their descendants, may the pilgrims of 1620 never be forgotten," Savage declared. Such acts of remembrance, he asserted, could even heal the nation. "Should a degenerate race ever rise in our land," threatening the people with "the poison of foreign influence," then, said Savage, "may the sight of the rock of Plymouth, like the brazen serpent in the wilderness, work miracles for their restoration." The brazen serpent, of course, referred to the bronze snake that Moses lifted on a pole to save the Israelites from disease and destruction. That was the way James Savage saw Plymouth Rock. The mere sight of it, the memory of it, the reverence and veneration for it that all should practice could restore and preserve the new nation of the United States. The duty of such collective remembering was incumbent on all Americans, Savage claimed. As he explained toward the end of his essay, "The frequent recollection of our pious ancestors should incite us to imitate their brilliant example. They have raised the temple; we should preserve it unpolluted."[10]

After graduating from Harvard, Savage tried to make his way in Portland, Maine, but he found "little room for a selection of companions." All he ever met were merchants, and all they seemed to care about was money. As a result, Savage mused, "My conversation must principally be with the absent and the dead. The spirits of those who lived in older days, must be summoned from the vasty deep, to instruct me." The letters he wrote from Portland to his adoptive mother, Mary Lincoln, express an incredible sense of loneliness, an aching loss of companionship. Savage needed to surround himself with others who cared about the same things he cared about, and what he cared most about was the past.[11]

Moving from Portland back to Boston, Savage started to make a lucrative career for himself primarily as a banker. Yet the main thing Boston offered him was not money but history. Savage devoted more and more of his time to reading, recording, and editing old texts. He attached himself to the Massachusetts Historical Society and began rising through the ranks, eventually serving as its fifth president, from 1841 to 1855. (His bust can still be found piled with many others in the attic.) With the support of the MHS, Savage began forming associations that eventually extended all the way out to the Midwest. In towns all across America, antiquarians gathered at historical societies, reclaiming, revisiting, and reviving the past. And in all their labors, they constantly sought the advice and affirmation of peers. The most successful antiquarians, like Savage, engaged in unceasing correspondence. As Belknap and Hazard pushed each other forward through their twenty-year exchange, so Savage found his partners and friends scattered from Massachusetts to Kansas. Together they became "gleaners in the by-ways of the past," seeking material, fixing errors, printing texts, and publicizing the results.[12]

Throughout Savage's life, these antiquarians formed his most abiding sense of community. So many wrote to him, with so many queries, comments, and discoveries, that his time was often consumed with correspondence. In 1851 he wrote his daughter, "in Boston, besides my social engagements, and numerous calls of business abroad, very numerous inquiries and communications about matters of local history or genealogy demand attention some times for one hour, not seldom for one day or one week."[13] The pursuit of American history—especially the pursuit of American historical material such as *A Model of Christian Charity*—required and produced a broad culture committed to the task.

There are, of course, many people who still do this kind of work today, who spend many hours and days and weeks and years with old records and lists and letters, searching out and sifting through the smallest facts in order to correct some larger story— and also finding in all this labor a great deal of joy. In Savage's day, that person was called an antiquarian, and antebellum America abounded with them. The inspiration for Savage's work and the glory he discovered in it depended on a vast network of colleagues and peers who engaged in these same pursuits and praised him for what he found.[14] James Savage, throughout his career, thrived at the center of a very large circle.

Perhaps nothing illustrates James Savage's sense of community and his underlying passions so much as his eventual trip to England in 1842—one of the few times in the last several decades of his life when he ever left Boston. By 1842, Savage had become the leading antiquarian of New England, and his wide network of peers pre-pared the way for a trip designed to bolster his research. Specifi-cally, Savage went to England to find out more about the Puritan roots of New England. Everything else was secondary. Various hosts kept trying to show him around, thinking he might like to ex-perience a bit of the old country while he was visiting, but Savage would have none of it. As he declared to his wife, "It shall never be said of me that my time was given to seeing sights, when it should have been occupied with the real business that brought me here." Idleness and pleasure could never lure him from his path.[15]

Still, Savage was not without delight. When he came to the var-ious storehouses of manuscripts and ancient books in London, he could hardly contain himself with excitement. In the British Mu-seum, James Savage found joy. At the State Papers Office, he expe-rienced real happiness—defined for him as five hours a day looking at rare manuscripts and copying out Puritan passenger names, one after another. When he went to Oxford, Savage spent four hours one day and two hours the next with the school registry, "finding graduates who went to our country in its earliest days." As his diary records, "the result of my labor yesterday and today has been to examine every *entry* of a student, beginning in 1615 down to 28 Apr. 1626 inclusive with a few of later date, none earlier." In June, he transcribed the names of 1,153 persons who passed to New England in 1634. Name after name, list after list, Puritan after Puritan, day after day—James Savage recorded it all. When the trip came to an end, he went to his "dearly beloved British Museum to ... cast one longing lingering look behind."[16] Savage kept his reading-room ticket all his life, a souvenir of extraordinary sights.

As demonstrated by the trip to England, the records James Savage loved best were what most people both then and now find impossible to read: wills, deeds, catalogues, ship logs, gravestones, and church registers of baptisms and marriages. So long as a record had not been seen or known before, it was as exciting to Savage as a first-rate novel. One peer remembered "his exuberant exultations, when his searches and researches were rewarded, by verifying some disputed date, or discovering some historical fact, or by lighting upon some lost historical manuscript."[17] The prospect of finding something new kept him devoted to the unprinted manuscripts stored in the State Papers Office, the British Museum, and the registry at Oxford University. His goal was to get history right, down to the smallest detail. And often enough, those details could only be found in the most tedious materials. The first folder in the first box of Savage Papers at the Massachusetts Historical Society is an undated set of documents that begins with "Description of Original Deeds in my possession." It is fair warning for what follows.

But getting history right also meant an active campaign to undermine and overthrow all that others got wrong. Old legends, however loved, had to be undone when the facts proved otherwise. This was the antiquarian's job. Two myths in particular demonstrate Savage's disregard for other people's feelings and his desire to set the record straight. The people of New Hampshire, for example, believed that the Puritan settler John Wheelwright had signed a deed with the Indians for the land on which they lived. They liked this story because it seemed fair and just and because it meant they properly owned the land. Savage, however, proved that the deed was false. It was a forgery. The governor of New Hampshire, William Plumer, raged against Savage, but Savage stuck to his claims. However much resistance his findings produced, he kept returning—with fierce passion—to the facts, believing that in the end the facts would win. In this case, he was right. The deed is now recognized as false.[18]

So, too, with "the martyr's Bible." John Rogers was one of the first Protestant martyrs to die during the reign of Queen Mary. He was a Bible translator who refused to recognize the legitimacy of the Roman Catholic Church, and in 1555, Queen Mary had him burned at the stake. Long family tradition claimed to have kept the very Bible that John Rogers once owned and read. James Savage was skeptical. With the help of a broader community, he tracked down this supposed martyr's Bible and found that it was published six years after Rogers died. It couldn't possibly have been the martyr's. Savage's friend George Livermore conveyed the excitement of the discovery: "I have this moment read my letters from England and have ascertained from them, *beyond all question*, that the so-called 'Martyr's Bible' was printed by John Cawood, in 1561, six years after blessed John Rogers was burnt at Smithfield!" Given the veneration for this martyr's Bible, Livermore advised Savage, "keep silent about the matter till we know all." Once he had the facts in full, Livermore would send a letter "putting at rest forever the story founded on a vague, foolish, and worthless tradition."[19] This was the antiquarian way: legends and traditions had to be tested. The facts would out. Myths would fall.

How important are these various corrections of tradition? In the case of a falsified deed with Native Americans, they remain hugely significant. This sort of debunking gets to the heart of relations with Native Americans, land ownership, rightful possession, and sovereignty still today. False deeds, like broken treaties, continue to reverberate. In the case of John Rogers's "martyr's Bible," however, the correction of the past seems a little less important: an old saint story comes out a little less saintly when a Protestant relic turns out to be a normal old Bible. What about private family traditions? What about the exact birthplace of Benjamin Franklin (another tradition Savage pursued)? How important is it to get exactly right the specific number of people present at a certain locale at a particular time? Savage didn't care what others thought. As one of his fellow workers explained, James Savage would "pursue the inquiry into the smallest incidents of history. They were not small to him." What mattered was getting it right. And to that end, he committed his life to a relentless pursuit of facts and evidence and authoritative sources. Antiquarians did not try to write histories or tell stories; they tried to verify details and set the record straight. They were, in that sense, the nineteenth century's most dedicated fact checkers.[20]

All the facts antiquarians checked were still guided by one underlying, unchecked premise: the Puritan origins of America. This fundamental supposition never came under scrutiny but instead enabled the examination of all the rest. It was fine for James Savage to debunk various myths related to such origins—the Wheelwright deed, the martyr's Bible, and so forth—but the idea of America as a nation arising from Puritanism was not, for New Englanders and many others, a *myth*. Instead, that assumption was simply the framework in which everything else cohered. As Savage rhapsodized in his 1838 introduction to Winthrop's "city on a hill" sermon, it was the Puritans' "spirit of stern patriotism and equal self denial" that laid the foundations of the United States. The glory of America was "all within their prophetic vision."[21] As the nation's foremost antiquarian, Savage honored that vision by devoting his life to the Puritan past.

Even so, the Puritan past was not without its faults. For all Savage's talk of venerating these ancestors, they also frequently got under his skin. In his early student essay "Reverence for Antiquity," he explained that patriotism did not entail a blindness for bigotry. "We should consider every virtue with enthusiastic admiration, and behold every failing in them with the eyes of candor." Those failings would become more and more apparent to him in the coming years, so that when he finally edited John Winthrop's *History of New England*—a three-volume manuscript in which Winthrop recorded the history of the Massachusetts Bay Colony from 1630 until the year he died—Savage's footnotes would record one Puritan fault after another, convicting them of tyrannical behavior, relentless intolerance, and unpardonable persecutions. The amount he criticized the Puritans would surprise someone who read only "Reverence for Antiquity" or considered James Savage part of the myth-making culture of Puritan New England. Yet Savage could criticize the Puritans so much *because* he considered them America's foundation. They had established its principles of civil and religious liberty. Given that story and framework, Savage condemned in no uncertain terms all Puritans who failed to meet their own high standard and calling.[22]

As a result, Savage's footnotes in Winthrop's *History of New England* are emphatic with criticism. The main problem, as Savage saw it, was the alignment of church and state, an arrangement that turned good religious principles and instincts into bad civil laws. Too often, he complained, "we are bound . . . to lament the undue dictation of the church." Modern states are not obliged to follow Mosaic law in their civic arrangements. God gave scripture, but he also gave reason. People should use it, Savage said. A new age required new norms.[23]

Because of these beliefs, Savage leveled a sustained fire at many different Puritan clerics and magistrates—anyone who failed to distinguish properly between church and state. Sir Henry Vane, the governor of Massachusetts Bay in 1636, Savage called the "prince of fanaticks." According to him, "Few men have done less good with greater reputation than this statesman." Thomas Dudley, another early Puritan governor, exercised "a hardness in public, and a rigidity in private life." Edward Johnson, a military man and public figure, could be called out by Savage for "his severe bigotry." As for Nathaniel Ward, who wrote a comedic defense of intolerance, his work was "very attractive for its humour, and curious for its execrable spirit." Altogether, James Savage had frequent opportunity to criticize Puritans for enforcing "incomprehensible jargon" with punishments that amounted to "extraordinary tyranny" and the "triumph of bigotry." "Of several parts of this history," Savage admitted, "many readers will perhaps form an unfavourable judgment."[24] The Puritans' superstitious sense of God's special providences, their punishment of dissidents, their treatment of Native Americans, and their union of church and state gave modern descendants much to lament and regret—all this from the pen of one who urged a "reverence for antiquity" and self-professedly venerated the first English settlers of New England.

One way to understand these dual tendencies is to realize that James Savage considered himself part of the family he criticized—as, of course, he was. He was a direct descendant of Thomas Savage, who arrived in 1635. These were *his* people, "our" people. Possessive pronouns reappear throughout the footnotes in Winthrop's *History of New England*. According to Savage, Winthrop's text recorded "*our* early affairs" in "*our* humble colony" as conducted by "*our* fathers," who leaned too heavily on "*our* church." Criticism can be most strident when it comes from within. Sharing a name, as Savage did, made Puritan failings personal. "With painful emotion," Savage remarked, "is the history of the intolerance of our fathers read by those of their descendants, who hold them in the highest veneration."[25]

Happily, there was one grand exception to all this bigotry and persecution: James Savage's great hero, John Winthrop. If the temporary failings of the Puritans must be separated from their lasting principles, one could accomplish that task by simply distinguishing John Winthrop from his peers. In fact, *A Model of Christian Charity* mattered so much to Savage because it detailed the underlying beliefs that alone could and would establish a superior American empire. As Savage wrote in his introduction, "Readers of the following homily of Governor Winthrop must, however, naturally have anticipated the success of the Massachusetts settlement, if his principles of action were diffused among his companions, and taught to their descendants."[26] For James Savage, *A Model of Christian Charity* summarized the greatness of Winthrop, and Winthrop was Puritanism at its best.

So much did James Savage love and venerate John Winthrop that he even, occasionally, adopted his name. "Good night my sweet Mrs. Governor Winthrop," Savage wrote his wife, Elizabeth, in 1828, "and tomorrow let me exult in having a letter from yourself and good stories of the children." Sometimes he just invoked Winthrop's goodwill: "I embrace my dear wife heartily as ever," Savage penned in 1831, "and with the blessing of Govr. Winthrop doubled upon you this night bid farewell." When he edited Winthrop's *History*, he included a facsimile of Winthrop's final letter to his wife sent from aboard the *Arbella* before sailing to New England. That touch of personal intimacy sheds light on the way Savage felt about the man. When later asked to work on the family pedigree of John Winthrop—a copy of which he kept for himself—Savage heartily agreed to the task, telling his daughter that he would do anything for "the family of my admirable friend, who has been dead to be sure more than two hundred years, Govr. Winthrop."[27]

James Savage, put simply, really loved John Winthrop. Others might be condemned, but never the first governor of Massachusetts Bay. Even in the case of Anne Hutchinson's banishment to Rhode Island—an act that has produced a good deal of harsh remarks about Winthrop through the years—Savage stood by his man and claimed that he exercised "general prudence." "The exasperation of the controversy did not, as usual, turn to gall Winthrop's gentleness of temper," Savage writes, though he allows that "it seems to me to have had an injurious influence on his judgment." This is as close as Savage ever came to criticism. Otherwise, Winthrop remained unblemished. In his introduction to *A Model of Christian Charity*, Savage wrote, "The name of that man is always sure to bring up to remembrance the virtues of our fathers, which will never find a better representative. That he practiced what in this essay is inculcated, the record of his life for nineteen years full discloses." John Winthrop was, in short, the best a Puritan could be—the "venerable father of Massachusetts."[28] And as the father of Massachusetts, he became, for James Savage, the founder of America itself.

In elevating John Winthrop and *A Model of Christian Charity*, James Savage denigrated and dismissed all other colonial settlements in America, just as Daniel Webster had done and just as countless others repeated in so many of the histories and textbooks being published at the time. Giving a lecture about "the different principles, on which the European Colonies in America were founded," Savage praised the founding tenets of Plymouth and Massachusetts and then emphasized their "wide difference" not just from "other European nations" but also from "the other plantations in general that were projected in England herself, even after our wonderful success ought to have been influential in leading undertakers to adopt the wisest policy." The Puritans, he claimed, were a unique breed, a distinct origin. No one else came close, especially those "bad settlers" farther south. In Winthrop's *History*, Savage noted Winthrop's report that Virginians were accustomed to drunkenness and explained, "Our neighbours of Virginia will not, I hope, be disconcerted at this report of customary drunkenness; or they must, at least, recollect that the materials of their infant colony were less select than those of New England."²⁹ By "materials," he meant "people": the settlers of New England were simply more select, a better people establishing a better colony at the opening of America.

As a result, Savage celebrated the United States only insofar as that nation descended from, and resembled, New England. While traveling through England in 1842, Savage made his allegiances abundantly clear. He was embarrassed by the political news coming out of America. "Still it is a sad thing to meet one's countrymen here," he wrote his wife, "when the country is hourly disgraced by the stupidity of its government." He feared being "pointed at as an American." This might seem to contradict the very patriotism that Savage so much praised. But Savage remained abidingly loyal to what he considered his real homeland—the region of New England. "I disclaim being answerable for, or acquainted with any part of the Western world, but New England," he pronounced.³⁰ New England mattered for the nation, he believed, but the nation might still lose sight of its roots and abandon the principles established by those special, self-denying, high-minded, true-hearted exiles of Massachusetts. If so, Savage would be a New Englander first, an American second.

In praising Winthrop and his fellow Puritans as the only true origin of America, Savage echoed sentiments that we have seen more broadly expressed in the era. The Puritans came for liberty and God, not for gain or greed. Savage rejoiced that the richer lands had been found by Spain and Portugal, which were "ruined by their unholy success." It was a "providential arrangement" that kept the English from losing their heads and diverting them from their holy purposes. Their "constant object" was a "higher and nobler freedom than any force or policy had ever established in the world." Savage described the Pilgrims as "a few high-souled men," and years later, at another Forefathers' Day celebration, he rejoiced that the nation was still "bestowing honor on the true hearted exiles." It was New England—and particularly that "devotion to the general good, which characterized the fathers of New England"— that set the example for the nation and prepared the way for all to follow.³¹ All these praises of the Puritans came together in Savage's 1838 introduction to *A Model of Christian Charity*.

In order for Savage to make his points clear about this sermon, he ended his introduction by quoting a long paragraph from John Winthrop's *History of New England*—the other text Savage so painstakingly edited and introduced. It is a paragraph from Winthrop's journal that describes the attempt of several Puritans to leave New England for a different settlement. Winthrop strongly opposed them, for a people who came together "into a wilderness, where are nothing but wild beasts and beastlike men," have promised in their "civil and church estate" to "bind themselves to support each other." According to Winthrop, when the Puritans came to America, they made a commitment to stay and aid one another indefinitely. They were bound to each other. They could not decide, willy-nilly, that the grass is greener and the skies are brighter somewhere else. Winthrop believed that only a dedication to the common good would enable their society to survive, and that meant setting aside personal desires or the lure of private gain. Ease and pleasure were not part of the agenda. They might come, they might not. Either way, those who set out in search of such things were imposters bent on destroying the pure patriotism and high ideals of the Puritans. In Winthrop's *History*, Savage took time in his footnotes to rhapsodize on this thought: "Few passages in this history are more gratifying than this faithful exhibition of the feelings, by which the early planters of New England were characterised."[32] This one passage, which Savage so much loved, demonstrated for him the exceptional nature of the first settlers of New England. It is the passage that he thought best summarized the whole message of Winthrop's "city on a hill" sermon—a corporate enterprise that set the common good over private gain.

In the first printing and first interpretation of Winthrop's "city on a hill" sermon, therefore, we have something quite different from the eventual vision of America that would be tied to Winthrop's sermon. The Puritans might have come for freedom, Savage agreed, but what he praised most in Winthrop's address was not the language of liberty but the commitment to community. Come what may, Savage claimed, these "high-souled" Puritan founders took on the burden of building a noble nation for later generations. "They seem to have anticipated the gratitude with which future ages should ascribe our present felicity to their fortitude."[33] And that gratitude owed itself to the spirit that bound Puritans to one another and to their common task. The Puritans did not come for profit, gain, or greed, Savage claimed, and they could not leave for ease or pleasure. This is what made the Puritans great. And this is precisely the greatness that James Savage saw exemplified in *A Model of Christian Charity*.

CHAPTER ELEVEN

Puritan Stock

T HE GREATNESS THAT JAMES SAVAGE found in the Puritans—especially as measured by *A Model of Christian Charity*—mattered to him in one other respect as well: racially. James Savage, the preeminent antiquarian of New England, thought of his New England homeland as a homogeneous settlement composed entirely of Anglo-Saxons, and its virtue depended on maintaining that racial and cultural purity. All those lists and registers he studied, all those deeds he collected, culminated in the great work of his life, *A Genealogical Dictionary of the First Settlers of New England*. Each enormous volume in this dictionary recorded in small print the precise date when individual Puritans had arrived, whom they had married, when they had died, and what children had come from those precious loins. The amount of labor that went into this project is staggering. As Savage says in the preface to the first printed volume, "One initial letter in this dictionary required a year and a quarter for its complete preparation, more than three months were given to each of several names, like Hall or Williams, and the progress of a page has often demanded a week." This he wrote in a book that came to 516 pages—the first of four volumes. "If my success has been less than my ambition," he continued, "it has not been owing to lack of industry, or to hurried operation." No one could argue with that. Nor could anyone deny the love that fueled this labor. As the last volume went to print, Savage wrote, "The task, that, near twenty years since, was assumed by me, is now ended; and no regret is felt for the time devoted to it. Pleasure and duty have been equally combined."[1]

Yet Savage was certainly not the only person engaged in such endeavors. In 1823, when the townspeople of Portsmouth, New Hampshire, resolved to commemorate "the First Settlement of our Country" as "a duty which we owe to the memory of our Ancestors," they sent their notice to James Savage and wrote, "Dear Savage, You will perceive by the above circular, that we have just discovered that we had ancestors." It was a discovery being made all over New England. Savage's personal desire to find his family roots tapped into a broader, rising interest in ancestry, especially prevalent among all those who hoped to trace their own town and family back to the first English settlers of New England. In a new republic that supposedly scorned ancestral pedigree, genealogy suddenly was everywhere on the rise. Benjamin Franklin had once proudly proclaimed himself "the youngest son of the youngest son for five generations back," arguing that in the United States the name of one's family did not matter. In a letter written to Franklin and later published with his *Autobiography*, one man praised him explicitly for that position: "You are ashamed of no origin; a thing the more important, as you prove how little necessary all origin is to happiness, virtue, or greatness."[2] That was in the late 1700s. By the 1820s and 1830s, origins began mattering a great deal to a whole host of Americans. And as a result, interest in genealogy swelled.

The man initially responsible for this boom in genealogy was John Farmer, a New Hampshire antiquarian who died two weeks before Winthrop's sermon first appeared. It was Farmer who began the search for familial roots in Puritan New England. In 1829, he published *A Genealogical Register of the First Settlers of New England*—the first dictionary of Puritan ancestors, whom Farmer hallowed by identifying for each "a residence, an office or military career, freeman status, English origin if known, . . . and whatever he could find on children and sometimes grandchildren through much of the seventeenth century." In pursuing this population with such minute researches, Farmer both assumed and bolstered the significance of the first generation of New England settlers.[3]

Farmer's success, which Savage extended, led to the whole idea
of a "Puritan stock"—the belief that special traits descended from
the precious blood of the Puritans to their various descendants and
heirs spread all across the United States. With four out of the first
five presidents coming from Virginia, New Englanders turned to
the superiority of their own moral principles, which they based increasingly in this sense of a "Puritan stock." Being associated with
such stock added character, prestige, and pride to all sorts of families. In 1859, James Savage received a typical letter from a man in
Chicago named Joseph Austin, who wrote to say that he had just
signed up to receive a copy of the *Genealogical Dictionary*. "My family being of the old Puritan Stock, though for some time out of
New England," he added, "I am anxious to learn its first point of
settlement."[4] He wasn't alone. Many Americans wanted to know
their first points of settlement and their first Puritan ancestors, associating themselves with the glory of the coming of the Puritans,
wherever they happened to live now.

As a result, genealogy took off. Farmer began the movement,
but Savage led it. When Savage finally proposed revising Farmer's
genealogical register in 1845, he met with widespread encouragement. For over twenty years, correspondence and visitors poured
in, checking on the work, aiding the labors, pushing Savage to
complete his studies. The manuscripts behind the printed volumes
of this dictionary fill eleven boxes at the Massachusetts Historical
Society. And what those boxes contain are not drafts of the finished
dictionary or notes about its construction but letters—endless letters, mountains of letters organized by the last name of each correspondent. In seeking out every detail of every Puritan ancestor,
James Savage wrote to people all over New England and beyond.
Many heard about Savage's work and simply wanted to know what
he had found. Others wanted to help however they could. Many
had begun their own family genealogies and sent what they had
discovered to Savage. "I am sorry I did not know of your purpose
before," one man wrote in 1858, "so that I could have furnished
you with historical and other correct materials for the notice of
Capt. George Denison, my ancestor. He has never had justice done
him in history."[5] This correspondent, like others, sent Savage an
elaborate, hand-drawn family chart. Most of the diagrams Savage

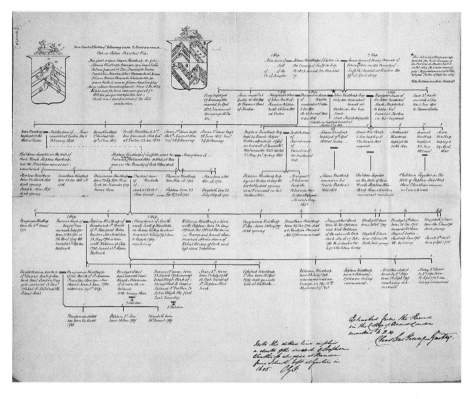

Figure 14: One of the many elaborate hand-drawn genealogical trees that engaged James Savage, here of the Winthrop family. Winthrop family chart, n.d., Ms. N-142, James Savage Genealogical Papers, Collection of the Massachusetts Historical Society.

received are today contained in an oversize box, and as you unfold them, they spread across the entire table—a beautiful, careful labor of love to trace family trees back to their first American root, to find an origin in the pure blood of the first Puritan settlers of New England (figures 14 and 15).

Because Savage had such a well-respected reputation, because his work touched on the interests of so many people at this time, many of the letters that came his way expressed their immense gratitude for the coming publication of his *Genealogical Dictionary*. "Permit me, dear sir, once more to recount my expressions of grateful acknowledgment to you for your invaluable service in the

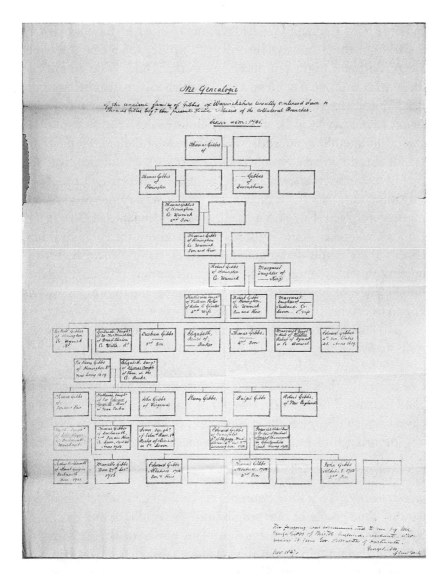

Figure 15: One of the many genealogical trees drawn and sent to James Savage to aid him in his labors. The Genealogie of the ancient family of Gibbes of Warkwickshire . . . , November 1847, Ms. N-142, James Savage Genealogical Papers, Collection of the Massachusetts Historical Society.

cause of New England Genealogy," one man wrote in 1848. Bringing to light these "musty" records is "a service for which the families of Puritan Origin can never be too thankful." "The number of those who will one day bless your unselfish efforts will be large indeed," another wrote in 1861. One man proclaimed that the *Genealogical Dictionary* "will be a treasure-house for all future explorers, 'usque ad finem' [to the end]." When it came time to seek purchasers for this dictionary, Savage could assert with confidence that "for the past thirty years, the study of family derivation has been spreading very rapidly in New England." It was. And it was spreading beyond New England as well. The descendants of New Englanders, wherever they lived, wanted to know their family lines, collect their family letters, and find their family records, reconnecting themselves to those first glorious settlers of New England. As the idea of a Puritan stock rose, more and more Americans hoped to catch a bit of glory trailing in their wake.[6]

It is not necessarily the case that someone interested in family roots is also interested in racial purity. Genealogical curiosity can flourish for any number of reasons. But in Savage's case, and in the case of many others in his day and age, those two pursuits often went hand in hand. There is a curious phrase that appears in the papers of Savage which illustrates this racial aspect of his work and its underlying importance to him. In a printed piece written for a Plymouth celebration, Savage explained that "it seems almost strict duty for the Historical Society to reverence whatever inheres in the *gentis incunabula nostrae*." That little Latin phrase could mean the "cradle of our nation," "the cradle of our people," or "the cradle of our race." For Savage, there was little distinction. The power of the Puritans inhered in their Anglo-Saxon blood. Such a belief helps explain why Savage loved and revered England so much. England had produced the race that had led to the Puritans who had codified the principles that had birthed the United States. England was, properly speaking, the fatherland and the alma mater, the "*gentis incunabula nostrae*," "the land of our fathers' sepulchres, the island of the blessed." Savage longed "to visit and examine the cities, towns, parishes, villages and hamlets where the ancestors of most of us resided."[7] The "us," again, is telling. He was a descendant of Anglo-Saxon Puritans, and he wrote to descendants of Anglo-Saxons all his life.

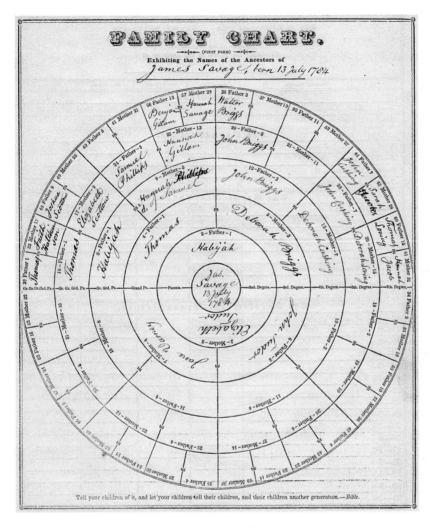

Figure 16: Because of the rise of genealogy in antebellum New England, many blank charts were printed for families to fill in their lineage. This one Savage filled out for his own family. Family Chart, Exhibiting the Names of the Ancestors of James Savage, born 13 July 1784, Ms. N-230, James Savage Papers, Collection of the Massachusetts Historical Society.

Yet Savage's conception of that descent went even beyond his immediate community of New England antiquarians. James Savage considered America itself to arise from Anglo-Saxon roots, and his *Genealogical Dictionary* begins with an extraordinary preface devoted to this very concept. Before he comes to the pages and pages of individual Puritans, Savage explains the importance of the compilation itself. During the entire period of colonization before 1776, he declares, "a purer Anglo-Saxon race would be seen on this side of the ocean than on the other." Savage then tries to deduce the relative purity of American racial descent over and against England's various mixtures. He says, "Within forty years a vast influx of Irish, with not a few thousand Scotch and Germans has spread over this new country, but certainly more than four fifths of our people still count their progenitors among the ante-revolutionary colonists." That is, according to Savage most Americans could still count as their ancestors those colonists who were here before the Revolution, and those colonists who were here before the Revolution were almost entirely Anglo-Saxon. He adds, "From long and careful research I have judged the proportion of the whole number living here in 1775, that deduce their origin from the kingdom of England, i.e. the Southern part of Great Britain, excluding also the principality of Wales, to exceed ninety-eight in a hundred."[8] Again, it is not clear whether Savage intends this number to cover all of America (as it seems) or just New England. In both cases, though, it is preposterous to believe that 98 percent of inhabitants were Anglo-Saxons from "the southern part of Great Britain" at the time of the Revolution. What about the Dutch? The Germans? The Swedish or French or Spanish? What about Native Americans? Africans? Savage looks past them all and equates the achieved independence of the new nation with its incredible racial purity—98 percent Anglo-Saxon, the purest stock in all the world.

We know that Savage based the success of America on this racial number because he specifically contrasted it with England's fall. While America kept its stock unmixed, England increasingly blended its population with an influx of people from all over Europe. During the colonial era, Savage writes, "great was the diversity of circumstances between the old and the new country so far as the increase of their respective numbers by incoming of strangers was affected." "Strangers" meant anyone other than Anglo-Saxons. With the return of Charles II, France's revocation of the Edict of Nantes, the invasion of William and Mary from the Netherlands, and the arrival of the House of Hanover from Germany, England repeatedly experienced "an infusion upon the original stock." But America, Savage believed, had no such problem, no incoming diversity in its early days. He rhapsodized, "A more homogeneous stock cannot be seen, I think, in any so extensive a region, at any time, since that when the ark of Noah discharged its passengers on Mount Ararat, except in the few centuries elapsing before the confusion of Babel." Savage concludes this extraordinary preface with an enthusiastic doxology for the supposed purity of this racial origin: "What honorable ancestry the body of New England population may assert, has often been proclaimed in glowing language; but the words of William Stoughton, in his Election sermon, 1668, express the sentiment with no less happiness than brevity: 'GOD SIFTED A WHOLE NATION THAT HE MIGHT SEND CHOICE GRAIN INTO THE WILDERNESS.'"[9] For Savage, "choice grain" arose from an Anglo-Saxon root.

That one line of Savage's in the preface to his *Genealogical Dictionary* reveals why all this immense labor mattered so much to him and others. The Puritans, many people believed, were able to accomplish extraordinary things because they represented a pure stock of Anglo-Saxon lineage particularly devoted to God and to one another. That stock, that blood, enabled them to establish principles of civil and religious liberty for a broad American empire. No other *race* could have accomplished as much. It was their blood, just as must as their principles, that made them great—or rather, to be more precise, their principles depended on and descended through their blood. For Savage, establishing Puritans as the origin of America meant making its racial heritage pure.

Savage was not alone in holding such a view. In his day, many Americans turned to the Puritans not just to elevate their own family line but also to give their nation's history a high purpose and destiny based in an Anglo-Saxon lineage. Race, culture, and nation were all bound up in the language of "Puritan blood" and a "Puritan stock." Such rhetoric could be used to indicate primarily a certain kind of New England culture spread throughout the nation, but that culture was itself thought to be the foundation of the

nation and a function of the blood flowing in one's veins.[10] For
many Americans, the superiority of ideas coming out of New England was based in the genealogies of those who bore such ideas in
their bodies, in their blood. They were pure, and that meant the
blood stayed pure. And none were purer than the Puritans.

According to George Bancroft—the renowned historian and
contemporary of James Savage—that pure blood was gradually
spreading throughout America, marriage by marriage and drop by
drop. Explaining why he "dwelt the longer on the character of the
early puritans of New-England," Bancroft asserted that "they are
the parents of one-third the whole white population of the United
States." As New England's political importance shrank through the
1800s, Bancroft reasserted its dominance through distribution. Puritan descendants, he declared, "are now not far from four millions.
Each family has multiplied on the average to one thousand souls.
To New-York and Ohio, where they constitute half the population,
they have carried the puritan system of free schools; and their example is spreading it through the civilized world."[11] Again we see
the link in Bancroft's mind between the blood in one's body and
the ideas in one's mind. The Puritans, the purest inheritors of Anglo-Saxon blood, were spreading Anglo-Saxon ideas of liberty and
education by moving those ideas physically outward and passing
them physically down through the reproduction of New England
culture and New England blood. Bancroft's influential histories
portrayed New England whitening the plains—and, in the process,
bringing civilization, liberty, and the proper love of God.

Such a position was not unusual at this time. Races were assumed to have characteristics, as were nationalities. The geogra-
phies that sold alongside history textbooks sketched the level of
civilization present in each region of the world, often linking that
level to the kind of people—the race, the blood—that lived there.
In sketch after sketch, in map after map, white Anglo-Saxons came
out ahead as the most advanced civilization in the world. These
maps argued that such an advanced level of civilization was not just
the result of peculiar circumstances related to a particular region
but a consequence of the character of the race who inhabited that
region. And freedom was carried most purely and most fully in the
blood of the Teutonic peoples—those Germanic tribes that de-

feated the Romans and created the Anglo-Saxons, who in turn produced the Puritans, who finally carried a pure form of Christianity along with civil and religious liberty to America. America was exceptional because it was founded by the Puritans; and the Puritans were exceptional because they were the latest, best, and purest extrapolation of Anglo-Saxon blood.[12]

In antebellum New England, those who wanted to trace their blood back to Puritan ancestors knew just where to turn. James Savage became famous through the course of his career for his careful scrutiny of old texts and his assemblage of vast genealogical information. "Dear Sir," John Farmer wrote him in 1826, "Your thorough acquaintance with the Massachusetts Colony Records give you a decided advantage over every one else in correcting the mistakes committed by our early and succeeding writers." Because of that reputation, the *Historical Magazine* once approached him for anything he might be willing to share on any subject whatsoever.[13] In antebellum America, anyone who wanted a fact from the Puritan past turned to Savage first.

That reputation extended broadly. Whenever a new historical society formed, it often sent a circular to James Savage and made him one of the society's first honorary members. His fame reached at least as far as Indiana and Kansas. In 1831, John Farnham, a member of the newly formed Indiana Historical Society, sent a letter to the great James Savage: "Dear Sir, Tho' I have not the honor of a personal acquaintance, permit me to say that I have long known you by reputation as a distinguished friend and advocate of Letters and liberal institutions." It was the missive of a devoted fan sent from what was still considered the American West. But Savage's reputation spread east as well. After his trip to England in 1842, all the greatest antiquarians and historians of England looked to him as their primary contact in the United States.[14] Throughout America and abroad, James Savage maintained his reputation as the quintessential antiquarian, the one person who knew the most details and held in his mind the most facts about the earliest days of New England.

Through the years, James Savage carefully considered his reputation and what might remain of it once he died. Suffering from a sickness in the 1840s, Savage felt "the uncertainty of life" and worried about finishing his genealogical work. "I care nothing about money, having enough and to share," he wrote; "but I am very solicitous for my reputation fifty or a hundred years hence." Taking up a second edition of Winthrop's *History of New England*—correcting errors, adding comments, producing a better and more careful copy—Savage admitted that the project would not bring him much money at all. But he wanted the public to see his "new devotion to Winthrop" so they could know, he said, "that my diligence is not relaxed nor my judgment weakened by the long lapse of time." Reputation, he added, "is a good thing to extend."[15]

Savage knew, moreover, that if any reputation would remain, it would have to come from his historical labors. He had been a minor politician, a mediocre lawyer, and a decently successful banker, whose Provident Institution for Savings in the Town of Boston, founded in 1816, served as the first chartered savings bank in the United States. With his money, contacts, and support, moreover, he helped his son-in-law, William Barton Rogers, establish the Massachusetts Institute of Technology. These activities were significant, certainly, but not of the sort that would gain him lasting fame. Instead, Savage thought only two productions would maintain enduring value: his edition of Winthrop's *History of New England* and his *Genealogical Dictionary of the First Settlers of New England*. Living to the age of eighty-nine, he had ample opportunity to see and experience the success of the first. "No labor has been so congenial to my feelings at any time, as that of publishing the true edition of Governor Winthrop's History of New England," he wrote in 1840, "nor can I ever again expect to satisfy the affectionate curiosity of students of our early annals by any work similar or second to that." That work, he knew, would make a difference. When a second edition was about to appear thirty years later, he considered this work with well-deserved pride. "Quite a good looking work will be the new edition," he told his daughter. "The work will be sought for, fifty years hence, in libraries." It might never be "a *popular* book," he admitted, but, he said, "my name will be kept up by it, when nobody alive can remember your assiduous father."[16] In that regard, he was absolutely right. His name has forever been associated with Winthrop's *History of New*

England—in part because he was the last person to see and edit the original manuscript of the second volume, which was destroyed when his office burned. If anyone knows James Savage today, they know him as the editor of Winthrop's *History*.

The *Genealogical Dictionary* is another matter. The longer Savage lived, the less he could be certain that this project would have any comparable impact. Genealogical interest rose, peaked, and began to wane during his lifetime, so that the tributes after he died actually mocked the labor of his last thirty years. Called upon to toast Savage's career and contributions, a young colleague named G. S. Hillard could not restrain himself from lighting into the *Genealogical Dictionary*. This work, he declared, "may well rank … with the most laborious works which the annals of literature have produced." Unlike other tedious works, however, "the Genealogical Dictionary possesses no element of general interest." Even a good, basic dictionary could occupy one's mind for thirty minutes or so, Hillard said, but not Savage's tome. "To a reader in search of amusement, it is the driest of dry bones, duller than the muster roll of an army, or the catalogue of the ships and warriors in the second book of the Iliad." Hillard used his tribute to deride and scorn Savage's biggest production, gawking at the size and boredom of it, even as he sought to honor the man for all his "immense toil" and "patient unwearied zeal."[17] But his inability to honor Savage's work demonstrated just how much the times had changed. James Savage lived so long that he outlasted not just three of his own children but also the greatest labor of his life. His *Genealogical Dictionary* went to the grave before he did.

Savage saw it happening. He could sense before he died that the *Genealogical Dictionary* was falling out of favor, and he learned to constrain his hopes. It wouldn't be crowds that would keep his name alive. It would be one lone scholar here and there, some person studying the Puritans who wanted to know a little more about their past and would turn to Savage to find the way. "One student in ten thousand will understand New England History better in its early days for my researches," Savage mused. "How unimportant that he may be ignorant of the humble benefactor that smoothed the way by levelling obstructions or filling gaps." In some of his last reflections on the labors of his lifetime, Savage wrote his daughter, "My genealogical, or perpetual, study is prosecuted with consistency, and the advantages to be derived from this occupation may not be realized in this generation; but some obscure inquirer a hundred years hence shall acknowledge how much he owes to that Mr. Savage who beat Job in his patience."[18] *Someone* would remember, Savage thought. *Someone* would know. Some "obscure inquirer" would still look him up, would still see the amount of effort he expended in getting the Puritans just right, would care enough to preserve his name.

Perhaps only one obscure inquirer in the last ten thousand visitors to the Massachusetts Historical Society has bothered to sift through all the papers of James Savage or understand his role as New England's foremost antiquarian. But I searched for him not because of his *Genealogical Dictionary* or because of his long-standing work on Winthrop's *History of New England*. I sought him out because he was the man who first printed and introduced a Puritan sermon by his great saint and hero, John Winthrop. That sermon would eventually exercise more influence on American culture than any of Savage's other productions. And yet it never surfaces in James Savage's self-reflections about his eventual fame and reputation. In 1838 it came and it went, and he never mentioned it again. The powerful story of America that he hoped to preserve and pass on—the history of America as originating in Puritan New England—would one day find its most important source and expression in *A Model of Christian Charity*, the sermon that Savage forgot.

CHAPTER TWELVE

The Mayflower Compact versus
A Model of Christian Charity

O NE YEAR AFTER THE discovery and publication of *A Model of Christian Charity*, John Winthrop's direct descendant Robert C. Winthrop took the lectern in New York. He had been called there by the New England Society to praise the Pilgrims in a grand oration. Founded in 1805, the first of its kind, the New England Society modeled a genealogical organization that began springing up wherever two or three wealthy New Englanders happened to gather. The point was to celebrate homogeneity, to find those who were "allied to each other by a similarity of habits and education."[1] For most who joined in the early days, the New England Society bound members together through a repeated practice of remembering Pilgrim and Puritan ancestors. And that cultural memory came to its culmination each year in December, when these societies hosted a banquet on the anniversary of Plymouth Rock. New York, having established the first and most eminent of all the New England Society chapters, always attracted the best speaker of the day.

In 1839, that speaker was Robert C. Winthrop. Born in Boston, educated at the best private schools, he took legal training directly from Daniel Webster and gleaned some of his oratorical prowess in the process. Having served in the Massachusetts state legislature, Winthrop, like Webster, went on to join the U.S. House of Representatives, where he also became its speaker. When Webster moved out of the Senate to accept his new role as U.S. secretary of state in 1850, Winthrop replaced him. From the law office to the state legislature, from the House to the Senate, the two had much in common. And that common bond included the widely admired ability to give a very good speech.

As Webster had done at Plymouth Rock in 1820, so Robert Winthrop came to New York in 1839 once again to lay the foundation of America in the landing of the Pilgrims. That settlement, he declared, "was of wider import than the confines of New Plymouth." In fact, he said, the fateful influences of the Pilgrims "have been coextensive with our country. They have pervaded our Continent. They have passed the Isthmus. They have climbed the farthest Andes. They have crossed the Ocean." Nothing could stop the spreading consequences of that momentous day. "The seeds of the Mayflower, wafted by the winds of Heaven, or borne in the Eagle's beak, have been scattered far and wide over the Old World as well as over the New."[2] By now, such rhetoric had already become a cliché. It was repeated by countless speakers in endless anniversary celebrations, retold and recycled by innumerable politicians. It was reprinted in textbooks, formed a central chapter in Bancroft's history, and became the "key" to understanding Alexis de Tocqueville's *Democracy in America*. Among Anglo-Americans in the North, this was just the talk of the day: the 1620 Pilgrims and their creation of America could not be repeated enough.

What matters here is just how much that Pilgrim influence hid from view John Winthrop's sermon *A Model of Christian Charity*. Plymouth Rock towered over every other potential origin of America, overshadowing and erasing from memory not just Indians, Africans, the Spanish, the French, and the English in Jamestown but also the Puritans, who came ever so slightly later and just a little to the north. In a speech that goes on for fifty printed pages, Robert Winthrop finds no occasion to discuss the founding of Boston or the coming of his dearly beloved ancestor. One year after James Savage had printed, introduced, and praised *A Model of Christian Charity*, associating it with the "prophetic visions" of

Puritan founders, Robert Winthrop took no notice of it at all. It had been found. It had been published. And it had once again been ignored—neglected not just by James Savage but also by all those who commemorated the memory of the "first settlers of New England." During the first hundred years of the sermon's life as a printed and public text, *A Model of Christian Charity* was never linked to the meaning of America and never situated as the origin of the nation. Most scholars and politicians didn't even know it existed. If they did know, they didn't care.

What enables or prevents a text's success? What makes it cited or ignored, famous or forlorn—or anything in between?

When it comes to understanding why Winthrop's sermon once again failed to strike a chord, small material factors play a surprisingly significant role. American origin stories and the texts they rely on come shaped by mundane constraints of how, where, and when texts come to print, their length, their ability to be summarized or reproduced, and their competition with other, similar documents being published or touted at the very same time. One simple reason Winthrop's sermon might have been too hard to hear in 1838, for example, was that it joined a cacophony of recovered texts. Alongside Winthrop's sermon, a massive number of early American documents and records were being collected, sorted, and printed. Texts kept surfacing. Archives swelled. The *Collections of the Massachusetts Historical Society* could hardly keep pace with all it found and preserved, publishing as much as it could in volume after volume but still selecting a smaller and smaller sample from all the society actually held. *A Model of Christian Charity* begins on page 31 and runs to page 47 in a volume that is 304 pages long. However important Winthrop's sermon might have been, it had to compete with a great deal of newly discovered and printed texts.[3]

In addition to the problem of competition, Winthrop's sermon faced a more basic constraint of size. The text was big. The writing comes to well over thirty pages in manuscript or sixteen in its first small print edition. If someone wanted to include this sermon in a textbook, they would have to devote a great deal of space to it. They might be able to put it in an appendix, but they could never fit the sermon into a footnote. Compare that problem of size to the portability of the Mayflower Compact. Coming in at a mere paragraph in length, the Mayflower Compact could easily be dropped into a text-book, collected in an anthology, or pasted into a history. Multiple schoolbooks simply transcribed the entire Compact in their narratives or included its text at the bottom of the page. These are small matters of materiality, but they have a huge impact on a text's success. How easy is the text to reprint? How much space does it take up? How much time does it require? Winthrop's sermon was just too long. Someone would have to crop it down to size before it could ever become useful. Eventually, that is exactly what happened: when Winthrop's sermon did start appearing in histories, anthologies, and textbooks, it often showed up only in part—and that reduction of the text eventually shaped how the whole sermon came to be received.

Robert Winthrop actually began the process. When he spoke to the New England Society in 1839, he was ascending through the ranks, and his future in national politics seemed bright. But that political career took a sudden turn after the death of Daniel Webster and the end of the Whig Party. Rather than meddle with the nation's political affairs, Winthrop turned to shoring up its history. Following the retirement of James Savage in 1855, Robert C. Winthrop became the sixth president of the Massachusetts Historical Society and served in that capacity until 1884—a lengthy and transformative reign in the life of the institution.

During Robert Winthrop's tenure as president, he gave the society a large trove of family papers dating all the way back to Adam Winthrop, the father of the famous first governor of Massachusetts Bay. So many papers were deposited, in fact, that the process of editing and publishing them continues still today. With these papers, Robert Winthrop decided to write a *Life and Letters* of John Winthrop. That was a common kind of book in the nineteenth century. Undertaken by a descendant on behalf of a notable ancestor, the *Life and Letters* genre mixed an ancestor's papers with contextual commentary and biographical details, all in the service of praise. When Robert Winthrop put together his book, he did not have the original manuscript of Winthrop's sermon, of course. No one did. But as president of the MHS, Robert Winthrop knew about *A Model of Christian Charity* in the *Collections of the Massachusetts Historical Society*, and he decided—unlike so many others in the nineteenth century—that this sermon deserved attention.

"It would seem ... that Mr. Phillips may not have been the only preacher on board the Arbella during this memorable voyage," Robert Winthrop began. And then, as if informing his audience of something nobody knew—as, in fact, few did—he wrote, "A discourse has been preserved." Presented as a surprise, the *Arbella* sermon appeared before the public in 1867 through the interpretative lens of Robert C. Winthrop. Winthrop called the sermon "an elaborate discussion of Christian charity or love" and claimed that it culminated in a discussion "of the great work in which they had embarked, and of the means by which it was to be accomplished."[4] Then to summarize the sermon, he reprinted its last few paragraphs. Those paragraphs contain what would become the most famous lines of John Winthrop's sermon, especially his declaration that "we shall be as a city upon a hill."

As we can see in this example, such lines became famous in part because figures like Robert Winthrop cut out the rest of the sermon and republished only this final bit. That is where he focused the reader's attention. That is all he printed. And that is why the end started to become so important to the sermon as a whole. The full discourse was still too much to reproduce, too much to process or filter or fit into a form that could easily be learned or passed along or integrated into the processes of collective memory. To become famous, Winthrop's sermon had to be reduced. And the best way to reduce it was to take the ending as the meaning and summary of the whole.[5]

Such reductions would affect the perceived meaning of Winthrop's sermon all the way to the present day. For many years, scholars, politicians, and commentators missed Winthrop's overt language of sympathy at the very center of his sermon, and they did so for a simple reason: it wasn't there. When *A Model of Christian Charity* began to enter print more broadly, it often lost the parts that emphasize a Christ-modeled, grace-endowed mutual affection—the idea that a true Christian community had a "sensibleness and sympathy of each other's conditions" and lived in "the sweet sympathy of affections."[6] Early editions of this sermon considered such language unnecessary and inessential to the message, so they cut it out.

We can see that development in some of the more influential publications to follow Robert Winthrop's edition of 1867. In 1938,

for example, the scholars Perry Miller and Timothy Johnson edited a
collection of Puritan documents for students that included a cropped
version of Winthrop's sermon. Miller and Johnson added back the
presumed beginning of this sermon—its "doctrine" that God Almighty had made some rich and others poor—but they, too, dropped
all talk of love or sympathy, defining *A Model of Christian Charity* primarily in terms of personal vocation, social hierarchy, and communal
covenant. That choice matters because their sourcebook became one
of the most widely used introductions to the study of Puritanism. For
almost half a century, a large number of students and future scholars
of Puritanism first read Winthrop's sermon without its middle. Fifty
years later, Alan Heimert and Andrew Delbanco printed a few more
passages from the sermon's interior, but anything considered a mere
example of mutual affection or sympathy was still removed—a pattern that persisted throughout the twentieth century.[7]

The point here is not to rebuke editors for making cuts. Books
are expensive, and decisions have to be made. Yet *what* gets cut from
the various editions of Winthrop's sermon reveals a great deal about
how *A Model of Christian Charity* has been read, understood, and
passed on to others. Winthrop's sermon is not about establishing a
proper form of government—all he says is that every society needs
"a due form of government both civil and ecclesiastical." Winthrop
never bothers to explain what a "due form" entails. More importantly, the language of social hierarchy at the beginning and the invocation of a covenant with God at the end become much more
significant if they are the only parts of the sermon printed. Between
the beginning and end, however, there is a middle, and that middle
turns this text from a logical command to a summons of the heart.
The language of sympathy lies at the center of Winthrop's vision.
But for most of its existence, that language went largely unnoticed—usually because it was removed. It was removed, moreover,
because the sermon was just too long. The material factors of a text,
down to the details of its length, have a large impact on the way it
comes to shape a broader cultural memory of the past.[8]

Material conditions matter, but they are not the only factors in a
text's failure or success. A new text must also, of course, match up
with some deeper ideological drives. As we have seen, American

origin stories do not just rely on texts; they are also largely *about* texts—about the writing of them, about the signing of them, about their long-lasting significance and the groundwork they laid for other, future American texts. As Jeremy Belknap and many others emphasized, American history was seen as unique because it all occurred within the time of modern writing, because it had been recorded with paper and ink in a European language that all could read. Ignoring Native Americans entirely, they claimed that this full written history is what made the history of America distinct. With a little diligence and care, all of it could be collected, housed, published, read, and known. For Belknap and many others both then and since, it is the *texts* that tell the tale.[9]

The story of America, therefore, had to begin with the right sort of text. And before *A Model of Christian Charity* came along, the Mayflower Compact had already claimed the opening spot. As Abiel Holmes wrote in his influential *American Annals* (1805), the Compact was born of necessity, but its consequences were extraordinary. Pilgrims agreed to "combine themselves into a body politic, to be governed by the majority," and to that end they drew up "a written instrument" and signed their names. "Thus did these intelligent colonists find means to erect themselves into a republic, even though they had commenced their enterprise under the sanction of a royal charter." This was the basic form of the story repeated in numerous textbooks. As the prize-winning textbook writer Salma Hale put it, "Previous to their landing, after prayer and thanksgiving, they formed themselves into a body politic, binding themselves by a written covenant to be governed by the decisions of a majority."[10] It all began with writing—with "a written covenant," "a written instrument," a *text*.

The Mayflower Compact mattered, moreover, because it could be used to create a textual genealogy that led straight from the Pilgrims to the Constitution. Consider how Emma Willard breaks up her history of America. After starting with Columbus and various acts of discovery and exploration, she turns to 1620. In that year, she writes in the table of contents, the Pilgrims landed "after having framed on board the May-Flower, the first written political compact of America." A special comment in the margin of the chapter again emphasizes the importance of the event: "Before landing," Willard adds, the Pilgrims "sign a civil compact, which was the first written constitution of the new world." The *first written political compact of America* and the *first written constitution of the new world*—for Emma Willard, American history consisted of a series of texts, a progression of New World constitutions leading through New England from the *first* in 1620 to the *best* in 1789.[11]

We can see that development in the further ways Willard breaks up the story of America. The next "epocha" of her history begins with another written constitution: the confederation of New England colonies in 1643. In 1643, the colonies of Massachusetts Bay, Plymouth, Connecticut, and New Haven banded together in mutual defense against Native Americans and Dutch settlers. Most Americans today have no cultural or collective awareness of this moment, but in the nineteenth century—especially in New England—it was considered a key turning point in American history. In multiple textbooks, the New England confederation of 1643 represented one of the most significant written prefigurations of a much larger, later union. After the 1643 confederation, meanwhile, Willard predictably turns to another written instrument: the 1692 charter for Massachusetts Bay. She makes these moves, from the Mayflower Compact (1620) to the New England Confederation (1643) to the second charter of Massachusetts Bay (1692), because in following a textual trail, she gets closer and closer to the Declaration of Independence, the United States Constitution, and George Washington's Farewell Address—the written instruments she would eventually describe as the nation's "political scriptures."[12]

This commemoration of the Mayflower Compact became more and more common through the 1800s and led to greater and greater expressions of praise. At the founding of the Society of Mayflower Descendants in 1894, the Mayflower Compact was described as "the germ of the American Constitution," and it became the text around which the whole society situated itself: "the keynote of our association, and its date our anniversary date." Two years later, the society published a small book of biographies called *Signers of the Mayflower Compact* (1896). Even more important than riding the *Mayflower* and landing at Plymouth Rock was *the signing of the Compact*. The first page of this book explains that it was drawn up and signed by forty-one men on November 11, 1620 (old style), "which gave to these people the claim of being the first 'signers' of this great and free United States of America." Of course, in 1620 there was no such thing as the United States of America, nor could such an eventual nation have entered the imagination of these English settlers. But no matter: for the Society of Mayflower Descendants, as for many others, the Mayflower Compact served as the textual origin of the entire nation. That is what the American origin story needed after all: not just the first landing but the first "signers"; not just the first event but the first written instrument, the *text* that could mark a new start.[13] To become part of an accepted tradition, to become canonical, a recovered text had to meet needs that other documents did not. In the nineteenth century, the Mayflower Compact already met all the needs and desires Americans associated with a great national origin.

The fact that Winthrop's sermon was delivered ten years after the Compact had been signed, moreover, did nothing to boost its standing. With a founding already fixed, it was doubly hard to move forward from 1620 to 1630 in order to proclaim a new origin of America. As Emma Willard's works make clear, 1620 marks *the* definitive break. It constitutes an important branch on her tree of time. But 1630 sports no branch, twig, or leaf. In Holmes's *American Annals*, Winthrop and the *Arbella* likewise pass by hardly mentioned. Instead, he dwells on Plymouth Rock. "It was on the eleventh of December 1620 . . . that the venerable fathers of New England first stepped on that ROCK, which is sacredly preserved in memory of their arrival."[14] Now *that* is an origin. The "fathers of New England" came on a specific date (December 11, 1620) with a specific action (a step) at a specific place (the rock) after having signed a particular written instrument (the Compact). It was considered one small step for Pilgrims, one giant leap for Western civilization.

In such moves, we see a subtle but significant distinction greatly affecting the reception of Winthrop's sermon. In general, when authors began America in New England, they defined that starting point as either Puritanism in general or Plymouth Rock in particular. People used phrases like "Puritan New England" or "Pilgrim Landing," but no one spoke of "Pilgrim New England" or

"Puritan Landing." The Mayflower Compact always initiated the story; the landing of the *Arbella* simply swelled the numbers. Tocqueville, for instance, explained that America owed its democratic character to Puritanism through "the principles of New England." But when it came to specifics, he, like others, turned to the Mayflower Compact—which he, like others, quoted in full. "This happened in 1620," he wrote, "and from that time forward the emigration went on." Tocqueville's text followed a general pattern: "Puritanism" as an idea could be an origin of America, but *its* origin went back to Pilgrim Landing. Thus, Pilgrims and Puritans were often blurred in American collective memory in such a way that Winthrop's sermon could not be seen as starting anything new. Before *Christian Charity* came to print in 1838, the American origin story that most people knew and accepted already had a different time line and text.[15]

When Winthrop's arrival on the *Arbella* does appear in history textbooks, therefore, the mention is hardly ostentatious. Insofar as Winthrop becomes the founder of anything, his establishment is *local*, not national. That would remain true from the earliest textbooks of American history in the 1820s all the way through the first public use of Winthrop's "city on a hill" sermon in 1930. Emma Willard reports in her 1833 abridged version of the *History of the United States*, for example, that "about 1500 persons, during the year 1630, sailed for Massachusetts Bay, and laid the foundation of Boston, and other towns in its vicinity." Notice the absence of any rhetorical flourish. Winthrop founded Boston—not New England writ large, not America, and not the other abstract origins that Americans loved to celebrate, such as self-government, religious liberty, civilization, and the love of God. All of that, these writers claimed, had already arrived.[16] In the writings of the nineteenth century, the year John Winthrop stepped ashore had nothing to do with grand beginnings. The *Arbella* just came too late.

Of course, plenty of historians and textbook writers had a great deal of love and praise for Winthrop. Many presented him as an able leader and a great governor, one of the firmest, mildest, best minds and hands of the early days. George Bancroft, for example, described him as "a man approved for piety, liberality and wisdom." But that view of Winthrop lifted up a separate text to celebrate:

John Winthrop's "little speech on liberty." This speech, delivered in a court of law fifteen years after he arrived, distinguished a right use of liberty from mere licentiousness, carefully outlining the subjection citizens owed their sovereigns. In the 1800s, many Americans loved it. It fit with early republican values that defined freedom not so much as a sphere of individual free choice but as the social good of virtuous behavior. Winthrop's speech appeared in multiple texts and was even proclaimed one of the greatest addresses of all ages, rivaling the classics. Students memorized and recited it. John Winthrop, in other words, maintained a solid reputation as a statesman, speaker, and writer, but that reputation relied on an entirely different text meeting an entirely different need.

A Model of Christian Charity, meanwhile, fell between the cracks. It could not be celebrated as the founding of America because the founding already occurred; and it could not be celebrated as a great statement on liberty because Winthrop's great statement on liberty was already well-known. When *A Model of Christian Charity* appeared, therefore, it became just one more Puritan document added to the huge number being recovered and reprinted every year.[17]

Beyond the problems of need and size, one other significant barrier stood in the way of celebrating *A Model of Christian Charity*: the Pilgrims had a better tale. The force of narrative makes a great difference, and the story surrounding Pilgrim Landing had much more action, adventure, courage, nobility, and power than any relating to the coming of the Puritans. As told by multiple chroniclers in nineteenth-century New England, Pilgrims squeaked their way out of Europe on a leaky ship with a hundred settlers who arrived in the midst of a hard winter, fell ill, struggled through to spring, and finally started recovering enough to plant a field and build a village. From the perspective of early Americans, this was nothing short of heroic. "In the whole history of Colonization, ancient or modern, no feebler Company, either in point of numbers, armament, or supplies, can be found, than that which landed, on the day we commemorate, on these American shores," Robert Winthrop declared.[18] John Winthrop's arrival, ten years later, with a thousand followers—with their relative stability, stateliness, grandeur, wealth, and health—had nothing on this little band of struggling believers.

The enduring courage of the Pilgrims appeared over and over in the writings of the nineteenth century, mostly by repeating in new ways one of the more poetic paragraphs in William Bradford's *Of Plymouth Plantation*. Recounting the moment that the Pilgrims first stepped ashore, Bradford wrote, "But here I cannot but stay and make a pause, and stand half amazed at this poor people's present condition; and so I think will the reader, too, when he well considers the same." From that point on, Bradford describes all that the Pilgrims lacked: "no friends to welcome them nor inns to entertain or refresh their weatherbeaten bodies; no houses or much less towns to repair to, to seek for succour." Meanwhile, "it was winter" and cruelly cold, and they were surrounded by enemies in "a hideous and desolate wilderness, full of wild beasts and wild men." It is, indeed, heroic. But from the perspective of Native Americans and many others both then and now, it also contains many of the problems that arise from European accounts of settlement, conquest, and encounter—a reduction of Indians to "savage barbarians" living in a supposed "wilderness" that Pilgrims feel divinely inspired to endure and subdue. Bradford's use of parallelism, his biblical allusions, negations, and contrasts, his points of emphasis—all of it shows that he knew his way with words. The writing of this single, vivid, powerful scene helped capture attention and fueled imaginations over two centuries later.[19]

The effect of Bradford's writing can be gauged by how often Anglo-American writers returned to it and incorporated it into their own retellings of American history. In book after book, they quoted and summarized this specific moment in Bradford's recollection. Sometimes it was recited in full. Sometimes it was given in part. Sometimes it was paraphrased instead of plagiarized. But almost always it appeared. Bradford's one paragraph describing the Pilgrims' first few moments ashore told in full the story that so many Americans in the nineteenth century wanted to remember and retell. And, like the Mayflower Compact, it had the distinct advantage of being small, portable, easily quotable, and easily paraphrased. Along with the Mayflower Compact, this single passage from *Of Plymouth Plantation* was one of the most recognizable seventeenth-century texts in nineteenth-century America.[20]

For all these reasons—text, time line, and tale—Winthrop's sermon stood little chance of becoming a new origin point for the story of America when it first appeared. Not only had historians and textbook authors already imagined an origin story that began in 1620; not only did orators and politicians annually remember and rehearse that origin in speeches, dinners, and commemorations; not only did the Pilgrims already produce a text that could easily be reprinted, repeated, and reused; but also, and even more simply, the story of the Pilgrims was far more compelling than the coming of Winthrop and his powerful fleet of Puritan followers. The Mayflower Compact held pride of place. For Winthrop's sermon to matter, his arrival would have to be reimagined into a better and more enthralling tale—a narrative that could compete with the coming of the Pilgrims by offering a fuller explanation of American identity, character, and purpose.

When *A Model of Christian Charity* finally started to become a national text, that is exactly what occurred.

PART V

Models

CHAPTER THIRTEEN

Creating a Usable Past

BEHIND ALL THE VARIED interpretations of Pilgrims and Puritans in the nineteenth century stood a series of questions about history itself: What is the purpose of studying the past? What is its benefit? How do you separate good history from bad, true history from false? As we have seen with Jeremy Belknap, Ebenezer Hazard, and John Pintard, these questions go a long way back. Those men wanted above all to be *useful*. And they eventually came to believe that their labors on behalf of "true history" were not just enjoyable to themselves but beneficial to others. A century later, a similar set of questions came to the fore in the 1884 founding of the American Historical Association (AHA)—the main professional organization of historians still today. Founders of the AHA debated not just how to do what they did but why it was finally worthwhile. And many of them raised such questions specifically in light of a broader debate about how to understand the Pilgrim and Puritan past.

Yet the questions were not contained by the growing cadre of specialists and professional historians, who carefully guarded their ranks. In the early 1900s, cultural and literary critics such as Van Wyck Brooks also raised and pressed these issues. Brooks wrote poetry, essays, history, biography, and criticism. And in his early work, he argued that national traditions are useful only insofar as they serve the purposes of the day. If they are uninspiring, they should be remade. For national traditions, he claimed, are not right or wrong assessments of the past but malleable interpretations created for the sake of the living. In his essay "On Creating a Usable Past" (1918), Brooks argued that the past has "no objective reality; it yields only what we are able to look for in it." With that premise, he then raised a crucial question: "If we need another past so badly, is it inconceivable that we might discover one, that we might even invent one?" All it takes, he said, is a bit of selection. "The past is an inexhaustible storehouse," he continued. It "opens of itself at the touch of desire; it yields up, now this treasure, now that, to anyone who comes to it armed with a capacity for personal choices." People can find in the past whatever they want or need.[1]

Many historians bristled at Brooks's notion of a "usable past." Part of becoming a professional discipline in the late 1800s had been a push to make history more scientific, and Brooks's essay opposed everything they hoped to build. The past, they insisted, is not an invention. It is not available to be used however one sees fit. It cannot be fabricated. It can only be *found*. The past consists of facts, and the facts tell the story. For those who were committed to such a perspective, history was either right or wrong, and historians had a duty to get it right. Brooks challenged such a view by focusing on history's purpose. What is history *for*? he asked. His own answer was clear: history is for the living.[2]

While Brooks may have added a new term in his call for a "usable past," he did not invent a new idea. These questions about the practice of history directly relate to the way Pilgrims and Puritans have so often been treated in American cultural memory. For many years, orators, authors of textbooks, historians, politicians, and others had been serving the needs and desires of the present day by creating multiple pasts out of Puritan New England. In particular, between 1870 and 1930, three competing models arose. Some scholars and politicians simply heightened the love of the Pilgrims. In a tradition flowing back to John Adams, they insisted that Plymouth Rock had initiated civil and religious liberty in the land and helped it flourish ever since. Others, in contrast, began to argue that Puritan New England opened a story of persecution and oppression: liberty had been achieved only by *escaping* from the clutches of the clergy. Finally, a third set of scholars, critics, and politicians set aside the question of liberty altogether and instead argued that industrious and enterprising Puritans had paved the way to American wealth. These were the dominant traditions of the early twentieth century. And not a single one of them relied on *A Model of Christian Charity* to make its point.[3]

The idea that Pilgrim Landing initiated American liberty climaxed in the early 1900s. During those years, many Americans seemed almost unchecked in their exuberant love of the Pilgrims, proclaiming ever more loudly that these early New England settlers had formed the very foundation of American freedom and flourishing—had established, in fact, the meaning, purpose, and destiny of America ever since. Their "coming, suffering and steadfastness," it was declared, "were the beginning of all our greatness."[4] In 1920, at the three hundredth anniversary of Plymouth Rock and Pilgrim Landing, the power and prevalence of this idea crested in an incredible wave of commemorations.

The planning for the Pilgrim anniversary began a full eight years earlier at the behest of a man named Walter Gilman Page. Page, who studied art in both Boston and Paris, established himself at Fenway Studios and founded the Boston Public School Art League. His paintings could vary, but his heart was steadfast: working with organizations such as the Preservation of New England Antiquities, the Sons of the Revolution, and the Massachusetts Historical Society, Page committed himself—as one brief biographical description reports—to "fostering the spirit of old New England." In 1916, during the Great War, he delivered a speech as chair of the Committee on the Tercentenary Celebration that more or less summarized all anyone would ever need to know about the Pilgrim tradition in America. "The Soul of the Nation," he proclaimed, "was born in the cabin of the Mayflower, the ideals set forth in the Compact gave us what is best and loftiest in the America of to-day, and throughout our National existence, our country never lacked the guidance of the Pilgrim Ideal." When the Great War ended, many Americans clamored to celebrate the spirit that had guided their nation from virtue to virtue and victory to victory. It was time, they said, to remember "the birth of a free people."[5]

And remember they did. An astonishing number of people attended an extraordinary series of events. According to a 1917 planning report, festivities for the commemoration of Pilgrim Landing would cost $1,884,300.[6] This was a large sum of money in 1917. The money raised eventually bought a memorial building on Cole's Hill, several plaques and statues throughout the area, and a gallant summer pageant. But it was the speeches and status of the attendees, more than the money they spent, that truly demonstrated the national significance of Plymouth Rock. Governors, senators, and presidents (past, present, and future) all showed up to remember and celebrate the Pilgrims.

The speeches of these statesmen established the meaning of America through the wonder-working providence of Pilgrim saviors in New England. The governor of Massachusetts, Calvin Coolidge—a man who would soon become vice president and then president of the United States—explained that the Pilgrims "sailed up out of the infinite. . . . They cared little for titles, still less for the goods of this earth, but for an idea they would die." That idea held world-historical consequences, he said, for the Pilgrims were "destined to free mankind." According to Coolidge, "No like body ever cast so great an influence on human history." Plymouth Rock, he proclaimed, "marks a revelation of that which is without beginning and without end,—a purpose shining through eternity with a resplendent light, undimmed even by imperfections of men."[7] The Pilgrims were a new creation, an almost incarnation. Their landing at Plymouth Rock changed world history by inaugurating truths that lay beyond and outside of history, giving purpose to all who had come before and all who had followed in their wake.

Coolidge's speech not only portrayed the Pilgrims as a divine revelation but also attempted to demonstrate the vast expanse of their legacy. Returning to Daniel Webster's commemoration of the Pilgrims in 1820—the speech that had first nationalized Pilgrim origins—Coolidge read off his famous prophecy that "the Rock of Plymouth, shall be transmitted through millions of the sons of the Pilgrims, till it lose itself in the murmurs of the Pacific seas." Just as Coolidge read these lines, a telephone rang onstage. As one account recalls, "Willard Parsons, local manager of the telephone company advanced from the wings, picked up the transmitter of the desk set and queried 'Is this the Governor of California? Just a moment. I introduce to you Governor Coolidge of Massachusetts.'" It turned out that the person on the other end of the line was not actually the governor of California; it was instead his secretary (the governor himself had literally gone fishing). Still, the stunt worked. The audience sat enthralled. Webster's prophecy, it seemed, had been fulfilled.[8]

For all of Coolidge's importance, the keynote address of the whole celebration came not from him but from the strikingly featured, nationalistic, imperialistic, combative, seventy-year-old historian and senator from Massachusetts Henry Cabot Lodge. Lodge embodied all the darker aspects of the Pilgrim origins myth. He believed deeply and sincerely in the superiority of the Anglo-Saxon race, and he had committed much of his life to studying, admiring, and protecting that race. In 1876, he received one of the first PhDs in history at Harvard University with a dissertation that concerned the Germanic roots of medieval Anglo-Saxon land law. The next year he was teaching American colonial history at Harvard. Soon, he turned to politics, rising from the House to the Senate and serving there from 1893 until his death in 1924. Those years saw one of the most massive waves of immigration in American history. In 1905, for the first time ever, more than a million immigrants flooded into the country, most coming from eastern and southern Europe. Lodge watched them come with a great deal of fear. And he responded by lending weight and voice to the Immigration Restriction League, doing all he could as a prominent speaker, writer, and politician to shore up the country's borders and keep the supposed Anglo-Saxon lineage of the nation pure.[9]

In Lodge's anti-immigrant speeches and essays, he focused on the particular danger of racial mixture. "There is a limit to the capacity of any race for assimilating and elevating an inferior race," he argued, "and when you begin to pour in in unlimited numbers people of alien or lower races of less social efficiency and less moral force, you are running the most frightful risk that a people can run." The threat of mixture—the danger of losing the purity, power, and dominance of Anglo-Saxonism—had already pressed in upon the nation, he warned. "There lies the peril at the portals of our land; there is pressing the tide of unrestricted immigration." In another speech he explained his love of the Puritans in precisely such terms. It was the purity of their blood, along with the ideas or culture carried in such blood, that defined their greatness: "We would not barter our descent from him [the Puritan] for the pedigree of kings. May we not now say that we also honor him because his race has shown itself able to break through its own trammels, and 'rise on stepping-stones of their dead selves to higher things'?"[10] If that race were to continue to rise, Lodge contended, it would have to keep all other races at bay. Eventually, Lodge's arguments gained sway. In 1917, Congress passed what became known as the Asiatic Barred Zone Act restricting the immigration of "undesirables," variously defined, tested, and judged.

Yet even as Lodge attempted to keep America pure, he also tried to extend its reach abroad. The Puritan origins thesis, as we have seen, often entailed an implicit imperialistic expansion, an unfolding of the origin that would gradually move west, claiming more and more territory, along with more and more people. Lodge, like others, combined an ideology of "Puritan stock" with a powerful sense of American influence. He strongly supported the Spanish-American War, as well as the annexation of Puerto Rico and the Philippines, and he would have preferred to take Cuba as well. In Lodge's conception, the American Anglo-Saxon race had to keep itself pure and dominant while simultaneously bringing its blessings—by force—to all others across the globe. These were the elements that went into his love of the Puritans and his praise of Pilgrim Landing.

And these are the reasons why in 1920 he was called upon to extol the Pilgrims once more. In his early days as a scholar, Lodge had written a biography of Daniel Webster, and now at the three hundredth anniversary of Plymouth Rock, he, like Coolidge, returned to Webster's speech. Citing large sections of that oration, Lodge presented Webster as someone who embodied "in varying forms the belief in progress, in the perfectibility of man," and he lamented that such a spirit had seemed to dissolve in the twentieth century. A formless, modern literature of pessimism had replaced the noble ideals of the nineteenth century, Lodge declared. But the Pilgrims could save us yet. In 1801, a young James Savage had called for a return to Plymouth Rock whenever a foreign element

threatened, comparing the very sight of it to Moses's brazen serpent. More than a century later, Lodge, facing what he perceived as
another foreign threat, called on the nation once more to return to
its Pilgrim values. "That which counted then and has counted ever
since," he concluded, "was that they set the spiritual above the material, the possessions of the mind and heart above those which
ministered to the body and made life easier and more comfortable."
The Pilgrims did not come here to make a better life for themselves or to get ahead. They came instead for *spiritual* reasons, for
pure and righteous worship, for self-government and the liberty of
conscience.[11] This was the principle that made America rise—and it
would continue to rise so long as Americans in the present day embraced the mind-set and meaning of their Pilgrim past.

The power of these statements and beliefs can best be seen in
the last event to commemorate Pilgrim Landing. In the final days of
the Tercentenary Celebrations, which actually came in August 1921,
a spectacular pageant praised all that the Pilgrims had supposedly
brought about. It played nightly for two weeks, and in the end,
President Warren G. Harding and Vice President Calvin Coolidge
both attended with their wives. The crowd swelled to over one hundred thousand, though the arena could only seat a tenth of them.
What they came to see was a pageant intended to "typify and illustrate the steps, not only of New England's advancement, but also
the progress of the Nation as well." Its underlying theme was "the
struggle of the Pilgrims and their forbears for religious toleration
and individual liberty," emphasizing that "individual liberty under
wise and tolerant laws" was "their gift to posterity."[12]

Here we cannot but stay and make a pause and stand half
amazed at the extraordinary final scene of George P. Baker's 1921
Pilgrim pageant. In the last celebration of Pilgrim Landing, in the
last scene of the last show, four Pilgrim leaders (Carver, Winslow,
Brewster, and Bradford) come out of the darkness and stand in the
center of the stage. Allegorical figures follow. "Tolerance" leads
from the dimness "the figures of Liberty, Law, Morality and Education," who take their place "just below the four leaders." As Tolerance points the way, "the Commonwealth, a female figure, . . .
passes to the highest point of the dais." She becomes the focus of
everyone's attention. "The eyes of all the figures are turned to her.

Tolerance hands her a great torch. Then from far and near youth, middle age and aged, men, women and children, of all nations, come to light their torches from that of the Commonwealth." This lighting ceremony continues with a multitude of people "half step-ping, half dancing" around the stage, filling the space "with torch-bearing figures." Finally, the boats that have been sitting behind the arena lift their searchlights to "the Rock." As everyone turns, "concealed choirs take up a great Hymn of Praise."[13]

Spotlighted, raised up, gazed at by all, Plymouth Rock shone out like the brazen serpent of Moses, held high to lead, heal, and guide the nation ever forward. For the celebration of seventeenth-century Pilgrims, the winter of 1920 and the summer of 1921 were as good as it would ever get. Fêted by national politicians, praised in elaborate pageants, memorialized in new stone carvings and plaques, venerated with a freshly built hall, the Pilgrims stood for the very foundations of American greatness, and they extended that greatness as a torch-bearing beacon of toleration, liberty, law, mo-rality, and education to all the world. A steam curtain concealed the actors as the last hymn swelled and the audience burst into ap-plause. In 1921, love of the Pilgrims seemed to know no bounds.

Yet for all that the audience applauded in Plymouth, plenty of oth-ers held back. Behind the celebrations, a growing number of crit-ics, historians, and scholars began condemning the first English settlers of New England for everything that had gone wrong with the country, especially for its oppressive moral norms and its mind-less commitment to making money. Criticism of the Pilgrims and Puritans went a long way back, of course, but in the 1880s a new chapter opened in the work of Brooks Adams. Adams belonged to the famous lineage of John Adams and John Quincy Adams, two American presidents who had done their fair share in the early days of the republic to build a heightened regard for the Pilgrims. But times had changed. Brooks Adams titled his 1887 history of New England *The Emancipation of Massachusetts*, a title suggesting that Puritan origins were a form of imprisonment from which later generations had struggled to escape. Whatever his true intentions might have been—and Brooks Adams complained bitterly all his life that his real motives and goals had never been understood—

almost every reviewer understood his book as an outright attack on the Puritan past.[14] Ardent Protestants hated Brooks Adams for taking such a line, and even those who were not particularly devout found his overwhelming diatribe a bit much to stomach. Still, readers recognized that someone—an *Adams*, no less—had finally punctured the overinflated ancestor worship that had ballooned out of control through the nineteenth century. And that, ultimately, is how the book made its mark. It was crude, everyone agreed, but at least it started something new.

That new tradition took shape in the hands of Brooks's brother Charles Francis Adams Jr., who expanded it with much more credibility and much better prose. It is "impossible to ignore the fact and more than useless to deny it," he argued, "that the New-England Puritans were essentially a persecuting race."[15] Charles wrote two books taking aim at the Puritan past, both of which helped establish him as a leading colonial historian. In 1895, he solidified that reputation by becoming president of the Massachusetts Historical Society—the same post that James Savage and Robert C. Winthrop once held—and six years later he presided over the American Historical Association. With such a figure at the helm, attacking Puritanism became an academic pastime.

Such work came to fruition in 1927 when Vernon Louis Parrington, an English professor at the University of Washington, published *Main Currents in American Thought*, his Pulitzer Prize-winning account of American literary history. This work was so influential that some scholars have called Parrington the founder of American Studies and the father of American literary history. For the first time ever, one reviewer raved, "the student of American literature . . . sees how political and economic thought flowers into literature, or how it strangles the impulse towards literature."[16] For Parrington, the Puritans landed squarely in the latter camp. They strangled everything they touched. A man who lost his university job in Oklahoma because religious groups purged the college of impure professors, Vernon Louis Parrington saw little to like and much to loath in the religious culture of American Puritanism. According to his basic division between the power of hierarchy and the forces of democracy, most of the ruling Puritans had brought the evil of English rule to America. In order for America to become *America*—in order for it to become the home of the brave and the land of the free—its inhabitants would have to destroy the power of Puritanism. For Parrington, the progress of liberty in America could be measured by how far it had traveled from those early New England days.

Alongside these new arguments about the coming of liberty in America—not *because* of the Puritans but *despite* them—other forceful attacks refocused attention on the underlying purpose of the Pilgrim and Puritan migration. During the early twentieth century, a new approach to historical studies, led by Charles and Mary Beard, began trying to understand the fundamental forces that determined the shape of historical events. This "new history," which often focused on economic drives, eventually eliminated the mainstay of Puritan origins: the idea that high-minded motives had supposedly driven them to set sail and defined the identity of America ever since. According to "progressive historians," as they have been called, it did not matter what these early Calvinists believed or what reasons and considerations they gave. What really drove the Puritans was the same motive that drove everyone else: money.[17]

Applying such arguments to New England offered a truly radical revision of its history. The acts of Puritans against Indians, Antinomians, Quakers, Baptists, and others had long been known and variously addressed throughout the nineteenth century. But according to most historians, whatever the Puritans might have done *after* they arrived, at least they had initially come for a holy cause. Persecuted in England, they came to America in search of God, religious liberty, self-government, freedom, *anything* other than just pure gold. This is what separated them from Jamestown, Spain, and all the rest. This is what separated the *United States* from all the rest. But in the early 1900s, that view began to change. More and more historians began to argue that the Puritans—just like everyone else—came for gain.

James Truslow Adams, unrelated to the famous family, lay at the heart of this new conception. In *The Founding of New England* (1922), he incorrectly claimed that 80 percent of the first English settlers in New England were not religious: they had no interest in esoteric theology or the forms and features of church polity. What they really wanted was a better life—the same as anyone else—but they had to struggle against the ruling theocracy. Devout Puritans, Adams claimed, held all the power, and they used that power to persecute dissenters far more than they themselves had ever been persecuted in England. As a result, the story of American liberty and economic empowerment owed itself not to the Puritans but to the fight *against* Puritanism. In the grand narrative of freedom's rise, James Truslow Adams proclaimed, the early opposition to Puritanism in the first decades of New England mattered just as much as the eventual fight against Britain in the American Revolution.[18]

James Truslow Adams, Brooks Adams, Charles Francis Adams Jr., Vernon Louis Parrington—all of these figures directly shaped the meaning of America linked to a Puritan past. But their efforts were not confined to the academy. An assortment of cultural critics, led by none other than Van Wyck Brooks, also pushed against the Puritan past. Brooks had begun writing about "a usable past" because he yearned for better art and literature in America. He assumed, as did many others at the time, that American literature had never been any good. It was rude, crude, imitative, and weak. And in *The Wine of the Puritans* (1908), Brooks blamed that deficiency on the Puritans. They were the nation's "first materialists," Calvinists so focused on "thrift and industry" that all other pursuits—including the fine arts—had dried up and disappeared. The perils of a new settlement had pushed out artistic inclinations in favor of frugality, thrift, and industry, and after three centuries those Puritan values still dominated. For Van Wyck Brooks, America was all work and no art—and *that* was the legacy of the Puritans. "Without doubt," he wrote a few years later, "the Puritan Theocracy is the all-influential fact in the history of the American mind."[19]

No one agreed more than H. L. Mencken, which was, in itself, surprising. In every other way Brooks and Mencken differed radically. They opposed each other on culture, art, politics, *everything*, but they found common ground in their condemnation of America's Puritan past. As one contemporary critic of both Brooks and Mencken wryly commented, "Now there is no other bond of union so strong as a common hate, and if our new men disagree widely in what they like, they agree wonderfully in what they dislike."[20] Mencken in particular lived and breathed a perfect hatred of the Puritans. A powerful critic with a wide audience throughout the

1920s, Mencken was loved, hated, revered, and despised by a whole host of American readers. In publication after publication, he consistently blamed the Puritans for every form of tyranny and repression known to modern humanity. Witty and wonderfully quotable, Mencken famously defined Puritanism as "the haunting fear that someone, somewhere, may be happy." As he lived through Prohibition, that definition applied more to Mencken's concerns with twentieth-century America than to any actual study or conception of seventeenth-century New England. According to Mencken, Puritans were still everywhere—censoring the press, suppressing joy, taking away your wine and liquor, turning everything into business and profit. They were a plight, a plague, a pest. Above all, they were a *symbol*. For Mencken, Brooks, and many others, the actual, historical Puritans hardly mattered. What mattered was the kind of traditions they had spawned.

For all that these critics hated the Puritans, however, they still seemed to agree that the meaning of America depended on them. *That* tradition, the tradition of Puritan origins—the idea that the meaning of America, for good or for ill, begins in Puritan New England and Pilgrim Landing—had been so strongly perpetuated in the publications of the 1800s that few could see their way around it. Some did, and often the alternative view came from someone other than an Anglo-American. "Before the Pilgrims landed we were here," W. E. B. Du Bois reminded readers in *The Souls of Black Folk* (1903).[21] He, like William Apess, hoped to reorient American perceptions of the past and their influence on the present. But these voices had to compete with a tradition of Pilgrim and Puritan origins that seemed only to expand through the early twentieth century. To some people, the Pilgrims and Puritans began all that was right with America. To others, they started all that was wrong. But to Anglo-Americans of all different stripes, these New England Calvinists still constituted the true heart of American history, "the all-influential fact in the history of the American mind."

In 1904, a German scholar named Max Weber visited America, took up the traditions he found around him, combined them with his own previous views of Calvinism, and formulated a new argument about Puritanism that became so famous and controversial that it has since become known simply as the "Weber Thesis." The crudest version of this thesis can be easily summarized: Calvinism gave us capitalism. Weber always objected to such a blunt paraphrase of *The Protestant Ethic and the Spirit of Capitalism*. Instead, he wanted to show that the religious ideas of Calvinism lent themselves to the development of a general disposition that was conducive to the rise of capitalism. That was something quite different—and quite new. Puritanism spiritualized work through its doctrines of predestination and calling, Weber argued. As a result, work became not just a means to an end (a way to get food, shelter, and clothing, for example) but an end in itself (a source of spiritual worth and assurance). In particular, Weber argued, Calvinists suffered from anxiety over their eternal fate—a fate that had been eternally decreed before they were ever born—and they turned to work as a way to prove to themselves and to others that they were saved. Though Puritans opposed the lure of prosperity and luxury, their doctrines of predestination and vocation created a view of labor that would later encourage and enable the coming of capitalism and the accumulation of wealth. In the end, Weber argued, "the Puritan philosophy of life" in some basic way "stood at the cradle of modern 'economic man.'"[22]

In making this argument, Weber relied on two dominant understandings of Puritanism. First, America had become what it was because of the "democratic traditions handed down by Puritanism as an everlasting heirloom." The United States, he declared, was "the great creation of the Anglo-Saxon spirit," and the "Protestant asceticism" of that spirit "laid the historical foundation for the special character of the contemporary *democracy* of the nations influenced by Puritanism, as distinct from that which is based on the 'Latin spirit.'" Second, Weber argued, Puritanism nurtured a hatred of fine arts, frivolous amenities, and indulgent luxuries. For a good Puritan, Weber said, all sensual pleasures were suspect. Wherever Puritans ruled, they put an end to good theater, great lyric poetry, all plastic arts, and any hint of beautiful music.[23] It was the same argument that Van Wyck Brooks was beginning to make at just about the same time; but while Brooks wanted to escape that antiartistic tradition and put the Puritans behind him, Weber folded this supposed hatred of fine arts into the development of his thesis. The rejection of indulgence meant that good Puritans could never spend money on themselves; and since the self could not be pampered, capital accumulated. More importantly, according to Weber, good Puritans could never relax or lessen their workload, because any such slackening would in itself signal that a person might not be saved. A Calvinist did not work to play; instead, true Calvinists, now and then, took a little time off in order to refresh their energies for work.

In the great twist of *The Protestant Ethic*, Weber argued that all these antiworldly attitudes finally led to the development of an all-too-worldly spirit. Benjamin Franklin represented for him the epitome of a secularized Puritan. Franklin had no great belief in God and certainly no vestige of Calvinist devotion. And yet, according to Weber, he always approached his work like a Calvinist. As Weber explained, "Moneymaking—provided it is done legally—is, within the modern economic order, the result and the expression of diligence *in one's calling* and *this diligence* is, it is not difficult to recognize, the real alpha and omega of Franklin's morality." While Weber eventually focused his treatise on England, not America, he began his account with the example of an American statesman and a comparison of American colonies. In his understanding of the North and the South, Weber flipped their motives with their outcomes. The Puritans were preachers, students, artisans, farmers, and the lower middle class who came for "*religious* reasons," Weber argued, while the founders of southern states were "great capitalists" who came "for *business* purposes." Yet the end result was the reverse of all expectation: the capitalist spirit, he proclaimed, flourished far more in New England—and that was *because* of the religious motivations that had founded it.[24] Quite unwittingly, Calvinist beliefs fostered the spirit of secular capitalism. A people worried about wealth and luxury created the ethic that would amass vast amounts of wealth. Weber saw history as essentially ironic. Consequences reverse intentions. And in the Puritans' case, he argued, the devout pursuit of Calvinist piety had brought about nothing less than the modern secular order.

With intricate reasoning, Weber wove together many of the Puritan traditions that were then winding their way through America. Though he did not gain all his insights from his travels, Weber managed to make an argument in which most American traditions about the Puritans could find a home.[25] We have seen how the Puritans could be celebrated as the forefathers of freedom, how they could be hated for their condemnation of literature and the arts, and how they could be feted as the foundation of American wealth and power. All of these traditions are deeply flawed, but Americans repeated one or the other ad nauseam in the early 1900s. More importantly, those who backed one view of the Puritans often virulently opposed the others. With Weber, that changed. He brought the traditions together and allowed them all to become reinforcing features of one overarching thesis. *Yes*, the Puritans came for high-minded religious purposes, Weber argued. And *yes*, those same Puritans hated and despised all art, literature, and pleasure. Yet in Weber's conception, it was precisely because Puritans prioritized religion and rejected sensual pleasure that they developed American capitalism, laying the groundwork for the nation's wealth and power.

When Max Weber finished the first half of this thesis—which simply posed the *question* of a relationship between Calvinism and capitalism—he put down his pen and took a steamer to the United States. He came as an invited speaker to the 1904 world's fair in St. Louis, which hosted an International Congress of Arts and Science. In late September, scholars from all different disciplines and many different institutions of higher learning descended on the campus of Washington University in St. Louis. Weber used the invitation to see as much of America as he could. He arrived in New York on August 31 with his wife, Marianne, and his friend Ernst Troeltsch. From New York they traveled north to Niagara Falls, then west to Chicago, before heading south to St. Louis. After Weber had given his talk, he also visited Oklahoma and then swung through several southern states before heading up to New England and back to Germany. As Tocqueville had done decades earlier, Weber traveled thousands of miles in only a few short months, passing through rural communities and Native American territories while also seeing New York, Buffalo, Chicago, St. Louis, New Orleans, Philadelphia, Washington, Baltimore, and Boston.[26]

Weber's talk at Washington University in St. Louis came at the midpoint of his travels and marked a break in his work on *The Protestant Ethic*. The lecture he gave (in German) supplemented his efforts to understand different forms of capitalism in the United States and Europe. In trying to explain the disparity between nations, Weber emphasized the effects of each place's underlying *Kultur*, which meant something more than our English word "culture." *Kultur* tried to get at "the realm of fundamental values," or "the values which determine the conduct of life taken as a whole," and it could best be understood as a combination of culture and civilization, a whole worldview and way of life. For Weber, the difference between American capitalism and its European counterpart came down to the meaning and impact of this one single word. The European nations each had an "old *Kultur*," he argued, stratified into an aristocracy, which had to be broken down for capitalism to flourish. America had no such impediments. It was instead a young country, with a young *Kultur*, expressing itself and expanding itself across limitless resources of land. As a result, Weber argued in *The Protestant Ethic*, the United States represented capitalism "at its most unbridled."[27]

In focusing so much attention on *Kultur*, Max Weber insisted—in contrast to the "new history"—that *ideas*, far more than material realities, shape the development of human history. History is determined by underlying values, by the fundamental outlook on life that different people bring to bear. *Kultur* gives meaning to material conditions, not the other way around. Europeans and Americans, Catholics and Protestants, quite simply *think* differently, Weber asserted. They exercise distinct foundational beliefs, so that even when they face the same material circumstances or conditions, results vary. Armed with that assumption, Weber went looking for the fundamental beliefs of America, and he found them in the Puritans. It was the Puritans, he said, who stood most clearly behind the coming of the modern world. That, for Weber, was the meaning of America.

Max Weber's 1905 thesis did not gain much traction until after 1930, when a scholar named Talcott Parsons traveled to Germany, encountered *The Protestant Ethic*, fell in love with it, translated it, and brought it back to America. At that point, Weber's reputation began to soar, and the links between religious motivations and capitalist outcomes became a newly thinkable thought. Yet in 1930, just as Weber's book appeared in English, the dominant traditions surrounding American Puritans still remained unbound. The Puritans could stand for *either* civil and religious liberty *or* for material prosperity, not both. The motive behind the migration and the outcome of that migration were assumed to be one and the same: *why* the Pilgrims came determined the meaning of America ever since. As a result, speakers, writers, and politicians who hoped to celebrate and commemorate the Pilgrims and Puritans had to sort through the various options and choose.

We can see that stark either/or choice already in the 1920 celebrations of Pilgrim Landing. As festivities were being planned for Plymouth, a separate, competing group of boosters suggested hosting a world's fair in Boston. Following a long and catastrophic war, they argued, people from all over the world could meet in Boston, "cement the bonds of comity and commerce between the Nations of the earth," and collectively marvel at "the different steps that have been taken by this country in attaining its present status of power and wealth, the foundation of which was the landing of the Pilgrims at Plymouth." That plan, had it gone forward, would have cost $17.5 million. It died, however, at the hands of Walter Gilman Page, the Boston artist and head of the Pilgrim Tercentenary planning committee. Defending Pilgrims as the origin of American liberty, Page condemned the notion that moneymaking schemes could ever play a part in their remembrance. On behalf of his commission, he strongly protested "any attempt to commercialize one of the greatest events in world history."[28] It wasn't the nation's wealth that made it great, he declared, but its spirit—its purpose. To make money out of celebrating the Pilgrims would betray the very ideals for which they stood.

The process of deciding why Pilgrims and Puritans came to America became equally explicit ten years later in the first public rendering of Winthrop's sermon. In 1930, *A Model of Christian Charity* appeared in stone. Not all of it, of course: the sermon was far too long for that. Instead, *A Model of Christian Charity* had been reduced to a few essential lines, including Winthrop's declaration that "we shall be as a city upon a hill." The words were carved on a new monument in Boston Common to celebrate the city's three hundredth anniversary. And the person who chose to inscribe those words was none other than old Walter Gilman Page—an aged man by now doing all he could to venerate the Pilgrims, the Puritans, and the spirit of old New England. These are the words he told the artist to carve:

> FOR WEE MUST CONSIDER THAT WE SHALL BE AS A CITTY VPON A HILL THE EIES OF ALL PEOPLE ARE VPPON US SOE THAT IF WEE SHALL DEALE FALSELY WITH OUR GOD IN THIS WORKE WE HAUE UNDERTAKEN . . . WE SHALL BE MADE A STORY AND A BY-WORD THROUGH THE WORLD—JOHN WINTHROP ON BOARD THE ARBELLA 1630.[29]

Page might have picked the words, but he could not decide their meaning. Try as he might, Walter Gilman Page died unable to stem the tide of the materialistic interpretations he so much hated—the economic understanding of early New England that linked the cause of the Puritans' coming to the rise of capitalism. At the dedication of the monument, Sherman L. Whipple, chairman of the Arrangements Committee, broached this key subject: "As to this purpose—whether religious or economic," he said, "historians are not yet fully in agreement. Probably both motives operated; but the evidence is preponderating that most came here to better themselves in civic, political and financial position. And this has been the underlying principle in the uprearing of our institutions and the founding of our government." In his commemoration of the Puritans, Whipple finally chose to celebrate Winthrop not for pursuing a higher cause or endowing America with a purer purpose but rather for establishing a place of material prosperity: "The land of opportunity!" he exclaimed. "A land where those who merit may achieve; where the humblest child, with nothing other than courageous will, industry and native talent, may find his chance to develop, unshackled by traditions, by social castes, or unfair laws. Thus John Winthrop's great purpose has run through all our three centuries of history and today inspires our future."[30] In the first public rendering of Winthrop's sermon—carved into stone on Beacon Street and facing Boston Common still today—the call to be a "city on a hill" became a message of material advancement through personal merit. *A Model of Christian Charity*, Whipple declared, inaugurated the American Dream.

Yet for all the praise Whipple lavished on Winthrop's vision, he still could not turn *A Model of Christian Charity* into a national text. This monument, these words, the dedication and celebration in 1930—all of it was distinctly local. The American Dream that Winthrop supposedly inaugurated was remembered only in relation to the founding of Boston, not the formation of America more broadly, not the region of New England, not even the state of Massachusetts. All of those foundings had their own days of celebration, and all the speakers at those celebrations were far more prominent than Sherman L. Whipple. The best it got for the Boston Monument was Charles Francis Adams III, the secretary of the Navy—not bad, certainly, but a man whose main distinction lay in his long Boston pedigree. No national politician and certainly no president or future president attended. When Winthrop's sermon made its public debut in 1930, the "city upon a hill" it glorified was quite literally the city of Boston, nothing more.[31]

The different celebrations for the Puritans (in 1930) and the Pilgrims (in 1920) reveal again those subtle but significant distinctions standing in the way of *A Model of Christian Charity*. While plenty of Americans praised Puritan New England in general, the particular origin they celebrated most was Plymouth Rock. The coming of the Pilgrims had national and world-historical implications, people said; the coming of the Puritans simply extended what others began. As a result, the commemoration of the Puritans in 1630 was relatively constrained. President Hoover and Congress appointed fifteen citizens "to represent the United States in connection with the Massachusetts Bay Tercentenary," but the commission "was not organized in time to participate in the Commonwealth's July celebration and so far as known took none of the action for which it was appointed." It was even hard to extend the celebration to all of Massachusetts. Those who lived outside "the original Bay Colony territory" (that is, beyond the eastern edge of the state) did not feel compelled to throw a party. Many celebrations occurred, to be sure, but plenty of people declined to participate.[32] Even accounting for the stock-market crash and the sudden onslaught of the Great Depression, the coming of the Puritans in 1930 was simply too inconsequential, too local, and too small to draw a crowd. All the way into the twentieth century, John Winthrop's arrival and

*Figure 17: Massachusetts Bay Tercentenary bronze plaquette, silver finish,
obverse, featuring a portrait of John Winthrop, with a copy of the colony's charter
and a symbolic book at the bottom corners. The plaquette is 2.5 × 3.25 inches,
and a larger (10 × 12) plaque was also made. Collection of the Massachusetts
Historical Society.*

John Winthrop's sermon were not in themselves a point of origin or
importance.

Insofar as the 1930 festivities celebrated a founding text, moreover, that text was never *A Model of Christian Charity*. In fact,
through all the state's anniversary gatherings—in the "2083 events
in 253 communities throughout the Commonwealth, attended by
11,041,625 people" and costing $1.5 million, all put together to
commemorate the state of Massachusetts (not the city of Boston)—
no mention of Winthrop's "city on a hill" sermon ever appears.[33] It
was the three hundredth anniversary of that sermon's first delivery,
and no one cared. Instead, commemorators focused on the colony's

Figure 18: Massachusetts Bay Tercentenary bronze plaquette, silver finish, reverse. Collection of the Massachusetts Historical Society.

charter. When a replica of the *Arbella* sailed into Salem on June 12, 1930, it carried on board a copy of "the Charter, the original of which formed a part of the earlier Arbella's precious cargo." When a scholar decided to commemorate the Puritans by republishing several of their documents, he gave a great deal of space to reprinting and explaining "the charter of Massachusetts Bay"—and no space at all to Winthrop's sermon. When an artist designed a medallion to be sold at the celebrations, he put Winthrop's portrait on the front and surrounded him with a representative "book" and, predictably, the charter of Massachusetts Bay (figures 17 and 18).[34] Insofar as any text of origin mattered in 1930, it was not *A Model of Christian Charity*.

Such was the status of Winthrop's sermon in 1930, one year before a young scholar named Perry Miller took up his first teaching post at Harvard University. All these traditions surrounding the Pilgrims and the Puritans shaped his education. Miller was born the year Max Weber first published his *Protestant Ethic and the Spirit of Capitalism* (1905); he attended high school, college, and graduate school through the period of Van Wyck Brooks, Vernon Louis Parrington, H. L. Mencken, and Henry Cabot Lodge; and he began his career just at the time when Talcott Parsons brought Weber's *Protestant Ethic* to America in an influential English translation (1930). In the period from the first printing of Winthrop's sermon to its eventual fame a century later, all these figures and their various texts offered multiple, competing models for the meaning of America. And all the meanings of America they offered—from the spiritual to the material, from the narrative of escape to the call for better art, literature, and culture—all of them took for granted that America was what it was because of its origins in Puritan New England and Plymouth Rock. Yet none of these traditions had a place for Winthrop's text. When Perry Miller finally made a case for *A Model of Christian Charity*, therefore, he did so by producing a new model, reimagining and reinventing what America really means.

CHAPTER FOURTEEN

A Meaning to Match Its Force

PERRY MILLER CAME OF age at a time when scholars, critics, journalists, and many others began explicitly seeking "the meaning of America." He joined this "symbolic quest" in 1931 and pursued the hunt in America, Europe, and Asia for over thirty years. Traveling back from Japan in 1952, he mused to a friend, "I have now looked seriously at America from both sides, West and East, and wish to Hell this country could say what, in the realm of ideas, it means commensurate with its force." That was the question that motivated him, the query that shaped his career: *what, after all, does America mean?* Miller dedicated his work to "America's unending struggle to make herself intelligible" and devoted his time "to unraveling the mystery of America." His obituary in the *Harvard University Gazette*, written by five friends who knew him well, claimed that Miller was consumed "by a Puritanical passion to make the facts of American history yield up the 'incalculable essence' of our national experience." Giving the keynote address at one seminar, he called on participants to hold more conferences that would force Americans to ask "what we as a nation mean in the chronicle of civilization." The subject, he believed, could hardly be exhausted. "As for that interminable field which may be called the meaning of America," he once asserted, "the acreage is immense, and the threshers few."[1] Through a lifetime of work, Perry Miller hoped to explain this nation to it-self—beginning at what he took to be the beginning and proceed-ing all the way through to the present day.

In taking up this task, Miller exerted an enormous influence on American history and literature. Well-known within the halls of ac-ademe still today, he nonetheless remains largely unknown by the broader public. Yet as one scholar has remarked, from 1931 to 1963, Miller "presided over most literary and historical research into the early forms of American culture." He helped establish the study of what he called "American Civilization," contributing to the rise of a new discipline (American Studies) just then taking in-stitutional shape. In a tribute for him after he died, the midcentury theologian Reinhold Niebuhr claimed that "Miller's historical la-bors were ... of such a high order that they not only gave delight to those who appreciated the brilliance of his imaginative and searching intellect, but also contributed to the self-understanding of the whole American Nation."[2]

That self-understanding, for Perry Miller, started with the Puri-tans. In graduate school, as Miller tells it, "it seemed obvious that I had to commence with the Puritan migration." And he wanted to make it obvious to others as well. In the short prologue of his most widely read book, *Errand into the Wilderness* (1956), he used the words "begin," "beginning," "began," "commence," and "origin" over twelve times in three short pages. Those words, for Perry Miller, all applied to the Puritans. And because he began America with the Puritans—because he did so in such an original way and with such overwhelming force—he left in his wake a long train of scholars who took up the study of early New England with fresh interest, making it one of the largest academic subjects of the twentieth century.[3]

Perhaps Perry Miller's most lasting influence, however, came not from his overall study of the Puritans but from his assertions about one particular text. In deciding that "the uniqueness of the American experience" was fundamentally Puritan, Miller turned to the precise moment when those Puritans first migrated. Or, rather, he turned to the moment marked as such in a mostly forgotten text. After all, other Puritans founded Salem in 1628; Separatists left for Plymouth in 1620; the Dutch arrived in Manhattan in

1609; the Spanish settled St. Augustine in 1565; and Native Americans had been here all along. Then, too, there was that other English colony farther south, Virginia, founded in 1607, which Miller dismissed for lacking the "coherence with which I could coherently begin." In other words, Miller did not seek an origin of America so much as an *expression* of origins: "the first articulate body of expression upon which I could get a leverage." For Miller, the Puritans "spoke as fully as they knew how, and none more magnificently or cogently than John Winthrop in the midst of the passage itself, when he delivered a lay sermon aboard the flagship Arbella and called it 'A Modell of Christian Charity.'"[4]

In order to turn John Winthrop's sermon into the origin of America, Perry Miller had to accomplish two tasks at once. First, he had to downplay the Mayflower Compact and remove Pilgrim Landing from its prized position in American culture; second, he had to reconceive and elevate the purpose and consequences of the *Arbella*'s 1630 arrival. Those tasks meant taking a stand against *both* the fulsome celebrations of Plymouth Rock *and* the critics of Puritanism who perceived nothing more than a narrow-minded, money-grubbing theocracy. As he explained late in his career, "I commenced my work within an emotional universe dominated by H. L. Mencken." He was, he admitted, "an adolescent campaigner in this anti-Puritan rebellion" but always "considered the intellect of Puritans worth serious examination." To that end, he rebuked the "hue-and-cry" of the cultural critic who railed "against the supposedly repressive and narrowing effects which Puritanism is accused of exerting on American culture." But he also, just as vehemently, rejected the "fustian and Fourth-of-July oratory" that claimed the "Puritans came to Massachusetts Bay, or pushed into Connecticut, in order to set up communities modeled on nineteenth-century ideals." Myths were everywhere, he asserted. The truth was in short supply. Nobody understood the history of the Puritans, their legacy, or why they actually mattered—nobody, that is, but Perry Miller. To get his version of Puritans accepted and adopted, Miller would have to explain why everyone else was wrong. That was a task he relished.[5]

Perry Miller had the perfect personality for busting up old myths. His brash, aggressive, and unruly temperament has been remembered in colossal terms by colleagues, students, and fellow scholars. Miller was "impatient with balderdash and decorum," one student recalled, "abrupt and snorting—perhaps not unlike one of Melville's magnificent whales." When Miller died, his obituary in the *Harvard Crimson* compared him to Melville's mad Captain Ahab: "Those brawling sentences, the brooding manner, the great, obscene chuckles whose delight it was impossible not to share, all were touched with something superhuman, something demonic. He lived intensely, self-destructively even." His "manners were rough," another student recalled; "his bearing was not quite what was expected of a professor; and his casual conversation was calculated to shock." Opening his courses with an attempt "to scare the overwhelming crowds away," Miller first recounted his "immense accomplishments" and then laid before the students an equally immense, almost impossible reading list. Such shows of force would seem to distance him from students, yet "you could not be in his presence without feeling that he cared about you and your ideas," one student reminisced. "Miller was not unkind," another added; "he was simply relentless." In one graduate seminar, a student said, "he forbade us to praise our fellow students' papers. 'Let us be brutal,' he said, 'for we love one another.'" According to at least one account, these lessons applied equally to himself. One student remembers hearing a violent argument in Miller's office while he waited outside the door. When the shouting died down, he knocked and entered, only to discover that Miller was alone. The argument had been with himself.[6]

That argument and agony, the snorting impatience and fierce devotion, the brutal caring—all of it applied to Miller's main topic of study: the life of the mind in America. Perry Miller committed himself to intellectual history, believing, like Max Weber, that ideas are the most crucial factor in the shaping of human events. He sensed in the broader culture "a sullen hostility to the entire notion that ideas ever have consequences."[7] Such an attitude filled him with a holy rage against complacency and an almost snide rejection of any historical work that failed to take seriously the content and consequences of thought. Ideas matter, he insisted, and getting them right requires patience, diligence, and devotion. It demands nothing less than a lifetime of study.

Miller gave as good as he talked. He committed his life to the sources. Spending vast energies on the published texts that Puritans left behind, he worked his way through the library one book or pamphlet at a time. If history is "the art of making an argument about the past by telling a story accountable to evidence," as Jill Lepore has usefully defined it, then Miller intended to have the most evidence of all. Edmund S. Morgan, a prolific student of Miller's, later claimed that Miller had "read everything written by Puritans in England or New England in the seventeenth century." He got that impression from Miller himself, who boasted that he had read through "the complete bibliography of early New England, with various additions, not merely once but many times over." As with Miller's other exaggerations, this claim is demonstrably false. He mostly read the published writings of the New England elite. In fact, he even disdained the kind of archival, handwritten, manuscript-driven research that prompted Jeremy Belknap, Ebenezer Hazard, and John Pintard to start the very institutions that would save and publish Winthrop's sermon. Still, at the time he wrote, Miller made his way through more published Puritan material than probably any other scholar. Whatever else he can be faulted for—and there is plenty—he cannot be accused of laziness. Long before the digital age, before texts could be searched, before catalogues could be clicked through, Miller meticulously picked through one Puritan text after another, piecing together a unified system of thought expressed through pages and pages of old published texts.[8]

Miller's work on this unified system of thought spurred his attack on America's accumulated myths. "There is nothing so idle as to praise the Puritans for being in any sense conscious or deliberate pioneers of religious liberty," he once proclaimed—"unless, indeed, it is still more idle to berate them because in America they persecuted dissenters." In fact, he explained, the Puritans were entirely consistent: in both England and New England they refused to tolerate falsehood. The Puritans knew exactly what God demanded of them, and they intended to follow it through. At the same time, Miller added, what God demanded of them was not a sexually repressed, antialcoholic, anti-intellectual campaign against all forms of pleasure, happiness, and joy. Instead, he said, they fixed their eyes "upon the positive side of religion, upon the beauties of salvation, the glory of God, and the joy of faith"; they "enjoyed a

vigorous and productive sexuality" and drank "staggering quanti-
ties of rum," loving their families and spending "pleasant evenings
with the neighbors."[9] Wherever Perry Miller found a caricature of
the Puritans, he rolled up his sleeves and set to work.

The myth that most animated Perry Miller, however, was Plymouth Rock. He hated the overblown celebrations of the Pilgrims because, according to him, their arrival showed no sense of purpose;
Pilgrims simply washed ashore. In contrast to Boston, "Plymouth
was a minute, relatively insignificant community, completely overshadowed by Massachusetts Bay. . . . The leaders of Massachusetts
Bay were aggressive, educated, philosophical; Plymouth was pious,
struggling, and desired chiefly to be let alone."[10] Given the tercentenary celebrations we have seen—the massive pageantry for the Pilgrims in 1920 and the restrained, local celebrations of the Puritans
in 1930—one can begin to understand just how radical these statements would have seemed. Essentially, Miller was saying that the
festivities should have been reversed. The president and vice president and their wives should have motored through Boston in 1930,
not Plymouth in 1920. Pilgrim Landing, Miller argued, didn't matter. The true origin of America lay farther north.

Miller had very clear reasons for moving America's origin from
Plymouth to Boston. If Winthrop and his fleet of followers constituted the first true society in America, he argued, then the story of
America would begin with a purposeful community of intellectually gifted and demanding preachers and politicians. Unlike the
Pilgrims, the Puritans had to be understood as the "outcome of a
long and matured program, the deliberate achievement of an objective deliberately sought after."[11] The Puritans knew what they
were about. They left England with a plan. They started America
with a complex system of ideas and a serious, ennobling purpose.
And the only way to guard that view of the past, Miller felt, was to
disregard the Pilgrims.

To understand these Puritans whom Miller made and placed at
the origin of America, it helps to know an old myth from ancient
Greece. In Plato's *Symposium*, a dialogue about the nature of love,
one character tries to explain romance by offering a new account
of creation. According to Aristophanes, everyone was initially doubled: we all had two bodies stuck together back-to-back, and we

moved around by rolling in a ball. As united bodies, we started off complete, experiencing a wholeness and unity that gave us tremendous power—so much power, in fact, that we even scaled Olympus and threatened the gods. Zeus responded by splitting us in half. Ever since, we forget the gods and instead spend our lives running around searching for the lost partner who will make us whole.

This old myth offers a remarkable picture of Perry Miller's Puritans and their place in American history. According to Miller, the Puritans sought "to integrate the divine and the natural, revelation and reason, into a single inspiration," maintaining "a symmetrical union of heart and head without impairment of either."[12] Miller's Puritans were the embodiment of a paradoxical union: emotional and intellectual, individual and communal, they were hard-bitten realists with undying hope. Filled with internal differences—facing different directions at the same time like two bodies stitched back-to-back—the Puritans nonetheless started America in a state of wholeness.

And then, as in the myth of Aristophanes, they fell. In their power, Miller taught, they tried to scale the heights of heaven. Some flung themselves to God in ever-greater emotional outbursts (the evangelicals); others tried to bring heaven down to earth in ever more rational explanations (the Unitarians). Eventually, the center could not hold. Puritanism split into "two distinct and contending things to two sorts of men." Successors, Miller argued, have "found themselves no longer capable of sustaining this unity, and it has yet to be re-achieved today, if achieved again it ever can be." Divided into the rational and the emotional, the individual and the communal, the spiritual and the material, American society could never be restored until its dueling elements reunited and restrained the worst elements of each other. In Miller's Harvard lectures on the Great Awakening, he came close to quoting Aristophanes directly. Explaining the tensions of the eighteenth century, he asked, "Who indeed can resist the suspicion that here, and here alone, was the fatal division, and that these severed fragments ~~of the complete man~~ must needs be joined somehow together again before we may again know completeness of humanity?"[13] Though he struck out the phrase "of the complete man" from his final lecture, the idea remained central to his paradigm. This was the myth that Miller made—a Puritan community of original wholeness that was fundamental to the meaning of America.

In 1938, Miller made that case by placing the Puritans before an American audience in the most influential way possible: he crafted a book for schools. As the first history textbooks of the 1820s spread a national story of Pilgrim origins, so the classroom anthology that Miller coedited brought Puritan writings to countless American students for most of the twentieth century. On the first page of that anthology, in the very first paragraph, Miller came out swinging: "Any inventory of the elements that have gone into the making of the 'American mind,'" he declared, "would have to commence with Puritanism." While acknowledging that many traditions have contributed to American culture along the way, Miller went on to erase them, claiming that Puritanism's "role in American thought has been almost the dominant one, for the descendants of Puritans have carried at least some habits of the Puritan mind into a variety of pursuits, have spread across the country, and in many fields of activity have played a leading part." In fact, he claimed, "Without some understanding of Puritanism, it may safely be said, there is no understanding of America." Again and again Miller claimed that the meaning of America could not be discovered apart from a thorough study of the Puritan past.[14]

In seeking to discover and describe the true meaning of America, Perry Miller found himself in very good company. Just as Miller's career began in 1931, a broad cultural dialogue emerged trying to define the "American way," the "American Dream," the "American creed," and the "American idea"—all terms that either first appeared or first flourished in the 1930s. Faced with the twin threats of fascism and communism, many intellectual and political leaders called for the "steadying effect of a vital cultural tradition." After the war ended, a surge of cultural nationalism further pushed for new celebrations and understandings of the United States. Publishers "besieged" Perry Miller "with requests for anthologies, introductions and monographs to satisfy the growing demand for American collections and studies." Old American texts reappeared; new interpretations mounted; book series spread. One new series, "Makers of the American Tradition" by the publisher Bobbs-Merrill, aimed to highlight individuals who contributed to "that strong and yet complex phenomenon that constitutes what we call the American tradition or the American way of life." The introduction voiced a common theme running throughout these works: that we must turn to our origins in order to understand the identity, purpose, and direction of the nation today. Faced with "external and internal threats to the American way of life," the general editor asked, how should Americans respond? "It seems to me," he answered, "that it is a constant in human nature at such times to turn inward, to return to one's roots, one's origins, to find such resources."[15]

One dominant and lasting development to emerge from these concerns was the discipline of American Studies. Institutionally, American Studies developed in colleges and universities as an attempt to define and defend the distinct meaning and culture of the United States. Miller contributed his talent to this project by insisting on the unique character and value of American literature. When he began his career, such a claim would still have seemed suspect. Until the 1930s, American literature had been routinely dismissed as uncouth and second-rate. English professors had been hired since the late 1800s; but few studied American literature, and hardly anyone devoted one's career to it. Perry Miller did. In 1933, he worked with his colleague F. O. Matthiessen to launch one of the first surveys of American literature to be found at any college in the country. With colleagues at Harvard, Yale, and the University of Minnesota, they started to make a sustained case for the study of American culture. Miller went on to become the first full professor of American literature at Harvard. And in all this work, he insisted that American writers had a great deal to offer, that American traditions had value and substance, that the Puritans— whom Miller always considered the *first* Americans—had an intellectual richness that it behooved Americans to revisit.[16]

The efforts of Miller and others to build up American Studies began receiving powerful support from the U.S. government in the 1940s, since many public officials saw in the new discipline a weapon to wield against communism. Scholars were considered diplomats who could spread understanding of America and the American way abroad. At a conference on "the American character" held in 1962, for example, Justice William O. Douglas argued that the United States should "be sending out a stream of scholars and a flood of democratic ideas that would be a positive force for democracy." He lamented that the nation was known mostly for its "oil companies"; instead, he insisted, we should be exporting "American ideas of liberty, justice, and equality."[17]

Some professors quickly joined the effort. Miller's colleague Howard Mumford Jones, for example, defended American Studies as a form of "propaganda." It represented "an attempt to explicate and make persuasive a set of values satisfactory to the American people." The American people, Jones explained, had undertaken "a mighty effort to make these values comprehensible both at home and abroad" precisely because they believed "these values, or some of them, may benefit other nations." In 1964, Jones won the Pulitzer Prize for taking this approach in his book *O Strange New World*. Another Pulitzer Prize–winning scholar, Daniel Boorstin, described his work as an "attempt to discover and explain to students, in my teaching and in my writing, the unique virtues of American democracy." Together, Boorstin, Jones, and many others helped initiate a "consensus school" of American Studies, focused on what they took to be the unity of the American people and dwelling at length on the exceptional qualities of American democracy.[18]

But that consensus school, despite its name, seldom agreed on the meaning of America or the scholar's proper role in studying it. Plenty of professors, including Perry Miller, took a far more ambivalent stance. For all that Miller asserted the unique values and character of the American tradition—for all that he hoped to unravel the mystery and meaning of America—he resisted all jingoistic, "propagandistic," nationalistic agendas and celebrations. When the Ford Foundation urged Miller to take his studies to India, for example, he flatly refused. "Mr. Thurber of the Ford Foundation argues that I should go," he told a friend, "that India is crucial in our diplomacy, and that after a year of such experience I shall be the better qualified to write about America." As such a letter reveals, American scholars were considered important actors in global diplomacy, but Perry Miller was not always willing to play his part.[19]

Miller had, however, played his part in the war. When the United States entered World War II, Miller believed that to speak about the meaning of America, he would have to experience its greatest struggle firsthand. He enlisted as soon as he could in 1941, working in the division on psychological warfare with the main goal of changing German minds and hearts. A few times, he came close to combat. He saw citizens bombed, mutilated, and killed in the streets of London. Two days after D-Day, he went to France and saw the American dead littered across the landscape—one "looking terribly young, crunched into the side of the road, his hand clutching a grenade which he had not had time to cock, his rifle lying across his chest and on the butt of it, pasted on with adhesive tape, a picture of his girl—young and fresh and smiling." Describing the scene, Miller wrote to his friends and family, "I have had the experience I needed and wanted, and I feel born out in my belief that for speaking with conviction to this generation, it is a valuable experience."[20]

Miller's instincts proved prescient. As one of his successful students later recounted, "Our respect for the historical imagination of these great teachers, our belief in its relevance to modern American life, and our eagerness to join them in the common enterprise of scholarship were surely reinforced by our belief that they had participated with us in the war against the Axis."[21] Miller's service gave him the credence to speak. His audience grew, and his graduate students—most of whom were former soldiers—trusted that whatever he was about, it *must* be important. Decorating his office with military equipment, standing his old boots next to his desk, Miller called in student after student and convinced them that the past mattered, that *ideas* matter. Wars, battles, conflicts, resolutions—the stuff of history arises from the strife of the mind.

In selling the relevance of history to students and audiences, Miller more and more attempted to make his scholarship apply directly and immediately to modern American life. He often said that a greater knowledge of the Puritan past would yield a better understanding of the American present. And to that end, he increasingly took his lectures into allusive leaps that allowed him to speak to the most pressing matters of the moment. World War II and its aftermath changed Perry Miller. When he returned to Harvard, he shifted from expounding and explaining toward preaching and prophesying. The Puritans became for him not just an origin of America, nor simply the best explanation of our subsequent cultural history; by the end of his career, they had also become America's best and earliest *guide*. According to the postwar writings and lectures of Perry Miller, what Puritans faced in the 1600s closely paralleled the crisis now confronting Cold War Americans. And the way the Puritans met their challenges—the way they succeeded and ultimately the way they failed—held monumental lessons for the present day. In the second half of his career, Perry Miller, the "goddam atheist," as he called himself, turned to the Puritans to preach.[22]

What he preached, primarily, was doom.

Following the outcome of World War II, at a time when the United States came into unquestioned world power, Perry Miller found it hard to rejoice. He was not alone. In conversations about American purpose and meaning during and after the war, a note of concern came prominently to the fore. On February 17, 1941, for example, the editor of *Life* magazine, Henry Luce, wrote an essay that would come to coin this period as "The American Century." This phrase would eventually sound like a grand proclamation, a ringing endorsement of American power put to the service of American ends, guiding efforts across the globe under the rhetoric of American ideals. But that is not where Luce began. Instead, he opened his essay with a fundamental problem: "We Americans are unhappy," he wrote. "We are not happy about America. We are not happy about ourselves in relation to America. We are nervous—or gloomy—or apathetic. As we look out at the rest of the world we are confused; we don't know what to do." Luce contrasted Americans with the British, who knew what they were about in fighting the Germans and so achieved a certain calmness, even a sense of peace. Americans, on the contrary, combined wealth and comfort with turmoil and anxiety. "We know how lucky we are compared to all the rest of mankind," he remarked. "At least two-thirds of us are just plain rich compared to all the rest of the human family—rich in food, rich in clothes, rich in entertainment and amusement, rich in leisure, rich."[23] But that material wealth had not solved America's problems. In fact, it only made Americans all the more guilty for their failures. Luce diagnosed America as filled with confusion and self-deceit, not knowing what direction or purpose would guide it forward.

That diagnosis led Luce to the proclamation for which his essay has since become famous. "The cure is this," he concluded: "to accept wholeheartedly our duty and our opportunity as the most powerful and vital nation in the world and in consequence to exert upon the world the full impact of our influence, for such purposes as we see fit and by such means as we see fit." Luce set America apart as a bastion of ideals. Here alone flourished "a love of freedom, a feeling for the equality of opportunity, a tradition of self-reliance and independence and also of co-operation." He described the United States as not just the "sanctuary" of these ideals but the place from which they would eventually spread across the globe: they were distinctively American and universally desired. By understanding that duality, Americans could embrace a mission to exert themselves in the world—on the world's behalf—and so find a purpose to guide their power. Closing his essay, Luce declared, "Other nations can survive simply because they have endured so long—sometimes with more and sometimes with less significance. But this nation, conceived in adventure and dedicated to the progress of man—this nation cannot truly endure unless there courses strongly through its veins from Maine to California the blood of purposes and enterprise and high resolve."[24]

Yet in making such a bold pronouncement, Luce and his peers were still guided by an underlying anxiety. The conversations about America's purpose and meaning grew only louder during the 1940s and 1950s. And in the course of those conversations, concern never seemed to diminish. It just kept rising. In the late 1950s, for example, Luce asked respected intellectual and political leaders once again to explain the purpose of the country to citizens who begged for an answer. "More than anything else," he remarked, "the people of America are asking for a clear sense of National Purpose." Respondents included politicians, poets, journalists, evangelists, and government officials—everyone from Billy Graham to Adlai Stevenson. Most in this august group assumed that the United States was the greatest nation on earth, but what did that greatness require? Or as Luce put it, "what shall Americans *do* with the greatness of their nation? And is it great enough? And is it great in the right way?"[25]

The sense of a nation that had lost its way haunted most who responded. As John Jessup, a prominent journalist, wrote, "Is there not a connection between the rise of nations and great purpose, between the loss of purpose and their decline?" Having achieved material success and become a world superpower, the nation seemed content to let private citizens seek private gains and private pleasures with no collective sense of a greater cause. According to Billy Graham, "History has many examples of nations that 'arrived' and then fell due to overconfidence, internal decay or neglect of the ideals and philosophies that made them great." The problem, it seemed, was complacency. Wealth had made Americans weak. "Part of our problem," John Gardner declared, "is how to stay awake on a full stomach." According to a wide range of well-known writers and thinkers, nothing was being asked of the American people. No sacrifices were being made. Adlai Stevenson, a presidential candidate and famous public intellectual of his day, summarized the situation this way: "The face which we present to the world—especially through our mass circulation media—is the face of the individual or the family as a high consumption unit with minimal social links or responsibilities." Having achieved material success and world power, the United States now seemed content to let private citizens go about spending and consuming, little caring about a higher cause.[26]

A whole culture of academics took up those concerns and tried to address them in a series of important books. David Brinkley, Betty Friedan, Richard Hofstadter, C. Wright Mills, David Reisman, William Appleman Williams, and so many others in their own ways condemned American consumerism and anti-intellectualism in works that were broadly consumed and debated by the American masses. Perry Miller, who portrayed himself as a "lone wolf," was by no means alone in his concerns. He, like others, believed that America's influence might be terribly short-lived. "History is littered with the corpses of civilization that reached the limit of expansion, dug in behind walls and moats, and there yielded to decay," he proclaimed. According to him, the materialistic culture of America would soon exhaust itself. It didn't require particular genius "to ask yourself, at least from time to time, whether this American way of life is not rushing at a steadily accelerating pace toward a massive megalopolis which finally, of sheer dead weight, shall grind to an agonizing stop, and then crumble into ruin by the force of inertia." As one of his students summarized, "He could imagine the end of America, if not of American affluence." Yet for Perry Miller, as for others, mere affluence constituted its own form of demise. The accumulation of wealth and power did not constitute a civilization. Rather, the very increase of America's pleasure, profit, and contentment entailed the destruction of its underlying structures.[27]

In taking this message of doom to America, Miller always claimed to be extending a fundamental American tradition. The most American thing to do, he argued, was to criticize America itself. To prove his point, he turned—per usual—to the Puritans. According to Miller, the minister John Cotton believed that the welfare of society depended on the number of godly members remaining in it. Individual salvation still mattered, of course, but if only one or two individuals cared about salvation, then their whole society would collapse and take them with it. "When the discrepancy becomes too great" between "the circle of the righteous" and "the national frontier," Perry Miller explained, then eventually "the minority of good men can no longer save the majority." Facing such a situation, Cotton had a choice to make: he could turn himself into a pariah by preaching against his peers, even though he could never convert enough to really save the nation; or he could comply with "the national ethos" and comfortably go down in the general demise: "In the one you resign yourself to unpopularity and ineffectiveness, in the other to conformity and destruction." What did Cotton do? He criticized with all his might. In case anyone might think it a stretch to move from this description of John Cotton's dilemma in seventeenth-century England to Perry Miller's situation in twentieth-century America, Miller made that move himself: "I think it is not too rough a modernization of Cotton's injunction to say that in times of public crisis we are not to submit or to sit apart, we are to become active critics of our society." Like a good preacher unfolding a sacred text, he applied the lessons of history to his audience: "The best patriotism in such emergencies is not conformity, it is speaking out against those abuses which have brought us into this dire predicament." Love of one's country demanded nothing less.[28]

The problem, Miller believed, was that a false love of one's country simply compounded its problems by refusing to acknowledge or address them. The "nationalistic ends" of American education especially worried him. Education has two goals, Miller explained; but they always exist in tension, and each period swings from pole to pole. On the one hand, education aims at the diffusion of information and the making of good citizens—"a profoundly democratic conviction that the schools should be so conducted as automatically to produce exactly what America wants." If America wants more workers, American schools will make them. If America wants more expressions of patriotism, expressions of patriotism will be practiced in the schools. But alongside this idea is a second principle: discovery. Education exists not just to pass things on but to find out what we do not know. Teachers and researchers do not just replicate society; they change it. And therefore, a true educator in a truly free society, Miller declared, "must stand, more firmly than ever he felt he would be called upon to stand, for the freedom of investigation, for the principle that nothing, not democracy itself, and not even the American way of life, is so sacred that it cannot be studied, analyzed, and criticized." Even as blind praise swept the nation, he insisted, criticism of the country must continue—a liberty of conscience and freedom of inquiry that had itself made the nation great. According to Perry Miller, those who treated this criticism as "heresy" were threatening their own civilization without knowing it.[29]

Miller asserted that freedom when he boycotted the University of Washington for its treatment of J. Robert Oppenheimer. Oppenheimer was a leading physicist who had helped develop the atomic bomb, and in the years after World War II, Oppenheimer openly worried about nuclear proliferation. Soon he began criticizing the policies of the United States. Eventually, it became too much for top officials to bear, and in 1954, Joe McCarthy put him on trial as a possible threat. Oppenheimer was never accused or convicted of espionage, but his name was smeared and his security clearance revoked. As a consequence, President Henry Schmitz of the University of Washington refused to let Oppenheimer speak on campus after an invitation had already been sent. Miller had been invited as well, but when the news broke about Oppenheimer, Miller withdrew. His letter to President Schmitz, which became public, began with his characteristic concern for academic freedom: "My dear Mr. Schmitz," Miller wrote, "It occurs to me that a university is supposed to be a place of free inquiry, and yet we read of your decision on Dr. Oppenheimer." After chastising Schmitz for defining "security" as "orthodoxy," Miller concluded, "One must hope that you will reconsider your decision, or it would seem that our great freedom loving institutions are in much greater danger from within than from without." In the 1950s, conservative administrators at universities refused speakers on the basis of their nationalistic credentials (weighing their approval with the judgment of the House Un-American Activities Committee). Perry Miller would have none of it.[30]

Throughout his career, then, Perry Miller maintained a strong conviction that love of country would always contain and nurture self-criticism. In that regard, Sinclair Lewis represented for him the characteristic case of a loyal American—a writer and thinker whom Miller loved, admired, and in many ways tried to emulate. Lewis, who was the first American to win the Nobel Prize for Literature, wrote novels like *Main Street, Babbitt,* and *Elmer Gantry* that tore into the idealized lives of small-town, middle-class America, portraying the values of capitalism and materialism as empty and hypocritical. Beginning with success, Lewis ended his career in alcoholic dissolution, touring Europe and drinking himself to death while producing fiction that received less and less acclaim. One year before he died, he visited the University of Leiden, where Miller happened to be teaching, and delivered a lecture that stunned his European crowd. What they found so surprising, according to Miller, was Lewis's self-evident love of America. Europeans had come to assume "that all our artists hate it and want, like Lewis, to escape to Europe." But in fact, Miller emphasized, the literature of protest was a literature of love. To demonstrate just how deeply the Europeans had gotten it wrong, Miller recounted a vivid image of Sinclair Lewis wandering drunkenly through the Swiss Alps, shouting, "'I love America' . . . into the unoffending European atmosphere; 'I love it, but I don't like it.'" Miller's career echoed Lewis's call into those canyons. "I aspire to be an honest expositor," he explained to one crowd, "and I count myself a patriotic American." He loved America, even if he did not like it.[31]

What Miller most disliked about America was its individualism and complacency. Describing the famous Puritan minister Thomas

Hooker once, Miller explained that for him, "the awakened sinner should actually be grateful to the minister who by his winged sermons had pierced the doors of his complacency, he should be overjoyed that he had been dragged against all his natural inclinations from the peace and security of false contentment into the heat and fury of this battle." That description of Hooker could serve as an equally valid description of his own professional goals. In class lectures, he rehearsed "how New England, or America, got from there to now, from the seventeenth-century solidarity to the present individualism," and he wondered aloud how the intimate cohesion of those first Puritans could ever be recovered. It seemed to him impossible. Individualism had become so much the dominant trait of the American character that modern citizens could hardly imagine the Puritan communal spirit. As he told one audience, "This deeply-lying instinct of oneness, this sense of the community, this fundamental trait of character, this major premise in all Puritan thinking has become so remote from us . . . that we resort to a hundred mechanical explanations of what we are incapable of appreciating, like some tone-deaf physicist explaining a Mozart aria as an affair of vibrations." Should the Puritans return to America now, he explained, they would "remain greatly distressed that religious freedom had meant the disappearance of the idea of a close-knit society."[32]

That lack of community went hand in hand with American materialism. The United States, Miller lamented, had become "a business civilization. That is the central point. It is the dominant theme of American history. Other things—religion, literature, scientific research—also form the image of America," he admitted, "but since about the year 1815, when the textile mills were opened in New England, ours has been a business civilization." The consequences of that fact—which Miller claimed too few Americans saw and not enough Americans feared—were dire. According to him, the Great Depression revealed business to be "intellectually, morally, and spiritually bankrupt," but the country had never changed course. The pursuit of profit was leading to moral self-righteousness, misplaced optimism, and a mass culture of cheap, vulgar, unthinking consumption—and it was doing so at an accelerating pace.[33]

At Brown University's graduate-student convocation in 1958, he made his views abundantly clear. Speaking to an audience of future researchers, he told them that by "unrepentantly own[ing] up to having minds," they would forever be "square pegs in the round American hole." In fact, "as long as you retain a vital connection with a laboratory, a library, a classroom—as long as you are investigating, endeavoring to discover something new, something hitherto unknown . . .—you have taken, in relation to the dominant pattern of this society, the vow not only of poverty but of failure." These students had refused to accept that "the business of America is business." They refused to "devise the slogans which hustle the American people to purchase gadgets they do not need and really do not want." It was not for them to propel others "into buying— buying just *anything*—and so receiving the plaudits of a patriotic nation or swimming pools in Bucks County donated by grateful sponsors." And because of their massive refusal to conform to a business civilization, these graduate students would pay the price. "In this sense," he said, "it is correct to insist that anybody within the American economy who deliberately decides to spend time in graduate school—rather than in an office, factory, or in professional training—stands convicted, by the nature of his act, of being un-American."[34] That, for Miller, was the fundamental problem with America.

It is no surprise, then, that though Miller hated Europeans for their snobbishness, he revered them for their love of literature. Teaching in Europe for a year, he confessed, "It was a relief . . . to get into a world where the people I dealt with took it for granted that literature is an index of civilization." A great nation values its writers, he argued, for writers are what make it great. "In America I have to spend time and energy maintaining that thesis. I don't complain, but I often wonder, as do my colleagues, whether I might make more progress were I not obliged to prove that my calling is not frivolous." In "a business civilization," a literature professor spends endless time defending the basic value of literature, while European professors use all that time to actually do their job—to read and write and study literature. On the one hundredth anniversary of Edgar Allan Poe's death, Miller reported, Europeans gathered in many different cities, held vigils, read his works, and remembered his contributions. Americans, meanwhile, did nothing. There was no question that America had great writers and great literature, Miller argued, but it remained an open question whether Americans would ever appreciate the fact.[35]

For Perry Miller, that is precisely why the Puritans mattered. America's present problems, he believed, could be understood and addressed by turning to the Puritan past. Teaching in the mid-twentieth century, Miller offered the early English settlers of Boston—the founders of Harvard, not the stragglers at Plymouth—as an alternative way of thinking, a different way of being in the world. They were the true origin of the nation, the opening that dedicated "American civilization" to the life of the mind long before the textile mills opened in New England. For this reason, Miller felt, the Puritans held all the crucial answers. Their successors, he explained, had "let something go which was once a source of strength to New Englanders and which, were it with us today, might enable us to meet our problems head-on with the resolution that so distinguished both the Puritan saint and sailor."[36] If we could study the Puritans as they really were, if we could just get back their dedication to the life of the mind and their commitment to community, we could finally recover the true purpose and meaning of America. That, in the end, was the message Miller preached. And that message became attached to one text in particular: *A Model of Christian Charity*.

CHAPTER FIFTEEN

Perry Miller's City on a Hill

T HE INFLUENCE OF PERRY MILLER on the story of Winthrop's sermon can be tracked in any number of ways.
Before Perry Miller began his career, no politician had
turned to *A Model of Christian Charity* as the origin of
America or sought national office by quoting, citing, or invoking it.
After Miller, this text has been quoted by almost every president to
hold office—beginning with John F. Kennedy and including Lyndon Johnson, Richard Nixon, Jimmy Carter, Ronald Reagan,
George H. W. Bush, Bill Clinton, and Barack Obama. Politics,
however, marks only one measure of Miller's influence. In the
many years that history textbooks hit the market before Perry
Miller began his career, none made the coming of the *Arbella* a
special new beginning to America, and none called the United
States a "city on a hill."[1] After Miller died, Winthrop's sermon
began spreading across textbooks at every level of schooling, so
that by 2010 a new textbook appeared taking *City upon a Hill* as its
title. Beyond politics and history, Miller's claims reshaped literature
as well. Through the mid-twentieth century, American literary history had no place in it for this 1630 sermon. After Miller died,
Winthrop's sermon gradually became the key text defining and explaining the development of American literature from its origins to
the present day. Percolating through new editions and anthologies

of American literature, rising in prominence as scholars continued to wrestle with Miller's work, by 1979 it opened and anchored *The Norton Anthology of American Literature*, the most dominant anthology on the market. A few years before, Norton had not included Winthrop's sermon at all. Almost in a flash, it became the foundation of American literature.

The importance this text has assumed in American culture begins with the place it achieved in Miller's career. So indispensable did this sermon become to Perry Miller that he actually began inventing facts to support its significance. By 1954, he was claiming that the sermon had been "printed," though it never was. One year later he explained that it "was sent back to London for printing, and was reimported to Massachusetts Bay, so that all might heed." It never was. The confidence with which he proclaimed these falsehoods can be startling, especially since he so frequently rebuked others for inventing falsehoods about the past. Miller made up facts about this sermon because he wanted so badly for this one piece of literature to matter. He found the sermon so compelling and so useful that he could not keep himself from exaggerating. It *had* to have been printed. It *had* to have been imported. It *had* to have been known by all, Miller insisted, because this one single text was vital to the entire venture, defining the meaning of America from the day it was preached all the way through World War II to the Cold War that followed.[2]

Why? What did this sermon do for Perry Miller? And through Miller, what did it do for mid-twentieth-century Americans that they so avidly adopted and promoted it?

Most importantly, *A Model of Christian Charity* began the story of America with purpose. "A society that is both clear and articulate about its intentions is something of a rarity in modern history," Miller lectured. "Most of the nations of Europe and Asia grew up by chance and by accident either of geography or politics." In other countries, so much had changed over so much time, he explained, "that even the most patriotic citizens would not dare say to what conscious purpose the nation was originally devoted."[3] This was the argument that the first writers of American origins had made in the histories and textbooks of the nineteenth century. Europe had legends and myths, a murky past misted over by a cloud of unknowing. But America had a *recorded* past—a *written* and *articulate* beginning. All one needed to do was gather up the texts. All one had to do was check the sources. All one really had to do, Miller said, was read Winthrop.

Winthrop's sermon, in other words, stood for the idea of an articulate and original mission. According to Miller, American society had been marked from its very beginning by this conscious and continuing need for a clear purpose. "A man *is* his decisions," he asserted, "and the great uniqueness of this nation is simply that here the record of conscious decision is more precise, more open and explicit than in most countries." His friend Archibald MacLeish, a prominent poet and the Librarian of Congress, agreed that "conscious purpose—a conscious national purpose—plays a more important part with us than it does with other peoples." As a result, in the United States "an American political leader has the prophet's role to play as well—or should." Leaders must state the purpose of the country because the country, quite simply, *began* with purpose. That is what carries it forward, what sets it apart.[4]

Such an argument, however, works in a perfect loop. If America, unlike Europe, began with a clear and articulate purpose, then the beginning of America would have to be located wherever a clear and articulate purpose could be found—*there* and nowhere else. That is what enabled Miller to bypass Virginia. Jamestown, he insisted, "lacked the coherence with which I could coherently begin." It did not record its purpose, or at least it did not do so in a clear enough way. One had to go to where the texts were, and the texts were in New England: "In the history of the mind in America the first chapter is written by the Puritans and is written by them because they are the articulate voice down through the seventeenth century." In this way, Miller set aside a host of possible beginnings and declared that the true origin of America came when the first Puritan governor of Massachusetts Bay proclaimed to his followers that "we shall be as a city upon a hill." "Chronologically speaking," Miller admitted, "Smith and a few others in Virginia, two or three at Plymouth, published works on America before the 'Modell,' but in relation to the principal theme of the American mind, the necessity laid upon it for decision, Winthrop stands at the beginning of our consciousness."[5]

In making this claim, Miller argued that *A Model of Christian Charity* mattered both in what it *marked* and in what it *said*. For Miller, this sermon meant that America's story held world-historical importance. According to him, Winthrop self-consciously established his society as a model for all to see, a monument intended to guide the rest of the nations to God. In one of his most famous metaphors, Miller explained that the Puritans engaged in a "flank attack" on Christendom. "New England was the culmination of the Reformation," he argued. It was "the climax of world history." That was what Winthrop's sermon signaled, Miller claimed. Winthrop "preached to the emigrants during the voyage that the eyes of the world would be upon them, that they would be as a city set upon a hill for all to observe." If this sermon were the origin of America, then America, from the first, had a role to play in putting the world right. That aspect of Winthrop's sermon would reappear frequently in the political speeches of President Reagan and many others in the years to come.[6]

But the content of Winthrop's sermon—what Miller thought Winthrop was actually saying or proposing as a model—differed radically from what Reagan and others would make of it. According to Miller, this sermon called Puritans to model radical communal solidarity. It had nothing to do with the American Dream, nothing to do with bettering one's life, nothing at all to do with making money or getting ahead. In fact, Miller claimed, Winthrop specifically rejected all such ideas. Going it alone, pulling ahead of others, getting rich or even trying to—these were the very dangers that Winthrop sought to guard against. Society's success depended instead on mutual affection, being "knit together in this work as one man." According to Miller, the Puritans exhibited "a mighty conviction of solidarity," a "living cohesion" and "concept of a fellowship united in a common dedication." Unlike today, Miller insisted, New England theorists thought of society "not as an aggregation of individuals, but as an organism functioning for a definite purpose, with all parts subordinate to the whole, all members contributing a definite share, every person occupying a particular status." "The individual could be free only *for* ends, not *from* ends," and those ends, for the Puritans, concerned the flourishing of the larger whole under the eternal guidance of God.[7]

For Miller, in other words, Winthrop's sermon stood against both materialism and individualism—the two dangers Miller himself most feared. By making communal purpose not just a fundamental part of the American way but the very origin of America, Winthrop's sermon could offer a different meaning to define and guide the nation forward. What was more, that meaning required repeated articulation. The audience, the congregation, the community had to be continuously educated into their place and purpose. As Miller put it, Winthrop was telling these "proto-Americans" that "they could not just blunder along like ordinary people, seeking wealth and opportunity for their children." Instead, this society "would have to know, completely understand, reckon every day with, the enunciated terms on which it was brought into being, according to which it would survive or perish." No one could shirk the responsibility of thought. "This duty of conscious realization lay as heavy upon the humblest, the least educated, the most stupid, as upon the highest, the most learned, the cleverest." As Miller insisted elsewhere, Puritan ministers believed that all people "should be lifted by main force to the highest possible pitch of understanding."[8]

That, in part, is what made the Puritans great. The responsibility of thought, the duty of conscious realization, the insistence on reaching the highest possible pitch of understanding—all of this entailed the establishment of a deep and broad intellectual culture. According to Miller, the Puritans never intentionally brought liberty to America, but they most definitely brought learning. In "the very throes of clearing land and erecting shelters, they maintained schools and a college." And it wasn't just the preachers and politicians who built Harvard; farmers and common folk sacrificed from their own "pecks of wheat" to make sure the college flourished.[9] The Puritans loved education. They loved the life of the mind. They needed, nurtured, and pursued learning from Winthrop's *Arbella* sermon forward. And, according to Perry Miller, that love of learning had long since been lost.

In the fall from intellect to wealth, the Puritans modeled for Perry Miller a failure he saw all around him in contemporary society. According to him, the commitment to a higher cause and the dedication to God had made the Puritan community unusually successful, and the success of their venture—the wealth it generated—had eventually undermined the venture itself. When Puritans started making money, their purposes collapsed. "A hundred years after the landings, they were forced to look upon themselves with amazement, hardly capable of understanding how they had come to be what they were," he wrote. They had lost sight of their cause and plan, their purpose and devotion. For Perry Miller, the point of this failure was clear: the demise of the Puritans did not arise from external opposition; rather, it came about from within. It was caused by the Puritans' own success.[10]

That was the story Miller saw playing out again in the 1950s: the success of the United States, its sudden wealth and power, would soon prove the nation's undoing. In fact, Miller found this paradigm repeated in a host of societies scattered through the leaves of history. The downfall of the Roman Empire, which Miller explicitly compared to America, also came about through dissolutions wrought by its own success. Its might and power made it weak, Miller explained. For him, history was fundamentally ironic. Victory and achievement produce disappointment and disaster; progress results from causes other than one's own intentions; and no advance is finally secure since all growth contains within it the seeds of a new and possibly more catastrophic decline. As Henry May once summarized, "His works on Puritanism all illustrate the slogan that nothing fails like success." Wherever Miller turned, he saw the same laws of history replayed, and in his mind's eye, the beginning of demise could be read in the modern riches of America's rise.[11]

In 1960, near the end of his life, Perry Miller summarized this whole basic story and retold one more time the tale he had been trying to narrate all along. Preparing for a talk on "American Puritanism" at Gonzaga University, he jotted down just a few notes to take with him. He knew his material so well by now that all he needed were a few cards of clipped clauses to summarize the whole story of America. The plot was simple: "Having come out to a city on a hill—dedicated to the intellect, they realized that people have a great inclination to make money, to tell the intellectual that he doesn't care about school, theology, etc."[12] The Puritans came with purpose; that purpose entailed a daily "conscious realization" of their ends; and that conscious realization established an intellectual culture in early New England. This is where America begins. This is its true origin. Only later, only when the Puritans succeeded and fell, did wealth replace intellect as America's pursuit. The culture that came for theology declined into consumerism, an ever-increasing accumulation of prosperity and power guided by no deliberate purpose and carried forward for no apparent reason. It had become a country in search of a meaning to match its force.

Beyond all the ways Perry Miller used the Puritans to preach against the perils of American society, one other aspect of their society drew him even deeper into the subject—a relevance in Calvinist thought that he believed touched the deepest anxieties and desires of his day and age. For Perry Miller, John Winthrop and his "city on a hill" sermon represented the beginning of a society that took seriously humanity's ultimate concerns. "His Puritans responded to what he took to be man's universal predicament," one scholar has explained. This was Miller's final answer when journalists asked him, as they sometimes did, "What relevance has this theological beginning of New England to modern America?" Puritan theology mattered, Miller argued, because the problems had never gone away. He read the Puritans not just for who they once were but for the philosophical lessons that still applied. "If we cannot find a common denominator for equating the ideas of the Puritans with ideas of today," he wrote, "we may possibly get at them by understanding the temperament, the mood, the psychology that underlay the theories. If Puritanism as a creed has crumbled, it can be of only antiquarian significance to us, but if Puritanism is also a state of mind, it may be something closer to home." In the end, Miller understood and approached the Puritans as just that—*a state of mind*. They were to him a way of being, a psychology, a whole philosophy of life.[13]

If it is possible to imagine what a Puritan would look like who had no faith and no religion, the resulting picture would be something like Perry Miller. Miller loved the Puritans because he found in them something he had experienced himself: an anxious feeling of alienation in a suffering world that too often did not add up. Jonathan Edwards was a particular hero of his—one of the last and greatest of the American Puritans—because Edwards "did not try to gloss over any difficulties": "he was as aware as you or I of all the reasons why anyone might find it difficult to reconcile the harshness and cruelty of life with the idea of a controlling God." For Miller, the Puritans were not a people of ironfisted, unwavering faith but a set of searchers who often failed to discover the meaning they hoped to find. That is why he loved them. As one perceptive reader of Perry Miller has put it, his Puritans "acutely felt the abyss that separated them from what they called God." The great American playwright Thornton Wilder sensed this same element in Miller. When he was living in Zurich, he sent Miller a picture of a mountain climber stretched across an impossible chasm, his feet pushing against rocks to hold him up over an endless abyss: "I send you this symbolic picture-postcard," he wrote. "Kierkegaard said life and faith are like walking over 70,000 fathoms of water."[14] It was a fitting image for Perry Miller, the fate Miller felt was common not just to him but to his entire generation.

Of course, plenty of people both then and now feel no dire predicament, no existential dread, at all. They go blithely about their lives without experiencing any crisis of meaning. Miller considered such people either blind or unthinking. "The whole tendency of western civilization since Edwards' day has been to put these reflections aside," he asserted.[15] And that became all the more true after Puritanism collapsed. With its disappearance, Miller argued, we have increasingly distracted ourselves with the baubles of materialism, pursuing an accumulation of goods and amenities that cannot finally resolve the underlying ills of the human mind. What Edwards knew, he lectured, was that a mere piling up of goods cannot begin to answer why tomorrow you should wake up and continue piling up more goods. In a dark moment of pause, in the minute before we rise for work, whenever we begin to ask our whys and wherefores, Perry Miller believed that the predicament of the modern era—the lack of purpose or meaning in a world no longer guaranteed purpose or meaning by a sovereign God—would begin to dawn.

Given the way Perry Miller admired the Puritans, I think it is safe to say that he desired a version of what he described in them as "grace." According to Miller, Puritans defined grace as "an elevation of reason, a freshening and quickening of the understanding; it is an imparting to man of that spark of imagination and that breadth of insight whereby he can at last perceive in part, and apprehend in the rest, the essential unity of life, and essential reasonableness of things." It was "as though one had listened many times to a piece of music which to his ears was meaningless, and then suddenly its form becomes clear to him and for the first time he really hears it, not merely with his ears, but with his whole being." Such a definition of grace focuses on finding meaning and form in the seemingly formless—piecing together and perceiving for a moment the world's essential reasonableness and unity. As many scholars have since demonstrated, this account of Puritan grace is not very accurate. The Puritans understood grace to be the implanting of a new heart. It was not an "elevation of reason" but rather an altered disposition bringing with it a whole new set of affections along with a renewing of the mind. What Miller's definition represents instead, I believe, is an account of his own striving. He longed to experience just such an "elevation of reason"—to perceive in part, and to apprehend in the rest, some essential unity and meaning in life.[16]

Miller remained an atheist all his life, but he always claimed to share in the longings of the religious. The theologian Reinhold Niebuhr described Perry Miller as a "believing unbeliever," and Miller described himself as "an atheist for Niebuhr." Even so, how could Perry Miller, the atheist, ever hope to find what he thought the Puritans had by faith? What could fit tragedy and joy together into a pattern with meaning, purpose, and sense? In place of God, Miller substituted human nature itself. Through a careful study of society and culture, he hoped to decipher the essential features of human beings that made them behave and believe in the ways they did. New England gave him a control group, a specific experiment to study. As he explained in one book, "The fascination of this region, for the first two hundred or more years of its existence, is that it affords the historian an ideal laboratory. It was relatively isolated, the people were comparatively homogeneous, and the forces of history played upon it in ways that can more satisfactorily be traced than in more complex societies." Like Jeremy Belknap, Emma Willard, and many others, Perry Miller finally approached the American past—especially New England—as a kind of experiment from which the fundamental laws of human nature and happiness might arise. In New England, the "forces of history" were on full display—or as Willard once argued, "Here effects may be traced to their causes." Miller considered history to be littered with failures, and he saw in Puritan New England a laboratory for the study of ruin, hoping to learn how *all* successful societies eventually, if only gradually, collapse. He wanted to understand human nature itself, and he thought, finally, that the Puritans could show him.[17]

Given this search for the underlying sense of things, it is no surprise that Perry Miller spoke freely of "the meaning of America." For Miller, there was no getting at the meaning of America without first going through metaphysical concerns. Each search flowed from his personal hunt for significance, some sense of purpose behind the disordered, chaotic, and disastrous. National identity and purpose were bound up with questions of human nature and experience. And it is for this reason that the story of Winthrop's sermon and its place in American culture passes irrevocably through the personal longings of Perry Miller. A sense of alienation and loneliness, a deep hunger to find how it all fits together, a belief that his own existential crises were common to the generation he taught and talked with—all this led Miller to the Puritans and helped, finally, to establish John Winthrop's sermon as the origin of America and the plaything of modern politicians. With deep longing, he hoped to be given a glimpse of how it all hung together. And in the last years of his life, he began a project that would force him to produce a vision of the whole—an "elevation of reason" that would fit it all together. It was a project he would never complete.

In the 1950s, Miller's ambitions entered a new phase. Midway through the decade he began work on a magnum opus called *The Life of the Mind in America*—his massive attempt to capture every facet of "the American mind" from the Revolution to the Civil War, the whole of it organized into nine coherent books: religion, law, science, education, political economy and association, philosophy, theology, nature, and the self. This compilation would serve as a capstone to all his efforts, the culmination to over three decades of dedicated study. All he had achieved, Miller once claimed, was just a preface and prolegomena to the real project—*this* project, the last.

When Miller began *The Life of the Mind in America*, he sought financial support from whatever foundations he could find. Not too many existed for supporting the humanities during his day, and few came forward to help. One organization supplied him enough money to hire a graduate student named Alan Heimert, who would soon replace him as the Powell M. Cabot Professor of American Literature at Harvard. Still, Perry Miller was not granted much assistance. Frustrated, he reported his limitations to his good friend Samuel R. Rosenthal, an eminent Chicago lawyer, and Rosenthal responded by funding Miller himself. In 1956, Samuel Rosenthal gave $30,000 to Harvard—enough to pay half of Miller's salary, plus benefits, for three years running, giving him one semester each year to write. Miller promised he would devote himself wholly to the "grand design" and "not do one particle of the hack work" he had from time to time let himself "get caught in."[18] Three years, it seemed, would be plenty of time.

Three years later, Miller wrote to Rosenthal to explain his lack of progress. He pleaded the intractability of the material and the ambition of the project itself: "I get overwhelmed from time to time at the arrogance implicit in my proposal," he admitted. Receiving the letter, Rosenthal simply offered more money. Miller refused. He claimed in 1960 that he had plenty of material, plenty of notes. All he had to do was write it up. The book would be finished soon. Still, Rosenthal insisted that his invented "D and R Fund" would give more if only Miller asked. Miller never asked. Instead, he kept pushing off his friend, promising Sam that the book was almost done. Considering what was left when he died in 1963—he completed only two parts out of the nine that were planned—there is no way that Perry Miller could have honestly believed he was ever close to finishing this book.[19]

The pressures, it seems, were mounting. Not only had his academic progress slowed, but his personal life was also falling apart. Betty Miller, his wife, kicked him out of the house. Their marriage had long been strained by Perry's heavy drinking and infidelity. He moved into a room at Leverett House and lived alone on Harvard's campus. At this point, he began to break down both mentally and physically. In his decline he had plenty of models to follow— colleagues, friends, and personal heroes who had spectacularly and catastrophically ended their lives. F. O. Matthiessen, who began the American survey with him three decades before, had jumped from a hotel window in 1951. Sinclair Lewis, one of his favorite novelists, drank himself to death in Europe. Ernest Hemingway—who embodied many of the personality traits of Perry Miller, who was born at the same time and grew up only a few blocks away, whom Miller always respected and with whom he seemed to identify—took a shotgun in 1961 and ended his life.[20]

What finally broke Perry Miller, however, was the assassination of John F. Kennedy. A committed liberal, Miller had placed his hopes in Kennedy to set America straight, to correct its course and bring it back to a sense of purpose, intellect, and direction. On November 22, 1963, a bullet brought those hopes to an end. "Perry felt Kennedy's death as a staggering personal blow," one friend later reported, "and reacted in the only way he has been able to react in recent months; he got drunk and stayed that way." Miller entered his classes in a stupor and "became incoherent, crying and babbling about Kennedy." Carried from the room, he "had to be helped to his apartment." This was not the first time that drinking interfered with teaching. So public was Miller's inebriation, so humiliating his behavior, that one dean began to talk seriously of having him fired. A friend warned him that no more spectacles would be tolerated, and Miller promised to shape up. It was a somber end to a spectacular career. This giant of American history and literature lived his last days alone in a Harvard dorm room, very close to losing his job.[21]

A spurt of energy marked the last week of Perry Miller's life. He seemed, briefly, to get his act together. By all appearances, he stopped drinking. "His lectures that week were brilliant," a friend related, "but on Thursday in the romanticism course, when he was about three-quarters through the lecture, he suddenly had trouble articulating his words. He knew what he wanted to say, but all that came out was gibberish. He turned to his assistant and asked, 'Am I having a stroke?'" He had a purpose, a point, but no words to express it. Class was dismissed, and students left, a little dazed to see their professor lose his speech. Miller returned the next day, seemingly suddenly well. He "apologized for his lapse" and then "gave such a brilliant lecture that the students applauded as he gathered his things and left the room." That lecture would be his last. The following Monday, December 10, 1963, a maid found Perry Miller's body alone and unattended. According to the coroner, "he had been dead at least twenty-four hours."[22]

The cause of death, officially, was "acute hemorrhagic inflammation of the pancreas," to which his drinking clearly contributed. As his great project mounted and his progress diminished, Miller turned increasingly to alcohol. A prominent student named David Levin once took his mother to meet the great scholar Perry Miller. "She had expected my eminent mentor to exude sober wisdom, but he had obviously been drinking heavily before he arrived to dine with us in the house we were renting in Cambridge that summer." After the dinner, Levin's mother had only one question: "Why . . . does a man with such a fine mind want to destroy himself?" Miller's doctor, seeing what was happening, tried to limit him to two drinks per day, telling him to measure them "with a jigger so you know just what you are taking." The advice didn't take. Warnings mounted, concerns increased, but no one could hold him back. Hearing of his death, one friend wrote that students and colleagues had "all watched helplessly . . . the mortal agony of a great life hopelessly possessed by the demon of self-destruction." According to either rumor or report, Miller died in his dorm room surrounded by empty bottles of liquor. Multiple students described it as a suicide.[23]

Perry Miller, having all his life admired the Puritans in their search for purpose, their desire for a pattern that could make sense of the whole, seems finally to have been overwhelmed by his own quest for meaning. He had begun with John Winthrop and *A Model of Christian Charity*—an articulate expression of origins, a coherence with which he could coherently begin—but as he moved forward, as the story broadened, as the arc of the narrative bent and shifted in multiple directions, he failed to find the paradigm that would hold it all together. He could not complete his last, great attempt to make an organic unity of American history and culture. He was not granted an "elevation of reason." Reading through his papers, one gets the sense that by the end of his life, Miller saw himself as having failed.

In a significant way he did fail, and that failure came about not despite his efforts but because of them—because of his relentless, lifelong commitment and dedication to the Puritans of New England

and *A Model of Christian Charity* as the ultimate, and in many ways the *only*, explanation of America. Such an insistence finally failed to address or explain the concerns that had come to dominate American society in the mid-twentieth century. At the opening of Miller's career, W. E. B. Du Bois published *Black Reconstruction in America* (1935), a searing account of the way historical studies had systematically excluded and denigrated the struggles and contributions of African Americans. The next year, 1936, Langston Hughes wrote "Let America Be America Again"—a plea that the promises of America extend themselves to African Americans at last. In 1941, the same year that Henry Luce published "The American Century," Richard Wright documented the diverse lives and hopes of "12 million black voices" in the Great Depression. A decade later, the civil rights movement erupted. And through all these years, millions and millions of African Americans migrated from the South to the North, from agricultural fields to urban centers such as the childhood neighborhood of Perry Miller. "The problem of the Twentieth Century is the problem of the color-line," Du Bois prophesied in 1903.[24] Yet the problem of the color line appears nowhere in all the mighty works of Perry Miller. No single book, and no single scholar, can address every issue, of course. But Miller explicitly set himself the task of explaining the "meaning of America," and that meaning never touched on one of the most vital issues engulfing the nation. If he felt that he had failed—if he felt that his story of America was increasingly hard to hold together and decreasingly important to the American people—he was right.

In one way, however, Perry Miller succeeded far beyond his grandest hopes. He brought John Winthrop's sermon *A Model of Christian Charity* before the public and turned it into the key text of American origins. Miller pronounced it the *first* articulate statement of community, a sermon expounding the idea that America would be dedicated to the life of the mind. He read in Winthrop's text a monumental testimony against the basic premises of the American Dream. The irony of history—one that Miller might well have appreciated—is that in promoting Winthrop's sermon, he caused it to become the key statement of all that he most feared and lamented. In the years to come, Winthrop's "city upon a hill" sermon would become "the shining city on a hill" of President

Reagan: a celebration of individual freedom, material prosperity, and American power—above all, a call for Americans to renew their optimism and believe in themselves again. Nothing breeds failure like success. And no one was more successful than Perry Miller in making Winthrop's sermon the cornerstone of American culture.

CHAPTER SIXTEEN

The American Jeremiad

THE FIRST AMERICAN PRESIDENT to cite John Winthrop's sermon was not Ronald Reagan. It was John F. Kennedy, who also happened to be the first Catholic president. This is not a coincidence. Since the nineteenth century, the claim that a "true history" of America started in New England—and nowhere else—offered a national purpose and identity wrapped up in Protestantism. The Pilgrims and Puritans had been touted as the origin of the nation in a bid to erase the history of slavery (sidelined off to the South) and celebrate civil and religious freedom, simultaneously condemning the absolutism, violence, and supposed indolence of Catholic conquistadors. Peaceful "settlement" versus violent "conquest" was a matter of ethnicity (English versus Spanish) tied closely to religion (Protestants versus Catholics). JFK knew this history. And when he left Boston for the nation's capital, he invoked Winthrop's sermon to graft American Catholics onto the Puritan stock.

Kennedy's campaign revealed just how much his Catholic identity remained a threat to American voters. On July 15, 1960, when he accepted the nomination, JFK voiced what many were thinking: "I am fully aware of the fact that the Democratic Party, by nominating someone of my faith, has taken on what many regard as a new and hazardous risk." He reassured listeners that he would not be controlled by the pope. "I am telling you now what you are entitled to know," he announced, "that my decisions on any public policy will be my own—as an American, a Democrat and a free man."[1] It was enough, though barely. Inspiring Americans, calling them to a "New Frontier," running a race premised on standing up for freedom against the advance of communism, JFK narrowly edged past Richard Nixon to become the thirty-fifth president of the United States.

Two months later, Kennedy gathered his things and prepared to leave for Washington, DC. He had been born in Boston, and for many years he had represented Massachusetts in Congress, first in the House of Representatives and then—after defeating the son of Henry Cabot Lodge—in the Senate. It was fitting, after so much service, that he "bid farewell to Massachusetts." It was equally fitting that when he addressed the Massachusetts General Court, he turned to the words of Winthrop. For JFK was not speaking to the nation when he cited *A Model of Christian Charity*; he was speaking to "the people of Massachusetts."[2] And while Perry Miller's efforts had begun to spread Winthrop's sermon through textbooks and academia, by January 1961 most Americans had not yet heard of this text or Winthrop's proclamation that "we shall be as a city upon a hill."

Other scholars have tried to determine how exactly JFK landed on *A Model of Christian Charity*. Richard Gamble, who first tracked the strange history of Winthrop's sermon, was able to interview Kennedy's longtime aide and speechwriter Ted Sorensen. But true to form, Sorenson, who died in 2010, attributed the "city upon a hill" speech to Kennedy and refused to disclose how the words had been chosen. Maybe the teachings of Perry Miller had made their way beyond the campus gates through a Harvard graduate. Or maybe, as Daniel T. Rodgers has suggested, Sorenson simply saw Winthrop's sermon while walking across Boston Common. After all, it had been carved in stone and sitting there since 1930. However it happened, in 1961, the words of Winthrop's sermon entered the vocabulary of an American president for the first time.[3]

They did so in an auspicious manner. For not only did Kennedy insert his Irish Catholic family into the Puritan origins of America; he also laid the foundation of the nation's principles in his home state of Massachusetts. Since the early 1800s, New Englanders had asserted their vital role in creating the nation, and Kennedy had grown up on that rhetoric. As a young teenager, he would have seen the 1930 tercentenary placards, announcing the importance of Boston and Massachusetts. His 1961 speech echoed those slogans. "I speak neither from false provincial pride nor artful political flattery," he declared. "For no man about to enter high office in this country can ever be unmindful of the contribution this state has made to our national greatness." Sounding the notes of Tocqueville and others, Kennedy claimed that Massachusetts's "principles have guided our footsteps in times of crisis as well as in times of calm. Its democratic institutions—including this historic body [the Massachusetts General Court]—have served as beacon lights for other nations as well as our sister states."⁴ In a few short lines, Kennedy artfully summarized a narrative that had been in the making for over 150 years. It was a story of Pilgrim and Puritan origins, a tale about the principles—the *ideals*—that had guided the nation from New England to the present day.

Tracing out the "enduring qualities of Massachusetts," Kennedy turned to Winthrop in order to demonstrate his own character and commitments. In constructing a national administration, he explained, "I have been guided by the standard John Winthrop set before his shipmates on the flagship *Arbella* three hundred and thirty-one years ago, as they, too, faced the task of building a new government on a perilous frontier." That standard was nothing less than what has since become Winthrop's most famous quote: "We must always consider, that we shall be as a city upon a hill—the eyes of all people are upon us.'" Broadening this vision from Massachusetts, Kennedy cast Winthrop across the country. "Today the eyes of all people are truly upon us," he continued, "and our governments, in every branch, at every level, national, state and local, must be as a city upon a hill—constructed and inhabited by men aware of their great trust and their great responsibilities."⁵ In such a statement, Kennedy treated Winthrop's sermon as the conditional it was. He did not declare that America had a God-given guarantee to succeed. He claimed that the world was watching and that leaders of the nation had better behave as though all could see. He used the Protestant, not the Catholic, form of Matthew 5:14.

In adopting and adapting *A Model of Christian Charity*, Kennedy took the mission of Perry Miller out of academic classrooms and into the halls of power. Since 1930, John Winthrop's "city on a hill" sermon had primarily celebrated the founding of Boston, not the establishment of the nation. Perry Miller had done a great deal to change that, and some other historians had begun to spread the word. Textbooks had begun to pick up the tale and spread it to students. And then, in 1961, JFK spoke the words as president-elect.

Even so, one local speech by one newly elected president would not, in itself, make Winthrop's sermon famous. Presidents only gradually discovered the power of Winthrop's words. While most since JFK have quoted Winthrop in some capacity, those quotations at first came infrequently. President Lyndon B. Johnson, for example, used Winthrop only once, in October 1964, when he paid tribute to Kennedy in Boston by turning to the former president's farewell. "In that speech," Johnson reminded listeners, "President Kennedy told us that John Winthrop, setting out for America, said to his shipmates, 'We must always consider that we shall be as a city upon a hill—the eyes of all people are upon us.'" Yet in citing Kennedy, Johnson transformed the text. "Well, America tonight *is* a city upon a hill," he continued. In that moment, in that statement, Johnson explicitly turned a simile into a metaphor. He took the conditional warning of JFK and made it a confident claim. Those who watch us, he went on, "look not to our tall buildings or our prosperous streets, or to our mighty arms. They look uncertainly, and hopefully, to see burning in the midst of the city a light of freedom, a flame of the spirit, the brightness of the nobility which is in man, and the arms of the Statue of Liberty awaiting them." It was not tall buildings or prosperous streets—not *wealth* or its pursuit—that set America apart. It was freedom, asylum, welcome. It was, in short, an exceptional set of *ideals* exceptionally realized in America alone. In other words, it was Lyndon B. Johnson, in 1964, who first turned the meaning of Winthrop's sermon into the vision of Reagan's career.[6]

Eventually, of course, Reagan would become the most famous person to use Winthrop's sermon and the person, in turn, who would make Winthrop's sermon most famous. But just as Reagan began touring through the United States citing *A Model of*

Christian Charity, the sermon itself became canonical far beyond political circles through the power and influence of Perry Miller, as picked up, repeated, and embellished by other scholars. The full story of Winthrop's "city on a hill" sermon in the latter half of the twentieth century thus involves two kinds of worlds working together at once, often despite themselves. For as Reagan went from being an actor to governor to president, bringing *A Model of Christian Charity* to politics in the most prominent way possible, scholars simultaneously built on Perry Miller's work to transform Winthrop's sermon from an interesting Puritan specimen into the guiding vision of New England and then, finally, the cultural key text explaining the entire meaning of America.

Once more, it was the work of a foreigner who created and consolidated this story of Puritan origins. In 1831, Alexis de Tocqueville came from France and traveled several thousand miles, observing, taking notes, and finally composing *Democracy in America*. Seven decades later, Max Weber toured America before finishing *The Protestant Ethic and the Spirit of Capitalism*. In 1961, Sacvan Bercovitch immigrated from Canada, traveling from Claremont Graduate School in California to his first job at Brandeis in Boston, back to San Diego, then on to Columbia before finally becoming the next great Puritan scholar at Harvard. Each of these foreigners—whether visiting or immigrating—would discover in the United States a powerful collective memory of Puritanism, and each would formulate a new thesis about its influence. For Tocqueville, Puritanism represented the source of American democracy. For Weber, Puritanism prepared the way for American capitalism. For Bercovitch, Puritanism served as the origin of American rhetoric. As he would explain throughout his career, Puritan New England produced the notion of a nation simultaneously chosen by God and committed to the rise of free enterprise.

Each of these writers—Tocqueville, Weber, and Bercovitch—built his claim on the basis of prior ones he found circulating in American culture. Tocqueville took a myth about New England origins and turned it into high political theory. Weber accepted from Tocqueville that America's "democratic traditions" had descended from the Puritans, then he wove that supposition into a new argument about the rise of capitalism. When Bercovitch emerged in the 1970s, he adopted and amplified *The Protestant Ethic*, threading Weber's thesis into a new explanation of American rhetoric. Democracy (Tocqueville), capitalism (Weber), and now the language of American exceptionalism (Bercovitch)—each of these features of American society has been laid at the Puritans' feet, most recently and most powerfully by Sacvan Bercovitch.

Sacvan Bercovitch, like Perry Miller, was a Harvard legend. Beginning in the 1970s, he exerted an enormous influence over the study of early America and the making of American Studies. When he died in 2014, obituaries praised him for his "academic bravery," for having "the courage to make large claims." His second book, *The American Jeremiad* (1978), has been described as "one of the most influential critical works in the study of American writing in any decade." For anyone who has studied the Puritans, for anyone invested in American Studies more generally, Sacvan Bercovitch has been unavoidable. His books have been translated into Chinese, Hungarian, German, French, Italian, and Portuguese.[7] And the underlying philosophical approach to his work—a study of American ideology through American literature—has been carried forward by a host of new scholars. Unlike Perry Miller, who directed only a handful of dissertations, Sacvan Bercovitch supervised over one hundred PhDs across a wide range of topics. Today, his talented students write and teach all across the country.

The startling disparity in these graduate-student numbers indicates the striking differences between Miller and Bercovitch. By all accounts, the many friends of "Saki" did not fear him; they loved him. According to one colleague, Saki was "whimsically self-questioning, disarmingly candid, and charmingly vulnerable." He was "deeply disinclined to plume his feathers or to expect the deference that is, nevertheless, due him and his scholarly work." Still others remembered him "for his warm and approachable character"— words and descriptions that would never have entered the same room as Perry Miller. Bercovitch had come from a life of hardship and poverty, earning his first degree through night school while working in a grocery store, and he always nourished a soft spot for an eclectic array of students. And an eclectic array of students have honored him in turn.[8]

Today, Bercovitch remains justly famous for formulating what he called "the American Jeremiad"—a way of speaking that he claimed came straight from John Winthrop's 1630 sermon *A Model of Christian Charity*. The *descent* of this rhetoric is rather dubious, but its *form* remains well worth knowing. Any bit of current news will probably demonstrate what Bercovitch first noticed and explained. In the summer of 2018, for example, the Trump administration began a "zero tolerance" policy of border control that separated over two thousand children from their parents. This action produced widespread protests, including criticism from the U.S. Conference of Catholic Bishops. When National Public Radio contacted Archbishop Thomas Wenski of Miami, the reporter asked him why Catholic leaders considered Trump's action immoral. "Well," Wenski answered, "it's—it goes against the values of our nation." That, said Bercovitch, is precisely how Americans talk. Whatever they admire or approve, whatever they think of as *moral*, they describe as the "nation's values." And when they do that, Bercovitch explained, they effectively pose an ideal America against the actual America. They set what America stands for against what Americans do.[9]

In order to consider just how strange this rhetoric can be, we have to remember that Archbishop Wenski spoke on behalf of the Catholic Church. Why should a Catholic bishop consider something "immoral" because it opposes "national values"? What do national values have to do with it? If something is "immoral" for Archbishop Wenski, presumably it contradicts his *Catholic* values, not his *national* ones. Yet in the United States, Bercovitch argued, something called "un-American" is considered wrong, and everything considered wrong is called "un-American." When Americans do that, he argued, they end up reasserting the righteousness of their nation and the rightness of their national ideals—however much they dispute those ideals and however little they ever get realized. Bercovitch called this way of speaking the American Jeremiad.

Moreover, Bercovitch added, that American Jeremiad has everything to do with Puritan New England. According to Bercovitch, the Puritans created it by conflating the sacred and the secular, turning the geographical space of America into a new Promised Land—the next step in God's plan of cosmic redemption from biblical times through New England to the end of days. Puritans thought of themselves as an "elect nation in New England," and in doing so they created a rhetorical legacy that would define American culture ever since. To the end of his life, Bercovitch never backed down from this fundamental claim. "In any case," he wrote in 2011, "it was the Puritan vision that became the language of the dominant culture."[10]

To make such claims, Bercovitch leaned heavily on several premises that Perry Miller first established. Like Miller, Bercovitch began with a basic sense of respect for the Puritans. He did not dismiss them as backward, unintelligent, hypocritical moralists but described them instead as an "outpost of the modern world," innovators who created American identity through an intricate and artful use of language. Like Miller, he also separated Puritans from all others in early America. The Spanish were not worth considering, but neither were the English farther south. As Perry Miller had taken one short paragraph in his most widely read work to dismiss the incoherence of Virginia, so Bercovitch, in his most influential book, briefly acknowledged and erased the South. The colony of Virginia was a common affair, led by a man who "urged English settlement for gold, glory, and gain." As a result, it "always retained its European cast." If you want to find the source of *American* identity, you cannot begin there. For Bercovitch, "The myth of America is the creation of the New England Way."[11]

Such an erasure of the South has a long history. It would not have taken the work of Perry Miller to hurry past Virginia and proclaim it irrelevant. But it did take Miller to dismiss the Pilgrims. That, as we have seen, was hardly conceivable until the middle of the twentieth century. In contrast to the usual celebrations of Plymouth Rock, Miller had turned to the Puritans—to John Winthrop, the *Arbella*, Boston, and *A Model of Christian Charity*—heightening the influence of 1630 while casting aside the Separatists as harried migrants who hoped only to be left alone. In contrast to the Pilgrims, the Puritans came with vision and purpose. They arrived with culture and intelligence. They founded Harvard, and they spread their ideas through all of New England and beyond.

Bercovitch accepted that narrative without question. For him the Pilgrims were nothing more than "an insulated group of about a hundred Separatists" who were guided solely by their desire "to worship God in peace." They did not have a grand design, and they did not see America as a holy place. It was the Puritans, Bercovitch asserted, who sanctified New England as an "elect nation" and tasked it with a divine mission. So much did this distinction matter to Bercovitch that he finally addressed the specific contest between *A Model of Christian Charity* and the Mayflower Compact. The Mayflower Compact, Bercovitch said, used only standard terms of the time, so much so that the Pilgrims even subscribed themselves the "loyal subjects of our dread sovreign Lord, King James."[12] The Puritans, in contrast, invented new rhetoric, sacralizing their leaders as fulfillments of old scriptural prophecy and subscribing themselves as God's chosen ones in a language that would shape the way Americans have conceived of themselves ever since. For Sacvan Bercovitch, the 1620 Mayflower Compact was *English*. But "America"—this new thing, this "language experiment," this "venture in rhetorical self-creation"—*that* was "launched in 1630."[13] It was *A Model of Christian Charity*, Bercovitch claimed, that inaugurated American identity.

In one last important way, Bercovitch built his work on the basis of Perry Miller. As Miller had once treated New England like a self-enclosed "laboratory"—a study of human nature and its fundamental laws—so Bercovitch found in New England "a sort of ready-made laboratory for examining the nature and effects of myth in a modern culture." The opportunity, he thought, was utterly unique. In most countries, national myths and heroes and legends "lie in the remote past, shrouded in legends of the supernatural and multiple oral traditions." Not so in America. As Jeremy Belknap, Emma Willard, and others had distinguished the United States by claiming that its full history could be fully known, so Bercovitch argued that "in the United States, the foundations were visible at every stage of construction, in published modern texts that spanned only a few hundred years. Here," he said, "you could follow the making of myth and symbol step by printed step, from definition to revision, sometimes from insertion to deletion to reinstatement." Here alone, he repeated, "the process of cultural formation stood open in plain sight."[14] New England, once again, would serve as history's lab.

Yet the experiment performed in that lab, Bercovitch implied, could only be viewed properly from the outside. Since he believed that all Americans were the *product* of the Puritan myth, Bercovitch seemed to assume that they could not adequately step back and analyze it. Only a foreigner could observe American rhetoric with detachment. And so, over the course of his career, Bercovitch began to repeat his life's story again and again and again. The son of Jewish, Marxist, anarchist, Ukrainian-Canadian radicals (he was named for Sacco and Vanzetti), his exceptional position gave him unique insights. When he came to the United States, he discovered "a country that, despite its arbitrary territorial limits, could read its destiny in its landscape, and a population that, despite its bewildering mixture of race and creed, could believe in something called an American mission, and could invest that patent fiction with all the emotional, spiritual, and intellectual appeal of a religious quest." In stumbling onto this rhetoric, Bercovitch felt "like Sancho Panza in a land of Don Quixotes."[15] Don Quixote, of course, is the hero who imagines himself a knight, though in reality he delusionally tilts at windmills. Sancho Panza, meanwhile, is the sidekick who sees a windmill for a windmill—who can distinguish (unlike Don Quixote) the real from the imagined. That, said Bercovitch, was exactly how he felt.

In other words, the force of his claims always depended on "the extreme marginality" of his outlook and his "own unrepresentative (not to say eccentric) experience." Presenting himself as one who "knew nothing about America" before coming to the United States, Bercovitch repeatedly described his wonder at discovering a rich rhetoric of sacred cause. So long as he did not get sucked into that rhetoric—as Tocqueville and other foreigners had, Bercovitch asserted—he could remain a scientific observer, revealing what was clear and apparent to anyone not trapped in the American cage. Bercovitch aimed only to point out and to put into words. With his autobiography comfortably in place, he presented himself as reporting back on experiments that were running out of a "sort of ready-made laboratory."[16]

Once Bercovitch had established his autobiography, he proceeded to pose in many ways the same inquiry that I have been seeking to answer: how did the myth of Puritan origins gain traction in the United States? How did it come to hide and erase so many other communities, cultures, and conflicts from early America? In fact, when Bercovitch focused specifically on Winthrop, he seemed to ask the very question of this book: "How and why did Winthrop's 'Model' become a key player" in the "social-symbolic game through which the United States has usurped the meaning of America?"[17] What, he wanted to know, explains the significance of Winthrop's sermon?

Yet the answer Bercovitch offered did not concern book history or the saving of texts; the creation of historical societies or the writing of textbooks; the rise of antiquarianism or the flourishing of genealogical interest; new racial investments in Anglo-Saxonism or Pilgrim anniversary celebrations; a crisis of identity in the wake of the Cold War or a burgeoning concern in the mid-twentieth century with the "meaning of America." These elements never surface in the work of Sacvan Bercovitch. Instead, Bercovitch's answer had everything to do with Winthrop's sermon itself. Assuming that *A Model of Christian Charity* had shaped American culture from 1630 forward, Bercovitch aimed to explain exactly how and why this one piece of rhetoric had produced so dramatic an effect. "The procession of references and allusions to Winthrop's 'Model,'" he once asserted, "runs more or less unbroken from colonial times to our own, and through all forms of discourse, from protest poetry to presidential orations." By the time Bercovitch published these lines in 1998, Winthrop's sermon had been canonized and quoted so often that no one knew or remembered its rather-recent rise to fame. Bercovitch assumed that the sermon had been famous from its very first day. In fact, Bercovitch explained that "familiarity has dulled the force of Winthrop's innovation."[18] As a result, he wanted to recover that "innovation," the "variation" in Winthrop's sermon that had given it so much force. For Bercovitch, it was what the sermon said, rather than what others did with it, that mattered most.

And what did Winthrop say? According to Bercovitch, America officially began when John Winthrop united the sacred to the secular and tied American history to the redemption of the world. Shortly before Bercovitch retired, he reemphasized that point by making Winthrop single-handedly the source of American identity. "My subject is the rhetoric of the dominant culture of the United States," he asserted, "my proof-text is John Winthrop's canonical lay-sermon of 1630, 'A Model of Christian Charity.'" In this sermon, Bercovitch argued, Winthrop offered his vision of society in "more or less familiar terms—and yet with a decisive turn in language and substance, a turn so sharp and compelling as to make it an abiding cultural legacy." From 1630 to the present day, Bercovitch believed, Winthrop's sermon exercised a "persistent and influential" impact on the meaning of America. And the whole thing—the whole sacred rhetoric of America and its divine mission descending from Winthrop's sermon—could be summarized by a simple four-word phrase. "My focus here is on one piece," Bercovitch explained, "Winthrop's 'city upon a hill,' which I assume provides an index to the significance of his address as a whole."[19]

Such an account of Winthrop's sermon is badly mistaken. Not only does it presume an influence that the sermon never had, but it also assumes that the Puritans saw themselves in such grand and prophetic terms. Yet, as we have seen, Winthrop never equated New England with the Promised Land, nor did any other Puritan. The Puritans of New England might have situated themselves in relation to sacred history—just like all Christians of different times and places have always done and still do today—but they did not see themselves as a specially chosen, unique step in God's plan of world redemption. Winthrop hoped to join his community to all other godly models spread all across the world. His was an international conception—a communion of saints never limited to the American strand. And it was always a *provisional* community: Winthrop genuinely feared failure. Sacvan Bercovitch, here and throughout his career, took a few phrases expressed in a few documents and amplified them into a unifying vision of American exceptionalism, further proclaiming that such a vision affected all of American culture. In fact, as scholars have since shown, New England Puritans spoke in much the same way as did other Protestants in England, Virginia, and elsewhere. "Winthrop's variation" turns out to be Bercovitch's innovation. Puritan origins did not invent the myth of America. Americans, much later, invented the myth of Puritan origins.[20]

So much did Bercovitch want to credit the Puritans, however, that he occasionally bent and warped the evidence to bolster his claims. He replaced "may" with "will" in one quote to make the Puritans sound more confident. And he used ellipses so liberally that hardly a Puritan quotation passes without missing some words from the middle. Most of his ellipses remain innocent attempts to shorten an old text while keeping the meaning intact. But a "..." here and another "..." there, dropping this word or that from what the Puritans actually said, combining one sentence with another, can make the Puritans of Sacvan Bercovitch sound quite different from the actual historical Calvinists who occupied New England.[21] It wasn't just later Americans who invented the myth of Puritan origins. Bercovitch himself created the Puritan origins he found everywhere on display.

In particular, Bercovitch heightened the significance of Winthrop's 1630 sermon as *the* Puritan origin that mattered most, and he did so—as Miller had done—by focusing more and more on this one text over the course of his career. In 1975, Bercovitch worked Winthrop's sermon into the middle of his treatise *The Puritan Origins of the American Self*. Three years later, he began *The American Jeremiad* with Winthrop's "provisional but sweeping prophecy of doom," which turned the people of New England—"here, as nowhere else"—into "instruments of a sacred historical design." In 1982, Bercovitch quoted almost directly from James Savage's 1838 introduction in order to argue that Winthrop's sermon embodied "a grand prophetic design" and launched a new community "summoned by God to a historic mission." A decade later, Bercovitch returned to Winthrop's "justly famous lay sermon" and reiterated once again that its power lay in proclaiming New England "the apex of history." Finally, just before he retired, he wrote, revised, and reprinted a last essay on the influence of Puritanism, which focused solely on the innovation and influence of John Winthrop's sermon *A Model of Christian Charity*.[22]

When Perry Miller came to dwell on *A Model of Christian Charity*, he invented a fact to serve his needs: he started to assert that the sermon had been printed in England and reimported so that all could heed. So, too, when Bercovitch turned to "Winthrop's innovation," he created a small piece of evidence to aid his claims. In order to demonstrate that Puritans saw John Winthrop as the leader of a literal and historical "New Israel," Bercovitch drew attention to the sermon's description of the Puritans as "Christian tribes." The phrase could be found, Bercovitch pointed out, right there on the very title page of Winthrop's sermon. That title page, however, comes from an unknown hand adding a doubtful cover note anytime between 1630 and 1838. Yet according to Bercovitch, it was "composed by Winthrop's son sometime in the mid-1630s."[23] He does not tell us what evidence supports this assertion or *which* son he has in mind (Winthrop had several). The claim, in other words, comes from nowhere. But Bercovitch added that detail because he placed so much weight on the title. He wanted it to matter.

The title page mattered so much to Bercovitch because it helped support one of his main claims about the Puritans. Right there on the cover page, he pointed out, the Puritans were described as a "company" headed by the "Honourable" John Winthrop, "Esquire." And those words—*company, honorable,* and *esquire*—allowed him to tie the whole story of Puritanism and its sacred mission to the ideology of the American Dream. The dubious title page demonstrated that this new Puritan venture was a modern economic undertaking leading all the way from Winthrop's sermon to modern middle-class ideals. For Miller, the Puritans had represented an intellectual, non-materialistic culture whose history could warn us against the dangers of capitalism. For Bercovitch, in contrast, the Puritans created American capitalism and sanctified it as sacred unto God. New England, he said, "evolved from its own origins, as it were, into a middle-class culture," and the enterprise of that culture "was consecrated, according to its civic and clerical leadership, by a divine plan of progress." Tracing this process back to its very root, Bercovitch turned, predictably, to *A Model of Christian Charity.*[24]

Sacvan Bercovitch's reading of the Puritans, as many scholars have since shown, is mistaken. The troubles with Max Weber's thesis are only amplified in his works. But it is hard to blame Bercovitch for coming to such a conclusion in the 1970s. At that time, he had good reason to emphasize the continuities of Puritan rhetoric. After all, the rise of Sacvan Bercovitch happened to coincide with the rise of Ronald Reagan. In 1966, Bercovitch got his first job at

Brandeis. In 1967, Reagan was elected governor of California. By 1974, Reagan was giving major addresses to conservatives and laying the groundwork for a national campaign. In 1975, Bercovitch published his first major monograph, *The Puritan Origins of the American Self*. Reagan ran for the Republican presidential nomination in 1976, and two years later, Bercovitch produced his second and most influential single-author book, *The American Jeremiad*. In 1980, Reagan entered the White House. In 1983, Bercovitch took up his prestigious post at Harvard. Side by side, these two men rose.

Of course, Ronald Reagan and Sacvan Bercovitch would never have seen each other in cahoots. One believed devoutly in an American exceptionalism guided and sustained through God's providence; the other relentlessly criticized such a belief while tracing its roots to Puritan New England. Yet the triumph of Winthrop's sermon required the success of both. During the 1970s, Bercovitch powerfully reshaped American literary history around the influence of the Puritans. In the same decade, Reagan's repeated use of Winthrop not only brought the words of a formerly unknown Puritan sermon to millions of Americans but also made Bercovitch's arguments seem self-evidently right. As Reagan invoked Winthrop to explain the fundamental identity and purpose of the nation, Bercovitch pointed out "the astonishing persistence of Puritan rhetoric from Winthrop to Reagan."[25] *Of course* students examining American thought and literature should begin their studies with Winthrop's sermon; after all, when they turned on the television at night, there was the American president still quoting it. Far more than the actual Puritan sources themselves, the public rhetoric of Ronald Reagan supported Bercovitch's claims. Through the 1970s and 1980s, these two formed a reinforcing loop. Bercovitch's works explained Reagan's language through Winthrop's sermon at the same time that Reagan used Winthrop's language to explain the nature and identity of the entire United States. Both, in their own ways, botched *A Model of Christian Charity*. But together, they made the sermon rise.

CHAPTER SEVENTEEN

American Exceptionalism and America First

R ONALD REAGAN FIRST TURNED to *A Model of Christian Charity* in 1969, in a low-stakes fund-raising event for Eisenhower College in upstate New York. By that point, Perry Miller had been dead for six years, Kennedy and Johnson had both invoked *A Model of Christian Charity*, and Bercovitch was about to be hired off to Columbia. It seems likely that when Reagan used Winthrop, he knew about Kennedy's 1961 farewell speech. In 1984, Reagan quoted JFK's address during his own appearance at a political rally in Boston. Just as his talk ended, he told the audience, "I understand how John Kennedy felt when he left to assume the Presidency." Then he quoted Kennedy, but even as he read from JFK's "city on a hill" speech, he specifically dropped Kennedy's invocation of that one famous phrase. By 1984, after all, "city on a hill" belonged to Ronald Reagan, and it may be that Ronald Reagan did not want to remind his audience who had quoted Winthrop first.[1]

Reagan took ownership of Winthrop's sermon on January 25, 1974, during the inaugural address of the first Conservative Political Action Conference (CPAC). As he would do throughout his career, he turned to American history in order to establish American policy. "I thought that tonight," he said, "rather than talking on the subjects you are discussing, or trying to find something new to say, it might be appropriate to reflect a bit on our heritage."[2] Then he offered his first formulation of a providential American exceptionalism. "You can call it mysticism if you want to, but I have always believed that there was some divine plan that placed this great continent between two oceans to be sought out by those who were possessed of an abiding love of freedom and a special kind of courage." Reagan was not talking about the crossing of the Bering Strait ten thousand years ago or the forced migration of enslaved Africans; he was talking about the willed crossing of the Atlantic by Europeans, and the *first* Europeans Reagan had in mind were none other than the 1620 Pilgrims. During a Fourth of July message in 1983, for example, Reagan repeated his belief "that by a Divine plan this nation was placed between the two oceans to be sought out and found by those with a special brand of courage and love of freedom." But then he specified whom he meant: "Can we imagine the courage it took back in 1620 to pick up family, bid goodbye to friends, board those small ships, and set sail across a mighty ocean toward a new future in an unknown world?" Apparently, the English settlers of Jamestown did not count—not to mention all others who came before. Instead, the Pilgrims retold an old story for Reagan, one that separated the motives of America's *true* founders from the greed and materialism characterizing everyone else. As Reagan explained for the National Religious Broadcasters in 1982, God's "divine plan" for America enabled the country to be "created by men and women who came not for gold but mainly in search of God. They would be free people, living under the law, with faith in their Maker and in their future."[3] Pilgrims told that story best.

As a result, when Reagan first began to find *A Model of Christian Charity* so useful, he turned the first Puritan governor of Massachusetts Bay into a fellow "pilgrim." Reagan knew perfectly well what he was doing. As Richard Gamble has observed, he even explained the difference to a correspondent who had complained about Reagan's use of the term. Reagan clarified that Winthrop was not part of the *Mayflower* crew, he knew, but was still very much a "pilgrim" (with a lowercase *p*) because he stood for "any such group of people who are embarked on a journey such as those who first came to this country."⁴ Again, by "those who *first* came to this country," Reagan meant the Pilgrims (with a capital *P*). All those who followed their example—coming with courage in search of freedom—could be considered a "pilgrim" (small *p*) as well. It is a pedantic argument, but it demonstrates an important point: Reagan consciously turned a Puritan into a Pilgrim and melded two origin stories into one. Thus, as Reagan proclaimed in many different speeches from 1969 to 1989, America started with John Winthrop "standing on the tiny deck of the Arbella in 1630 off the Massachusetts coast," declaring to his fellow "pilgrims" that "we shall be as a city upon a hill."⁵ With his subtle use of a single term, Reagan could insert a new text—*A Model of Christian Charity*—into a very old tale.

Yet even as Reagan honored Pilgrims for their courage and ideals, he also turned Winthrop's "city on a hill" into a celebration of material progress. Freedom, for Reagan, always included free enterprise. John Winthrop's "city on a hill" sermon came to serve the very drive of capitalism and accumulation that Perry Miller most feared. The "tall, proud city" of Reagan's rhetoric was defined by "free ports that hummed with commerce and creativity," busy and bustling in the absence of government regulations. During his 1974 CPAC address, Reagan praised the United States for its enormous wealth, its vast economic activity, and its high standard of living. "Ninety-nine percent have gas or electric refrigeration, 92 percent have televisions, and an equal number have telephones. There are 120 million cars on our streets and highways." Recognizing that such numbers could serve as "proof of our materialism—the very thing that we are charged with"—Reagan then praised Americans for having "more churches" and "more libraries" and supporting "voluntarily more symphony orchestras, and opera companies, nonprofit theaters," and for publishing "more books than all the other nations of the world put together."⁶ America would always be idealized apart from its prosperity, its materialism. And yet, for Reagan, the ideals of America are precisely what made it prosper. Staying true to the country's covenant with God, Americans had grown fabulously rich. That, for Reagan, was the point of Winthrop's sermon.

By making *A Model of Christian Charity* so famous during the course of his presidency, Reagan essentially turned it into a text that Democrats had to adopt and adapt. Much as Catholic usages of Matthew 5:14 in the seventeenth century forced Protestants to reinterpret it, so in the twentieth century Reagan heightened the significance of Winthrop's sermon so much that it could no longer be ignored. As a result, in the 1980s, Democrats began to reconstruct and redeploy *A Model of Christian Charity*, offering a competing account of what Winthrop really meant—and, in turn, what his sermon meant for the making of America.

Mario Cuomo began the process. Entering the second year of his first term as governor of New York in 1984, Cuomo found himself tasked with the keynote address of the Democratic National Convention, which nominated Walter Mondale to run against Reagan. In order to present a competing vision of America, Cuomo addressed head-on the "shining city on a hill" that had become the slogan and catchphrase of Reagan's career. The city shines for only a few, Cuomo charged: "not everyone is sharing in this city's splendor and glory." For the rest, a different city, a darker town, marked the realities of daily life. The United States had been divided into a "Tale of Two Cities," Cuomo argued, and he called on Americans to build a better sense of community. "We must convince them that we don't have to settle for two cities, that we can have one city, indivisible, shining for all of its people."[7] Cuomo's call rang out so loudly that he soon became the focus of Democrats' ambitions. After the success of this single speech, many wanted him to run for president, but he never did.

Instead, the Democratic nomination in 1988 went to Michael Dukakis, the governor of Massachusetts, who in his acceptance speech turned once again to *A Model of Christian Charity*. The rhetorical move that Dukakis made in that speech proved even more powerful than Cuomo's, and despite Dukakis's defeat, his innovation has largely defined Democratic usage of this text ever since. Rather than redirect the language of a "shining city on a hill" into a "Tale of Two Cities," Dukakis focused on a *separate passage* from Winthrop's sermon. Emphasizing community as the keynote of the Democratic Party, Dukakis made that idea foundational to American history, and he did so through his use of Winthrop. "The idea of community," he proclaimed to cheering listeners: "an idea that was planted in the New World by the first Governor of Massachusetts." Then Dukakis quoted *A Model of Christian Charity*: "'We must,' said John Winthrop, 'love one another with a pure heart fervently. We must delight in each other, make each other's condition our own, rejoice together, mourn together, and suffer together … We must,' he said, 'be knit together as one.'" Dukakis closed off this quotation by clarifying exactly what Winthrop intended: "John Winthrop wasn't talking about material success," he explained. "He was talking about a country where each of us asks not only what's in it for some of us, but what's good and what's right for all of us."[8]

Of course, John Winthrop wasn't talking about a "country" at all. Nor did he "plant" the idea of community in the New World. Plenty of people formed plenty of communities for plenty of centuries before the Puritans arrived. Moreover, when Winthrop spoke of mutual affection, he primarily meant a love that flourished within the Body of Christ; he was speaking of the church, not a nation. These differences are not insignificant. Yet in focusing on community, Dukakis narrowed his attention to what was in fact the real intent of Winthrop's text. The point of that sermon, as we have seen, was not the American Dream or the pursuit of wealth. Instead, *A Model of Christian Charity* records Winthrop's fear that a selfish pursuit of gain would corrupt and destroy a "community in peril." When Democrats after Dukakis began to recite Winthrop's lines about rejoicing together, mourning together, laboring and suffering together as one—all lines that went back to the Apostle Paul in Romans 12—they came far closer to capturing the essence of Winthrop's text. What matters, however, is not whether Republicans or Democrats had the better interpretation; what matters is that by 1988, both sides felt the *need* to read and interpret this 1630 sermon. By the time of Dukakis's nomination, *A Model of Christian Charity* had become fundamental to the meaning of America. No one knew that the manuscript itself had been lost, forgotten, and largely ignored for most of American history.

In the coming years, rather than remembering this text's initial irrelevance, Democrats and Republicans both continued to highlight its continuing significance. On the right, Winthrop's "city on a hill" line became part of the official Republican platform. "America had its rendezvous with destiny in 1980," the party announced in 1992. "Faced with crisis at home and abroad, Americans turned to

Republican leadership in the White House." By cutting taxes and bureaucracy, Republicans "vanquished the idea of the almighty state as the supervisor of our daily lives." And that move had far-reaching implications: "In choosing hope over fear, Americans raised a beacon, reminding the world that we are a shining city on a hill, the last best hope for man on earth."[9] Building on this rhetoric, Republicans officially embraced American exceptionalism in their party platform twenty years later. "We are the party of peace through strength," they announced. "Professing American exceptionalism—the conviction that our country holds a unique place and role in human history—we proudly associate ourselves with those Americans of all political stripes who, more than three decades ago in a world as dangerous as today's, came together to advance the cause of freedom."[10] Such an account went straight back to John Winthrop's "city on a hill" sermon, which was fully on display in the 2012 Republican nomination. Apart from Reagan, no political figure has recited Winthrop's "city on a hill" line more often than the Republican presidential candidate of that year, another former governor of Massachusetts, Mitt Romney.

Meanwhile, on the left, Democrats turned increasingly to the lines Dukakis first invoked. Speaking to the Democratic Leadership Council in 1997, President Bill Clinton laid out a "philosophy of opportunity, responsibility, and community"—three key terms to serve as "America's guideposts to the 21st century." When it came time to summarize, Clinton cited Winthrop. "The first American social compact," he proclaimed, "was forged by the Pilgrims braving stormy seas to flee religious persecution and begin anew." One might think he had in mind the Mayflower Compact. For the first 150 years of the United States, that had been the history most often traced—a "social compact" forged aboard the *Mayflower* by Pilgrims in search of civil and religious liberty and leading ultimately to the U.S. Constitution. But instead, Clinton followed that remark by reciting lines from *A Model of Christian Charity*. "As he came to join this colony, John Winthrop told his shipmates gathered in the hold of their ship that in America we must be knit together in this work as one man—rejoice together, mourn together, labor and suffer together, always having before our eyes our community in the work, our community as members of one body." Once again, the Pilgrims and Puritans became one, so that Winthrop's sermon could serve as the starting point of America. Winthrop became for Democrats the prophetic voice of American community.[11]

When Barack Obama took office, he dutifully carried this tradition forward. On May 1, 2013, the National Day of Prayer, he offered the Puritans as the first Americans and used *A Model of Christian Charity* to make his point. "Americans have long turned to prayer both in times of joy and times of sorrow," he explained. "On their voyage to the New World, the earliest settlers prayed that they would 'rejoice together, mourn together, labor, and suffer together, always having before our eyes our commission and community in the work.'" Invoking the blended tradition of Pilgrim and Puritan origins, relying on Winthrop's sermon as the text that mattered most, Obama proclaimed these English colonists "the earliest settlers" of America. And "*from that day forward*," he continued, "Americans have prayed as a means of uniting, guiding, and healing." For Barack Obama, the Pilgrims and the Puritans—through *A Model of Christian Charity*—became the origins of America, the fundamental starting point for all that America means.[12]

Yet the adoption of this story by the Left has also, in recent years, involved a return to the phrase "city on a hill." Dukakis once cut that line in order to shift the focus of Winthrop's sermon and reinterpret it for the modern Left. Obama, two decades later, brought it back. "It was right here, in the waters around us, where the American experiment began," he told a Boston audience in 2006. "As the earliest settlers arrived on the shores of Boston and Salem and Plymouth, they dreamed of building a City upon a Hill. And the world watched, waiting to see if this improbable idea called America would succeed."[13] For Obama, that "improbable idea" meant a difficult yet continuous progress toward a more perfect union. "This union may never be perfect," he claimed, "but generation after generation has shown that it can always be perfected."[14] As Langston Hughes yearned for American promises to be fulfilled and extended to *all* Americans in 1936, so Barack Obama, picking up that rhetoric, tried to turn the story of American exceptionalism into a tale of potential progress. His American exceptionalism told a story of ever-greater inclusion, diversity, dignity, and opportunity. America was not, as it had been for Reagan, "still a beacon, still a magnet for all who must have freedom." Instead, it was *becoming* a beacon, gradually, through the course of time.[15]

So it went through the 1980s, 1990s, and 2000s. On the one side, citation after citation of Winthrop's sermon quoted the "city on a hill" line, from Reagan (the most) to George H. W. Bush to John McCain, Sarah Palin, Herman Cain, Michele Bachmann, Ted Cruz, Marco Rubio, Newt Gingrich, and, most often in recent years, Mitt Romney. On the other side, by and large (though not exclusively), came a competing call to create or revive America's social compact by reciting Winthrop's *other* stirring words and telling a tale of progress, diversity, and community—from Dukakis's innovation to Bill Clinton, Elizabeth Warren, E. J. Dionne, Barack Obama, Hillary Clinton, and many others.[16] In both cases, there lay an underlying sense that *A Model of Christian Charity*, this 1630 lay sermon by the first governor of Massachusetts Bay, had established the essence of the United States ever since—a national character and destiny that had continued "from that day forward."

Yet as Democrats and Republicans both turned increasingly to Winthrop's sermon, the whole idea of "Puritan origins" fell apart in academic circles. If Sacvan Bercovitch and Ronald Reagan had once, unwittingly, reinforced each other's claims, the 1990s saw a radical divergence in how scholars and politicians approached New England. Not only did scholars object to the exceptionalism that often accompanied studies of the Puritans; they also turned against any academic work that treated the past as a set of stepping stones leading *inevitably* from some supposed origin to the present day. Far from a unique origin—isolated, set apart, and driven by an exceptional purpose—early New England increasingly made sense to scholars only within an interconnected frame that spanned the Atlantic Ocean and engaged with events and people all across the Americas. Today, the early English settlers of New England, who always thought of themselves as *English*, can no longer be approached without considering a much broader context of religion, trade, culture, politics, and war. Puritan scholars study the landscape of the seventeenth century through the lens of a vast early American world—all kinds of people and cultures interacting, adapting, and contributing to the making of many different Americas. As Winthrop's "city on a hill" sermon made its way into political rhetoric through the 1990s and beyond, scholars, in contrast, forcefully abandoned the myth of Puritan origins.[17]

Such an abandonment, however, has not necessarily translated beyond the confines of certain academic departments. Some of the best scholars in other disciplines still trace the modern day to a starting point in Puritan New England.[18] Beyond academia, meanwhile, Pilgrims and Puritans still get deployed to explain the meaning of America. Far from the origin of civil and religious liberty, the Puritans have now been called the starting point and cause of religious fanaticism, "fake news," and the "fantasyland" of modern America.[19] Whatever the case or cause, whether in praise or condemnation—and despite all that recent scholars keep trying to say, write, and teach—many Americans continue to locate in Pilgrim Landing and Puritan New England the source of all our successes or woes.

One American who resists this tendency, oddly enough, is Donald Trump. The rhetoric of "America First"—which defines President Trump's agenda—can sometimes seem like the same thing as American exceptionalism, and many Americans no doubt equate the two. In reality, however, these two ways of talking and thinking offer radically different visions of the United States' place and purpose in the world, both with their own long histories. Campaigning without Reagan's "city on a hill," never once quoting *A Model of Christian Charity*, Trump specifically rejected the rhetoric of American exceptionalism.[20]

The main difference between America First and American exceptionalism—on full display during Trump's presidency—concerns the use of origin stories. When President Reagan ended his career on Winthrop's sermon, he called Americans to study history, for as he declared, "if we forget what we did, we won't know who we are." So, too, in 1997 President Clinton asserted, "At the dawn of the new century, we ought to remember Mr. Winthrop as we write a new social compact."[21] Historically, American presidents have often told us to remember; we must learn and study our past in order to move forward in the right direction. Often, that past has been more imagined than actual, but it has always been considered essential: American exceptionalism ties a sense of what America stands for to a claim about how America began.

America First, in contrast, dispenses with history. President Trump campaigned on the vague notion that once we were great and now we are not, but he never offered any details about what he meant or how he understood America's past. *When* were we great? What did greatness mean? How did it look or feel?[22] The history of America did not matter and almost never appeared. Instead, America First offers a philosophy of nations. It claims that all countries are the same, *including the United States*, and all share the same fundamental goal: to win. In that sense, "greatness" has nothing to do with historic ideals or bedrock values rooted somewhere deep in the American past. It is, rather, a measure of material wealth. It amounts to having the most money, the biggest military, the best airports. And for that reason—because greatness amounts to gain—there is nothing that finally sets America apart. Trump has consistently proposed a universal purpose for all nations: *every* country protects itself, advances its interests, and prospers its own. That, and that alone, is the point and purpose of a nation.

Both forms of rhetoric have their own particular hazards. The idea that our country has a distinct history and unique purpose has always implied both a higher morality to guide us and a sense of God's election—a belief long rooted in a myth of Puritan origins and more recently tied to Winthrop's sermon. That conviction not only has erased from memory all kinds of other people and events in the American past but also has led the nation down some very dubious and dangerous paths. John O'Sullivan, who coined the phrase "Manifest Destiny," declared that the destiny of the United States would be "to establish on earth the moral dignity and salvation of man—the immutable truth and beneficence of God. For this blessed mission to the nations of the world, which are shut out from the life-giving light of truth, has America been chosen."[23] Expressed in the language of Manifest Destiny, that "mission to the nations of the world" involved a brutal confiscation of land; an unwillingness or inability to recognize the civilization, culture, or contributions of other peoples; and an extension of American interests dressed up in the guise of being good for all the world. If we call or consider our nation the special messenger of God, we are not likely to be found listening to, or learning from, others.

The hazards of America First, in contrast, come not from a sense of election but from a worldview based in the utter absence of any higher moral good. America First urges self-interest in a world seen as a survival of the fittest, where winners make losers and losers have no claim to the sympathy of others. The rich get richer; the poor stay poor; and the bonds between individuals and nations remain abstract, insubstantial, and unimportant. In utter contrast to *A Model of Christian Charity*, the goal in America First is to get ahead, and getting ahead means leaving others behind.

For all the ways that words spin out of control whenever Trump attempts to use them, he has actually been quite clear when it comes to talking about this national purpose. In his inaugural address, for example, he announced, "At the center of this movement is a crucial conviction: that a nation exists to serve its citizens." In such a pronouncement, the United States became, again, just "*a* nation"—not the "city on a hill" or "the indispensable nation" or the "nation of nations" or "the last best hope of mankind," as others have proclaimed. It was just one nation among many. And, Trump continued, "it is the right of all nations to put their own interests first." Therefore, "from this day forward, a new vision will govern our land. From this moment on, it's going to be America First."[24]

The basic premise of "America First," in other words, contradicts the main assumptions of American exceptionalism. American exceptionalism has always said that because of the country's unique history, emanating from Pilgrim Landing and Puritan New England, the United States stands for a distinct set of values that it must model and spread, whatever they might be—democracy, religious liberty, freedom, free enterprise, diversity, human dignity, self-government, and so on. It is a thousand points of light, a candle, a beacon, a city on a hill. America First, however, claims that such views have caused a great deal of harm. It is "a dangerous idea," Trump has insisted, to believe "that we could make Western democracies out of countries that had no experience or interests in becoming a Western democracy." According to him, "We've made other countries rich while the wealth, strength and confidence of our country has dissipated over the horizon." In the 2005 inaugural,

President George W. Bush announced, "It is the policy of the United States to seek and support the growth of democratic movements and institutions in every nation and culture, with the ultimate goal of ending tyranny in our world." In 2015, Trump declared, "I want to take everything back from the world that we've given them."[25] According to Trump, American exceptionalism has created the very problems that America First must solve.

The difference between American exceptionalism and America First can be seen most clearly in President Trump's speeches to foreign nations. Addressing the United Nations on September 19, 2017, Trump called all countries to "lift the world to new heights" and shape a "better future." That kind of soaring rhetoric tied Trump to typical American rhetoric, but he soon took his own path by emphasizing one particular word: *sovereignty*. Winthrop's sermon has been used to advance all sorts of different values, projects, and policies through the years, but never once has it been cited to strengthen or defend the idea of sovereignty. For Trump, however, sovereignty—tied to self-interest—is always what has mattered most. "We do not expect diverse countries to share the same cultures, traditions, or even systems of government," he explained. "But we do expect all nations to uphold these two core sovereign duties: to respect the interests of their own people and the rights of every other sovereign nation." A few months later, Trump repeated these positions. "We are not going to let the United States be taken advantage of anymore," he asserted. "I am always going to put America first the same way that I expect all of you in this room to put your countries first." The doctrine of America First alleges, in short, that the whole world will improve if every nation maintains its sovereignty and becomes *more*, not less, self-interested. For if we all seek our own gain, Trump asserts, all will be better off. When he speaks to foreign leaders, therefore, Trump envisions "strong, sovereign, and independent nations, thriving in peace and commerce with others."[26] When he speaks to Americans, however, he simply calls on us to win. Either way, his rhetoric has offered no moral vision of freedom, democracy, opportunity, immigration, asylum, or any other traditional term of American exceptionalism. The "city on a hill" of Winthrop's sermon—which has defined the vision of the Right from Reagan to Romney—has no place in the rhetoric of Donald Trump.

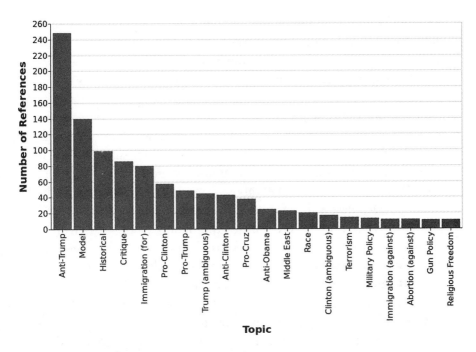

Figure 19: This graph represents the analysis of eleven hundred published usages of "city on a hill" during the 2016 campaign, indicating the number of references found by topic. Courtesy Humanities Digital Workshop, Washington University in St. Louis.

It should not surprise us, therefore, that during the 2016 presidential campaign, the "city on a hill" phrase showed up most often in *opposition* to Donald Trump. Sorting through over 1,100 articles, letters, and blogs that used this line in the 2016 election, we can see exactly what it meant in that campaign (figure 19). Of all the publications where it appeared, nearly 250—almost a quarter of the total—were written against Donald Trump. Less than 50 supported him. That usage remained true regardless of party. We sorted the findings into "right," "left," and "unclear," primarily through the self-identification of writers, and when we focused only on the 350 cases of conservative writers, 85 appearances of the phrase "city on a hill" came in anti-Trump articles; only 48 supported him. By a margin of almost two to one, *conservatives*, not liberals, used the main slogan of American exceptionalism to oppose the candidacy of

Donald Trump. In other words, searching for the phrase "city on a hill" during the 2016 election turned out to be a good way of locating blogs, articles, and public comments critical of Donald Trump.[27]

Beyond opposing Trump, the phrase "city on a hill" was frequently used in support of immigrants and refugees. That makes sense, since a strong and clear difference between America First and American exceptionalism arises in the case of immigration. America First, in short, sees immigrants as present-day threats. It never thinks of immigration or asylum in relation to American history. Trump has never talked about Americans as a nation of diverse peoples descended from those who came here long ago. He has offered no story or memory of the nation at all, apart from a vague notion of lost greatness. In his rhetoric, there has been no rise from immigration, no mix of cultures, no fleeing from oppression in the American past—not even the Pilgrim voyage supposedly undertaken in pursuit of civil and religious liberty. For Donald Trump, there has always been only the present day, only sovereignty and self-interest now. It is as though he has attempted to freeze time, to keep people in place, to remove from memory any history of passage, settlement, migration, or colonization. Without any understanding of the development of America, he has no way of incorporating a movement of people from one land to another.

American exceptionalism, in contrast, has often been used to emphasize a story of immigration and asylum. That was the story that guided Jeremy Belknap as he founded the MHS. And that was the story that remained in place for President Reagan, who explicitly compared John Winthrop—the supposed founder of America—to a *refugee*. According to Reagan, Winthrop was the first of the world's oppressed who came here in search of freedom. Throughout his career, Reagan used *A Model of Christian Charity* to draw a history lesson leading from the Pilgrims to the present day, a story in which America had always served as a beacon of liberty and a land of hope "for all the pilgrims from all the lost places who are hurtling through the darkness, toward home." Unsurprisingly, then, when the phrase "city on a hill" pinpointed a specific policy during the 2016 election, it showed up most often in the context of immigration. And in almost eight times as many articles (eighty to twelve), "city on a hill" *supported* the cause of immigrants and refugees. Writers called on the country to be an asylum of liberty *in keeping with historic values*, claiming that we ought to open our borders to the oppressed, that we should embrace all those who are searching for freedom and opportunity—that we should, in short, be a "city on a hill."

In the age of Donald Trump, therefore, *A Model of Christian Charity* seems to have moved into a new phase. Whereas it once served as the opening text in a tale of American exceptionalism embraced by the Right and adapted by the Left, it now (as of early 2019) serves primarily as a wedge text between two types of conservatives. It separates the Reagan remnant from the tribe of Trump. More than any other document, it seems, Winthrop's sermon isolates the striking differences between American exceptionalism and America First. In one form of rhetoric, an American story beginning in Puritan New England makes the United States the leading player in a divinely guided history of liberty, leading the world to redemption by modeling and spreading any number of national values. In the other form of rhetoric, the United States has the same two values as every other nation: sovereignty and self-interest, which aim at nothing other than what everyone everywhere is presumed to want—material wealth.

The more the rhetoric of America First rises, therefore, the farther *A Model of Christian Charity* will fall. Politicians may soon ditch it as a relic of the past, no longer able to deliver an election. If this happens, then Winthrop's sermon will have thrived and perished in a relatively short period of time. Unimportant in its own day, not printed until 1838, mostly neglected for the next hundred years, *A Model of Christian Charity* first became popular at the opening of the Cold War, reached its apex of fame in the 1980s, embedded itself in political rhetoric for the next twenty years, and now, perhaps, is passing away. Searches for the phrase "city on a hill" will bring an endless series of hits, but the politicians most devoted to that line seem—in 2019 at any rate—least able to win. Plenty of politicians may still be able to defeat the rhetoric of "America First," its proponents, and the president who stands at its helm, but they may do so now without ever calling the United States a "city on a hill." Winthrop's sermon, first considered fundamental to the meaning of America in the middle of the twentieth century, may not last long in the twenty-first.

Coda
The Death of a Sermon

O N DECEMBER 5, 2018, Americans gathered for the funeral of their forty-first president, George Herbert Walker Bush. A little more than halfway through the ceremony, the Reverend Randolph Hollerith, dean of Washington National Cathedral, rose and read from Matthew 5:14. "Jesus said that you are the light of the world," he pronounced. "A city on a hill cannot be hidden."

It was a fitting text for President Bush. Following the eight years of Reagan's administration, he extended his predecessor's vision, overseeing the breakup of the Soviet Union and the close of the Cold War. These were the last two presidents of that great strife, and both came to the end of their life with the phrase "city on a hill" ringing in the hall. When Reagan died, in 2004, it was George H. W. Bush himself who reminded Americans of those all-important words. "He believed in America," Bush declared, "so he made it his shining city on a hill." Justice Sandra Day O'Connor explicitly linked that line back to *A Model of Christian Charity*. Pulling a few quotes from the last couple paragraphs of the text—the only paragraphs that had appeared in Robert C. Winthrop's popular 1867 printing of the *Life and Letters of John Winthrop*—O'Connor offered "a reading from a sermon delivered in 1630 by the Pilgrim leader John Winthrop, who was aboard the ship the *Arbella* on his way from England to the Massachusetts Bay Colony."[1] Winthrop, we know, was not a "Pilgrim," and he almost certainly did not deliver this sermon aboard the *Arbella* to a handful of Puritan followers. But the story had become so famous that by the time Reagan died, it would have been impossible to bury him without it.

In 2016, twelve years after Reagan's funeral, Americans elected a president who saw no need for Winthrop's sermon or the "city on a hill." Donald Trump rejected American exceptionalism in favor of America First, offering little by way of American history and declaring that it is the right of all nations to put their own interests first. Have the deaths of Reagan and Bush spelled the end of *Christian Charity*? Did these two presidents take that sermon to the grave?

It is impossible to know. The story of a text is not like the biography of a person. A person is born, lives, and dies. But the death of a sermon can never be pronounced. Texts come into the world, live, speak, die, reappear, pass away, resurrect. Some rise to prominence and become as public and as visible as a city upon a hill. Others remain present though no one sees them—latent texts filled with possible lives, whiling away the time in a national archive or a forgotten drawer. Still others pass away so completely that it seems they could never be found, known, studied, interpreted, or put to use again. These trajectories are not mutually exclusive. After all, Winthrop's sermon itself seemed to have died and disappeared, passing out of the world almost at the very moment it was proclaimed. One letter written sometime in the seventeenth century testifies that someone knew about this text. Beyond that one man, no one else seems to have noticed or cared.

This first death of Winthrop's sermon can be seen in the Capitol Rotunda, the place where both Ronald Reagan and George H. W. Bush lay in state. Eight large paintings line the wall, depicting various origin stories of America. They begin with the nation itself: *The Declaration of Independence*, *The Surrender of General Burgoyne*, *The Surrender of Lord Cornwallis*, and *General George Washington Resigning His Commission*. The artist John Trumbull painted these images after the War of 1812, and all were hung in the Capitol in 1826, celebrating fifty years since the United States had declared itself independent. A decade later, Congress cast the country's origins further back. In the midst of anti-immigrant and anti-Catholic

fervor, at a time when Andrew Jackson pursued a ruthless campaign of Indian Removal, as slavery continued to spread its horrors
both in the nation and beyond its borders, American exceptionalism seemed everywhere on the rise. It was the age of Emerson, the
dawn of O'Sullivan, the era of Tocqueville. And it was at this moment, in 1836, that Congress commissioned four new paintings to
capture the true history of America.

Two focus on the Spanish and two on the English. The Spanish
paintings take a typical approach, celebrating them for finding the
"New World" while condemning them for barbarous conquests.
Swords, spears, and crosses angle against each other in a sea of
metal. The images of English settlement, meanwhile, offer a very
different tale. *The Baptism of Pocahontas* commemorates the conversion of a Native American as a sign of English civilization, while an
even more powerful narrative informs Robert W. Weir's *Embarkation of the Pilgrims*. There we find the story of a nation founded by
Pilgrims in search of civil and religious freedom, committed from
its very conception to the care and providence of God. Weir's Pilgrims surround military gear, but unlike in the paintings of the
Spanish, it is piled on the floor, unused, while a minister opens the
New Testament above. In this painting, we encounter the influential myth of white civilization and stability that would continue to
spread throughout the nineteenth century—the dissemination of
Anglo-Saxon Protestantism from New England to the nation as a
new sort of revelation for the world.[2]

Among these eight paintings in the Capitol Rotunda, which
surrounded Reagan and Bush as they lay in state, many absences
appear. Native Americans emerge only as conquered or converted.
African Americans are nowhere to be found.[3] But in addition to
these clear voids and vacancies, another silence becomes strikingly
apparent: there is no image of Winthrop. The paintings, after all,
had been commissioned before *A Model of Christian Charity* was
ever found or known. Even after Winthrop's sermon materialized,
it languished for over a century—cast aside as contributing nothing
to the American tale. For that reason, Winthrop and the *Arbella*
make no entrance in the Frieze of American History that circled
Reagan's casket just above the eight historic paintings. These stone
carvings were first sketched in 1859, two decades after Winthrop's

"city on a hill" sermon had been printed. But again, no one paid it any mind. Eventually, only in the pressures of the Cold War—and only through the labors of Perry Miller—Winthrop's sermon emerged as fundamental to the meaning of America.

When George H. W. Bush passed away, many commentators spoke in elegiac tones of his legacy. Something, they felt, had been lost with his death. Some significant period in American history had come to a close. For some, it seemed as though the time of great politicians facing great strife had reached its end. If Winthrop's sermon is closely identified with the Cold War in American history, then it may be that the election of Donald Trump and the funeral of George H. W. Bush will mark the beginning of the end of Winthrop's text.

Or, conversely, it may be that Bush's funeral will give an old phrase new life—a stage in the "city on a hill" that may return Winthrop to his place in history, while restoring the words of Jesus to his Sermon on the Mount. For when Rev. Hollerith recited Matthew 5:14, he did not reference Winthrop at all. He did not attempt to define a two-hundred-year-old nation through a four-hundred-year-old sermon or a two-thousand-year-old passage of scripture. Most markedly, he did not stop at verse 14. "A city on a hill cannot be hidden," he read. "Neither do people light a lamp and put it under a bowl. Instead, they put it on its stand, and it gives light to everyone in the house. In the same way, let your light shine before men that they may see your good deeds and praise your father in heaven." In the context of Bush's funeral, the "city on a hill" seemed, for the first time, *personal*. It was about the behavior of one man, not the calling of a nation. And it seemed to mourn, along with the other speeches of that day, the passing of a time—regardless of politics—when the elected representatives of the nation might garner some basic sense of respect for their leadership. If "city on a hill" survives this period, it may come to signal new values altogether: civility, decorum, stateliness, grandeur, the dignity of elected office. It might shift from identifying our nation as a model civilization to hoping that any future president will act as a model citizen.

It might. It might not. The possible lives of a text, like its potential death, lie forever in suspense. The story of Winthrop's sermon demonstrates nothing less. After being lost, forgotten, and ignored for over three centuries, *A Model of Christian Charity* suddenly emerged in the twentieth century as "the best sermon of the millennium" and the "cultural key text" of American history. Its rags-to-riches rise reveals the way national stories take shape and shows us in dramatic fashion how those tales continue to influence competing visions of the country—the many different meanings of America that emerge from rediscoveries, reinventions, and reinterpretations of its literary past.

Notes

Introduction

1. For the data, see Jeremy Yamashiro, Abram Van Engen, Henry L. Roediger III, "American Origins: Political Divides in U.S. Collective Memory," *Memory Studies* 15, no. 1 (2022). We used the word "America" to test whether people associated it primarily with the United States or with a territory beyond the United States. Throughout this book, I use "America" as the writers did whom I study, who often meant the United States, but most scholars today do not refer to the United States of America as "America," a term that designates a much broader territory than a single nation. Similarly, throughout this book I capitalize "Puritan" to indicate the *idea* of a coherent people that came to stand as the origin of the nation. But most scholars today do not capitalize "puritan" in order to indicate the vast disagreements and variety covered by the term.

2. John Winthrop, "A Modell of Christian Charity," in *Winthrop Papers*, vol. 2 (Boston: Massachusetts Historical Society, 1931), 295; Ronald Reagan, "Farewell Address to the Nation," January 11, 1989, accessed at the American Presidency Project, https://www.presidency.ucsb.edu/docu ments/farewell-address-the-nation.

3. Andrew Delbanco, *The Puritan Ordeal* (Cambridge, MA: Harvard University Press, 1989), 72; Sacvan Bercovitch, "Puritan Origins Revisited: The 'City on a Hill' as a Model of Tradition and Innovation," in *Early America Re-explored: New Readings in Colonial, Early National, and Antebellum Culture*, ed. Klaus Schmidt and Fritz Fleischmann (New York: Peter Lang, 2000), 31; Peter Gomes, "A Pilgrim's Progress: The Bible as Civic Blueprint," *New York Times Magazine*, 1999, https://archive.nytimes.com/ www.nytimes.com/library/magazine/millennium/m1/gomes.html. Gomes offers a solid, quick reading of the sermon, despite the misleading title.

4. For the sermon as commonplace, see Francis Bremer, "The Heritage of John Winthrop: Religion along the Stour Valley, 1548–1630," *New England Quarterly* 70, no. 4 (1997): 515–547. For the 1640s letter, see Henry Jacie [Jessey] to John Winthrop Jr., ca. February 1635, in *Winthrop Papers*, vol. 3 (Boston: Massachusetts Historical Society, 1945), 188–189. As Jerome McGann has pointed out, the contents of this letter indicate it was written after 1642. Jerome McGann, "'Christian Charity,' A Sacred American Text: Fact, Truth, Method," *Textual Cultures* 12, no. 1 (2019): 27–52. I am grateful to Jerry for sharing this manuscript with me before publication and for our conversations about "Christian Charity."

5. See Richard Gamble, *In Search of the City on a Hill: The Making and Unmaking of an American Myth* (London: Continuum, 2012), chap. 4; Daniel T. Rodgers, *As a City on a Hill: The Story of America's Most Famous Lay Sermon* (Princeton, NJ: Princeton University Press, 2018).

6. Charles F. Richardson, *American Literature: 1607–1885* (New York: Putnam, 1910), 91.

7. Google Books scans printed works, mostly gathered from research libraries, and then converts them into searchable text files through optical character recognition (OCR). We approached Google Books through the Google Books Corpora (https://googlebooks.byu.edu/x.asp), which is essentially a more scholarly version of the database. There are obvious problems with using such a large collection to represent the rise or fall of a single phrase or sermon. First, the OCR does not always work well. Second, for as large as this collection might be, it still has certain limitations. Since it mostly gathers books from university libraries, its collections are skewed (dime novels and genre fiction, for example, will not be well represented). Finally, and most obviously, all this scanning requires texts that have been printed. Manuscripts go missing. Our collection and findings therefore offer a representative, but not comprehensive, account of how the phrases "city on a hill," "city upon a hill," "city set on a hill," and "city set upon a hill" have been used from 1800 to 2015. Other databases (EEBO and Evans in particular) can be searched for how these phrases appear in pre-1800 publications, but to maintain consistency and to see in particular what happened after Winthrop's sermon was printed in 1838, we graphed the Google Books data. The graphs and data can be found online at The City on a Hill Archive we are constructing. See https://doi.org/10.7936/cityonahill.

8. Reagan, "Farewell Address."

9. Reagan.

10. Reagan.

11. Reagan (emphasis added).

12. See Kathleen Donegan, *Seasons of Misery: Catastrophe and Colonial Settlements in Early America* (Philadelphia: University of Pennsylvania Press, 2014).

13. For the most complete and authoritative biography of John Winthrop, see Francis J. Bremer, *John Winthrop: America's Forgotten Founding Father* (New York: Oxford University Press, 2003), which includes a very good reading of Winthrop's sermon. For an older, still excellent biography of Winthrop and his world, see Edmund S. Morgan, *The Puritan Dilemma: The Story of John Winthrop*, 3rd ed. (London: Pearson, 2006).

14. For a recent history of the Pilgrims, see Francis J. Bremer, *One Small Candle: The Story of the Plymouth Puritans and the Beginning of English New England* (New York: Oxford University Press, forthcoming). For a recent history of transatlantic Puritanism, see Michael P. Winship, *Hot Protestants: A History of Puritanism in England and America* (New Haven, CT: Yale University Press, 2019).

Chapter One. The Mystery of Winthrop's Manuscript

1. John Winthrop, "A Modell of Christian Charity," in *Winthrop Papers*, vol. 2 (Boston: Massachusetts Historical Society, 1931), 282. Winthrop's language of affection, some scholars have claimed, is nothing more than a "sleight of hand," a good trick to make people accept and obey the authorities in place. See, for example, Scott Michaelsen, "John Winthrop's 'Model' Covenant and the Company Way," *Early American Literature* 27 (1992): 90; and Sacvan Bercovitch, "Puritan Origins Revisited: The 'City upon a Hill' as a Model of Tradition and Innovation," in *Early America Re-explored: New Readings in Colonial, Early National, and Antebellum Culture*, ed. Klaus Schmidt and Fritz Fleischmann (New York: Peter Lang, 2000), 36.

2. Mark Valeri, *Heavenly Merchandize: How Religion Shaped Commerce in Puritan America* (Princeton, NJ: Princeton University Press, 2010), 57. Stephen Innes, who also focuses on the economics of the sermon, mashes the two halves together as "communal capitalism." Innes, *Creating the Commonwealth: The Economic Culture of Puritan New England* (New York: Norton, 1995), 92. Various commentators have noted the division in Winthrop's sermon and sought various ways to unite it. Francis Bremer, for example, notes that Winthrop "emphasize[s] both the hierarchical and communal elements of society" and links them as "commonplaces of the time." Bremer, *John Winthrop: America's Forgotten Founding Father* (New York: Oxford University Press, 2003), 175–176. Michael Colacurcio argues that Winthrop has an "unmistakably affective center" to an "otherwise crisp version of 'contractual absolutism.'" Colacurcio, *Godly Letters: The Literature of the American Puritans* (Notre Dame, IN: University of Notre Dame Press, 2006), 429. Edmund S. Morgan resolves the dual emphases by seeing the sermon as part of a communion service at sea. Morgan, "John Winthrop's 'Modell of Christian Charity' in a Wider Context," *Huntington Library Quarterly* 50 (1987): 145. Ivy Schweitzer

asserts that Winthrop's sermon "yoke[s] together two contradictory images of 'Christian Charity'"—the secular world of business and the sacred world of regenerate saints—through the implications of "familiar Commerce." Schweitzer, "John Winthrop's 'Model' of American Affiliation," *Early American Literature* 40, no. 3 (2005): 446. Daniel T. Rodgers, meanwhile, splits the sermon into four parts, each concerned with a different theme or idea. See Rodgers, *As a City on a Hill: The Story of America's Most Famous Lay Sermon* (Princeton, NJ: Princeton University Press, 2018), chap. 1. Matthew Holland also divides the sermon into four parts. See Holland, *Bonds of Affection: Civic Charity and the Making of America—Winthrop, Jefferson, and Lincoln* (Washington, DC: Georgetown University Press, 2007), part 1.

3. Winthrop, "Christian Charity," 284, 289; Winthrop, *The Journal of John Winthrop, 1630–1649*, ed. Richard S. Dunn, James Savage, and Laetitia Yeandle (Cambridge, MA: Harvard University Press, 1996), 726. Hugh Dawson was the first to note corruptions in the surviving manuscript. See Dawson, "'Christian Charitie' as Colonial Discourse: Rereading Winthrop's Sermon in Its English Context," *Early American Literature* 33 (1998): 114–148. Rodgers compares the language of *Christian Charity* to Winthrop's language elsewhere to argue for his authorship. See Rodgers, *As a City on a Hill*, chap. 1. For the challenge to Winthrop's authorship, see Jerome McGann, "'Christian Charity,' a Sacred American Text: Fact, Truth, Method," *Textual Cultures* 12, no. 1 (2019): 27–52. McGann argues that the sermon was by George Philips, the minister on board the *Arbella*. That is plausible. In discussion, we also considered that the verses in Winthrop's journal could have been notes Winthrop took while listening to another (George Philips) preach. In what follows I still assume that this sermon was given by Winthrop, in part because it sounds like what he says elsewhere, but I find some of McGann's evidence compelling. Since I am most interested in how this sermon has come down to us (especially its mythic usage in American culture), the actual authorship is not as critical to my claims. Suffice it to say, a great deal of mystery surrounds the composition and delivery of this sermon.

4. William Perkins, *The Art of Prophesying* (first translated into English 1606; repr., Carlisle, PA: Banner of Truth Trust, 1996), 48.

5. On Robert Cushman's sermon and its possible influence on John Winthrop, demonstrating similarities and contrasts in emphasis, see David A. Lupher, *Greeks, Romans, and Pilgrims: Classical Receptions in Early New England* (Leiden: Brill, 2017), 290–294. Both Gamble and Rodgers claim that it is not a sermon. I disagree. See Richard Gamble, *In Search of the City on a Hill: The Making and Unmaking of an American Myth* (London: Continuum, 2012), 31; and Rodgers, *As a City on a Hill*, 24–29. Rodgers argues in part that because Puritan ministers did not write out their sermons, this text cannot be a sermon. But we have reams of Puritan ser-

mons from the seventeenth century, which had to be written out at some point to be published. As Mark A. Noll reports, "Massachusetts was the only colony where more sermons (2,067) . . . were published than government items (1,931) and the colony where by far the most sermons were printed (65 percent of the colonial total)." Noll, *In the Beginning was the Word: The Bible in American Public Life, 1492–1783* (New York: Oxford University Press, 2016), 112. It is true that Puritan ministers did not typically write out their sermons; but listeners did, and they circulated those texts. The fact that we do not have an original in Winthrop's handwriting actually makes it more likely that this was a sermon Winthrop preached, which was then heard, noted, and composed by listeners within the massive sermon culture of seventeenth-century Puritanism. The essential starting point on Puritan sermons is Harry S. Stout, *New England Soul: Preaching and Religious Culture in Colonial New England* (New York: Oxford University Press, 1986). See also Meredith Neuman, *Jeremiah's Scribes: Creating Sermon Literature in Puritan New England* (Philadelphia: University of Pennsylvania Press, 2013). As Francis Bremer explains, *A Model of Christian Charity* "was the first recorded lay sermon preached by Winthrop, but it would not be the last." Bremer, *Lay Empowerment and the Development of Puritanism* (Basingstoke, UK: Palgrave Macmillan, 2015), 76. For the first argument that Winthrop delivered the sermon in England, see Dawson, "'Christian Charitie' as Colonial Discourse," 117–148. For the most compelling reading of the sermon within that place and context, see Bremer, *John Winthrop*, 173–186.

6. Even scholars such as Richard Gamble, who do not think of this text as a sermon, admit that "in its structure, the *Arbella* discourse certainly does resemble the classic Puritan sermon format as developed by the Cambridge minister William Perkins in his influential book, *The Art of Prophesying*" (Gamble, *In Search*, 31).

7. Geneva Bible (1599), 1212.

8. Theodore Dwight Bozeman offers an excellent analysis of the so-called national covenant, demonstrating that the covenant of grace, as preached and applied, tied together self and society in similar ways. See Bozeman, "Federal Theology and the 'National Covenant': An Elizabethan Presbyterian Case Study," *Church History* 61, no. 4 (1992): 394–407.

9. Winthrop, "Christian Charity," 288 (italics added).

10. That remains true even if my claim about the missing opening verse for this sermon is wrong. Suppose that this text is a complete "discourse" or "treatise" rather than an incomplete sermon. It remains the case that these Pauline verses are central to understanding it. A web of biblical passages in the Geneva Bible links Galatians 5:13–14 to Romans 13:8–10, and these passages inform Winthrop's imagination as he attempts to describe a godly society. For a further elaboration of that point and discussion of the other Pauline models informing Winthrop's sermon, see

Abram Van Engen, "Origins and Last Farewells: Bible Wars, Textual Form, and the Making of American History," *New England Quarterly* 86, no. 4 (2013): 543–592.

11. Winthrop, "Christian Charity," 289–290.

12. Winthrop, "Christian Charity," 288–289, 293. For a fuller explanation of how sympathy forms the heart of this sermon and fits with Puritan culture more broadly, see Abram Van Engen, *Sympathetic Puritans: Calvinist Fellow Feeling in Early New England* (New York: Oxford University Press, 2015), chap. 1.

13. Or as Winthrop put it, so "that every man might have need of other, and from hence they might be all knit more nearly together in bonds of brotherly affection" ("Christian Charity," 282). Winthrop's model dipped into a deep well of Calvinist thinking about gratitude. See B. A. Gerrish, *Grace and Gratitude: The Eucharistic Theology of John Calvin* (Minneapolis: Fortress, 1993).

14. Ronald Reagan, "Farewell Address to the Nation," January 11, 1989, accessed at the American Presidency Project, https://www.presidency.ucsb .edu/documents/farewell-address-the-nation.

15. As David Hall has observed, "Allusions to 'liberty' were everywhere [in Puritan writing], in part because English Protestants appropriated the concept from passages in the New Testament where St. Paul contrasted the obligations of Jewish law with the freedom of Christians 'called unto liberty' (Galatians 5:13)." He explains, "Here as elsewhere, the word denoted responsibility or obedience, in contrast to a liberty that was lawless." Hall, *A Reforming People: Puritanism and the Transformation of Public Life in New England* (New York: Knopf, 2011), 15.

16. For Winthrop's "little speech" on liberty (1645), see *Winthrop's Journal: History of New England, 1630–1649*, vol. 2, ed. J. Franklin Jameson, Elibron Classics Reprint (New York: Scribner, 1908), 237–239.

17. John Cotton, *Gods Promise to His Plantation* (London, 1630), 6; Cotton, "Cotton's Reasons for His Removal to New-England," in *Chronicles of the First Planters of the Colony of Massachusetts Bay, 1623–1636*, ed. Alexander Young (Boston, 1846), 441 (emphasis added); Cotton, "To Lord Say and Sele, 1636," in *Puritans in the New World: A Critical Anthology*, ed. David D. Hall (Princeton, NJ: Princeton University Press, 2004), 172–175.

18. This point is best explained in Theodore Dwight Bozeman, *To Live Ancient Lives: The Primitivist Dimension in Puritanism* (Chapel Hill: University of North Carolina Press, 1988). On Puritans' reforms and their relation to politics, see Hall, *Reforming People*, and Michael Winship, *Godly Republicanism: Puritans, Pilgrims, and Massachusetts' City on a Hill* (Cambridge, MA: Harvard University Press, 2012). For an excellent review of these books, see Mark Peterson, "Why They Mattered: The Return of Politics to Puritan New England," *Modern Intellectual History* 10, no. 3 (2013): 683–696.

Chapter Two. The Significance of Winthrop's Bible

1. Some scholars have known the actual verses Winthrop quotes. See, for example, Sacvan Bercovitch, *The American Jeremiad* (1978; repr., Madison: University of Wisconsin Press, 2012), 40. For the full analysis of this error in the Norton and Heath anthologies, along with Winthrop's use of scripture here and throughout his sermon, see Abram Van Engen, "Origins and Last Farewells: Bible Wars, Textual Form, and the Making of American History," *New England Quarterly* 86, no. 4 (2013): 543–592. Since the publication of that article, the *Norton Anthology of American Literature* has corrected its error for the ninth edition.

2. John Winthrop, "A Modell of Christian Charity," in *Winthrop Papers*, vol. 2 (Boston: Massachusetts Historical Society, 1931), 283, 284. This assertion is based on analyzing fifty-five biblical passages in Winthrop's sermon. In all cases, the quotations match the Geneva Bible or diverge from all known translations.

3. On the popularity of the Geneva Bible, see David Daniell, *The Bible in English: Its History and Influence* (New Haven, CT: Yale University Press, 2003), 294–295. For a good, quick history of English Bible translations, see Mark A. Noll, *In the Beginning Was the Word: The Bible in American Public Life, 1492–1783* (New York: Oxford University Press, 2016), chap. 2. As Noll writes of the publication of the Geneva Bible in 1560, "Almost immediately it became the dominant version" (58).

4. "In all, the commentary exceeded 300,000 words in length and constituted, in effect, a self-contained theological library for common readers." Harry S. Stout, "Word and Order in Colonial New England," in *The Bible in America: Essays in Cultural History*, ed. Nathan Hatch and Mark A. Noll (New York: Oxford University Press, 1982), 21.

5. On this point, Christopher Hill is right. Admitting that the "marginal notes which have possible social or political significance ... are only a small part of the message of the Geneva translation," he insists, "Nevertheless, the 'seditious' notes were there to be seized on by students of the scriptures who were looking for them; they had all the authority of the printed text, and of the Geneva." Hill, *The English Bible and the Seventeenth-Century Revolution* (London: Penguin, 1993), 62. One does not need to endorse all of Hill's conclusions to accept his account of these marginal notes.

6. William Barlow, *The Summe and Substance of the Conference . . . at Hampton Court, January 14, 1603* (London, 1604), 46–47. King James specifically cited the notes on 2 Chronicles 15:16 and Exodus 1:19–20, which endorsed disobeying civil rulers out of a deeper obedience to God.

7. Andrew Barnaby and Joan Wry argue that the KJV project aided King James in his desire "to promote the status of the Crown." Barnaby and Wry, "Authorized Versions: Measure for Measure and the Politics of Bible Translation," *Renaissance Quarterly* 51, no. 4 (1998): 1228.

8. On Bible usage, see P. Marion Simms, *The Bible in America: Versions That Have Played Their Part in the Making of the Republic* (New York: Wilson-Erickson, 1936), 90. Daniell calls the inception of the KJV "a political act by reactionary bishops against Geneva Bibles" (*Bible in English*, 294). See also Hill, *English Bible*, 63–64; and David Norton, *A History of the English Bible as Literature* (Cambridge: Cambridge University Press, 2000), 90–91. Numerous scholars have tempered the idea of deeply divided loyalties, asserting that a Calvinist consensus persisted throughout the reign of James I and splintered with the rise of Charles I. See, for example, Patrick Collinson, *The Elizabethan Puritan Movement* (London: Jonathan Cape, 1967); and Peter Lake, *Moderate Puritans and the Elizabethan Church* (Cambridge: Cambridge University Press, 1982). Yet even if one does not accept a divide between Puritans and anti-Puritans in 1604, it is clear that James I sided with bishops against Puritan leaders. For the anti-Puritanism of King James, see Michael Winship, *Godly Republicanism: Puritans, Pilgrims, and a City on a Hill* (Cambridge, MA: Harvard University Press, 2012), 68–71.

9. Stout, "Word and Order," 22; Arnold Hunt, *The Art of Hearing: English Preachers and Their Audiences, 1590–1640* (Cambridge: Cambridge University Press, 2010), 68–69.

10. For a good book on the closed canon of scripture, helping to make sense of how Puritans could both quote and alter scripture, see David Holland, *Sacred Borders: Continuing Revelation and Canonical Restraint in Early America* (New York: Oxford University Press, 2011).

11. Richard Gamble sets these texts next to each other as well. For his reading of the differences, see Gamble, *In Search of the City on a Hill: The Making and Unmaking of an American Myth* (London: Continuum, 2012), 58–61.

12. Sacvan Bercovitch became one of the foremost exponents of Americans' sense of "chosenness." For more on him, see chapter 16. In the latest version of this story, the sociologist Philip Gorski explains, "However we re-tell it today, the Puritans understood their story as that of a new Israel established in a new England." Gorski, *American Covenant: A History of Civil Religion from the Puritans to the Present* (Princeton, NJ: Princeton University Press, 2017), 38. As I hope to show, that is simply not true. It is important to note that there are roughly two ways Winthrop's sermon and the Puritans have been used to start histories of American exceptionalism: first, as here, in comparisons between New England and Israel; and second, in Winthrop's declaration that "we shall be as a city upon a hill." These two elements are often conflated, but it is better to recognize how they are distinct. Each had its own context and meaning, and each relied on different parts of the Christian Bible (the Old and New Testaments, respectively). Here I consider Winthrop's invocation of Moses and comparisons to Israel. In chapter 3, I take up the context of Winthrop's "city on a hill."

13. See especially Reiner Smolinski, "Israel Redivivus: The Eschatological Limits of Puritan Typology in New England," *New England Quarterly* 63, no. 3 (1990): 357–395. The best account of "New Israel" language is coming soon in the work of Richard Cogley, who kindly shared his manuscript with me. For an excellent, quick review of this point, see Mark A. Noll, "'Wee Shall Be as a City upon a Hill': John Winthrop's Non-American Exceptionalism," *Review of Faith & International Affairs* 10, no. 2 (2012): 5–11. Noll concludes, "We are left with the substantial question of why a persistent misapplication of Winthrop, the Puritan experiment, and this particular speech prevails so widely" (11). For a careful elaboration of this "Israelite paradigm" in England, see especially Michael McGiffert, "God's Controversy with Jacobean England," *American Historical Review* 88, no. 5 (1983): 1151–1174. Of the many jeremiads comparing *England* to Israel beginning in the late sixteenth century, Patrick Collinson explains, "The message is always the same: most favored, most obligated, most negligent." Collinson, "Biblical Rhetoric: The English Nation and National Sentiment in the Prophetic Mode," in *Religion and Culture in Renaissance England*, ed. Claire McEachern and Debora Shuger (Cambridge: Cambridge University Press, 1997), 28.

14. *The Bible and Holy Scriptures*, trans. William Wittingham (Geneva, 1560), n.p. Winthrop's father, Adam Winthrop, would almost certainly have owned one of these older Geneva Bibles, considering what else he held in his library. On Adam Winthrop's book collection, see Francis Bremer, "The Heritage of John Winthrop: Religion along the Stour Valley, 1548–1630," *New England Quarterly* 70, no. 4 (1997): 525–526. Richard Gamble finds a source for the "eyes" line in Calvin's commentary on Matthew, which is certainly plausible and does not rule out that Winthrop found the same sentiment expressed in the Geneva Bible's prefatory letter to the queen. See Gamble, *In Search*, 53–55.

15. John Winthrop, "Reasons to Be Considered and Objections with Answers," in *The Founding of Massachusetts: Historians and the Sources*, ed. Edmund S. Morgan (Indianapolis: Bobbs-Merrill, 1964), 176–177; Winthrop, "Christian Charity," 293, 295.

16. Theodore Dwight Bozeman, *To Live Ancient Lives: The Primitivist Dimension in Puritanism* (Chapel Hill: University of North Carolina Press, 1988), 92.

Chapter Three. The Meaning of Winthrop's City on a Hill

1. James Sharpe, *The Triall of the Protestant Private Spirit* (1630), 177 (italics in original); *Holy Churches Complaint, for Her Childrens Disobedience* (1600), A4v; Samuel Hieron, *An Answere to a Popish Ryme* (London, 1604); see also John Rhodes, *An Answere to a Romish Rime* (London, 1602), 6. Such

arguments already appear in Leonard Pollard, *Fyve Homiles of Late* (London, 1556). As one Catholic writer pressed, "you in the meane tyme, without any lineall Descente from those whome you pretend to have beene your Auncestors, . . . do still remayne in the darcknes of your invisible Church, tossed in the Sea of Error, *with every winde of new Doctrine,* not knowing certainly whome to follow, nor what to believe." L.D., *A Defence of the Appendix* (1624), 30. This state of affairs was contrasted to the Catholic Church, which was called, predictably, a "city on a hill." Protestants drew from Augustinian tradition for their idea of an "invisible church," but Catholics pointed out (quite rightly) that "invisible church" never occurs in scripture. For more examples and evidence to the points in this chapter, see Abram Van Engen, "Claiming the High Ground: Puritans, Catholics, and the City on a Hill," in *American Literature and the New Puritan Studies,* ed. Bryce Traister (New York: Cambridge University Press, 2017), 206–219.

2. John Lightfoot, *Some Genuine Remains of the Late Pious and Learned John Lightfoot, D.D.* (London, 1700), 244; Alexander Ross, *Pansebeia, or, A View of All Religions in the World* (London, 1655), 437–438.

3. Sir Humphrey Lynde, *Via Tuta: The Safe Way* (London, 1628), 292, 305 (emphasis in original). This entire treatise concerns the relation of truth to the visible church. Lynde emphasized that "the paucitie of true beleevers were the special Caracter of the true Church" (292). The Protestant minister Thomas Taylor specifically addressed the Catholic claim to Matthew 5:14 by describing the true church, again, as "a selected company called out of the world, a little flock." Taylor, *Christs Victorie over the Dragon* (London, 1633), 295. See also John Prime, *An Exposition and Observations upon St Paul to the Galatians* (London, 1587), 223–224. As Theodore Dwight Bozeman has shown, this claim to be the "little flock" could be used by dissenters of all sorts against the larger, established church. Even in the 1570s and 1580s, he writes, "the godly chose and indeed accented and savored a minority status within their church and town," so that godly clergy often called themselves "a 'very smal' presence, 'a smal, poore, . . . flocke.'" Bozeman, *The Precisianist Strain: Disciplinary Religion and Antinomian Backlash in Puritanism to 1638* (Chapel Hill: University of North Carolina Press, 2004), 53.

4. Hieron, *Answere to a Popish Ryme,* C3r; Lynde, *Via Devia,* "Epistle Dedicatorie" (no page number or printer's signature), see also pp. 672–673; Taylor, *Christs Victorie,* 296. Taylor repeated this point throughout his treatise. See also the Archbishop of Canterbury, George Abbot, *A Treatise of the Perpetuall Visibilitie, and Succession of the True Church in All Ages* (1624).

5. John Calvin, *Institutes of the Christian Religion,* vol. 1, ed. John T. McNeill, trans. Ford Lewis Battles (Louisville, KY: Westminster John Knox Press, 1960), 24; Prime, *Exposition,* 227; John Owen, *A Vindication of the Animad-*

versions on Fiat Lux (London, 1664), 382. In a section labeled "Errors of the Nature of the Church" from Calvin's prefatory address to King Francis, he goes on at length about this particular error of visibility: "Our controversy turns on these hinges," he explains: "first, they contend that the form of the church is always apparent and observable. Secondly, they set this form in the see of the Roman Church and its hierarchy." Moreover, he adds, "They rage if the church cannot always be pointed to with the finger." But Calvin rejects such a view of the true church. "How long after Christ's coming was it hidden without form?" he asks. "How often has it since that time been so oppressed by wars, seditions, and heresies that it did not shine forth at all?" (*Institutes*, vol. 1, 24–25).

6. Prime, *Exposition*, 227; Thomas Bayly, *Certamen Religiosum* (London, 1651), 154 (italics in original). This was a point that Protestants frequently reiterated by reference to the moon. Rhodes's Protestant "answer" to a "Romish Rime" explained, "So that sometimes as Sunne and Moone, / it [the church] is eclip'st and hath her doome, / In mans conceit to shine no more: / but God againe doth her restore" (*Answere to a Romish Rime*, 6). God knows the members of the true church at all times, even if they are unknown to the world, and he will "restore" them to glory eventually. See also Hieron, *Answere to a Popish Ryme*, C3r; and Abbot, *Perpetuall Visibilitie*, 23–24. Lynde, in his anti-Catholic treatise, summarized the approach: "I speake not this in any sort to decline the visibility of our *Church*; for the Church is like the *Moone*, which hath often waxings & waynings, and wee know the Moone at full, and the Moone at the waine, is one and the same Moone, although not alike conspicuous" (*Via Devia*, "Epistle Dedicatorie," no page number or printer's signature).

7. Lynde, *Via Tuta*, A2v–A2r (italics in original); Abbot, *Perpetuall Visibilitie*, A2r–A3v.

8. Delbanco goes on to claim that Winthrop "had more fear of notoriety, of 'shipwracke,' of being revealed as the leader of 'a perjured people,' than he had appetite for fame." Andrew Delbanco, *The Puritan Ordeal* (Cambridge, MA: Harvard University Press, 1989), 72. For other Protestants using Luke 12:32 and Revelations 12, see Avihu Zakai, *Exile and Kingdom: History and Apocalypse in the Puritan Migration to America* (Cambridge: Cambridge University Press, 1992), 143–144. Several scholars have looked at Winthrop's line about "the eyes of all people" and noted its emphasis on failure. Bozeman, for example, claims, "The projected impact upon 'all people' ... presupposed the *failure* of New England's enterprise"; success, meanwhile, could be ignored. Theodore Dwight Bozeman, *To Live Ancient Lives: The Primitivist Dimension in Puritanism* (Chapel Hill: University of North Carolina Press, 1988), 92 (emphasis in original). See also Joseph Conforti, *Saints and Strangers: New England in British North America* (Baltimore: Johns Hopkins University Press, 2006), 40–41; Michael Winship, *Godly Republicanism: Puritans, Pilgrims, and a*

City on a Hill (Cambridge, MA: Harvard University Press, 2012), 172; Darrett Rutman, *Winthrop's Boston: A Portrait of a Puritan Town, 1630–1649* (1965; repr., New York: Norton, 1972), chap. 1; Andrew Delbanco, "The Puritan Errand Re-viewed," *Journal of American Studies* 18 (1984): 343–360; Theodore Dwight Bozeman, "The Puritans' 'Errand into the Wilderness' Reconsidered," *New England Quarterly* 59 (1986): 231–235. Perhaps such insistence that Winthrop was not intent on modeling anything for anyone has been necessary to correct for the overblown readings of Perry Miller and Sacvan Bercovitch, but the extreme position of Miller and Bercovitch has been sufficiently challenged by now. It is the more nuanced sense of demonstrating godliness in a community of love (just as Winthrop claims others had done) that must be acknowledged. Winthrop knew both meanings of the "city on a hill" phrase (the negative and the positive, the unwanted scrutiny and the possibility of leading by example), and he invoked that ambiguity to describe *both* his fear *and* his hope for New England.

9. During the Antinomian Controversy, when the colony nearly split in two over the assurance of salvation, dissenters such as John Wheelwright and Anne Hutchinson frequently turned to classic Protestant rhetoric in order to defend their positions and bolster their claims. In one very public instance, Wheelwright called his particular followers a "little flock" opposed to the larger New England establishment. Seeking to identify "true beleevers" in an important Fast Day sermon, he admitted that the "enimyes to the Lord and his truth are many" and added, "I must confesse and acknowledge the saynts of God are few, they are but a little flocke." Wheelwright, "A Fast-Day Sermon," in *The Antinomian Controversy, 1636–1638: A Documentary History*, 2nd ed., ed. David D. Hall (Durham, NC: Duke University Press, 1990), 154, 163. For the mentality of persecution and martyrdom in early New England, including how it surfaces in the Antinomian Controversy, see Adrian Chastain Weimer, *Martyrs' Mirror: Persecution and Holiness in Early New England* (New York: Oxford University Press, 2011), chap. 3.

10. Francis Bremer, "To Live Exemplary Lives: Puritans and Puritan Communities as Lofty Lights," *Seventeenth Century* 7, no. 1 (1992): 37.

11. Wilkinson, quoted in Bremer, 30.

12. My thanks to Edward O'Reilly, curator and head of the Manuscript Department of the Patricia D. Klingenstein Library at the New-York Historical Society, for pointing this out to me. He has written up his finding. See O'Reilly, "John Winthrop's 'City upon a Hill' Sermon and an 'Erasure of Collective Memory,'" *From the Stacks* (blog), New-York Historical Society, December 5, 2018, http://blog.nyhistory.org/21991-2/.

13. Ronald Reagan, "Farewell Address to the Nation," January 11, 1989, accessed at the American Presidency Project, https://www.presidency.ucsb.edu/documents/farewell-address-the-nation.

Chapter Four. A True History of America

1. *Massachusetts Gazette and Boston News-Letter*, February 2, 1764, 2. "Only 404 volumes escaped incineration; some hadn't yet been shelved in the building, and 144 were out on loan." "Saved from the Flames," *Harvard Magazine*, May 1, 2001, https://harvardmagazine.com/2001/05/saved -from-the-flames.html.

2. Jeremy Belknap to Dr. Andrew Eliot, June 18, 1774, Letterbook, 1768– 1788, Jeremy Belknap Papers (JBP), MHS, Boston, MA.

3. Hazard quoted in Fred Shelley, "Ebenezer Hazard: America's First Historical Editor," *William and Mary Quarterly* 12, no. 1 (1955): 48. Hazard's collection of political pamphlets eventually contained "150 bound volumes of 8 or 10 pamphlets each" (Shelley, 46).

4. Thomas Jefferson to Ebenezer Hazard, February 18, 1791, National Archives Founders Online, accessed April 11, 2019, https://founders.ar chives.gov/documents/Jefferson/01-19-02-0059. This connection is also made by Alea Henle, who offers an excellent account of the rise of historical societies in the early United States. See Henle, "Preserving the Past, Making History: Historical Societies in the Early United States" (PhD diss., University of Connecticut, 2012).

5. Jeremy Belknap to Ebenezer Hazard, May 18, 1787, and Belknap to Hazard, September 29, 1787, Belknap Papers, Part I, in *Collections of the Massachusetts Historical Society*, 5th ser., vol. 2 (Boston: MHS, 1877), 481, 494.

6. Burr quoted in Margaret Heilbrun, "NYORK, NCENTURY, N-YHS," *New York Journal of American History* 65, no. 1 (2003): 22; Walter Muir Whitehill, "John Pintard's 'Antiquarian Society,'" *New-York Historical Society Quarterly* 45 (1961): 356. Larry Sullivan writes, "Never a well-known politician, statesman, or president of voluntary societies or political parties, Pintard was nevertheless a highly significant person, because he performed the very important but less glamorous function of the organizer and secretary of a variety of organizations." Sullivan, "Books, Power, and the Development of Libraries in the New Republic: The Prison and Other Journals of John Pintard of New York," *Journal of Library History* 21, no. 2 (1986): 408. For a history of Pintard and the New-York Historical Society, see R. W. G. Vail, *Knickerbocker Birthday: A Sesqui-centennial History of the New-York Historical Society, 1804–1954* (New York: New-York Historical Society, 1954).

7. Belknap to Hazard, August 10, 1789, Belknap Papers, Part II, in *Collections of the Massachusetts Historical Society*, 5th ser., vol. 3 (Boston: MHS, 1877), 157; Hazard to Belknap, September 5, 1789, Belknap Papers, Part II, 165. Hazard's "character" of Pintard read, "Mr. P[intar]d is a lively, chearful man, who appears to me not to want understanding as much as he does solidity. I can hardly form a determinate character of him in my own mind, and yet in some respects I am disposed to think favourably of

him too. I think him a singular mixture of heterogeneous particles." Hazard to Belknap, August 27, 1789, Belknap Papers, Part II, 162.

8. Belknap to Hazard, 19 February 1791, Belknap Papers, Part II, 245. "Introductory Address to the Public," *Collections of the Massachusetts Historical Society,* 1st ser., vol. 1 (1792), 3.

9. NYHS, *To the Public: The Address of the New-York Historical Society,* September 15, 1809, NYHS-RG 1, Management committee records (1804–1938), New-York Historical Society Records, Patricia D. Klingenstein Library, New-York Historical Society, New York; hereafter cited as NYHSR. This 1809 one-page broadside is signed by the recording secretary, John Pintard. It was originally printed as two pages with the society's constitution in 1805. Pintard added that the two institutions hoped to coordinate efforts rather than compete: "Without aiming to be rivals, we shall be happy to co-operate with that laudable institution in pursuing the objects of our common researches; satisfied if, in the end, our efforts shall be attended with equal success."

10. On the numbers tripling in the 1820s, see Henle, "Preserving the Past," 17. On seventy-two societies by 1861, see George Callcott, *History in the United States, 1800–1860: Its Practice and Purpose* (Baltimore: Johns Hopkins University Press, 1970), 25. On two hundred societies by 1884, see Julian Boyd, "State and Local Historical Societies in the United States," *American Historical Review* 40 (1934): 26. The annual report of the American Historical Association in 1905 "required 1,375 pages of small print to publish Appleton Prentiss Clark Griffin's *Bibliography of American Historical Societies* with entries dating back to 1791." H. G. Jones, preface to *Historical Consciousness in the Early Republic: The Origins of State Historical Societies, Museums, and Collections, 1791–1861,* ed. H. G. Jones (Chapel Hill: North Caroliniana Society and North Carolina Collection, 1995).

11. There are no biographies of Pintard or Hazard. Two exist of Belknap: George Kirsch, *Jeremy Belknap: A Biography* (New York: Arno, 1982); and Russell Lawson, *The American Plutarch: Jeremy Belknap and the Historian's Dialogue with the Past* (Westport, CT: Praeger, 1998).

12. MHS, "Constitution of the Historical Society," in *Collections of the Massachusetts Historical Society,* 1st ser., vol. 1 (Boston: MHS, 1792), 1; NYHS, *To the Public.*

13. Jeremy Belknap, *A Discourse Intended to Commemorate the Discovery of America by Christopher Columbus* (Boston, 1792), 36–37.

14. Hazard to Belknap, February 18, 1780, Belknap Papers, Part I, 31; Belknap to Captain [Thomas Westbrook] Waldron, July 17, 1772, in Jane Marcou, *Life of Jeremy Belknap, D.D.: The Historian of New Hampshire, with Selections from His Correspondence and Other Writings* (New York: Harper and Bros, 1847), 47.

15. Belknap to Waldron, July 17, 1772, in Marcou, *Life of Jeremy Belknap,* 47. For both Belknap and Hazard, the pursuit of history had to be "animated

by motives of benevolence and public utility." Charles Deane and Charles C. Smith, introduction to *Proceedings of the Massachusetts Historical Society, 1791–1835*, vol. 1 (Boston: MHS, 1879), xxx.

16. Belknap to Hazard, August 27, 1792, Belknap Papers, Part II, 307; Hazard to Belknap, October 18, 1789, Belknap Papers, Part II, 195. On "public good," see Belknap to Hazard, February 2, 1779, Belknap Papers I, 2; on its "utility," see Hazard to Belknap, August 31, 1779, Belknap Papers I, 13. "I will join you as far as I am able in making useful discoveries," Hazard wrote, "and I will join you in publishing them for the common good." Hazard to Belknap, February 18, 1780, Belknap Papers, Part I, 34. For Pintard, see Sullivan, "Books, Power, and the Development of Libraries," 414.

17. Pintard quoted in Sullivan, "Books, Power, and the Development of Libraries," 419; Thomas Jefferson to Ebenezer Hazard, April 30, 1775, National Archives Founders Online, accessed April 11, 2019, https://founders.archives.gov/documents/Jefferson/01-01-02-0102; MHS, "The Act of Incorporation," in *By-Laws of the Massachusetts Historical Society* (Boston: MHS, 1882), 7; Gouverneur Morris, untitled address, September 4, 1816, NYHS-RG 11: Manuscripts of lectures and addresses (1809–1957, 2001, 2015–2016), NYHSR. For most people in this period, as Trevor Colbourn explains, "history was above all useful." Colbourn, *The Lamp of Experience: Whig History and the Intellectual Origins of the American Revolution* (Chapel Hill: University of North Carolina Press, 1965), 5.

18. According to Colbourn, Jefferson believed that "the foundation for a working democratic republic had to be an educated electorate," while John Adams "kept returning to his theme that knowledge was the road to freedom" (*Lamp of Experience*, 175, 89). For the definitive account of this idea and its consequences, see Richard D. Brown, *The Strength of a People: The Idea of an Informed Citizenry in America, 1650–1870* (Chapel Hill: University of North Carolina Press, 1996). The idea that liberty and education required each other flowed from a republican ideology that helped shape the entire Revolutionary period. For good overviews see Daniel T. Rodgers, "Republicanism: The Career of a Concept," *Journal of American History* 79, no. 1 (1992): 11–38; and Joyce Appleby, *Liberalism and Republicanism in the Historical Imagination* (Cambridge, MA: Harvard University Press, 1992). On the extent of education, Belknap preached, "There are as many good capacities among the children of the poor, who are not able to give them a good education, as of the rich who are," and he declared that daughters should be "set off to the best advantage by due cultivation and improvement," which included a broader education than was then available. Jeremy Belknap, *Election Sermon* (Portsmouth, NH, 1785), 14, 8. Like many New England ministers, Belknap preached on this theme repeatedly. As Nathan Hatch writes, "New England ministers devote as much rhetoric to the necessity of proper education as they do to

any other single theme." Hatch, *The Sacred Cause of Liberty: Republican Thought and the Millennium in Revolutionary New England* (New Haven, CT: Yale University Press, 1977), 164n65.

19. Hazard quoted in Shelley, "Ebenezer Hazard," 54; Andrew Eliot to Jeremy Belknap, 1785, Belknap Papers, Part III, *Collections of the Massachusetts Historical Society*, 6th ser., vol. 4 (Boston: MHS, 1891), 286. Callcott observes that already in the 1780s, "Americans were coming to think of their history not as the account of an English colony but as the emergence of a new people with a new way of life" (*History in the United States*, 13). At the same time, as David Van Tassel explains, "Many Americans realized that the colonies had to be welded into a nation, not only by the establishment of a common political system, but by the creation of a cohesive heritage." Van Tassel, *Recording America's Past: An Interpretation of the Development of Historical Studies in America, 1607–1884* (Chicago: University of Chicago Press, 1960), 31. George Pilcher likewise highlights the importance of "the many attempts to preserve a now common past through the collection and publication of historical documents and narratives." Pilcher, "Ebenezer Hazard and the Promotion of Historical Scholarship in the Early Republic," *Pennsylvania History: A Journal of Mid-Atlantic Studies* 56, no. 1 (1989): 3. Meanwhile, exalting America through education was a large part of the plan for Belknap, Hazard, and Pintard. In 1782, for example, Belknap imagined a nation known internationally for its learning. "Why may not *a Republic of Letters* be realized in America as well as a Republican Government?" he asked. "Why may there not be a Congress of Philosophers as well as of Statesmen?" As he went on to explain, "I am so far an enthusiast in the cause of America as to wish she may shine Mistress of the Sciences, as well as the Asylum of Liberty." Belknap to Hazard, February 4, 1780, Belknap Papers, Part I, 255. If America was going to be great, it had to be great in learning, Belknap assumed, and that would require interlinked educational institutions all over the country. Pintard also had the idea of linked educational and historical societies. When he worked to engraft "an antiquarian scheme of a museum upon" the Tammany Society in New York, he told Belknap, "If your society succeeds, we will open a regular correspondence & interchange of communications, duplicates, etc." Pintard to Belknap, April 6, 1791, Belknap Papers, Part III, 491. For broader context about learned societies in the early republic, see David Shields, "The Learned World," in *An Extensive Republic: Print, Culture, and Society in the New Nation, 1790–1840*, ed. Robert A. Gross and Mary Kelley, vol. 2 of *A History of the Book in America* (Chapel Hill: University of North Carolina Press, 2010), 247–265.

20. On the support of Belknap, see, for example, the encouragement from Governors Wentworth and Weare in Belknap Papers, Part III, 54, 136. See also Abigail Adams to Jeremy Belknap, May 1798, in Marcou, *Life of*

Jeremy Belknap, 236–238. On Jefferson's support of Hazard, see Thomas Jefferson to Ebenezer Hazard, April 30, 1775, National Archives Founders Online, accessed April 11, 2019, https://founders.archives.gov/documents/Jefferson/01-01-02-0102.

21. Worthington C. Ford et al., eds., *Journals of the Continental Congress, 1774–1789*, vol. 11 (Washington, DC: Government Printing Office, 1908), 705–706.

22. Shelley, "Ebenezer Hazard," 58; Thomas Jefferson to Ebenezer Hazard, February 18, 1791, National Archives Founders Online, accessed April 11, 2019, https://founders.archives.gov/documents/Jefferson/01-19-02-0059. See also Pilcher, "Ebenezer Hazard."

23. Joshua Brackett to Jeremy Belknap, 1778, Belknap Papers, Part III, 135; Belknap, "Petition to the General Court of New Hampshire," Belknap Papers, Part III, 301–302; Bartlett to Belknap, February 25, 1791, Belknap Papers, Part III, 480. For the cost of the books, see Kirsch, *Jeremy Belknap*, 125–127. Both thankful and maddened, Belknap asked his friend how to express gratitude. "You will excuse my saying that I cannot view it as 'a recompense,' when you consider my attention & labour for more than eighteen years past in collecting, compiling, digesting, & copying the History, together with the expense & risqué which I have incurred." Belknap to Nathaniel Peabody, March 23, 1791, Belknap Papers, Part III, 485.

24. This story of seeking funds, along with the related letters, can be found in Vail, *Knickerbocker Birthday*, 36–39.

25. Hazard to Belknap, January 14, 1796, Belknap Papers, Part II, 361; Belknap to Hazard, August 21, 1795, Belknap Papers, Part II, 357; Deane and Smith, introduction to *Proceedings of the Massachusetts Historical Society, 1791–1835*, vol. 1, xxxi. For Hazard's lack of encouraging sales, see Hazard to Belknap, September 9, 1792, Belknap Papers, Part II, 309.

26. Belknap to Hazard, March 22, 1798, Belknap Papers, Part II, 365.

27. See Vail, *Knickerbocker Birthday*, 63–68. State support for historical societies continued for many years, especially in the Midwest. By the early twentieth century, the historical societies of Iowa and Kansas, for example, rivaled East Coast societies, and the size of the collections in the Wisconsin Historical Society exceeded the Massachusetts Historical Society—all because of state support. See Boyd, "State and Local Historical Societies," 28–30.

Chapter Five. A Providential History of America

1. The fact that Belknap, Hazard, and Pintard were deeply religious has not gone entirely unnoticed, but it has usually been set apart from their historical work. Belknap "was miscast as a minister," claims Louis Tucker. "His primary interest was in secular matters of the mind, not theology or servicing the spiritual needs of parishioners." Tucker, *Clio's Consort:*

Jeremy Belknap and the Founding of the Massachusetts Historical Society (Boston: MHS, 1990), 11. Tucker is especially insistent on this division. But that is the usual view. Lester Cohen approaches Belknap within the context of arguing "for the secularization of historical thought." Cohen, *The Revolutionary Histories: Contemporary Narratives of the American Revolution* (Ithaca, NY: Cornell University Press, 1980), 21. Considered a "child, or step-child, of the Enlightenment and proto-Unitarian," Belknap and his coterie came to be seen as writing history "in the image of their liberal rationalism." Lawrence Buell, *New England Literary Culture: From Revolution through Renaissance* (New York: Cambridge University Press, 1986), 216; Sidney Kaplan, "*The History of New-Hampshire*: Jeremy Belknap as Literary Craftsman," *William and Mary Quarterly* 21, no. 1 (1964): 21. The few mentions of providence that make it into Belknap's historical writing are considered nothing more "than a bow to piety, a nod to stale tradition" (Kaplan, "*History of New-Hampshire*," 21–22). On this point, only Russell Lawson offers a more nuanced view. Lawson, *The American Plutarch: Jeremy Belknap and the Historian's Dialogue with the Past* (Westport, CT: Praeger, 1998).

2. See Joyce Goodfriend, "The Last of the Huguenots: John Pintard and the Memory of the Diaspora in the Early American Republic," *Journal of Presbyterian History* 78, no. 3 (2000): 185. Though Pintard's books were organized according to distinct categories, as Larry E. Sullivan notes, "we must remember that they all form one construct. And its nucleus was religion." Sullivan, "Books, Power, and the Development of Libraries in the New Republic: The Prison and Other Journals of John Pintard of New York," *Journal of Library History* 21, no. 2 (1986): 416. While Pintard did not hold to the same doctrines as his ancestors, theological innovations could still make him uneasy. He always professed to practice "christian charity," but "he could not 'patiently endure' the liberal Christians." Conrad Edick Wright, *The Transformation of Charity in Postrevolutionary New England* (Boston: Northeastern University Press, 1992), 8. Hazard's baptism was performed by his grandfather Gilbert Tennent, and in his youth he was educated under Samuel Finley. Russell Lawson, *Ebenezer Hazard, Jeremy Belknap and the American Revolution* (London: Pickering and Chatto, 2011), 28.

3. Hazard to Belknap, November 18, 1784, Belknap Papers, Part I, in *Collections of the Massachusetts Historical Society*, 5th ser., vol. 2 (Boston: MHS, 1877), 406. For more on the universalism of Belknap, Hazard, and their friends—and how to distinguish it from other forms—see Conrad Wright, *The Beginnings of Unitarianism in America* (Boston: Starr King, 1955), chap. 8. On their rejection of prodigies and superstitions, see Belknap to Hazard, June 5, 1780, Belknap Papers, Part I, 54–55. On their rejection of original sin and predestination, see Hazard to Belknap, April 17, 1781, and Belknap's response, Belknap to Hazard, April 23, 1781,

Belknap Papers, Part I, 90, 96–97. A belief in the equal revelations of both reason and scripture led people like Belknap to reject creeds and confessions as static and stultifying. "But creeds, either in philosophy or divinity," Belknap declared, "should never be imposed, because they tend to fetter the mind and stop its genuine excursions into the field of truth." Belknap to Hazard, April 11, 1784, Belknap Papers, Part I, 325. Compare against Belknap's earliest formulation of his faith: Belknap, "Confession of Faith, February 10, 1767," in Belknap Papers, Part III, in *Collections of the Massachusetts Historical Society*, 6th ser., vol. 4 (Boston: MHS, 1891), 18–22. Even as these men's approaches to theology led them out of Calvinism, they still held firmly to the Trinity and the divinity of Christ, causing them to oppose deists and Socinians. Spencer McBride points out that clergymen's opposition to deism could be self-interested, since more deists meant fewer people in the pews. See McBride, *Pulpit and Nation: Clergymen and the Politics of Revolutionary America* (Charlottesville: University of Virginia Press, 2016), 136. For more on Belknap's religious beliefs, including a nuanced sense of their complexity, see George Kirsch, *Jeremy Belknap: A Biography* (New York: Arno, 1982), 24–42.

4. Jeremy Belknap, *Election Sermon* (Portsmouth, NH, 1785), 42. This combination of natural and revealed religion has been called "supernatural rationalism," and it is best (and first) described in Wright, *Beginnings*, chap. 6; and in Conrad Wright, *The Liberal Christians: Essays on American Unitarian History* (Boston: Beacon, 1970), 1–21. See also Lauri Bauer Coleman, "Rain Down Righteousness: Interpretations of Natural Events in Mid-Eighteenth-Century Boston," in *Remaking Boston: An Environmental History of the City and Its Surroundings*, ed. Anthony Penna and Conrad Edick Wright (Pittsburgh: University of Pittsburgh Press, 2009), 233–258. Anthony Delbourgo describes this framework as "physico-theology." See Delbourgo, *A Most Amazing Scene of Wonders: Electricity and Enlightenment in Early America* (Cambridge, MA: Harvard University Press, 2006), 63–72.

5. Hazard to Belknap, March 28, 1789, Belknap Papers, Part II, in *Collections of the Massachusetts Historical Society*, 5th ser., vol. 3 (Boston: MHS, 1877), 113. Belknap assured another father that afflictions were "the discipline of our heavenly father to reduce us from our wanderings and make us partakers of his holiness." Jeremy Belknap to Mr. Maclintock, 1779, Letterbook, 1768–1788, Jeremy Belknap Papers (JBP), MHS, Boston, MA. As Benjamin E. Park writes of New England clergymen, "An acute sense of particular providence—the belief that God was in charge of the intricate details of life and events—saturated these ministers' sense of nationalism." Park, *American Nationalisms: Imagining Union in the Age of Revolutions, 1783–1833* (New York: Cambridge University Press, 2018), 88.

6. Jeremy Belknap, *A Discourse Intended to Commemorate the Discovery of America by Christopher Columbus* (Boston, 1792), 36 (italics in original). David Ramsay quoted in Cohen, *Revolutionary Histories*, 175. "It is both

amusing and instructive," Belknap wrote, "to review our former notions
of liberty, both civil and religious; and to see what imperfect ideas we had
on these subjects, derived by tradition from our European ancestors"
(*Discourse*, 37).

7. Belknap, *Discourse*, 36; Belknap, *Election Sermon*, 42, 11. On these men's belief that virtue led to happiness and thus that the Christian religion was in
everyone's own best interest, see, for example, Belknap to Hazard, March 8,
1781; Hazard to Belknap, April 17, 1781; and Belknap to Hazard, July 2,
1784, Belknap Papers, Part I, 86, 90, 365–366. See also Jeremy Belknap, *A
Plain and Earnest Address from a Minister to a Parishioner on the Neglect of the
Publick Worship* (Salem, MA, 1771), 11.

8. Hazard to Belknap, October 2, 1780, Belknap Papers, Part I, 77–78;
Belknap, *A Sermon, Delivered on the 9th of May, 1798, the Day of the National Fast* (Boston, 1798), 19; Belknap, *Discourse*, 43; Eliot to Belknap,
March 26, 1776, Belknap Papers, Part III, 96. These men saw direct in-
tervention in the ratification of the Constitution as well. See, for example, Hazard to Belknap, March 5, 1788, and Hazard to Belknap, August 7,
1788, Belknap Papers, Part II, 24, 57. Still, they usually approached the
study of God's providence indirectly. On the role of providentialism in
the creation of American national identity, the essential starting point is
Nicholas Guyatt, *Providence and the Invention of the United States, 1607–
1876* (New York: Cambridge University Press, 2007). Guyatt's excellent
book demonstrates how a providential understanding of America was
radically reshaped by the American Revolution. Spencer McBride has
demonstrated that *both* Federalists and Anti-Federalists read the ratification contest in providential terms. See McBride, *Pulpit and Nation*, 103.
As John Berens has written, "Providential thought during the early national period sanctified the nationalist themes of special nation, special
destiny, and special mission." Berens, *Providence and Patriotism in Early
America, 1640–1815* (Charlottesville: University of Virginia Press, 1978),
6. While it is true that providence does not appear much in Belknap's
History of New Hampshire, the places where it does appear are telling. For
example, at one point Belknap writes, "Never was the hand of divine
Providence more visible, than on this occasion." Belknap, *The History of
New-Hampshire, Volume II: Comprehending the Events of Seventy Five Years,
from MDCCXV to MDCCXC* (Boston, 1791), 232. By putting providence
in such terms, Belknap assumes that the reader can carry on the task
without his help. Such an approach had broad appeal, for this was one of
Belknap's sentences that many other early American historians, such as
Hannah Adams and John Marshall, chose to quote in their own accounts
of America. It is accurate to say, though, that Belknap's focus on indirect
causes represents an important shift. For more on Puritan historians and
their writing, see Francis Bremer, "John Winthrop and the Shaping of
New England History," and Reiner Smolinski, "'Seeing Things Their

Way': The Lord's Remembrancers and Their New England Histories," both in *Massachusetts Historical Review* 18 (2016): 1–64.

9. Belknap, *Election Sermon*, 34–35. For a good analysis of the Federalist position, see Jonathan Den Hartog, *Patriotism and Piety: Federalist Politics and Religious Struggle in the New American Nation* (Charlottesville: University of Virginia Press, 2015). As Den Hartog explains, Federalists like Belknap "hoped to create a Protestant, Christian nationalism in which citizens voluntarily worshipped properly and lived morally" (4).

10. Jeremy Belknap, Sermon on Job 11:7, Sermon Notebook: 1790–1798, Jeremy Belknap Papers (JBP), MHS, Boston, MA; Hazard to Belknap, April 17, 1781, Belknap Papers, Part I, 90; George Callcott, *History in the United States, 1800–1860: Its Practice and Purpose* (Baltimore: Johns Hopkins University Press, 1970), 186. As Belknap wrote to his friend Benjamin Rush, "The main business of all philosophical researches is to fix our attention to the great 'Cause uncaus'd,' & the deeper we penetrate the arcana of Nature, the more reason do we find for wonder, love, & praise." Belknap to Rush, July 29, 1789, Belknap Papers, Part III, 442.

11. Jeremy Belknap to Captain [Thomas Westbrook] Waldron, ca. October 1772, in Jane Marcou, *Life of Jeremy Belknap, D.D.: The Historian of New Hampshire, with Selections from His Correspondence and Other Writings* (New York: Harper and Bros, 1847), 49.

12. Jeremy Belknap, Thanksgiving Sermon on Psalm 122:6-8, 19 February 1795, Sermon Notebook: 1790–1798, JBP.

13. Hazard, *Historical Collections*, vol. 1 (Philadelphia, 1792), A2r. Pintard likewise "regarded the American experiment as a special event in world history," and as such, "it deserved to be recorded" (Tucker, *Clio's Consort*, 77).

14. Belknap, Thanksgiving Sermon. Again, such a position was not unique to Belknap: see Park, *American Nationalisms*, chap. 2. After the Revolution, that sense of being specially chosen became particularly strong in New England, but it also spread elsewhere. As McBride points out, the statesmen who made the Constitution utilized no comparisons to the Bible or to a supposed "Hebrew Republic," but when ministers began supporting its ratification, they turned the Constitution into a religious act as a form of "Federalist propaganda" (*Pulpit and Nation*, 111). See also Nathan Hatch, *The Sacred Cause of Liberty: Republican Thought and the Millennium in Revolutionary New England* (New Haven, CT: Yale University Press, 1977); and Eran Shalev, *American Zion: The Old Testament as a Political Text from the Revolution to the Civil War* (New Haven, CT: Yale University Press, 2013).

15. In a 1780 letter to Nathaniel Greene, for example, John Adams writes, "America is the City, set upon a Hill, I do not think myself guilty of Exaggeration, Vanity or Presumption, when I say, that the proceedings of Congress are more attended to, than those of any Court in Europe, and the Motions of our Armies than any of theirs. And there are more politi-

cal Lies made and circulated about both, than all the rest: which renders genuine Intelligence, from good Authority, the more interesting and important." Adams to Greene, March 18, 1780, National Archives Founders Online, accessed April 11, 2019, https://founders.archives.gov/documents/Adams/06-09-02-0041. See also John Adams to David Sewall, January 10, 1821, National Archives Founders Online, accessed April 11, 2019, https://founders.archives.gov/documents/Adams/99-02-02-7452.

Chapter Six. A White History of America

1. Jeremy Belknap to Reverend [Samuel] Haven, January 1, 1766, in Jane Marcou, *Life of Jeremy Belknap, D.D.: The Historian of New Hampshire, with Selections from His Correspondence and Other Writings* (New York: Harper and Bros, 1847), 20. For the best account of Belknap's views regarding Native Americans and African Americans, see George Kirsch, "Jeremy Belknap and the Problem of Blacks and Indians in Early America," *Historical New Hampshire* 34 (1979): 202–222. Belknap was avidly opposed to slavery and worked for African American rights, but Native Americans represented a particular problem for the history of America he wanted to tell.

2. Jeremy Belknap's Journal, 1774, in Marcou, *Life of Jeremy Belknap*, 69–71; Hazard to Belknap, April 1, 1780, Belknap Papers, Part I, in *Collections of the Massachusetts Historical Society*, 5th ser., vol. 2 (Boston: MHS, 1877), 46. In 1783, Belknap had already concluded, "As to the plan of civilizing or converting them, it is indeed highly benevolent, but totally impracticable in any methods that have yet been adopted here." Belknap to Hazard, June 28, 1783, Belknap Papers, Part I, 227–228.

3. On the ideal of faithfulness and impartiality, see Hazard, *Historical Collections*, vol. 2 (Philadelphia, 1792), A2v.

4. For the letters discussing and debating this idea, see Belknap Papers, Part I, 135–141, 151–153, 158–168, 177, 186, 413–414, 417; and Belknap Papers, Part III, in *Collections of the Massachusetts Historical Society*, 6th ser., vol. 4 (Boston: MHS, 1891), 219–222, 226.

5. Jeremy Belknap, "Report of a Committee, Who Visited the Oneida and Mohekunuh Indians in 1796," in *Collections of the Massachusetts Historical Society*, 1st ser., vol. 5 (Boston: MHS, 1798), 29.

6. Jeremy Belknap, "To Henry Knox, *Esquire*, Late Secretary of War," *Columbian Centinel*, January 24, 1795, 1. In his last publication with the Massachusetts Historical Society, Belknap printed and endorsed a letter from General Benjamin Lincoln that concluded, "On the whole, I am fully in opinion with my friend, Dr. Ramsay, that the Indian nations will never be civilized," and added, "Nature forbids civilized and uncivilized people possessing the same territory" (Belknap, "Report of a Committee," 11).

7. Jeremy Belknap, *The Foresters, an American Tale: Being a Sequel to the History of John Bull the Clothier* (1792; repr., Gainesville, FL: Scholar's Facsimiles and Reprints, 1969), 58–60, 68.

8. Belknap to Hazard, December 21, 1783, Belknap Papers, Part I, 287–288; Belknap to Hazard, January 13, 1784, Belknap Papers, Part I, 298; Belknap to Hazard, February 2, 1787, Belknap Papers, Part I, 455; Hazard to Belknap, January 16, 1784, Belknap Papers, Part I, 298. The "Kentucke people," Belknap reported, "are said to be almost as savage as the Indians." Belknap to Hazard, September 29, 1787, Belknap Papers, Part I, 493. On his way to an exploration of the White Mountains, he observed that Indians considered the mountains "possessed" and refused to ascend them; then he noted, "The same superstition is common among the people of the towns through which we passed." Belknap to Hazard, August 19, 1784, Belknap Papers, Part II, in *Collections of the Massachusetts Historical Society*, 5th ser., vol. 3 (Boston: MHS, 1877), 184.

9. Jeremy Belknap, *Election Sermon* (Portsmouth, 1785), 23. Building a library, his friend enthused, "would be a means of diffusing knowledge thro' all ranks of people, of dissipating the ignorance & darkness that obscure the human mind, & better preparing men for the reception of the truth." John Eliot to Belknap, January 30, 1775, Belknap Papers, Part III, 75. Belknap was involved in multiple institutions aimed at expanding education; as his granddaughter Jane Marcou later wrote, "he was one of the Overseers of Harvard College, and one of the Library committee, a member of the Humane society, one of the committee for visiting the public schools, and a member of the American Academy of Arts and Sciences" (*Life of Jeremy Belknap*, 148). Such zeal defined the work of Pintard, too. As Larry E. Sullivan explains, Pintard's "solution to ameliorating this vice-prone nature [in the people] was education, and that meant books, reading, libraries, schools, benevolent associations, and ultimately prisons." Sullivan, "Books, Power, and the Development of Libraries in the New Republic: The Prison and Other Journals of John Pintard of New York," *Journal of Library History* 21, no. 2 (1986): 414. In this way, they were very Arminian: "Righteousness or morality, for the Arminians," as Conrad Wright has explained, "was the fruit not so much of a deep religious experience as of education and training." The stress lay on "man's development rather than his sudden conversion." Wright, *The Beginnings of Unitarianism in America* (Boston: Starr King, 1955), 132–133.

10. Jeremy Belknap, *Jeremy Belknap's Journey to Dartmouth in 1774*, ed. Edward Lathem (Hanover, NH: Dartmouth, 1950), 1, 5, 5, 19, 22; Jeremy Belknap, "Dr. Belknap's Tour to Oneida, 1796," in *Proceedings of the Massachusetts Historical Society* 19 (1881–1882): 397, 398, 400, 404; Belknap, *Foresters*, 3–4. "A leading theme" in the first volume of Belknap's *American Biography*, according to George Kirsch, "is the westward march of civilization across the Atlantic and its ultimate clash with the more primitive

cultures of the New World." Kirsch, *Jeremy Belknap: A Biography* (New York: Arno, 1982), 131.

11. They were Edward Andrews, *Native Apostles: Black and Indian Missionaries in the Boston Atlantic World* (Cambridge, MA: Harvard University Press, 2013); Julie Fisher and David Silverman, *Ninigret, Sachem of the Niantics and Narragansetts: Diplomacy, War, and the Balance of Power in Seventeenth-Century New England and Indian Country* (Ithaca, NY: Cornell University Press, 2014); and Sean Harvey, *Native Tongues: Colonialism and Race from Encounter to the Reservation* (Cambridge, MA: Harvard University Press, 2015). For an essential corrective to where Belknap began, see Susan Sleeper-Smith, Juliana Barr, Jean M. O'Brien, Nancy Shoemaker, and Scott Manning Stevens, eds., *Why You Can't Teach United States History without American Indians* (Chapel Hill: University of North Carolina Press, 2015).

Chapter Seven. The Rise of National History

1. Ralph Waldo Emerson, "The American Scholar," in *Emerson's Poetry and Prose*, ed. Joel Porte and Saundra Morris (New York: Norton, 2001), 56, 68.

2. John O'Sullivan, "The Great Nation of Futurity," *United States Democratic Review* 6, no. 23 (1839): 428; O'Sullivan, "The True Title," *New York Morning News*, December 27, 1845. As Adam Gomez writes, "In [O'Sullivan's] thought, America's sinlessness and divine mission in world history exempt it from the legal and moral norms that bind other nations, and there exists no legitimate constraints in its providential mission to expand the global reach of liberty." Gomez, "Deus Vult: John L. O'Sullivan, Manifest Destiny, and American Democratic Messianism," *American Political Thought* 1 (2012): 240.

3. Lyman Beecher, *A Plea for the West* (Cincinnati, 1835), 11, 38–39, 20.

4. Tocqueville quoted in George Wilson Pierson, *Tocqueville and Beaumont in America* (New York: Oxford University Press, 1938), 6. Details of travel from Isaac Kramnick, introduction to *Democracy in America*, by Alexis de Tocqueville, trans. Gerald Bevan (New York: Penguin Classics, 2005). For more on the travels, see Alexis de Tocqueville and Gustave de Beaumont, *Alexis de Tocqueville and Gustave de Beaumont in America*, ed. Oliver Zunz, trans. Arthur Goldhammer (Charlottesville: University of Virginia Press, 2010). See also James Schleifer, *The Making of Tocqueville's "Democracy in America,"* 2nd ed. (Indianapolis: Liberty Fund, 2000).

5. Alexis de Tocqueville, *Democracy in America*, trans. Henry Reeves, ed. Isaac Kramnick (New York: Norton, 2007), 27–28. Of nations, he explained that "the circumstances which accompanied their birth and contributed to their rise, affect the whole term of their being" (27). Here and throughout I cite the Norton Critical Edition because it uses the 1838 translation that Americans would have been reading at the time.

6. Tocqueville, 30–31.

7. "New England is the cradle of American Democracy," Sparks told Tocqueville, and he kept reiterating it. Pierson, *Tocqueville and Beaumont in America*, 399; Lawrence Buell, *New England Literary Culture: From Revolution through Renaissance* (New York: Cambridge University Press, 1986), 204.

8. For more on the shaping of national narratives in this period, see Jonathan Arac, *The Emergence of American Literary Narrative, 1820–1860* (Cambridge, MA: Harvard University Press, 2005).

9. As Joyce Appleby has aptly explained, "Because political union preceded the formation of a national identity, the first generation was forced to imagine the sentiments that might bind the nation together." Appleby, *Inheriting the Revolution: The First Generation of Americans* (Cambridge, MA: Harvard University Press, 2000), 262. For two essential starting points on the role of culture and imagination in the creation of nationalism, see Benedict Anderson, *Imagined Communities: Reflections on the Origin and Spread of Nationalism*, rev. ed. (New York: Verso, 1991); and Eric Hobsbawm and Terence Ranger, eds., *The Invention of Tradition* (Cambridge, UK: Cambridge University Press, 1983). At the same time, I am cognizant of the critiques by ethnosymbolists like Anthony D. Smith, who remind us that nations are "*felt* and *willed*" by citizens, not just invented or constructed by elites. Smith, *The Nation in History: Historiographical Debates about Ethnicity and Nationalism* (Hanover, NH: University Press of New England, 2000), 105. For good, brief introductions to nationalism and its vast scholarly literature, see Craig Calhoun, *Nationalism* (Minneapolis: University of Minnesota Press, 1997); Steven Grosby, *Nationalism: A Very Short Introduction* (New York: Oxford University Press, 2005); Smith, *Nation in History*; and Smith, *Nationalism: Theory, Ideology, History* (Cambridge, UK: Polity, 2003).

10. On rites, see David Waldstreicher, *In the Midst of Perpetual Fetes: The Making of American Nationalism, 1776–1820* (Chapel Hill: University of North Carolina Press, 1997). On maps, see Martin Brückner, *The Geographic Revolution in Early America: Maps, Literacy, and National Identity* (Chapel Hill: University of North Carolina Press, 2006). As Brückner emphasizes, "In the first decades of the United States' existence, the image of the national map was one of the few visual artifacts demonstrating what many perceived to be either an abstract or even untenable fiction, namely that there could be a national union between disjointed regions and politically disparate people" (*Geographic Revolution*, 121). See also the works of Susan Schulten, especially *Mapping the Nation: History and Cartography in Nineteenth-Century America* (Chicago: University of Chicago Press, 2012); and Bruce A. Harvey, *American Geographics: U.S. National Narratives and the Representation of the Non-European World, 1830–1865* (Stanford, CA: Stanford University Press, 2001).

11. Daniel Walker Howe, *What Hath God Wrought: The Transformation of America, 1815–1848* (New York: Oxford University Press, 2007), 71; see especially chap. 2. Eileen Ka-May Cheng likewise writes that American exceptionalism became more strident following the war, making it "all the more incumbent on historians to provide an account of the nation's past that would articulate and explain what made the United States distinctive." Cheng, *The Plain and Noble Garb of Truth: Nationalism and Impartiality in American Historical Writing, 1784–1860* (Athens: University of Georgia Press, 2008), 19. See also Jean Matthews, "'Whig History': The New England Whigs and a Usable Past," *New England Quarterly* 51, no. 2 (1978): 193–208.

12. On the importance of history and forgetting to the formation of nations and nationalism, the fundamental starting point is the 1882 lecture by Ernst Renan, reprinted as "What Is a Nation?," trans. Martin Thom, in *Nation and Narration*, ed. Homi K. Bhabha (London: Routledge, 1990), 8–22. As Renan explains, "Forgetting, I would even go so far as to say historical error, is a crucial factor in the creation of a nation, which is why progress in historical studies often constitutes a danger for [the principle of] nationality" (11). For a good, brief overview and introduction to collective memory, see James V. Wertsch and Henry L. Roediger III, "Collective Memory: Conceptual Foundations and Theoretical Approaches," *Memory* 16, no. 3 (2008): 318–326. On collective remembering, see Wertsch, *Voices of Collective Remembering* (New York: Cambridge University Press, 2002).

13. Buell, *New England Literary Culture*, 195. On the sales of the *Collections*, see George Callcott, *History in the United States, 1800–1860: Its Practice and Purpose* (Baltimore: Johns Hopkins University Press, 1970), 43, 111; and Leslie Dunlap, *American Historical Societies, 1790–1860* (Philadelphia: Porcupine, 1974), 105. Meanwhile, between 1820 and 1860, more than fifty novels were written specifically about the Puritans. For a bibliography, see Michael Davitt Bell, *Hawthorne and the Historical Romance of New England* (Princeton, NJ: Princeton University Press, 1971), 243–248. For more on the dramatic rise of historical interest in the 1820s and 1830s, especially in New England, see Harlow Sheidley, *Sectional Nationalism: Massachusetts Conservative Leaders and the Transformation of America, 1815–1836* (Boston: Northeastern University Press, 1998), chap. 5.

14. Samuel Hazard, *The Register of Pennsylvania: Devoted to the Preservation of Facts and Documents and Every Other Kind of Useful Information Respecting the State of Pennsylvania* (Philadelphia: Wm. F. Geddes, 1828), accessed May 28, 2019, https://archive.org/details/registerofpennsy12haza/page/n5. For more on Samuel Hazard, see Roland M. Baumann, "Samuel Hazard: Editor and Archivist for the Keystone State," *Pennsylvania Magazine of History and Biography* 107, no. 2 (1983): 195–215.

15. For schooling laws, see Catherine Reef, *Education and Learning in America* (New York: Facts on File, 2009), 25, 37. For Massachusetts, see Gretchen

Adams, *The Specter of Salem: Remembering the Witch Trials in Nineteenth-Century America* (Chicago: University of Chicago Press, 2008), 49. For the state laws about teaching history, see Susan Schulten, "Emma Willard and the Graphic Foundations of American History," *Journal of Historical Geography* 33, no. 3 (2007): 546. The states were Massachusetts, Vermont, New York, Virginia, and Rhode Island. "In New York alone," Trudy Hanmer reports, "the number of schoolchildren grew from 176,449 in 1816 to 508,848 in 1833." Hanmer, *Wrought with Steadfast Will: A History of Emma Willard School* (Troy, NY: Emma Willard School, 2012), 132. As Callcott summarizes, "At the time of the Revolution almost no one studied history academically, but by the time of the Civil War it was at least as prominent in the elementary and secondary schools—though not in the colleges—as it is today" (*History in the United States*, 55).

16. Salma Hale, *History of the United States* (New York, 1823), iii; Barry Joyce, *The First U.S. History Textbooks: Constructing and Disseminating the American Tale in the Nineteenth Century* (Lanham, MD: Lexington, 2015), 43. For the numbers of editions per decade, see George Callcott, "History Enters the Schools," *American Quarterly* 11, no. 4 (1959): 473. Callcott claims that five editions appeared between 1775 and 1820. John Nietz says that "only eight or nine American history textbooks were published in our country before 1820, and apparently none had a wide circulation." Nietz, *Old Textbooks* (Pittsburgh: University of Pittsburgh Press, 1961), 234. The journals devoting book reviews to textbooks were the *United States Literary Gazette* (established 1824) and the *American Journal of Education* (established 1826). See David Van Tassel, *Recording America's Past: An Interpretation of the Development of Historical Studies in America, 1607–1884* (Chicago: University of Chicago Press, 1960), 89–90. For the top four textbook writers, see Alfred Goldberg, "School Histories of the Middle Period," in *Historiography and Urbanization: Essays in American History in Honor of W. Stull Holt*, ed. Eric Goldman (Baltimore: Johns Hopkins University Press, 1941), 171–188. Gretchen Adams names the top six: these four plus Jesse Olney and Marcius Wilson. Adams, *Specter of Salem*, 50. For the rise and role of schoolbooks more generally in the era, see Charles Monaghan and E. Jennifer Monaghan, "Schoolbooks," in *An Extensive Republic: Print, Culture, and Society in the New Nation, 1790–1840*, ed. Robert A. Gross and Mary Kelly, vol. 2 of *A History of the Book in America* (Chapel Hill: University of North Carolina Press, 2010), 304–318. Monaghan and Monaghan, like others, identify 1820 as a turning point.

17. In this sense, national history textbooks are the essential place to find a middle ground between versions of nationalism that insist on social constructivism and those that insist on its rootedness in more objective realities and in the will and feelings of those who inhabit the territory to be nationalized. On the role of narratives in creating a nation, see Simon During, "Literature—Nationalism's Other? The Case for Revision," in

Nation and Narration, ed. Homi K. Bhabha (London: Routledge, 1990), 139–153. For a good review of debates about nationalism and its relation to representation, see Thomas Allen, *A Republic in Time: Temporality and Social Imagination in Nineteenth-Century America* (Chapel Hill: University of North Carolina Press, 2008), 1–16.

18. Van Tassel, *Recording America's Past*, 91. Joyce observes, "Textbook publishers targeted entire families as likely consumers of their product" (*First U.S. History Textbooks*, 56). Gerald F. Moran and Maris A. Vinovskis call the antebellum classroom a "scene of confusion." Moran and Vinovskis, "Schools," in Gross and Kelly, *Extensive Republic*, 296. Joyce explains, "The very things that presumably eroded the possibilities for effective classroom learning . . . further elevated the role that textbooks played as bodies of knowledge as the most consistent and accessible source of the American tribal narrative" (*First U.S. History Textbooks*, 54).

19. See Callcott, *History in the United States*, 68. As the literary historian Joseph Conforti aptly summarizes, "New Englanders dominated American historical writing from the seventeenth well into the twentieth century." Conforti, *Imagining New England: Explorations of Regional Identity from the Pilgrims to the Twentieth Century* (Chapel Hill: University of North Carolina Press, 2001), 6.

20. Joyce, *First U.S. History Textbooks*, 114.

21. William Grimshaw, *History of the United States, from Their First Settlement as Colonies, to the Cession of Florida*, 3rd ed. (Philadelphia, 1822), 48, 48, 50, 57, 51, 58.

22. Frederick Butler, *A Complete History of the United States of America* (Hartford, CT, 1821), iii, v, 9. Butler returns to this point more than once, asking rhetorically, "Who that surveys this adventure in all its parts, from the rise of the Puritans, to the landing of these pilgrims, does not see the hand of God as conspicuously displayed, as in the call of Abraham, through the whole history of his family, to their settlement in the land of Canaan" (104).

23. Hawthorne quoted in Buell, *New England Literary Culture*, 206. Cheng notes that "historical novelists played an important role in developing a more critical view of the Puritans during this period" (*Plain and Noble Garb*, 170). As Buell details, the usual type of female heroine in Puritan historical novels was "the enlightened female outsider who functions as critic of provincial rigidity, risks getting into trouble for her outspokenness, but escapes unscathed" (*New England Literary Culture*, 242). The enlightened, anachronistic modern mind-set placed in a harsh Puritan society remains a popular literary device, as can be seen, for example, in the work of Geraldine Brooks. For a great work on historical novels about the Puritans, see Philip Gould, *Covenant and Republic: Historical Romance and the Politics of Puritanism* (New York: Cambridge University Press, 1996). Michael Colacurcio has done the most detailed work exam-

ining especially Hawthorne's study of the Puritan past. See especially Colacurcio, *The Province of Piety: Moral History in Hawthorne's Early Tales* (Cambridge, MA: Harvard University Press, 1984).

24. Though others have since taken up New Amsterdam's cause. See Russell Shorto, *The Island at the Center of the World: The Epic Story of Dutch Manhattan and the Forgotten Colony That Shaped America* (New York: Vintage, 2005).

25. On this point, see especially Jean O'Brien, *Firsting and Lasting: Writing Indians Out of Existence in New England* (Minneapolis: University of Minnesota Press, 2010).

Chapter Eight. The Spread of National Pilgrims

1. Webster quoted in Frederic Austin, *Daniel Webster* (Philadelphia: George W. Jacobs, 1914), 110. In four short years, Webster left an enormous legacy on the making of American law. For details, see Robert Remini, *Daniel Webster: The Man and His Time* (New York: Norton, 1997), chap. 7. Many scholars agree that Webster's speeches of the 1820s were integral to making Pilgrim Landing and Plymouth Rock into a national origin myth. As Joseph Conforti summarizes, "The founding of Plymouth itself remained an uncommemorated, even obscure, local event overshadowed for most of the colonial era by the 'Great,' expansive Puritan migration to New England." Conforti, *Imagining New England: Explorations of Regional Identity from the Pilgrims to the Twentieth Century* (Chapel Hill: University of North Carolina Press, 2001), 171. Webster would change that. For a summary of Webster's influence, see Harlow Sheidley, *Sectional Nationalism: Massachusetts Conservative Leaders and the Transformation of America, 1815–1836* (Boston: Northeastern University Press, 1998), chap. 5. For my account of Daniel Webster and his speech, I have relied primarily on Irving Bartlett, *Daniel Webster* (New York: Norton, 1978); Conforti, *Imagining New England*, 183–185; Paul D. Erickson, "Daniel Webster's Myth of the Pilgrims," *New England Quarterly* 57, no. 1 (1984): 44–64; Remini, *Daniel Webster*; and John Seelye, *Memory's Nation: The Place of Plymouth Rock* (Chapel Hill: University of North Carolina Press, 1998), 73–85.

2. Daniel Webster, *A Discourse, Delivered at Plymouth, December 22, 1820, in Commemoration of the First Settlement of New-England* (Boston, 1821), 5–6, 64, 16, 11, 16, 25.

3. Webster, 60, 100.

4. Webster, 60, 16–17.

5. The essential book on Whig culture is Daniel Walker Howe, *The Political Culture of the Whigs* (Chicago: University of Chicago Press, 1979). For a good account of the contrast between Whigs and Democrats on American expansion, see Reginald Horsman, *Race and Manifest Destiny: The*

Origins of American Racial Anglo-Saxonism (Cambridge, MA: Harvard University Press, 1981). As Sandra Gustafson observes, when Webster spoke of the United States expanding its democratic experiment, he entertained "relatively modest expectations about the spread of that system, which, he emphasized repeatedly, should be accomplished by moral example and not by physical force." Gustafson, "Histories of Democracy and Empire," *American Quarterly* 59, no. 1 (2007): 121.

6. Webster, *Discourse*, 30–40.

7. Webster, 41–42. Later editions of this speech changed this line to claim that "the first night of their repose saw the Pilgrims already *at home* in their country."

8. Webster, 42.

9. Webster, 10–11, 90.

10. George Ticknor quoted in Bartlett, *Daniel Webster*, 83; John Adams quoted in Remini, *Daniel Webster*, 186. Henry Cabot Lodge, in his own enthusiastic biography of Webster, claimed that the Plymouth oration "was received with a universal burst of applause. It had more literary success than anything which had at that time appeared, except from the pen of Washington Irving." Lodge, *Daniel Webster* (Boston: Houghton, Mifflin, 1887), 123.

11. In 1855, Willard reported to Lyman Draper, the man behind the State Historical Society of Wisconsin, that Robert Winthrop read and loved her textbook and had procured it "on the recommendation of Daniel Webster, who not only wrote an unsolicited letter to me, saying that he kept it by him, . . . but he told Mr. Winthrop that he hardly traveled without it." Willard to Lyman Draper, November 10, 1855, Emma Willard School Archive, Troy, NY.

12. In 1818, Emma wrote her friend that it was still uncertain what John planned to do and how it would affect her plans to teach. See Willard to Hannah Davis, March 16, 1818, copy, Emma Willard School Archive, Troy, NY, from Sheldon Museum, Middlebury, VT. The standard biography of Emma Hart Willard remains Alma Lutz, *Emma Willard, Daughter of Democracy* (Boston: Houghton Mifflin, 1929), which was adapted as *Emma Willard, Pioneer Educator of American Women* (Boston: Beacon, 1964). Recently, Trudy Hanmer has written an impressive history of the Emma Willard School that includes an important biographical account of Emma Willard as well. See Hanmer, *Wrought with Steadfast Will: A History of Emma Willard School* (Troy, NY: Emma Willard School, 2012).

13. In 1815, she wrote that she first thought to assist her husband by "assuming my former employment" but soon she found far more: "my fondness for my former favorite occupation has revived," she explained. Willard to Benjamin and Mrs. Tappan, March 12, 1815, Emma Willard School Archive, Troy, NY. As one scholar reports, "The new school was scarcely underway when she set herself the goal of making it better than 'any

heretofore known,' and to 'inform myself, and increase my personal influence and fame as a teacher, calculating that in this way I might be sought for in other places, where influential men would carry my project before some legislature.'" John Lord, *The Life of Emma Willard* (New York: Appleton, 1873), 34–35. This biography includes several of Willard's letters.

14. For "magna carta," see Hanmer, *Wrought with Steadfast Will*, 46; Emma Willard, *An Address to the Public: Particularly to the Members of the Legislature of New-York, Proposing a Plan for Improving Female Education*, 2nd ed. (Middlebury, VT, 1819), 18, 59. The idea that women had a moral role to play in keeping the character of the nation, especially through the upbringing of children, has been called "republican motherhood." See Linda Kerber, *Women of the Republic: Intellect and Ideas in Revolutionary America* (Chapel Hill: University of North Carolina Press, 1980).

15. Clinton to Willard, December 31, 1818, Emma Willard School Archive, Troy, NY.

16. Willard to Gideon Granger, March 4, 1820, copy, Emma Willard School Archive, Troy, NY, from Gideon Granger Papers, Library of Congress, Washington, DC.

17. See Lutz, *Emma Willard, Pioneer*, 39; Hanmer, *Wrought with Steadfast Will*, 72.

18. Emma Willard, *Letter, Addressed as a Circular to the Members of the Willard Association, for the Mutual Improvement of Female Teachers* (Troy, NY: Elias Gates, 1838); George Combe to Willard, 1837, Emma Willard School Archive, Troy, NY. "By the mid-1830s, institutions modeled on the 'Troy plan' sprang up in South Carolina, Maryland, Ohio, Vermont, and other parts of the country." Angelo Repousis, "'The Trojan Women': Emma Hart Willard and the Troy Society for the Advancement of Female Education in Greece," *Journal of the Early Republic* 24, no. 3 (2004): 456. Anne Firor Scott counts more than twelve thousand pupils at Troy between 1821 and 1872. Scott, "What, Then, Is the American: This New Woman?" *Journal of American History* 65 (1978): 680–681. See also Scott, "The Ever Widening Circle: The Diffusion of Feminist Values from the Troy Female Seminary, 1822–1872," *History of Education Quarterly* 19, no. 1 (1979): 3–25. For more on the rise of female education in this period, see Mary Kelley, *Learning to Stand and Speak: Women, Education, and Public Life in America's Republic* (Chapel Hill: University of North Carolina Press, 2006).

19. Susan Schulten, "Emma Willard and the Graphic Foundations of American History," *Journal of Historical Geography* 33, no. 3 (2007): 545. See also Nina Baym, "Women and the Republic: Emma Willard's Rhetoric of History," *American Quarterly* 42 (1991): 1–23.

20. As Schulten remarks, "Willard believed that information presented *spatially* and *visually* would facilitate memory by attaching images to the

mind through the eyes" ("Emma Willard," 545). For Willard's pedagogical innovations, see Schulten's work as well as Brückner, *Geographic Revolution*, 246–248; and Daniel Calhoun, "Eyes for the Jacksonian World: William C. Woodbridge and Emma Willard," *Journal of the Early Republic* 4.1 (1984): 1–26, especially 13–14.

21. John Hart Willard to Emma Willard, March 16, 1844, Emma Willard School Archive, Troy, NY. As one paper reported, "The works of Mrs. Willard, late of the Troy Female Seminary, are receiving the stamp of approbation wherever they are made known." *District School Journal, of the State of New-York* 5, no. 3 (1844): 93. For printing counts, see Baym, "Women and the Republic," 5. Baym adds, "The intended audience for this text, then, was the entire literate population" (4–5). For the figure of a million copies sold, see Barry Joyce, *The First U.S. History Textbooks: Constructing and Disseminating the American Tale in the Nineteenth Century* (Lanham, MD: Lexington, 2015), 45. Letters show direct evidence of Willard's history textbooks extending to Mississippi (C. Davies to Emma Willard, August 31, 1842), Wisconsin (Emma Willard to Lyman Draper, November 10, 1855), and Georgia (Elizabeth [Twiss] to Emma Willard, October 11, 1829), but presumably most of her pupils, who learned American history from her textbooks, would have then used her textbooks to teach. All letters at Emma Willard School Archive, Troy, NY.

22. Emma Willard, *History of the United States, or Republic of America* (New York, 1828), iii–v.

23. Willard, 46. On Pilgrim origin stories, see especially John Seelye, *Memory's Nation: The Place of Plymouth Rock* (Chapel Hill: University of North Carolina Press, 1998). See also Ruth Miller Elson, *Guardians of Tradition: American Schoolbooks of the Nineteenth Century* (Lincoln: University of Nebraska Press, 1964), 113. For a great source concerned more broadly with memory and the making of "New England," see Conforti, *Imagining New England*.

24. Salma Hale, *History of the United States* (New York, 1825), 24; John Howard Hinton, *The History and Topography of the United States of North America, from the Earliest Period to the Present Time*, with additions and corrections by Samuel L. Knapp, vol. 1 (Boston, 1834), 39, 43–44.

Chapter Nine. The Creation of an Exceptional New England

1. George Chalmers quoted in Abiel Holmes, *American Annals; or, A Chronological History of America from Its Discovery in MCCCCXCII to MDCCCVI in Two Volumes* (Cambridge, MA, 1805), 1:156. For Willard, see Gretchen Adams, *The Specter of Salem: Remembering the Witch Trials in Nineteenth-Century America* (Chicago: University of Chicago Press, 2008), 51. John Seelye explains, "For if the United States was an exception among

nations, it was because the Pilgrims were an exceptional group of people and the Landing and the Signing exceptional events, having no parallels in human history, a distinction often enforced by comparisons not with ancient history but colonial Virginia." Seelye, *Memory's Nation: The Place of Plymouth Rock* (Chapel Hill: University of North Carolina Press, 1998), 59.

2. Frederick Butler, *A Complete History of the United States of America* (Hartford, CT, 1821), 113; J. L. Blake, *The Historical Reader, Designed for the Use of Schools and Families* (Rochester, NY, 1827), 296. As William Grimshaw noted, "In about seventeen years after the first emigration to New England, negroes were imported there, as a regular branch of traffic with the West Indies." Grimshaw, *History of the United States, from Their First Settlement as Colonies, to the Cession of Florida*, 3rd ed. (Philadelphia, 1822), 68. On slavery in New England, see Wendy Warren, *New England Bound: Slavery and Colonization in Early America* (New York: Liveright, 2016).

3. Holmes, *American Annals*, 205; Butler, *Complete History*, 108; Charles Goodrich, *A History of the United States of America*, 3rd ed. (Hartford, CT, 1824), 30. For more on what Seelye calls "this logic of adversity" in relation to the Pilgrims, see Seelye, *Memory's Nation*, 86–100.

4. John Howard Hinton, *The History and Topography of the United States of North America, from the Earliest Period to the Present Time*, with additions and corrections by Samuel L. Knapp, vol. 1 (Boston, 1834), 44; Salma Hale, *History of the United States* (New York, 1825), 25–26. As Stephanie Kermes says, competing denominations often tried "to claim the New England heritage for their own branch of Protestantism." Kermes, *Creating an American Identity: New England, 1789–1825* (New York: Palgrave Macmillan, 2008), 181. Margaret Bendroth is particularly good on this point. See Bendroth, *The Last Puritans: Mainline Protestants and the Power of the Past* (Chapel Hill: University of North Carolina Press, 2015). For the positive use of an imagined Puritan heritage by abolitionists of all different sorts—white and black, male and female—see the excellent new book by Kenyon Gradert, *Puritan Spirits in the Abolitionist Imagination* (Chicago: Chicago University Press, 2020); as well as Gradert, "Swept into Puritanism: Emerson, Wendell Phillips, and the Roots of Radicalism," *New England Quarterly* 90, no. 1 (2017): 103–129. For additional readings of these flexible and contested origins, see Lawrence Buell, *New England Literary Culture: From Revolution through Renaissance* (New York: Cambridge University Press, 1986), 207–217. Seelye is emphatic on this point: see Seelye, *Memory's Nation*, especially chaps. 9–10.

5. Hinton, *History and Topography*, 6; John O'Sullivan, "The Great Nation of Futurity," *United States Democratic Review* 6, no. 23 (1839): 427. This rhetoric is closely related to the form of American exceptionalism that Sacvan Bercovitch famously excavated in *The American Jeremiad* (1978; repr., Madison: University of Wisconsin Press, 2012). But Bercovitch's jere-

miad involved a castigation of the current generation for falling away from ancestors. Most textbooks record an unending celebration of America for the progress unfolding from its origin. Bercovitch comes closer to explaining this form of rhetoric in his description of George Bancroft. See Bercovitch, *The Rites of Assent: Transformations in the Symbolic Construction of America* (New York: Routledge, 1993), chap. 6.

6. Hinton, *History and Topography*, 42. (Hinton was probably making an allusion to the last lines of *Paradise Lost*: "The World was all before them, where to choose / Their place of rest, and Providence their guide: / They hand in hand with wandring steps and slow, / Through Eden took their solitary way.") Emma Willard, *History of the United States, or Republic of America* (New York, 1828), 3–4. This way of thinking had a long history. As John Locke famously stated in the seventeenth century, "Thus in the beginning all the world was *America*." Locke, *Second Treatise of Government*, ed. C. B. Macpherson (Indianapolis: Hackett, 1980), 5.49 (italics in original). It was common to celebrate the transformation of the "wilderness" into towns of "houses, churches, and other public edifices." Samuel Goodrich, *The First Book of History* (Cincinnati, 1832), 20. On the assumption of progress in nineteenth-century historiography, see Dorothy Ross, "Grand Narrative in American Historical Writing: From Romance to Uncertainty," *American Historical Review* 100, no. 3 (1995): 651–677.

7. As Schulten notes, "By naming this an 'introductory' map, Willard reinforced the contemporary assumption that Native Americans existed in a timeless space prior to human history." Schulten, *Mapping the Nation: History and Cartography in Nineteenth-Century America* (Chicago: University of Chicago Press, 2012), 25. Schulten has done the best and most detailed work on Willard's maps.

8. Emma Willard, *A Series of Maps to Willard's History of the United States, or Republic of America; Designed for Schools and Private Libraries* (New York, 1828). All of these maps and images are accessible through the Library of Congress at https://www.loc.gov/item/2002624002/. For more on Emma Willard's maps, see Martin Brückner, *The Geographic Revolution in Early America: Maps, Literacy, and National Identity* (Chapel Hill: University of North Carolina Press, 2006), chap. 7; Daniel Calhoun, "Eyes for the Jacksonian World: William C. Woodbridge and Emma Willard," *Journal of the Early Republic* 4, no. 1 (1984): 1–26; and Susan Schulten, "Emma Willard and the Graphic Foundations of American History," *Journal of Historical Geography* 33, no. 3 (2007): 542–564.

9. Andrew Jackson quoted in Robert A. Gross, introduction to *An Extensive Republic: Print, Culture, and Society in the New Nation, 1790–1840*, ed. Robert A. Gross and Mary Kelley, vol. 2 of *A History of the Book in America* (Chapel Hill: University of North Carolina Press, 2010), 2.

10. Calhoun, "Eyes for the Jacksonian World," 18; Hale, *History of the United States*, 15. As Daniel Walker Howe comments, "Almost all Americans re-

garded their country as an example and a harbinger of popular government to the rest of the world, and even non-church-members found millennial expectations an appropriate metaphor for this destiny." Howe, *What Hath God Wrought: The Transformation of America, 1815–1848* (New York: Oxford University Press, 2007), 285.

11. Adams, *Specter of Salem*, 60. Bancroft says in the opening of his first volume that he "sought to collect truth from trustworthy documents and testimony," desiring "to give to the work the interest of authenticity." George Bancroft, *A History of the United States*, vol. 1 (Boston, 1834), v. Eileen Ka-May Cheng observes, "Ultimately, then, what made Bancroft's account of American history—and his vision of American exceptionalism—so compelling was not just its mythic quality but its claims to impartial truth, for by making his account appear to be impartial, he conferred on myth the mantle and legitimacy of objective reality." Cheng, *The Plain and Noble Garb of Truth: Nationalism and Impartiality in American Historical Writing, 1784–1860* (Athens: University of Georgia Press, 2008), 159. As Jonathan Arac aptly puts it, "Bancroft did not think of himself as an inventor. He conceived his task to resemble that of a primitive bard. He wanted to articulate what his people already knew and believed and had been telling each other, but to give it a shape and scope that would include as much of the story as possible, more than could be directly known by any single person or local tradition, and that would thus make possible the continuation of the people, their knowledge, and their story." Arac, *The Emergence of American Literary Narrative, 1820–1860* (Cambridge, MA: Harvard University Press, 2005), 24. For important works on Bancroft, see Michael Kraus, *The Writing of American History* (Norman: University of Oklahoma Press, 1953); David Levin, *History as Romantic Art: Bancroft, Prescott, Motley, and Parkman* (Stanford, CA: Stanford University Press, 1959); Dorothy Ross, "Historical Consciousness in Nineteenth-Century America," *American Historical Review* 89, no. 4 (1984): 909–928; and Bercovitch, *Rites of Assent*, chap. 6.

12. Bancroft, *History*, vii, 338.

13. Bancroft, vii, 204. Cheng points out that "his critics saw his work as a sectional vehicle that promoted the interests of New England at the expense of other regions of the country" (*Plain and Noble Garb*, 165).

14. Bancroft, *History*, 327, 328, 338.

15. Bancroft, 349–350.

16. There has been controversy about the end of William Apess's life. Historically, he was taken to have died of alcoholism. According to Robert Warrior, Apess "found himself in a state of intellectual despair that was exacerbated by excessive drinking." Warrior, *The People and the Word: Reading Native Nonfiction* (Minneapolis: University of Minnesota Press, 2005), 6. But Apess's conditions seem consistent with appendicitis. And it is now widely believed that he took up the name of a Seneca revivalist

named Handsome Lake in some of his final lectures, still working and writing and speaking to the end. The case for Apess's continued activities, and his death by appendicitis, is most convincingly made by Drew Lopenzina, *Through an Indian's Looking-Glass: A Cultural Biography of William Apess, Pequot* (Amherst: University of Massachusetts Press, 2017), 243–252.

17. Scott Manning Stevens reminds us that "one should not overlook the appeal of Apess's regional identity.... Like many people living in post-Conquest America, Apess would have been surrounded by the cultural triumphalism of the new independent United States." Stevens, "William Apess's Historical Self," *Northwest Review* 35, no. 3 (1997): 68. Apess's *Eulogy on King Philip*, as many scholars have pointed out, "uncomfortably placed Native experiences at the heart of the American story." Daniel Richter, *Facing East from Indian Country: A Native History of Early America* (Cambridge, MA: Harvard University Press, 2003), 238. Apess was "establishing New England as Native space into which Europeans entered." Lisa Brooks, *The Common Pot: The Recovery of Native Space in the Northeast* (Minneapolis: University of Minnesota Press, 2008), 199. For one of the foundational starting points on "settler colonialism," giving context to Apess's work, see Patrick Wolfe, "Settler Colonialism and the Elimination of the Native," *Journal of Genocide Research* 8, no. 4 (2006): 387–409.

18. "He was perhaps the most successful activist on behalf of Indian rights in the antebellum United States." Patricia Bizzell, "(Native) American Jeremiad: The 'Mixed Blood' Rhetoric of William Apess," in *American Indian Rhetorics of Survivance: Word Medicine, Word Magic*, ed. Ernest Stromberg (Pittsburgh: University of Pittsburgh Press, 2006), 34. Though William Apess was himself erased from memory for a long time, the 1990s saw a rebirth of interest in him. There is now a voluminous literature on him, including two recent biographies: Philip Gura, *The Life of William Apess, Pequot* (Chapel Hill: University of North Carolina Press, 2015); and Lopenzina, *Through an Indian's Looking-Glass*. The starting point for studies of Apess is the compilation of his writing that Barry O'Connell produced: *On Our Own Ground: The Complete Writings of William Apess, a Pequot* (Amherst: University of Massachusetts Press, 1992).

19. For the significance of the date, see Maureen Konkle, *Writing Indian Nations: Native Intellectuals and the Politics of Historiography, 1827–1863* (Chapel Hill: University of North Carolina Press, 2004), 131–133. For the wider cultural context of remembering King Philip in the early nineteenth century, see Jill Lepore, *The Name of War: King Philip's War and the Origins of American Identity* (New York: Vintage, 1998), chap. 8.

20. As Stevens states, "For Apess it would be the *rhetoric* of history and not that of religion that came ultimately to provide him with the best means for giving voice to a Native identity and its place in American culture" ("William Apess's Historical Self," 75).

21. As Anna Brickhouse has explained, "The term *settlement* . . . has tradition-
    ally been used in the historiography of the Anglo-American colonies, and
    it has always functioned as more than just another word for colonialism:
    it has from its earliest usages connoted a specifically *English* and particu-
    larly Protestant style of colonialism that is in contrast to its . . . Spanish
    foil: *conquest.*" Brickhouse, *The Unsettlement of America: Translation, Inter-
    pretation, and the Story of Don Luis de Velasco, 1560–1945* (New York: Ox-
    ford University Press, 2015), 2. Apess understood that well. Peyer Bernd
    points out Apess's awareness of other "current intellectual trends" as well.
    See Bernd, *The Tutor'd Mind: Indian Missionary-Writers in Antebellum
    America* (Amherst: University of Massachusetts Press, 1997), 159.
22. William Apess, "Eulogy on King Philip," in O'Connell, *On Our Own
    Ground*, 282, 284, 277, 285, 285, 304, 308.
23. Apess, 290, 277.
24. Apess, 280, 301, 279, 304. Apess actually writes, "December (O.S.) 1620"
    referring to the "Old Style" calendar.
25. Apess, 287, 305. As Sandra Gustafson summarizes, Apess's *Eulogy* serves
    as "a powerful analysis of the Puritan roots of American racism." Gus-
    tafson, "Nations of Israelites: Prophecy and Cultural Autonomy in the
    Writings of William Apess," *Religion and Literature* 26, no. 1 (1994): 32.
26. Apess, "Eulogy on King Philip," 286, 286, 306, 310, 310. As Deborah
    Gussman summarizes, Apess "invites his audience to see the connection
    between history, representation, and political practice and to reject the
    official narratives and reconstruct a new, more just, and more inclusive
    American society." Gussman, "'O Savage, Where Art Thou?': Rhetorics
    of Reform in William Apess's 'Eulogy on King Philip,'" *New England
    Quarterly* 77, no. 3 (2004): 463. Because of this message, many scholars
    have linked Apess's address to Frederick Douglass's "What to the Slave Is
    the Fourth of July?" See, for example, Patricia Bizzell, "The 4th of July
    and the 22nd of December: The Function of Cultural Archives in Per-
    suasion, as Shown by Frederick Douglass and William Apess," *College
    Composition and Communication* 48, no. 1 (1997): 44–60.
27. Apess, "Eulogy on King Philip," 279, 282. Richter says of Apess's address,
    "Exaggerated, one-sided, propagandistic? Certainly; but no more so than
    Webster's skewed view of the continent's past" (*Facing East*, 251). Many
    scholars, like Richter, have seen Apess directly responding to the
    speeches of Daniel Webster.

Chapter Ten. Antiquarian America

1. James Savage, "Prefatory Remarks by a Member of the Massachusetts Historical Society," in *Collections of the Massachusetts Historical Society*, 3d ser.,
   vol. 7 (Boston: MHS, 1838), 32. Notably, George Folsom references the
   same line as James Savage does. When Folsom discovered the sermon at

the NYHS, he admitted that he was "unable to furnish any additional information relative to this interesting relic of the 'brave leader and famous Governor' of the Colony of Massachusetts Bay." Folsom, introductory letter, "Model of Christian Charity by John Winthrop Esq. First Governor of the Colony of the Massachusetts Bay," in *Collections of the Massachusetts Historical Society*, 3d ser., vol. 7 (Boston: MHS, 1838), 31.

2. As one historian writes, "the great surge of local historical writings came after 1815 in reaction to the rapid growth of nationalism and as a reflection of the competition between the states." Each historical society "originated as a weapon in the battle to dominate the writing of national history." David Van Tassel, *Recording America's Past: An Interpretation of the Development of Historical Studies in America, 1607–1884* (Chicago: University of Chicago Press, 1960), 55, 59. In 1838, meanwhile, the NYHS issued a resolution to hold "a general meeting to be composed of delegates from all the historical and antiquarian Societies in the United States; with the view of promoting concert of action in the great work of historical research into matters connected with our own history." Quoted in Leslie Dunlap, *American Historical Societies, 1790–1860* (Philadelphia: Porcupine, 1974), 115. The meeting, incidentally, was never held.

3. Folsom to Thaddeus Harris, January 31, 1838, MHS Archives, MHS, Boston, MA.

4. Harris to Folsom, February 15, 1838, MHS Archives, MHS, Boston, MA.

5. "Catalogue of Manuscripts Belonging to the N-YHS, ca. 1820?," NYHS-RG 21: Library Department records (1815–2016), NYHS Records, Patricia D. Klingenstein Library, NYHS, New York, NY.

6. Charles Deane, "Tribute by Mr. Deane to James Savage," *Proceedings of the Massachusetts Historical Society* 12 (1871–1873): 439.

7. James Savage, "Savage Genealogy," 1839, James Savage Papers I, 1757–1891, MHS, Boston, MA (hereafter cited as JSP I). Savage, "Personal Memoir," written for his daughter, Emma Rogers, n.d., JSP I. Savage to Mrs. James Otis Lincoln, August 20, 1818, in *Letters of James Savage to His Family* (Boston, 1906), 9.

8. James Savage, "Nil magnum sine labore," School Essays 1799–1803, JSP I.

9. James Savage, "Reverence for Antiquity," School Essays 1799–1803, JSP I.

10. Savage, "Reverence for Antiquity," School Essays 1799–1803, JSP I.

11. James Savage to Mary Lincoln, October 10, 1803, James Savage Papers II, 1770–1940, MHS, Boston, MA (hereafter cited as JSP II).

12. As one of Savage's colleagues once explained, "It belongs to the antiquary ... to gather up the small facts of history, the fragments of truth, to be a gleaner in the by-ways of the past." In this regard, James Savage "was at that day—and with those surroundings—the perfect impersonation of an Antiquary, in form and feature, in speech and in spirit." Deane, "Tribute," 439.

13. James Savage to Emma Rogers, March 3, 1851, in *Letters*, 133.

14. As Savage's colleague G. S. Hillard reported after Savage died, "The high reputation which he had gained as a New England Antiquary by that work led to an extensive correspondence with persons interested in similar pursuits. The letters he received often required a considerable degree of research before they could be answered satisfactorily to himself." Hillard, "Memoir of the Hon. James Savage, LL.D.," *Proceedings of the Massachusetts Historical Society* 16 (1878): 141.

15. James Savage to his wife [Elizabeth], July 7, 1842, in *Letters*, 70. Hillard, who eventually read Savage's diary of this trip, accurately reports that it leaves no trace "of his having visited any of those places in Great Britain which are of most interest to the generality of cultivated Americans" ("Memoir," 142).

16. Savage, "Diary," 1842, JSP I, 89.

17. Deane, "Tribute," 436.

18. On this dispute and James Savage's role in it, see JSP I, box 1, folders 1824 and 1829.

19. Livermore to Savage, May 26, 1855, JSP I.

20. Deane, "Tribute," 439. Hillard perhaps summed up this attitude best: "A wrong date, a false statement, a careless narrative, he resented as if it were a personal grievance; and it made no difference whether the offender had been sleeping in his grave a hundred years or more, nor was the energy of his feeling at all proportioned to the importance of the subject" ("Memoir," 151). On the difference between antiquarians and historians, see Lawrence Buell, *New England Literary Culture: From Revelation through Renaissance* (New York: Cambridge University Press, 1986), 111.

21. Savage, "Prefatory Remarks," 32.

22. Savage, "Reverence for Antiquity." As Hillard tried to summarize, Savage "loved the fathers of New England judiciously, but not extravagantly. He was very kind to their virtues, but not blind to their faults or the faults of the time in which their lot was cast" ("Memoir of James Savage," 137).

23. John Winthrop, *The History of New England from 1630–1649*, ed. James Savage, 2 vols. (Boston: Phelps and Farnham, 1825), 1:179n1. "Our fathers looked too much to a special divine appointment in their management of secular concerns," he complained, "often forgetting that reason was no less the gift of God, than the ritual of Moses" (1:121n4). As Savage also remarked, "Church and state were too often playing into each other's hands—if so irreverent a phrase may be allowed—and thus sanctifying principles and conduct, which either would not have, singly, ventured to adopt or enforce" (1:163m1).

24. Winthrop, 1:12n1, 1:17on2, 1:51n4, 1:84n1, 1:154n1, 1:23n2, 1:289n1, 1:21n2, 1:132n1.

25. Winthrop, 1:30n2, 1:26n3, 1:64n1 (italics added), 1:174n1. It is no coincidence that in several places, Savage traces out the ancestral names that have been honored by Puritan descendants. On the clergyman Thomas Hooker,

for example, Savage noted that a "line of pious, useful and honourable descendants have embalmed the memory of their ancestor" (1:88n1).

26. Savage, "Prefatory Remarks," 32.

27. Savage to his wife [Elizabeth], August 4, 1828, in *Letters*, 17; Savage to his wife [Elizabeth], August 26, 1831, in *Letters*, 34; Savage to his daughter [Emma Rogers], April 21, 1852, in *Letters*, 151. For an excellent analysis of how and why Savage would turn to facsimiles of Winthrop's letters in his modern edition of *The History of New England*, see Patricia Roylance, "Winthrop's Journal in Manuscript and Print: The Temporalities of Early-Nineteenth-Century Transmedial Reproduction," *PMLA* 133, no. 1 (2018): 88–106.

28. Winthrop, *History of New England*, 1:250n1, 1:404, 2:338n1; Savage, "Prefatory Remarks," 32. The worst aspects of the Antinomian Controversy Savage attributed to Thomas Weld, not John Winthrop. He fought a long duel with another antiquarian about the authorship of the notorious *Short Story*, which had long been credited to Winthrop, insisting that Weld was responsible for the majority of it. For more on Savage's love of Winthrop and his defense of Winthrop in the Antinomian Controversy, see Lindsay DiCuirci, "History's Imprint: The Colonial Book and the Writing of American History, 1790–1855" (PhD diss., Ohio State University, 2010), 64–100. For the authorship, publication, and circulation of *Short Story*, see David D. Hall, *Ways of Writing: The Practice and Politics of Text-Making in Seventeenth-Century New England* (Philadelphia: University of Pennsylvania Press, 2008), chap. 2.

29. James Savage, "The different principles, on which the European Colonies in America were founded. A Lecture delivered 25 Nov. 1835 at the Athenaeum," JSP I; Winthrop, *History of New England*, 2:22n2.

30. James Savage to his wife [Elizabeth], July 7, 1842, in *Letters*, 76.

31. Savage, "Different principles"; James Savage, Plymouth Celebration cutout from 1853 (in folder for 1830–1831), JSP I; Savage, "Prefatory Remarks," 32.

32. Winthrop, *History of New England*, 2:87, 2:87n1. "Ask again, what liberty thou hast towards others, which thou likest not to allow others towards thyself," Winthrop pressed: "for if one may go, another may, and so the greater part, and so church and commonwealth may be left destitute in a wilderness, exposed to misery and reproach, and all for thy ease and pleasure" (2:87). This passage is repeated in Savage, "Prefatory Remarks," 32.

33. Savage, "Different principles."

Chapter Eleven. Puritan Stock

1. James Savage, *A Genealogical Dictionary of the First Settlers of New England*, 4 vols. (Boston: Little, Brown, 1860–1862), 1:x, 4:iii. Of Savage's four-volume *Genealogical Dictionary*, Hillard admitted that "these volumes,

seemingly so unattractive, were to Mr. Savage a labor of love, which never degenerated into mere task work." G. S. Hillard, "Memoir of the Hon. James Savage, LL.D.," *Proceedings of the Massachusetts Historical Society* 16 (1878): 145.

2. Citizens of Portsmouth, NH, "Resolution to Honor Ancestors," March 3, 1823, James Savage Papers I, 1757–1891, MHS, Boston, MA (hereafter cited as JSP I); Benjamin Franklin, *Autobiography*, ed. Joyce E. Chaplin (New York: Norton, 2012), 72.

3. As one biographer explains, "In this work Farmer became the first American antiquarian to study an entire population—in this case, the Great Migration of immigrants to New England between 1620 and 1643." Ralph J. Crandall, "Farmer, John," *American National Biography Online*, February 2000, http://www.anb.org/articles/20/20-00336.html. "As the nation matured and as pride in its origins grew," Francois Weil has explained, "Farmer and his peers succeeded in persuading their fellow citizens that genealogy was central to their understanding of American family, local, and national history; they succeeded, in short, in inventing and legitimating ideologically acceptable forms of genealogical interest." Weil, "John Farmer and the Making of American Genealogy," *New England Quarterly* 80, no. 3 (2007): 409. For these reasons, Farmer has justly been called "the father of genealogical studies in the United States." Crandall, "Farmer, John."

4. Joseph Austin to James Savage, January 31, 1859, in James Savage Genealogical Papers, 1705–1868, MHS, Boston, MA (hereafter cited as JSGP). As Weil points out, this language of a Puritan stock "emerged in early nineteenth-century New England as one of several answers to what many New Englanders perceived as the relative political and cultural decline of their region in the new republic." Francois Weil, *Family Trees: A History of Genealogy in America* (Cambridge, MA: Harvard University Press, 2013), 91.

5. Charles Denison to James Savage, July 23, 1858, JSGP. Charles Denison, the descendant, had for the past year been putting together his own family genealogy and had actually printed and distributed a circular, explaining that he intended "to publish,—as soon as circumstances will permit,—a complete genealogy of the DENISON family, from the time of the landing of WILLIAM DENISON, at Boston, in the year 1630, to the present generation." Denison Circular, 1857, sent to Savage with Denison to Savage, July 23, 1858. Laboring away at this great *Genealogical Dictionary* many years after he first began, Savage wrote his son-in-law, William Rogers, "Visitors are very numerous, wishing to see what I have gathered about their forefathers." Savage to Rogers, December 11, 1850, in *Letters of James Savage to His Family* (Boston, 1906), 131.

6. Payne Kenyon Kilbourn to James Savage, 1848, JSGP; letter to James Savage, December 5, 1861, JSP I; Edward Herrick to James Savage,

January 22, 1862, JSP I; "Proposals by Little, Brown and Company, Boston, for Publishing by Subscription A Genealogical Dictionary of the First Settlers of New England," 1858, JSP I. A few years earlier, Savage had similarly explained to one correspondent that "the spirit of genealogical research is very widely spreading in our country, and in not a few cases it works deeply into the soil, so as to turn up from the earliest hour of colonisation all the direct and collateral ramifications of families." James Savage to Joseph Hunter, 1855, JSP I. This created a self-reinforcing loop in the argument for Puritan origins. As Weil writes, "Because New England held dominion over the fledgling enterprise of antiquarianism, its proponents were able to argue successfully that the region's local history was the history of the nation in the making" ("John Farmer," 414).

7. James Savage, Plymouth Celebration Cutout from 1853 (in folder for 1830–1831), JSP I. See letters from folder 1839–1840, JSP I. Letter from James Savage, July 6, 1860, JSP I. These sorts of sentiments were repeated frequently, especially in his preparations for his trip to England in 1842.

8. Savage, *Genealogical Dictionary*, 1:v–vi.

9. Savage, 1:vi, vii. As Matthew Jacobson has shown, the rise of the category of "Anglo-Saxon" whiteness begins especially in the 1840s, right when Savage turned to the project of his *Genealogical Dictionary*, and it did so in response to an influx of Irish Catholic immigrants. See Jacobson, *Whiteness of a Different Color: European Immigrants and the Alchemy of Race* (Cambridge, MA: Harvard University Press, 1998), chap. 2.

10. As another history writer from the period explained, "Our forefathers put in no claims for ancestral honours or splendid alliances, but they were justly proud of a pure honest blood; there were no left-hand marriages among them, and none of the poison of licentiousness, or the taint of crime." John Howard Hinton, *The History and Topography of the United States of North America, from the Earliest Period to the Present Time*, rev. ed., vol. 1 (Boston, 1834), 44.

11. George Bancroft, *A History of the United States*, vol. 1 (Boston, 1834), 507. As John Seelye notes, "[Henry Ward] Beecher's emphasis on the restless spread of Puritan institutions by means of Yankee migrations is a constant feature of New England Society speeches, indeed is inescapable, given the very nature and spirit of those organizations." Seelye, *Memory's Nation: The Place of Plymouth Rock* (Chapel Hill: University of North Carolina Press, 1998), 498.

12. As Bruce A. Harvey explains, "The nation as a whole ... defined itself through hierarchical, racial taxonomies of foreign regions." Harvey, *American Geographics: U.S. National Narratives and the Representation of the Non-European World, 1830–1865* (Stanford, CA: Stanford University Press, 2001), 5.

13. John Farmer to James Savage, June 19, 1826, JSP I. The editor of the *Historical Magazine* wrote, "If, at any time, you shall feel inclined, and physically able, to add to our many obligations, by noticing, even most briefly, your views, on either the subject under consideration, or any other, I shall feel honored by being permitted to give them a place in the pages of *The Historical Magazine*." *Historical Magazine* to Savage, n.d., box 1, folder 2, JSP I.

14. John Farnham to James Savage, November 1, 1831, JSP I. "He had corresponded with them all," Charles Deane reported, "and had known them all personally, while he was visiting England." Deane, "Tribute by Mr. Deane to James Savage," *Proceedings of the Massachusetts Historical Society* 12 (1871–1873): 437.

15. James Savage to Sylvester Judd, September 2, 1846, JSP I; Savage to his daughter and her husband [the Rogerses], November 23, 1852, in *Letters*, 168.

16. James Savage, "Savage Genealogy," folder: 1839–1840, JSP I; Savage to his daughter [Emma Rogers], February 27, 1853, in *Letters*, 175.

17. Hillard, "Memoir," 145.

18. James Savage to his daughter [Emma Rogers], July 1, 1867, in *Letters*, 282, 278–279.

Chapter Twelve. The Mayflower Compact versus *A Model of Christian Charity*

1. New England Society, *Constitution of the New-England Society, in the City and State of New-York* (New York, 1806). The New England Society continues to this day, though its membership has broadened beyond lineage. See New England Society, "Application Process," accessed May 30, 2019, http://www.nesnyc.org/join.

2. Robert C. Winthrop, "Address (1839)," in *The New England Society Orations: Addresses, Sermons, and Poems Delivered before the New England Society in the City of New York, 1820–1885*, vol. 1, ed. Cephas Brainerd and Eveline Warner Brainerd (New York: Century, 1901), 220–221.

3. In the single volume containing Winthrop's sermon, for example, one can also find papers related to D'Aulnay and La Tour (governors of Nova Scotia), Whalley and Gaffe (famous regicides who fled to America), the commission of James II to Sir Edmund Andros (a hated governor of Massachusetts Bay), the memoirs of Rev. John Hale (a doctor during the Salem witch trials), the memoirs of Rev. Dr. Abiel Holmes (an early American historian), a description of coins, a list of portraits, and more.

4. Robert C. Winthrop, *Life and Letters of John Winthrop: Governor of the Massachusetts-Bay Company at Their Emigration to New England, 1630*, 2 vols. (Boston: Ticknor and Fields, 1867), 2:17–18.

5. Robert Winthrop's book went through three editions in the nineteenth century, suggesting a fairly broad audience—certainly much broader than

the first publication of the sermon in the *Collections of the Massachusetts Historical Society*.

6. John Winthrop, "A Modell of Christian Charity," in *The Winthrop Papers*, vol. 2 (Boston: Massachusetts Historical Society, 1931), 289–290. All citations are from this edition unless otherwise specified.

7. R. Winthrop, *Life and Letters*, 1:18–20; John Winthrop, "A Modell of Christian Charity," in *The Puritans: A Sourcebook of Their Writings*, ed. Perry Miller and Thomas Johnson (Mineola, NY: Dover, 2001), 195–199; J. Winthrop, "A Model of Christian Charity," in *The Puritans in America: A Narrative Anthology*, ed. Alan Heimert and Andrew Delbanco (Cambridge, MA: Harvard University Press, 1985), 81. For a comparison of various editions, see our attempt to visualize them at The City on a Hill Archive: https://doi.org/10.7936/cityonahill.

8. J. Winthrop, "Christian Charity," 294. Today, many scholars and commentators see mutual affection—or sympathy—as central to Winthrop's sermon, but that is a relatively recent development. See especially Peter Coviello, "Agonizing Affection: Affect and Nation in Early America," *Early American Literature* 37, no. 2 (2002): 439–468; Ivy Schweitzer, *Perfecting Friendship: Politics and Affiliation in Early American Literature* (Chapel Hill: University of North Carolina Press, 2006), 73–102; and Matthew Holland, *Bonds of Affection: Civic Charity and the Making of America—Winthrop, Jefferson, and Lincoln* (Washington, DC: Georgetown University Press, 2007), part 1.

9. Trish Loughran puts this nicely: "Americans have historically had a mundane faith in the infallibility of their own written origins. When asked where America began, many will answer '*in print*.'" Speaking of the Revolutionary era, she explains how "the founding has long been understood as a text-based process" and how American Studies has repeated that narrative. This is a narrative, however, that goes back to the Revolutionary era itself, and it is one cause behind the rise of the Puritan origins thesis. Loughran's own work challenges the basic premises of this argument for a nationalized print public sphere. Loughran, *The Republic in Print: Print Culture in the Age of U.S. Nation Building, 1770–1870* (New York: Columbia University Press, 2007), xviii (italics in original).

10. Abiel Holmes, *American Annals; or, A Chronological History of America from Its Discovery in MCCCCXCII to MDCCCVI in Two Volumes* (Cambridge, MA, 1805), 200; Salma Hale, *History of the United States* (New York, 1823), 26.

11. Emma Willard, *History of the United States, or Republic of America* (New York, 1828), 24, 45. As Barry Joyce writes, "Our veneration for the written word as authority . . . is manifested within the creation story itself, with its shipboard compacts, petitions to the king, declarations of independence, written constitutions, bills of rights, and other key signifiers of the past." Joyce, *The First U.S. History Textbooks: Constructing and Dissemi-*

nating the American Tale in the Nineteenth Century (Lanham, MD: Lexington, 2015), 8. For an excellent account of how the Mayflower Compact came to be mythologized, starting in the early 1800s, see Joseph Conforti, *Imagining New England: Explorations of Regional Identity from the Pilgrims to the Mid-Twentieth Century* (Chapel Hill: University of North Carolina Press, 2001), 171–196.

12. Willard, *History of the United States*, vi. On these political documents as a kind of national scripture, see Pauline Maier, *American Scripture: Making the Declaration of Independence* (New York: Vintage, 1998).

13. Quoted in Wesley Craven, *The Legend of the Founding Fathers* (Ithaca, NY: Cornell University Press, 1965), 151; Annie Arnoux Haxtun, *Signers of the Mayflower Compact* (New York: Mail and Express, 1896), preface. Almost thirty years later, the Society of Mayflower Descendants put forward a motion to have the Compact read annually in all "city and town schools of the United States on the last school day before Thanksgiving of each year." Quoted in John Seelye, *Memory's Nation: The Place of Plymouth Rock* (Chapel Hill: University of North Carolina Press, 1998), 612. The motion did not pass.

14. Holmes, *American Annals*, 207n1.

15. Alexis de Tocqueville, *Democracy in America*, ed. Isaac Kramnick (New York: Norton, 2007), 30, 34. Robert Winthrop's 1839 address to the New England Society is a case in point. He freely admitted that "the direct and immediate influence of the passengers in the Mayflower, either upon the destinies of our land or of others, may, indeed, have been less conspicuous than that of some of the New England Colonists who followed them." But in praising the Pilgrims, he proclaimed, "it was the bright and shining wake they left upon the waves, it was the clear and brilliant beacon they lighted upon the shores, that caused them to have any followers." According to Robert Winthrop, Pilgrims begin the story that Puritans only embellish. Winthrop, "Address (1839)," 228. Many authors followed this pattern.

16. Emma Willard, *Abridgment of the History of the United States; or, Republic of America*, 3rd ed. (New York, 1833), 35. The same kind of language appears in other textbooks as well. Salma Hale, for example, explains that "in 1630, more than fifteen hundred persons came over, and founded Boston and several adjacent towns" (*History of the United States*, 38).

17. George Bancroft, *A History of the United States*, vol. 1 (Boston, 1834), 383. Michael Ditmore, in an unpublished manuscript, argues that Winthrop's "little speech" was "perhaps the most famous and cited of all New England Puritan discourses" in the nineteenth century, celebrated by Tocqueville, Savage, and countless others. I am grateful to Michael for sharing this work with me and for our conversations about Winthrop's sermon. For the creation and celebration of Winthrop's reputation in the nineteenth century, see Lindsay DiCuirci, *Colonial Revivals: The Nine-*

teenth-Century Lives of Early American Books (Philadelphia: University of Pennsylvania Press, 2018).

18. Winthrop, "Address (1839)," 222.

19. William Bradford, *Of Plymouth Plantation, 1620–1647*, ed. Samuel Eliot Morison (New York: Knopf, 2006), 61–62.

20. Here, for example, is how Frederick Butler rewrites Bradford: "Without one solitary hut to shelter themselves in; surrounded by the ocean, on the one side, and the dreary waste, of the barren sands of Cape Cod, on the other; and without the least knowledge of the local geography of that country on which they had landed, and to which they had committed their destiny; without the knowledge of even one spring of water where they might cool their thirst, they gave themselves up to God their deliverer, and preserver, and submitted entirely to the guidance of his providence." Butler, *A Complete History of the United States of America* (Hartford, CT, 1821), 104. Samuel Goodrich, in his popular *First Book of History*, offered a shorter version of the same scenario: "There were no houses to receive them, there were no friends to welcome them; there was nothing before them but a gloomy forest, inhabited by savages and wild beasts. There was nothing behind them but the vast ocean, rolling between them and their native land." Goodrich, *The First Book of History* (Cincinnati, 1832), 28. Rev. J. L. Blake likewise paraphrased: the conditions of the Pilgrims had "ill prepared them to endure and brave the rigors of a North American winter, and in a wilderness too, where there was no asylum prepared for them, no house built, no fresh and wholesome provision, no vegetation, no friend to receive them, or to bid them welcome." Blake, *The Historical Reader, Designed for the Use of Schools and Families* (Rochester, NY, 1827), 235. In Emma Willard's *Abridgment of the History of the United States*, she similarly pauses to describe the Pilgrims' plight: "The situation of these wanderers was desolate in the extreme. They were in an uncultivated wilderness: they were exposed to the inclemency of a dreary winter, their supplies of food were scanty, and they had no prospect of future harvest. They were surrounded by a savage enemy, and were visited by a raging disease" (*Abridgment*, 30). No history of America could be considered complete without commenting on the feeble origins of the small band of Pilgrims and their lack of provisions. Though Bradford's manuscript had not actually been published, much of it had leaked out through the years in various other writings, and this particular paragraph was key among them. For a quick history of Bradford's manuscript and its almost full appearance in print in 1856, see Michael Ditmore, "What Do We Know about the New England Puritans, and When Did We Know It? Twenty-First Century Reconsiderations of William Bradford and John Winthrop," in *American Literature and the New Puritan Studies*, ed. Bryce Traister (New York: Cambridge University Press, 2017), 191–205.

Chapter Thirteen. Creating a Usable Past

1. Van Wyck Brooks, "On Creating a Usable Past," *Dial*, April 11, 1918, 338–339. Commenting on Brooks's influence, Richard Ruland notes that "even a cursory acquaintance with the period reveals that it accepted no *single* national heritage." Ruland, *The Rediscovery of American Literature: Premises of Critical Taste, 1900–1940* (Cambridge, MA: Harvard University Press, 1967), 7. That lack of unity prompted a broader discussion, which Brooks's essay powerfully articulated.

2. For the main history of these debates, including their nuances and effects, see Peter Novick, *That Noble Dream: The "Objectivity Question" and the American Historical Profession* (New York: Cambridge University Press, 1988).

3. For two very good accounts about the changing perception of Puritanism during this period, see Francis Bremer, "Remembering—and Forgetting—John Winthrop and the Puritan Founders," *Massachusetts Historical Review* 6 (2004): 38–69; and Jan C. Dawson, *The Unusable Past: America's Puritan Tradition, 1830 to 1930* (Chico, CA: Scholars, 1984).

4. Massachusetts Pilgrim Tercentenary Committee 1917 Report, 43, 37, Massachusetts Historical Society Archives, Massachusetts Historical Society, Boston, MA.

5. Nantucket Historical Association, "Walter Gilman Page (1862–1934)," in *The Nantucket Art Colony, 1920–45*, digital exhibition, accessed May 30, 2019, https://www.nha.org/digitalexhibits/artistcolony/walterpage.htm; Walter Gilman Page, untitled paper, December 11, 1916, Papers on the Pilgrim Tercentenary at Plymouth Given by Walter Gilman Page, 1912–1919, Ms. S-753, Pilgrim Tercentenary Commission Records, 1912–1919, Massachusetts Historical Society, Boston, MA (hereafter cited as PTCR). After the Great War, Page declared, "The principles of self-government which are imbedded in the Compact of the Mayflower have been fought for during a period of over four years and our boys, the Pilgrims of today, return to us victorious." Page, untitled, Papers on the Pilgrim Tercentenary at Plymouth, 1912–1919, PTCR.

6. *Report of the Pilgrim Tercentenary Commission* (Boston: Wright and Potter, 1917), 9, box 1917, PTCR.

7. *Exercises on the Three Hundredth Anniversary of the Landing of the Pilgrims: Held at Plymouth, Massachusetts, Tuesday, December 21, 1920*, 17–18, box L-1920, PTCR.

8. Frederick W. Bittinger, *The Story of the Pilgrim Tercentenary Celebration at Plymouth in the Year 1921* (Plymouth, MA: Memorial, 1923), 15–16.

9. As John Higham writes, "When Lodge raised the banner of race against the new immigration, it acquired its most dangerous adversary." Higham, *Strangers in the Land: Patterns of American Nativism, 1860–1925* (New Brunswick, NJ: Rutgers University Press, 1955), 96; for immigration numbers and effects in this period, see especially 95–110. As T. J. Jackson Lears

comments, "Such impressions [of the waning of Anglo-Saxons] were strengthened by more precise evidence: a declining birthrate among old-stock Americans. Respected statisticians like Francis A. Walker and Frederick L. Hoffman warned that decadent Anglo-Saxons were being replaced by inferior immigrant stock." Lears, *No Place of Grace: Antimodernism and the Transformation of American Culture, 1880–1920* (New York: Pantheon, 1981), 30. The Immigration Restriction League sought "to arouse public opinion to the necessity of a further exclusion of elements undesirable for citizenship or injurious to our national character." "Constitution of the Immigration Restriction League," ca. 189?, Harvard University Library Digital Collections, https://curiosity.lib.harvard.edu/immigration-to-the -united-states-1789-1930/catalog/39-990100087120203941. See also Matthew Jacobson, *Whiteness of a Different Color: European Immigrants and the Alchemy of Race* (Cambridge, MA: Harvard University Press, 1998); and Matthew Pratt Guterl, *The Color of Race in America, 1900–1940* (Cambridge, MA: Harvard University Press, 2001).

10. Henry Cabot Lodge, "The Restriction of Immigration," speech in the Senate, March 16, 1896, in *Speeches and Addresses, 1884–1909* (Boston: Houghton Mifflin, 1909), 264, 266; Lodge, "The Puritans," speech at the New England Society of Philadelphia, December 22, 1887, ibid., 36.

11. Henry Cabot Lodge, *The Pilgrims of Plymouth: An Address at Plymouth, Massachusetts, on the Three Hundredth Anniversary of Their Landing, December 21, 1920* (Boston: Pilgrim Tercentenary Commission, 1921), 20, 38, box 1921, PTCR.

12. *Report of the Pilgrim Tercentenary Commission*, 6, 26. Since winter is no time to hold a pageant in Massachusetts, the planners postponed the tribute to the following summer.

13. *Report of the Pilgrim Tercentenary Commission*, 28–29.

14. It is not hard to see why. Brooks Adams noted that it took a long while to establish "the freedom of individual thought" in America and that all who worked for it had to fight against the abuse and intransigence of Puritan ministers: "long years of bloodshed passed before the victory was won; and from the outset the attitude of the clergy formed the chief obstacle to the triumph of a more liberal civilization." Adams, *The Emancipation of Massachusetts* (Boston: Houghton Mifflin, 1887), 2–4.

15. This quote ("impossible to ignore the fact") from Charles Francis Adams Jr.'s *Three Episodes of Massachusetts History* was used by a reviewer for the *New York Times* to summarize the book. See "Adam's Boston Bay Book," *New York Times*, October 23, 1892, 19. In taking up this theme, Perry Miller later explained, Charles "directed a much more concentrated attack than had Brooks upon 'the filio-pietistic' school of New England historians, naming them specifically and holding up passages of their apologetics to scorn." Miller, introduction to Brooks Adams, *The Emancipation of Massachusetts: The Dream and the Reality* (New York: Houghton Mifflin, 1962), xxix.

16. Stanley Williams, review of *Main Currents in American Thought* by Vernon L. Parrington, *New England Quarterly* 1, no. 1 (1928): 90. Thinking back on the appearance of this book years later, Perry Miller wrote, "Anyone alive in 1926 who was responding to the fresh interest in things American which blew like a gale across the country will remember the excitement of Parrington." Miller, *The Responsibility of Mind in a Civilization of Machines*, ed. John Crowell and Stanford J. Searl Jr. (Amherst: University of Massachusetts Press, 1979), 164–165.

17. Basically anything beyond political or constitutional history—anything beyond great politicians and wars—could be considered "new history" in this era, but the influence of the Beards led many at this time to focus on economic forces. For more on the rise of "new history" and the "progressive historians," see Novick, *That Noble Dream*, chap. 4. See also Richard Hofstadter, *The Progressive Historians: Turner, Beard, Parrington* (New York: Knopf, 1968). Critical of the methods and findings of these historians, Hofstadter nevertheless states his appreciation: "The Progressives opened up arguments in areas where there had been too much agreement and too much complacency. . . . They attempted to find a usable past related to the broadest needs of a nation fully launched upon its own industrialization, and to make history an active instrument of self-recognition and self-improvement" (xvi–xvii).

18. James Truslow Adams wanted "to show how, in the period treated, the domestic struggle against the tyranny exercised by the more bigoted members of the theocratic party, was of greater importance in the history of liberty than the more dramatic contest with the mother-country." The Puritans, according to Adams, had fought in England "not for toleration, but for control," which they then exercised ruthlessly in New England. J. Adams, *The Founding of New England* (Boston: Atlantic Monthly Press, 1921), x, 71.

19. Van Wyck Brooks, *The Wine of the Puritans* (London: Sisley's, 1908), 11–13; Brooks, *America's Coming-of-Age* (New York: B. W. Huebsch, 1915), 8. For more on Van Wyck Brooks and his influence, see Randall Fuller, *Emerson's Ghosts: Literature, Politics, and the Making of Americanists* (New York: Oxford University Press, 2007), chap. 3.

20. Paul Elmore More quoted in Ruland, *Rediscovery of American Literature*, 50. *The Wine of the Puritans*, as Fuller has explained, was the "founding text in an anti-Puritan movement," but that movement "would soon reach its apogee in the denunciations of H. L. Mencken" (*Emerson's Ghosts*, 55).

21. W. E. B. Du Bois, *The Souls of Black Folk*, ed. David Blight and Robert Gooding-Williams (New York: Bedford, 1997), 94.

22. The full quote reads as follows: "Wherever the power of the Puritan philosophy of life extended, it always benefited the tendency toward a middle-class, economically *rational* conduct of life, of which it was the

most significant and only consistent support. This is, of course, far more important than merely encouraging the formation of capital. It stood at the cradle of modern 'economic man.'" As Weber says at another point, he aimed in his essay to "highlight those particular points in which the Puritan concept of the calling and the insistence on an ascetic conduct of life *directly* influenced the development of the capitalist style of life." Weber sometimes offered lines like these, which sound like a direct causal link between Puritanism and capitalism; at other times, he backed off such a strong claim, simply highlighting *affinities* between Puritanism and capitalism. He insisted that he was not "defending any such foolishly doctrinaire thesis as that the 'capitalist spirit' . . . let alone capitalism itself, *could only* arise as a result of certain influences of the Reformation." Max Weber, *The Protestant Ethic and the Spirit of Capitalism and Other Writings*, ed. Peter Baehr and Gordon C. Wells (New York: Penguin, 2002), 117, 112, 36. As Baehr and Wells nicely put it, "the general thrust of his argument is that the *ethos* of modern capitalism—that is, its distinctive moral attitudes toward economic activity and work, its methodical, specialized style of life— is historically indebted to (caused by, congruent with) the Protestant *ethic*: the ascetic movement that arose out of the Protestant Reformation and its aftermath." Baehr and Wells, introduction to *Protestant Ethic*, xvii–xviii. Weber's notion of "Puritanism" was a broad version of "ascetic Protestantism" that reached its clearest example in Calvinism but also could be found in Quakers, Methodists, and Baptists. See Peter Ghosh, "Max Weber's Idea of 'Puritanism': A Case Study in the Empirical Construction of the Protestant Ethic," *History of European Ideas* 29 (2003): 183–221. For two essential sources on the influence, context, and history of *The Protestant Ethic and the Spirit of Capitalism*, see Hartmut Lehmann and Guenther Roth, eds., *Weber's Protestant Ethic: Origins, Evidence, Contexts* (New York: Cambridge University Press, 1993); and William H. Swatos Jr. and Lutz Kaelber, eds., *The Protestant Ethic Turns 100: Essays on the Centenary of the Weber Thesis* (London: Routledge, 2005). For the best and most recent account of Calvinism's relationship to capitalism in early New England, see Mark Valeri, *Heavenly Merchandize: How Religion Shaped Commerce in Puritan New England* (Princeton, NJ: Princeton University Press, 2010).

23. Peter Ghosh, "Max Weber on 'The Rural Community': A Critical Edition of the English Text," *History of European Ideas* 31 (2005): 333, 345. On Puritan hatred of sensual pleasure, see for example Weber, *Protestant Ethic*, 112–114. According to Weber, the antiartistic situation remained true "among the Anglo-Saxon peoples" still today. "In America," he argued, the only churches that had any halfway decent music were the black churches and the white ones wealthy enough to hire professionals. Otherwise, he remarked, a person "only hears the screeching that passes for 'congregational singing' and is so unbearable for the German listener" (Weber, *Protestant Ethic*, 191–192). To illustrate his point about

Puritanism's democratic antiauthoritarianism, Weber claimed that Puritanism could even be considered "the basis, historically speaking, for the 'disrespectfulness' of Americans, which some find repugnant and others refreshing" (Weber, *Protestant Ethic*, 172).

24. Weber, *Protestant Ethic*, 12–14.

25. As Paul Michael Lützeler writes, "Weber had formed preconceptions about this topic long before he came to St. Louis. On the other hand, it is hard to imagine that he could have written with such certainty about life and conditions in the United States had he not traveled in the States for a couple of months." Lützeler, "The St. Louis World's Fair of 1904 as a Site of Cultural Transfer: German and German-American Participation," in *German Culture in Nineteenth-Century America: Reception, Adaptation, Transformation*, ed. Lynne Tatlock and Matt Erlin (Rochester, NY: Camden House, 2005), 69.

26. Baehr and Wells, introduction to *Protestant Ethic*, xiv. See Lawrence A. Scaff, *Max Weber in America* (Princeton, NJ: Princeton University Press, 2011).

27. Weber, *Protestant Ethic*, 121. The St. Louis speech is reprinted as "Capitalism and Rural Society in Germany" in *From Max Weber: Essays in Sociology*, ed. and trans. Hans Gerth and C. Wright Mills (New York: Oxford University Press, 1946). Here I use the critical edition produced by Ghosh. See Ghosh, "Max Weber on 'The Rural Community,'" 327–366; for "the realm of fundamental values," see 347–348. See also Ghosh's accompanying explanation of the speech's meaning and importance: Peter Ghosh, "Not the *Protestant Ethic*? Max Weber at St. Louis," *History of European Ideas* 31 (2005): 367–407. As Ghosh explains, "Weber had no interest in pure economics without its foundation in *Kultur*, the realm of men's ultimate values, religious and otherwise" ("Not the *Protestant Ethic*?," 377). Even though he considered America a young country with a young *Kultur*, he predicted that the land would soon run out, social stratification would increase, and America would gradually be Europeanized. According to Weber, "while it is correct to say that the burden of historical tradition does not overwhelm the United States and that the problems arising from the power of tradition do not exist here, yet the effects of the power of capitalism are [all] the stronger and will, sooner or later, further the development of land monopolies." When that happens, "then, indeed, the desire of the capitalistic families to form a 'nobility' will arise, probably not in form though in fact" (Ghosh, "Max Weber on 'The Rural Community,'" 344). Weber thus predicted the Americanization of Europe and the Europeanization of America, both converging on a new form of society from different ends through the power of modern capitalism.

28. *Report of the Pilgrim Tercentenary Commission*, 35.

29. James M. Curely, comp., *Tercentenary of the Founding of Boston* (Boston, 1930), 140.

30. *Tercentenary of the Founding of Boston*, 143–144.

31. It was all about "this city of ours set upon a hill," as the mayor said in his dedication speech. Again, the line between local celebration and national influence could often blur. They very much celebrated Boston, but they considered Boston an "outpost of civilization on the Western Hemisphere which has led the way in every important undertaking that has placed America in the front rank of the nations of the world." Even so, the United States and the nations of the world did not send dignitaries to the Boston celebrations. *Tercentenary of the Founding of Boston*, 151, 82.

32. Everett B. Mero, comp., *Celebrating a 300th Anniversary: A Report of the Massachusetts Bay Tercentenary of 1930* (Boston: Tercentenary Conference of City and Town Communities, 1931), 57. In a report intended to aid those who were planning the presumed four-hundredth-year celebration in 2030, Everett B. Mero admitted, "It cannot be said that the Massachusetts Bay Tercentenary was a thorough-going New England celebration, although that end was sought by interests anxious for tourist trade, and although there was historical as well as present day justification for such inclusiveness" (58).

33. Mero, 17; for the cost, see 21. To clarify, a quote from the sermon shows up on the Boston monument only for the commemoration of Boston, a local affair, not for any of the commemorations of Massachusetts Bay.

34. Mero, 54. Stewart Mitchell, ed., *The Founding of Massachusetts: A Selection from the Sources of the History of the Settlement, 1628–1631*, tercentenary ed. (Boston: Massachusetts Historical Society, 1930). The "book" on the medallion was intended to typify "education as well as religion, as the Charter typifies the law and social and civic affairs—and likewise a freedom much greater than the makers of it foresaw." Edward Elwell Whiting, *Story of the Medallion* (Boston: Massachusetts Bay Tercentenary, 1929), 7.

Chapter Fourteen. A Meaning to Match Its Force

1. Michael Kammen, "The Problem of American Exceptionalism: A Reconsideration," *American Quarterly* 45, no. 1 (1993): 9–10; Perry Miller to Samuel R. Rosenthal, September 14, 1952, HUG 4572.9—Correspondence and Other Papers, ca. 1918–1963, Perry Miller Papers, Harvard University Archives, Cambridge, MA (hereafter cited as PMP); Miller, untitled address, folder: "Corcoran 1958," 24, HUG 4572.15—Notes and Papers for Addresses and Lectures, PMP; Phillip R. Wheeler to Mrs. Miller, December 12, 1963, HUG 4572.5—Correspondence, L–Z, PMP; "Perry Miller," *Harvard University Gazette*, January 10, 1964, 108; Miller, "The American Humanities in an Industrial Civilization," July 6, 1956, 2, HUG 4572.15—Notes and Papers for Addresses and Lectures, PMP; Miller, *Errand into the Wilderness* (Cambridge, MA: Harvard University Press, 1984), ix.

2. Michael Clark, "Perry Miller," in *Dictionary of Literary Biography*, vol. 63, *Modern American Critics, 1920–1955*, ed. Gregory S. Jay (Detroit: Gale, 1988): 164; Reinhold Niebuhr, "Perry Miller and Our Embarrassment," *Harvard Review* 2, no. 2 (1964): 51. "He authorized us," Everett Emerson later explained. "He encouraged us—and still does—to undertake the study of early American literature by his magnificent example." Emerson, "Perry Miller and the Puritans: A Literary Scholar's Assessment," *History Teacher* 14, no. 4 (1981): 460. Miller's influence is well-known. As Michael McGiffert wrote, "It is possible in the 1960's to speak of American Puritan studies as a field of scholarship, and to appraise its estate and activity, because Perry Miller, above all others, made the American Puritans studiable." McGiffert, "American Puritan Studies in the 1960's," *William and Mary Quarterly* 27, no. 1 (1970): 64. Murray Murphey, meanwhile, claims that Perry Miller is "the most important single figure in launching American civilization." Murphey, "Perry Miller and American Studies," *American Studies* 42, no. 2 (2001): 5. That's debatable, but accounts of the rise of American Studies (especially its institutionalization) should include the influence of Perry Miller.

3. Miller, *Errand into the Wilderness*, viii. As Miller tells it, he had been in the Congo seeking "adventure" and unloading drums of American oil after the First World War, when he had a sudden "epiphany" about what he should do with his life. "It was given to me, equally disconsolate on the edge of a jungle of central Africa, to have thrust upon me the mission of expounding what I took to be the innermost propulsion of the United States." That took him to graduate school and began his exploration of Puritan New England. This "epiphany" scene is almost surely fabricated, but it embedded in Miller's account of American history what became strikingly obvious to later scholars: the absence of people of color. Africa served as a "barbaric tropic" against which he set out to explore America. For the classic critique based in this moment, see Amy Kaplan, "'Left Alone with America': The Absence of Empire in the Study of American Culture," in *Cultures of United States Imperialism*, ed. Amy Kaplan and Donald E. Pease (Durham, NC: Duke University Press, 1993), 3–21. As Kaplan writes, "Beginning with Jamestown would evoke a counternarrative of migration to that of the Puritans: the forced migration of Africans on slave ships" (7). It is an incisive critique, but it misses the fact that historians had been skipping past Jamestown for precisely such a reason since the early 1800s. Such a move is not unique to Miller.

4. Miller, *Errand into the Wilderness*, viii–ix, 4.

5. Perry Miller, "Preface to the Beacon Press Edition," in *Orthodoxy in Massachusetts, 1630–1650* (Boston: Beacon, 1959), xviii; Miller, lecture for Penn State and Toronto, 1958, 1, HUG 4572.15—Notes and Papers for Addresses and Lectures, PMP; Miller, lecture notes on the Great Awakening, n.d., 2, HUG 4572.10—Lecture notes for courses at Harvard, box

1 of 2, PMP. "I was, and remain, in many respects a child of the 1920's," he told one audience. Miller, lecture for Penn State and Toronto, 1. At the same time, in taking a new approach to Puritanism, Miller did not solely denigrate others. He had his debts, he admitted, and occasionally he gave credit to former scholars and critics. Whatever the merits of previous writers, however, they were still, in his mind, essentially misguided.

6. David Binder to Perry Miller, August 20, 1962, HUG 4572.5: Correspondence A–K, box 1 of 2, PMP; Perry Miller obituary, *Harvard Crimson*, December 10, 1963; Edmund S. Morgan, "Perry Miller and the Historians," *Proceedings of the American Antiquarian Society* 74 (1965): 11; Stephen Schlesinger, "A Memorial to Perry Miller," *Harvard Review* 2, no. 2 (1964): 3; Morgan, "Perry Miller and the Historians," 18; David Levin, "Perry Miller at Harvard," *Southern Review* 19, no. 4 (1983): 804, 807. This last story comes from a personal conversation with Andrew Robertson of CUNY Graduate Center and Lehman College, CUNY. Robertson reports it as an experience of the late William McLoughlin, the historian of U.S. religion at Brown. As Robertson wrote to me in personal correspondence, "Like so many graduate students of Puritanism at Harvard in that era, McLoughlin stood in awe of Miller but wound up doing his dissertation with Oscar Handlin." Miller tried to awe his students, but he could often terrorize them instead.

7. Miller, "Preface," xx.

8. Jill Lepore, *The Story of America: Essays on Origins* (Princeton, NJ: Princeton University Press, 2012), 14; Morgan, "Perry Miller and the Historians," 13. For Miller's boast and the definitive critique of Miller's source material, see George Selement, "Perry Miller: A Note on His Sources in *The New England Mind: The Seventeenth Century*," *William and Mary Quarterly* 31, no. 3 (1974): 453–464. Miller sought his whole life to recover "the majesty and coherence of Puritan thinking" (Miller, "Preface," xx). For an excellent overview of Perry Miller's approach to Puritanism and the usual criticisms of it, see McGiffert, "American Puritan Studies." It is important to note here that for Miller, a coherent system of thought required published *texts*—European writings. For Miller, consciousness in America began with the coming of the Puritans because Puritans left the published texts that he could read.

9. Perry Miller and Thomas H. Johnson, "The Theory of the State and of Society," in *The Puritans: A Sourcebook of Their Writings*, ed. Perry Miller and Thomas H. Johnson (Mineola, NY: Dover, 2001), 184–185; Miller and Johnson, "This World and the Next," in *Puritans*, 288; Miller, Bangor Theological Seminary Lectures, n.d., Part III, 11, HUG 4572.15—Notes and Papers for Addresses and Lectures, PMP.

10. Miller and Johnson, "History," in *Puritans*, 88–89.

11. Miller, *Orthodoxy in Massachusetts*, xiii. When Puritans wrote out their system of church and society in the Cambridge Platform of 1648, there-

fore, what they produced "was not the whimsical or capricious result of a chance encounter. It was not a fortuitous creation; it was a summing up and a codification of a long development." Perry Miller, "The Cambridge Platform in 1648," in *The Responsibility of Mind in a Civilization of Machines*, ed. John Crowell and Stanford J. Searl Jr. (Amherst: University of Massachusetts Press, 1979), 52.

12. Miller and Johnson, "Theory of the State," 191; Miller and Johnson, introduction to *Puritans*, 11.

13. Miller, lecture notes on the Great Awakening.

14. Miller and Johnson, introduction to *Puritans*, 1. Based on the way Miller explains who wrote what in this book, it is clear that this account of the Puritans is his own. As Avihu Zakai nicely summarizes, "In Miller's view, Puritanism was not merely a historical phenomenon of seventeenth-century New England, but rather a fundamental component underlying the entire American past from its beginning until his own time." Zakai, "'Epiphany at Matadi': Perry Miller's *Orthodoxy in Massachusetts* and the Meaning of American History," *Reviews in American History* 13, no. 4 (1985): 628. It is important to remember that Miller was not the first to make this argument. Not only had nineteenth-century scholars made this claim repeatedly, but twentieth-century scholars of American literature had also begun articulating this view. Russell Reising offers an account of the "Puritan origins" school in American literary history. See Reising, *The Unusable Past: Theory and the Study of American Literature* (New York: Methuen, 1986).

15. See Wendy L. Wall, *Inventing the "American Way": The Politics of Consensus from the New Deal to the Civil Rights Movement* (New York: Oxford University Press, 2008), chap. 1. General editor of Bobbs-Merrill Hiram Haydn quoted in Nicholas Guyatt, "'An Instrument of National Policy': Perry Miller and the Cold War," *Journal of American Studies* 36 (2002): 134–135.

16. The roots and origins of American Studies have been reassessed and contested by countless scholars. Certainly American Studies has "radical roots" that extend back to all sorts of persons both inside and outside the academy, such as W. E. B. Du Bois, Wilber Cash, C. L. R. James, Constance Rourke, and Carey McWilliams. See Elaine Tyler May, "'The Radical Roots of American Studies': Presidential Address to the American Studies Association," *American Quarterly* 48, no. 2 (1996): 179–200. But Perry Miller was an essential part of its *institutional* development, especially in making a case for American literature. As May remarks, most professors ignored and dismissed American literature as "beneath the standards of literary merit set by authors of classic British texts," and thus the first task of American Studies entailed "retrieving American literature from the margins of academic consideration" ("Radical Roots," 182–183). Miller developed the American literature survey with Matthiessen, and together they ran it for many years. For a great account of "the extensive

revival of interest, both popular and academic, in American literature witnessed by the first fifty years" of the twentieth century, see Richard Ruland, *The Rediscovery of American Literature: Premises of Critical Taste, 1900–1940* (Cambridge, MA: Harvard University Press, 1967) (quote on ix).

17. Center for the Study of Democratic Institutions, *The American Character: A Conversation* (Santa Barbara, CA: Fund for the Republic, 1962), 8. Accounts of the rise of American Civilization programs and the birth of American Studies are voluminous. Philip Gleason offers a good explanation of the role of World War II, and his notes are a great place to start for studying traditional accounts of the rise of American Studies. See Gleason, "World War II and the Development of American Studies," *American Studies* 36, no. 3 (1984): 343–358.

18. Jones quoted in Reising, *Unusable Past*, 39; Boorstin quoted in Guyatt, "Instrument of National Policy," 126–127. Daniel T. Rodgers includes good work on Daniel Boorstin, emphasizing his role in elevating American exceptionalism and the "city on a hill." Daniel T. Rodgers, *As a City on a Hill: The Story of America's Most Famous Lay Sermon* (Princeton, NJ: Princeton University Press, 2018), chap. 16.

19. Perry Miller to Samuel R. Rosenthal, January 18, 1956, HUG 4572.9—Correspondence and Other Papers, ca. 1918–1963, box 1 of 2, PMP. Randall Fuller has explained that he belonged to programs "created to perform the ideological work of anticommunism," but he and others nonetheless "tended to understand their work as Jeremiadic: an assertion of American exceptionalism that was celebratory, to be certain, but celebratory of an ideal all too obviously betrayed by the dominant culture." Fuller, "Errand into the Wilderness: Perry Miller as American Scholar," *American Literary History* 18, no. 1 (2006): 119.

20. Perry Miller to Betty Miller and the Murdocks, July 29, 1944, HUG 4572.5: Correspondence A–K, box 1 of 2, PMP.

21. Levin, "Perry Miller at Harvard," 803.

22. Perry Miller quoted in Kenneth Lynn, "Perry Miller," *American Scholar* 52, no. 2 (1983): 225. As Fuller nicely puts it, Perry Miller "struggled for much of his professional life with Emerson's call for intellectual activism as well as with the contradictions engendered by that call" ("Errand into the Wilderness," 102). Guyatt has carefully tracked this development in Miller and nicely phrases the dilemma he faced: "When does intellectual history become instrumental history in the service of some cause, and when it does become instrumental history is it no longer intellectual?" ("Instrument of National Policy," 113). Guyatt and Fuller should be read together for their competing accounts of Miller's investment in public scholarship.

23. Henry R. Luce, "The American Century," *Life*, February 17, 1941, 61.

24. Luce, 63, 65, 65.

25. Henry Luce, foreword to *The National Purpose*, ed. Henry Luce (New York: Time, 1960), v.

26. John Jessup, "A Noble Framework for a Great Debate"; Billy Graham, "Men Must Be Changed before a Nation Can"; John Gardner, "Can We Count on More Dedicated People?"; Adlai Stevenson, "Extend Our Vision . . . to All Mankind," all in Luce, *National Purpose*, 2, 63, 72–73, 26. See also John Jeffries, "The 'Quest for National Purpose' of 1960," *American Quarterly* 30, no. 4 (1978): 451–470.

27. Perry Miller, "The Social Context of the Covenant," in *Responsibility of Mind*, 134–135; Ann Douglas, "The Mind of Perry Miller," *New Republic*, February 3, 1982, 30. For "lone wolf," see Perry Miller, "The Plight of the Lone Wolf," in *Responsibility of Mind*, 8–14. As Michael Clark summarizes, Miller "returned almost obsessively to the theme of the isolated scholar, holding out against a society bent on self-destruction" ("Perry Miller," 166). But he was not actually isolated in his fear of American materialism. Still, he was forceful. As Kenneth Lynn wrote, "Miller spoke of America's horror that its 'gigantic exertion' was heading toward 'some nightmare of debauchery.'" Lynn, "Perry Miller," *American Scholar* 52, no. 2 (1983): 223.

28. Miller, "Social Context," 140.

29. Miller assumed that an American educator would be "loyal to his country," but that loyalty would be manifested "by meticulously remaining faithful to the pursuit of learning, and to the transmission of learning to posterity, no matter how many conflicts this devotion may lead him into." Perry Miller, "Education under Cross Fire," in *Responsibility of Mind*, 82, 96. "Toward all the possible themes of triumph," his friend Henry May explained, "Miller was deeply and even agonizingly ambivalent." May, "Perry Miller's Parrington," review of *The Life of the Mind in America*, by Perry Miller, *American Scholar* 35, no. 3 (1966): 564.

30. Copy of a letter from Perry Miller to President Schmitz, March 9, 1955, HUG 4572.5—Correspondence, L–Z, box 2 of 2, PMP. A host of responses are preserved in the Perry Miller Papers. Many are grateful for Miller's public stance, though Miller also kept some of the more vociferous letters accusing him, Oppenheimer, and other leftist professors of undermining the country.

31. Perry Miller, "The Incorruptible Sinclair Lewis," in *Responsibility of Mind*, 117, 121; Miller, "Europe's Faith in American Fiction," *Atlantic Monthly* 188, no. 6 (December 1951), 56.

32. Miller and Johnson, "This World and the Next," 283; Perry Miller, lecture notes on the Great Awakening, 2; Miller, John Franklin Jameson Lecture, n.d., 23, HUG 4572.9—Correspondence and Other Papers, ca. 1918–1963, box 1, PMP; Miller, "Religious Background of the Bay Psalm Book," in *Responsibility of Mind*, 24.

33. Center for the Study of Democratic Institutions, *American Character*, 23. Perry Miller should not be thought of as a curmudgeon who hated all comfort, luxury, and ease. He did not oppose amenities. Nor were

business leaders bad people, he admitted. "Some of my best friends are businessmen," he told one audience. "And hundreds of them have a wider-ranging curiosity, a larger appetite for ideas, than the average professor of an erudite specialty." Miller, "Liberty and Conformity," in *Responsibility of Mind*, 188. What he opposed was not material luxury but rather the way material desires had become the overriding thrust of American culture, crowding out all other concerns and scorning anyone devoted to any good other than the making of money.

34. Miller, "Liberty and Conformity," 187–189.

35. Miller, "Europe's Faith," 52. The Europeans, he continued, seemed to be suggesting that his work was better needed across the sea: "shouldn't I go home and proselytize my own people rather than preach to those who needed not my ministrations?"

36. Miller, "Individualism and the New England Tradition," in *Responsibility of Mind*, 35.

Chapter Fifteen. Perry Miller's City on a Hill

1. I spent two days searching the Gutman Library's holdings of forty-five hundred American history textbooks, and I did not discover Winthrop's sermon or the phrase "city on a hill" in any one of them published before the 1950s.

2. Perry Miller, "The Social Context of the Covenant," in *The Responsibility of Mind in a Civilization of Machines*, ed. John Crowell and Stanford J. Searl Jr. (Amherst: University of Massachusetts Press, 1979), 137; Miller, "Equality in the American Setting," in *Responsibility of Mind*, 145.

3. Perry Miller, "Centrifugal Puritanism," lecture at the University of Delaware, March 10, 1953, 3, HUG 4572.15—Notes and Papers for Addresses and Lectures, Perry Miller Papers, Harvard University Archives, Cambridge, MA (hereafter cited as PMP).

4. Perry Miller, "The Shaping of the American Character," *New England Quarterly* 28, no. 4 (1955): 453; MacLeish to Miller, January 23 (no year), HUG 4572.5—Correspondence, L–Z, box 2, PMP. For Miller's clearest account of how national purpose shapes America, see "The Shaping of the American Character," which ends by arguing that a search for purpose defines America yet settling for any *one* purpose only narrows it. "He who endeavors to fix the personality of America in one eternal, unchangeable pattern not only understands nothing of how a personality is created, but comprehends little of how this nation has come along thus far." The only "Un-American" thing to do, Miller concluded, was to fix unalterably on one and only one purpose for America, whether "in politics, diplomacy, economics, literary form, or morality itself" ("Shaping of the American Character," 453–454).

5. Perry Miller, "American Puritanism," lecture notes for talk at Gonzaga University, July 1960, 1, HUG 4572.15—Notes and Papers for Addresses and Lectures, PMP; Miller, "Shaping of the American Character," 443. Elsewhere Miller claimed that he did not really intend to elevate New England above the rest of America or to denigrate or dismiss Virginia, Maryland, or the Dutch, but that is simply how the texts played out: "because under the peculiar conditions of the settlement, the issues were in that region made more articulate—the dedication to a specific ecclesiastical program required the leaders more to expound their conception—than elsewhere" ("Equality in the American Setting," 144).

6. Perry Miller and Thomas H. Johnson, "History," in *The Puritans: A Sourcebook of Their Writings*, ed. Perry Miller and Thomas H. Johnson (Mineola, NY: Dover, 2001), 86. This theme of an American mission is what Richard Gamble and Daniel T. Rodgers emphasize in their accounts of Perry Miller's influence. See Gamble, *In Search of the City on a Hill: The Making and Unmaking of an American Myth* (London: Continuum, 2012), chap. 5; Rodgers, *As a City on a Hill: The Story of America's Most Famous Lay Sermon* (Princeton, NJ: Princeton University Press, 2018), chap. 15.

7. Perry Miller, John Franklin Jameson Lecture, n.d., 23, HUG 4572.9—Correspondence and Other Papers, ca. 1918–1963, box 1, PMP; Miller and Johnson, "The Theory of the State and of Society," in *Puritans*, 183; Miller, "Individualism and the New England Tradition," in *Responsibility of Mind*, 43.

8. Miller, "Shaping of the American Character," 444; Miller and Johnson, introduction to *Puritans*, 13n1. Embellishing his point, Miller wrote, "We who are today being made all too familiar with the horrors of the art of 'popularization,' can only marvel at how little allowance the divines made for the ignorance or the simplicity of the average man in the addresses and sermons they delivered to him" (Miller and Johnson, introduction to *Puritans*, 12).

9. Miller and Johnson, introduction to *Puritans*, 12–14. Reading the words of Puritans about the importance of learning engraved in the iron gates of Harvard, Miller was moved. He told one audience, "Often in the summertime I weep silent tears as I watch the bemused but uncomprehending stolidity with which sightseers barely pause to spell them out." Miller, "The Paradoxes of Puritanism" lecture, 1955, 16, HUG 4572.10—Lecture notes for courses at Harvard, box 2, PMP.

10. Perry Miller, foreword to *The New England Mind: From Colony to Province* (Boston: Beacon, 1961), vii. As Francis Butts aptly summarizes, "Miller's point is ironical. Behind economic activity was pious intention, and the unforeseen consequence of that intention was a weakening of the original utopian ideals. Industry was mandated as a way to glorify God, yet the fruit of industry distracted the Saints from their initial errand. Success

bred failure." Butts, "The Myth of Perry Miller," *American Historical Review* 87, no. 3 (1982): 683.

11. Henry May, "Perry Miller's Parrington," review of *The Life of the Mind in America*, by Perry Miller, *American Scholar* 35, no. 3 (1966): 568. For the comparison to Rome, see Miller, "Shaping of the American Character," 439. More famously, he compared his inspiration and his historical labors to Edward Gibbon, the great Enlightenment historian who wrote *The Decline and Fall of the Roman Empire*, feeling himself "equally disconsolate" and poised on the edge of another empire's downfall. Perry Miller, *Errand in the Wilderness* (Cambridge, MA: Harvard University Press, 1984), viii. The best article on this topic is Gene Wise, "Implicit Irony in Perry Miller's *New England Mind*," *Journal of the History of Ideas* 29, no. 4 (1968): 579–600.

12. Perry Miller, "American Puritanism," lecture notes for talk at Gonzaga University, July 1960, 1, HUG 4572.15—Notes and Papers for Addresses and Lectures, PMP.

13. Perry Miller, "The Paradoxes of Puritanism" lecture, 1955, 10, HUG 4572.10—Lecture notes for courses at Harvard, box 2, PMP; Miller and Johnson, introduction to *Puritans*, 59. The real issue, he sometimes explained, was simply one of translation: "The principal problem to be confronted is that of making outmoded and now almost forgotten terminology of a theological age meaningful in ordinary human or philosophical terms." Miller, "Thought and Expression in New England, 1630–1730," prospectus for a book (probably *The New England Mind*), n.d., addressee unknown, HUG 4572.9—Correspondence, box 2, PMP.

14. Miller, lecture notes on Jonathan Edwards, HUG 4572.10—Lecture notes for courses at Harvard, box 1, PMP; Butts, "Myth of Perry Miller," 670; Thornton Wilder to Perry Miller, February 29 (no year), HUG 4572.5—Correspondence, L–Z, box 2, PMP.

15. Miller, lecture notes on Jonathan Edwards.

16. Miller and Johnson, introduction to *Puritans*, 39, 53–54. The turn to the heart was taken up by many scholars who felt Miller invested too much in the intellectual side of Puritanism, and the better understanding of grace appears in many such works. It is a line of argument I summarize in *Sympathetic Puritans: Calvinist Fellow Feeling in Early New England* (New York: Oxford University Press, 2015), introduction and chap. 1.

17. Reinhold Niebuhr, "Perry Miller and Our Embarrassment," *Harvard Review* 2, no. 2 (1964): 50; Perry Miller, "The Influence of Reinhold Niebuhr," *Reporter*, May 1, 1958, 40; Miller, foreword to *New England Mind*, viii; Emma Willard, *History of the United States* (New York, 1828), 3. Ormond Seavey describes Miller as "a sort of fellow traveler with the founders of neo-orthodoxy." Seavey, "Sacvan Bercovitch and Perry Miller: Parricide Regained," *Studies in Puritan American Spirituality* 3 (1992): 158. The obituary in the *Harvard University Gazette* explained

that "Miller's relationship to Puritanism—and to the Christian religion in general—was more complex than he allowed. For when Miller proclaimed himself an unbeliever, or derided various believers as men of shallow faith, he did so with a profane gusto which concealed a sacred rage." Obituary of Perry Miller, *Harvard University Gazette*, January 16, 1965, 108. As Murray Murphey writes, Miller could "appreciate their [the Puritans'] anguish without accepting their answers." Murphey, "Perry Miller and American Studies," *American Studies* 42, no. 2 (2001): 9.

18. Miller to Rosenthal, February 19, 1956, HUG 4572.9—Correspondence and Other Papers, ca. 1918–1963, box 1, PMP. The deal was arranged and carried out by McGeorge Bundy, the youngest dean of Arts and Sciences ever at Harvard and a man who would shortly become a national security adviser for President Kennedy. Bundy, who gladly accepted the money, told Rosenthal "that while many people feel they have a great book within them, few in the opinion of the authorities have it. However, he and his colleagues feel that Perry has it and therefore they are very happy that he will have the chance to write it." Rosenthal to Miller, May 3, 1956, HUG 4572.9—Correspondence and Other Papers, ca. 1918–1963, box 1, PMP.

19. Miller to Rosenthal, January 18, 1956, HUG 4572.9—Correspondence and Other Papers, ca. 1918–1963, box 1, PMP.

20. Lynn makes the link to Hemingway explicit. "With Hemingway's suicide [1961]," he writes, "Miller's determination to destroy himself entered its climactic phase." Lynn, "Perry Miller," 226–227. After Miller died on December 9, 1963, his brother explained that he had "slowed up considerably in the last two or three years, and very noticeably during the four or five months before 9 December." Charles T. Miller to Samuel Rosenthal, January 7, 1964, HUG 4572.9—Correspondence and Other Papers, ca. 1918–1963 (box 1), PMP.

21. George to Kenneth B. Murdock, December 16, 1963, HUG 4589.7: KBM, Correspondence and some other papers, c. 1932–1971, box 3, Kenneth B. Murdock Papers, Harvard University Archives, Cambridge, MA (hereafter cited as KBMP). "George" was evidently a close friend to both Perry Miller and Kenneth Murdock, but I have not been able to identify him beyond his first name. He wrote a detailed letter of the last three weeks of Miller's life. Ann Douglas recounted that Miller frequently taught "hung over and ill." Douglas, "The Mind of Perry Miller," *New Republic*, February 3, 1982, 26–27.

22. George to Murdock, December 16, 1963.

23. Curtis Prout to Perry Miller, November 3, 1961, HUG 4572.5—Correspondence, L–Z, box 2, PMP; George to Murdock, December 16, 1963; David Levin, "Perry Miller at Harvard," *Southern Review* 19, no. 4 (1983): 815. "Several empty quart bottles of liquor were reportedly found by the side of his corpse" (Douglas, "Mind of Perry Miller," 27). Kenneth Lynn

and Ann Douglas both saw his death as suicide. David Levin allowed for suicide as an explanation, voicing a common opinion that no one could really know the source of the self-destruction: "I cannot explain the mystery of self-destruction any more than the marvel of creativity" ("Perry Miller at Harvard," 815).

24. W. E. B. Du Bois, *The Souls of Black Folk*, ed. David Blight and Robert Gooding-Williams (New York: Bedford, 1997), 6. For an excellent account of how the Civil War was remembered and remade in ways that Du Bois found so dubious and damaging, see David Blight, *Race and Reunion: The Civil War in American Memory* (Cambridge, MA: Harvard University Press, 2001).

Chapter Sixteen. The American Jeremiad

1. John F. Kennedy, speech at the 1960 Democratic National Convention, July 15, 1960, accessed at the John F. Kennedy Presidential Library and Museum, https://www.jfklibrary.org/Asset-Viewer/AS08q50YzoS FUZg9uOi4iw.aspx.

2. John F. Kennedy, "MR65-221 Massachusetts General Court," January 9, 1961, accessed at the John F. Kennedy Presidential Library and Museum, https://www.jfklibrary.org/Asset-Viewer/ohJztSnpVo6qFJUT9etUZQ .aspx.

3. Richard Gamble, *In Search of the City on a Hill: The Making and Unmaking of an American Myth* (London: Continuum, 2012), 133–134; Daniel T. Rodgers, *As a City on a Hill: The Story of America's Most Famous Lay Sermon* (Princeton, NJ: Princeton University Press, 2018), 223–227.

4. Kennedy, "MR65-221 Massachusetts General Court."

5. Kennedy.

6. Lyndon B. Johnson, "Remarks in Boston at Post Office Square," October 27, 1964, accessed at the American Presidency Project, https://www.pres idency.ucsb.edu/documents/remarks-boston-post-office-square (emphasis added).

7. David Holland quoted in Jalin P. Cunningham, "Sacvan Bercovitch, Courageous Literary Scholar, Dies at 81," *Harvard Crimson*, January 13, 2015. "Certainly not every scholar agreed with those claims," Holland added, "but everyone has to deal with them." Mason Lowance Jr., "Sacvan Bercovitch and Jonathan Edwards," in "Sacvan Bercovitch and the American Puritan Imagination," special issue, *Studies in Puritan American Spirituality* 3 (1992): 54; Corydon Ireland, "Sacvan Bercovitch, 1933–2014: Renowned Scholar of Puritan America," *Harvard Gazette*, December 12, 2014.

8. Christopher Looby, "Scholar and Exegete: A Tribute to Sacvan Bercovitch, MLA Honored Scholar of Early American Literature, 2002," *Early American Literature* 39, no. 1 (2004): 4; Cunningham, "Sacvan Berco-

vitch." As Corydon Ireland reports, "From 1992 to 2008, as a form of re-payment to his own academic origins, he once said, Bercovitch taught at the Harvard Extension School" ("Sacvan Bercovitch").

9. "Religious Groups Criticize Trump Immigration Policies," *Weekend Edition Saturday*, National Public Radio, June 16, 2018, https://www.npr .org/2018/06/16/620611526/religious-groups-criticize-trump-immigra tion-policies. Bercovitch repeated his position in 2012, explaining that Americans always posit a "True America" and then set it "against the ac-tual (but inessential, correctible) evils of the Real America." Sacvan Berco-vitch, "2012 Preface," in *The American Jeremiad* (Madison: University of Wisconsin Press, 2012), xvi. As Gerald Graff has summarized, Bercovitch identified "the belief that, though the United States repeatedly betrays its founding ideals of justice and fairness, it is uniquely willing to measure its betrayals against those ideals and to try to change itself accordingly." Graff, "On *The American Jeremiad*," in "Short Reflections on Sacvan Bercovitch's *The American Jeremiad*," special issue, *Common-Place* 14, no. 4 (2014), http://www.common-place-archives.org/vol-14/no-04/ looby/#.WyQd5RJKjOQ. Graff adds that if something is wrong, it should simply be *wrong*: "its wrongness has nothing to do with whether it is un-American or not." For a more recent, good book that nuances and builds on Bercovitch's insights while analyzing various forms of the American jeremiad today, see Andrew R. Murphy, *Prodigal Nation: Moral Decline and Divine Punishment from New England to 9/11* (New York: Oxford Univer-sity Press, 2009).

10. "Elect Nation in New England" is the title of chapter 3 in Sacvan Berco-vitch, *The Puritan Origins of the American Self* (1975; repr., New Haven, CT: Yale University Press, 2011). Bercovitch, "2011 Preface," in *Puritan Origins*, xl. Bercovitch made this claim in multiple ways. "The New Eng-land Puritans gave America the status of visible sainthood," he announced early in his career. As a result, "The importance of their vision to subse-quent American thought can hardly be overestimated." Bercovitch, intro-duction to *The American Puritan Imagination: Essays in Revaluation*, ed. Bercovitch (New York: Cambridge University Press, 1974), 12. In his first major monograph, he explained, "The New England Puritans swept away that crucial distinction [between sacred and secular history]. In their 'spe-cial commission,' they proclaimed, redemptive merged with secular his-tory. With an arrogance that astounded their contemporaries, Protestants no less than others, they identified America as the new promised land, foretold in scripture, as preparatory to the Second Coming" ("2011 Pref-ace," xiii). In a review essay skeptical of Bercovitch's claims, Nina Baym summarizes, "The purpose of the argument is to compel us to recognize the relevance of the Puritans in a culture from which their values would seem to have disappeared." Baym, "Rev. of *The American Jeremiad* and *The Puritan Origins of the American Self*," *Nineteenth-Century Fiction* 34, no. 3

(1979): 348. As Jonathan Arac added years later, *Puritan Origins of the American Self* "culminated four decades of recovering Puritanism as the foundation of American literature." Arac, "The American Jeremiad after Thirty-Five Years," in "Short Reflections." See also Arac, "Fragments of Bercovitch's America," *RSA Journal: Rivista di Studi Americani* 19 (2008): 86–88.

11. Bercovitch, *American Jeremiad*, 20; Bercovitch, *Puritan Origins*, 139–143. For more on the relationship between Miller and Bercovitch, see Arne Delfs, "Anxieties of Influence: Perry Miller and Sacvan Bercovitch," *New England Quarterly* 70, no. 4 (1997): 601–615; David Harlan, "A People Blinded from Birth: American History According to Sacvan Bercovitch," *Journal of American History* 78, no. 3 (1991): 949–971; Daniel W. Howe, "Descendants of Perry Miller," *American Quarterly* 34, no. 1 (1982): 88–94; Donald Weber, "Historicizing the Errand," *American Literary History* 2, no. 1 (1990): 101–118; and Ormond Seavey, "Sacvan Bercovitch and Perry Miller: Parricide Regained," in "Sacvan Bercovitch and the American Puritan Imagination," 149–167.

12. Bercovitch, "2011 Preface," xliin2, 44; Bercovitch, *American Jeremiad*, 38 (for a reiteration of this supposedly fundamental difference, see 95); Bercovitch, "The Winthrop Variation: A Model of American Identity," *Proceedings of the British Academy* 97 (1998): 90.

13. Bercovitch, "2011 Preface," xxxviii. For a very good review essay criticizing this distinction and demonstrating how fast it falls apart when we recognize that the Puritans, not just the Pilgrims, subscribed themselves as loyal subjects of the king and always considered themselves English (not American), see Norman Pettit, "God's Englishman in New England: His Enduring Ties to the Motherland," *Proceedings of the Massachusetts Historical Society*, 3rd ser., 101 (1989): 56–70.

14. Bercovitch, introduction to *American Puritan Imagination*, 10; Bercovitch, *Puritan Origins*, 2; Bercovitch, "2011 Preface," xvi. As Bercovitch explained late in his career, "The particular advantage of studying 'America' for me was its transparently fictive quality and the relatively recent period of its creation. What fascinated me was the extraordinary prospect this offered for explaining the process of cultural formation" ("Winthrop Variation," 78).

15. Bercovitch, *American Jeremiad*, 11.

16. Sacvan Bercovitch, "Investigations of an Americanist," *Journal of American History* 78, no. 3 (1991): 972; Bercovitch, "Discovering America: A Cross-Cultural Perspective," in *The Translatability of Cultures: Figurations of the Space Between*, ed. Sanford Budick and Wolfgang Iser (Stanford, CA: Stanford University Press, 1996), 150; Bercovitch, "Discovering America," 147. Bercovitch called the rhetoric of America—descending from Puritan New England—"the America-trap" and the "America cage." Because of his autobiography, Bercovitch presented himself as specially

able to see the bars for what they were—even if he did not necessarily know how Americans could escape. Bercovitch, "2012 Preface," xxiii. A year earlier, Bercovitch contrasted himself with Karl Marx, Albert Bierstadt, Alexis de Tocqueville, and Philip Schaff as foreigners who fell for the American myth in various ways. "Evidently these sophisticated foreigners had also come under the enchantments of the rhetoric," Bercovitch asserted. "And their enchanted 'observations' had in turn cast their spell on American historians and critics" ("2011 Preface," xx). What Bercovitch implicitly offered in contrast were unenthralled, disenchanted, more *scientific* observations of American rhetoric. Moreover, by using Weber's metaphor of a "cage," he could show his updated account: the "cage" was not capitalism, per se, but the rhetoric that supported free enterprise and dressed it up as a mission from God. For the best piece on the critical role of autobiography in the work of Bercovitch, see Arne Delfs, "Sacvan Bercovitch and the Revision of American Studies," *European Contributions to American Studies* 40 (1998): 258–267. For the fullest intellectual biography of Bercovitch, see Susanne Klingenstein, *Enlarging America: The Cultural Work of Jewish Literary Scholars, 1930–1990* (Syracuse, NY: Syracuse University Press, 1998), chap. 11. See also Rael Meyerowitz, *Transferring to America: Jewish Interpretations of American Dreams* (Albany: State University of New York Press, 1995), chap. 5.

17. Bercovitch, "Winthrop Variation," 77.
18. Sacvan Bercovitch, "Puritan Origins Revisited: The 'City on a Hill' as a Model of Tradition and Innovation," in *Early America Re-explored: New Readings in Colonial, Early National, and Antebellum Culture*, ed. Klaus Schmidt and Fritz Fleischmann (New York: Peter Lang, 2000), 31; Bercovitch, "Winthrop Variation," 75, 82.
19. Bercovitch, "Puritan Origins Revisited," 31; Bercovitch, "Winthrop Variation," 76, 79; Bercovitch, "Puritan Origins Revisited," 32.
20. Bercovitch admitted at one point, early in his career, "All this they announced in imagery which, we have seen, was thoroughly traditional" (introduction to *American Puritan Imagination*, 11). It *was* thoroughly traditional, more so than he realized. For important criticisms of Bercovitch (in addition to previous cited sources), see Pascal Covici Jr., "God's Chosen People: Anglican Views, 1607–1807," *Studies in Puritan American Spirituality* 1 (1990): 97–128; Giles Gunn, "Beyond Transcendence or Beyond Ideology: The New Problematics of Cultural Criticism in America," *American Literary History* 2, no. 1 (1990): 1–18; Philip Gura, "What Hath Bercovitch Wrought?," *Reviews in American History* 21, no. 4 (1993): 562–568; and Russell Reising, *The Unusable Past: Theory and the Study of American Literature* (New York: Methuen, 1986). See also "Symposium on *The Puritan Origins of the American Self*," *Early American Literature* 47, no. 2 (2012): 377–442.

21. As the historian Michael Winship has pointed out, one "overstretched ellipsis" even drops *sixty pages* between the beginning of the quote and its end. See Winship, "What Puritan Guarantee?," in "Symposium on *The Puritan Origins of the American Self*," 411–420. For the earliest and harshest criticism of how Bercovitch handled Puritan sources, see David Hirsch, "Hermeneutics as Free-Floating Fantasy: Rev. of *The Puritan Origins of the American Self* and *The American Puritan Imagination*," *Sewanee Review* 85, no. 3 (1977): lxxii–lxxix. Hirsh's position was unusual in 1977, but it became more common two decades later.

22. Bercovitch, *American Jeremiad*, 3, 7–8; Bercovitch, "Rhetoric as Authority: Puritanism, the Bible, and the Myth of America," *Social Science Information* 21, no. 1 (1982): 8; Bercovitch, *The Rites of Assent: Transformations in the Symbolic Construction of America* (New York: Routledge, 1993), 74. Bercovitch's essay on Winthrop's sermon was first printed in 1998 as "The Winthrop Variation" and then slightly revised and reprinted as "Puritan Origins Revisited" (1998) and "Rhetoric as Cultural Work: The Example of John Winthrop's 'A Model of Christian Charity,'" in *Making America: The Cultural Work of Literature*, ed. Susanne Rohr, Peter Schneck, and Sabine Sielke (Heidelberg: Universitatsverlag C. Winter Heidelberg, 2000), 15–32.

23. Bercovitch, "Winthrop Variation," 78.

24. Bercovitch, 86–87. "I think it can be said without hyperbole," he added, "that the process of consecration began with the two prototypic American jeremiads of 1630" (Bercovitch, *American Jeremiad*, 20). The other "jeremiad" that Bercovitch emphasized was John Cotton's *Gods Promises to His Plantations*. In his old age, Bercovitch saw little to change. Admitting that plenty of other colonists and settlers came with capitalistic aspirations, he nonetheless distinguished the venture in New England. In New England, he said, "the Puritans gave a special supernatural legitimacy to the Protestant work ethic in the New World." The American Jeremiad they generated "sanctified the capitalist way of life that developed in the United States as the American Dream" ("2012 Preface," xiii–xiv). As Daniel Walker Howe summarized, "Bercovitch identifies Puritanism with emergent capitalism—indeed, he does so even more closely than Max Weber ever did." Howe, "Descendants of Perry Miller," *American Quarterly* 34, no. 1 (1982): 91. Again, the great Nina Baym offers a deft summary: Bercovitch, she explains, "returns to the same documents that Miller used and, attempting to counter Miller's estrangement, produces precisely that reading of the Puritans against which Miller argues, turning them into the comfort-loving capitalists of the First Thanksgiving"; Bercovitch makes Puritans into the "Founding Fathers of the free enterprise nation in which we now pretend that we live" ("Rev. of *American Jeremiad* and *Puritan Origin*," 349–50).

25. Bercovitch, "Rhetoric as Authority," 16.

Chapter Seventeen. American Exceptionalism and America First

1. Ronald Reagan, "Remarks at a Reagan-Bush Rally in Boston, Massachusetts," November 1, 1984, accessed at the American Presidency Project, https://www.presidency.ucsb.edu/documents/remarks-reagan-bush-rally-boston-massachusetts. As Richard Gamble has pointed out, Reagan's first invocation of Winthrop's sermon stayed fairly close to Winthrop's text. Reagan included the warning of possible failure and judgment, and he did not describe Winthrop's city as "shining." Over time, Winthrop's warning of possible failure would gradually disappear. See Gamble, *In Search of the City on a Hill: The Making and Unmaking of an American Myth* (London: Continuum, 2012), 144–145.

2. Ronald Reagan, "We Will Be a City upon a Hill," January 25, 1974, accessed at the Patriot Post, http://reagan2020.us/speeches/city_upon_a_hill.asp.

3. Ronald Reagan, "Message to the Nation on the Observance of Independence Day," July 3, 1983, accessed at the American Presidency Project, https://www.presidency.ucsb.edu/documents/message-the-nation-the-observance-independence-day; Reagan, "Remarks at the Annual Convention of the National Religious Broadcasters," February 9, 1982, accessed at the American Presidency Project, https://www.presidency.ucsb.edu/documents/remarks-the-annual-convention-the-national-religious-broadcasters-5.

4. Gamble, *In Search of the City on a Hill*, 148.

5. Reagan, "We Will Be a City upon a Hill."

6. Ronald Reagan, "Remarks at a Dinner Marking the 10th Anniversary of the Heritage Foundation," October 8, 1983, accessed at the American Presidency Project, https://www.presidency.ucsb.edu/documents/remarks-dinner-marking-the-loth-anniversary-the-heritage-foundation; Reagan, "Farewell Address to the Nation," January 11, 1989, accessed at the American Presidency Project, https://www.presidency.ucsb.edu/documents/farewell-address-the-nation; Reagan, "We Will Be a City upon a Hill." As Richard Gamble has explained, the sermon embodied three themes for Reagan: "economic growth and opportunity; democratic revolution and world peace; and America's global and eternal mission" (*In Search of the City on a Hill*, 151). All three themes supported one another in Reagan's rhetoric.

7. Mario Cuomo, "1984 Democratic National Convention Keynote Address," July 16, 1984, accessed online at American Rhetoric: Top 100 Speeches, http://www.americanrhetoric.com/speeches/mariocuomo1984dnc.htm.

8. Michael Dukakis, "Address Accepting the Presidential Nomination at the Democratic National Convention in Atlanta," July 21, 1988, accessed on-

line at the American Presidency Project, http://www.presidency.ucsb.edu/ ws/index.php?pid=25961&st=delight+in+each+other&st1. The ellipsis is from the original speech.

9. "Republican Party Platform of 1988," August 16, 1988, accessed at the American Presidency Project, http://www.presidency.ucsb.edu/ws/index .php?pid=25846.

10. "2012 Republican Party Platform," August 27, 2012, accessed at the American Presidency Project, http://www.presidency.ucsb.edu/ws/?pid=101961.

11. William J. Clinton, "Remarks to the Democratic Leadership Council," October 27, 1997, accessed at the American Presidency Project, https:// www.presidency.ucsb.edu/documents/remarks-the-democratic-leader ship-council-0. That sense of prophetic community has proven effective rhetoric in many different circumstances. When two bombs went off at the 2013 Boston Marathon, for example, Senator Elizabeth Warren responded by turning once more to Winthrop's sermon. And once more, his text appeared as her closing exhortation. "In times of calamity, in times like these," she declared, "we remember the words of John Winthrop, who counseled the founders of Boston 'to do justly, to love mercy, to walk humbly with our God. For this end, we must be knit together, in this work, as one man. . . . We must delight in each other; make others' conditions our own; rejoice together, mourn together, labor and suffer together. . . . So shall we keep the unity of the spirit in the bond of peace.'" Sabrina Siddiqui, "Elizabeth Warren Speech on Boston Marathon Bombings: 'We Will Not Be Broken,'" *HuffPost*, April 17, 2013, https://www .huffingtonpost.com/2013/04/17/elizabeth-warren-speech_n_3102775 .html. This includes the full transcript of Warren's speech.

12. Barack Obama, "Proclamation 8974—National Day of Prayer, 2013," May 1, 2013, accessed at the American Presidency Project, https://www .presidency.ucsb.edu/documents/proclamation-8974-national-day -prayer-2013 (italics added).

13. Barack Obama, "University of Massachusetts at Boston Commencement Address," June 2, 2006, accessed at Obama Speeches, http://obamaspeeches .com/074-University-of-Massachusetts-at-Boston-Commencement -Address-Obama-Speech.htm.

14. "Text of Sen. Barack Obama's 'A More Perfect Union' Speech,'" *Los Angeles Times*, March 8, 2008, http://www.latimes.com/nation/la-na-cam paign19mar19-speech-story.html.

15. For an excellent, early account of Obama's American exceptionalism and its difference from Reagan's, see Philip Gorski and William McMillan, "Barack Obama and American Exceptionalisms," *Review of Faith and International Affairs* 10, no. 2 (2012): 41–50. Obama's rhetoric often deployed what Andrew R. Murphy called "the progressive jeremiad." See Murphy, *Prodigal Nation: Moral Decline and Divine Punishment from New England to 9/11* (New York: Oxford University Press, 2009), 114–118. See

also Peter Manseau, "The Past Imperfect of Barack Obama," *Religion and Politics*, April 14, 2015, http://religionandpolitics.org/2015/04/14/the -past-imperfect-of-barack-obama/.

16. For Dionne's good, brief reading of Winthrop's sermon, see E. J. Dionne Jr., *Our Divided Political Heart: The Battle for the American Idea in an Age of Discontent* (New York: Bloomsbury, 2012), 77–78. For Hillary Clinton, see Daniel White, "Read Hillary Clinton's Speech Touting 'American Exceptionalism,'" *Time*, September 1, 2016, http://time.com/4474619/read -hillary-clinton-american-legion-speech/.

17. For introductions to where Puritan studies stand today, see Bryce Traister, "Introduction: The New Puritan Studies," in *American Literature and the New Puritan Studies*, ed. Bryce Traister (New York: Cambridge University Press, 2017), 1–20; and Sarah Rivett and Abram Van Engen, "Postexceptionalist Puritanism," *American Literature* 90, no. 4 (2018): 675–692, which this paragraph summarizes.

18. See, for example, Philip Gorski, *American Covenant: A History of Civil Religion from the Puritans to the Present* (Princeton, NJ: Princeton University Press, 2017). Gorski begins his account of American civil religion with what he calls "America's first founding: the establishment of Puritan New England." There is certainly some rationale for Gorski's position: since scholars of civil religion study collective memory more than actual history, he begins with the *imagined* origin of America. His account, however, then explains the *historical* influence of Puritanism on all American society through the flawed paradigms of Perry Miller and Sacvan Bercovitch. See especially chap. 2. This is the same underlying problem with George McKenna, *The Puritan Origins of American Patriotism* (New Haven, CT: Yale University Press, 2007). McKenna offers some great readings of how the Puritans were rediscovered and remade throughout American history, but he nonetheless insists, through Bercovitch, that it all originally came from the Puritans themselves. "It may be an exaggeration to characterize the Puritans as America's original founders," McKenna writes, "but it would not be out of place to call them the founders of America's political culture and rhetoric" (4).

19. Kurt Andersen, *Fantasyland: How America Went Haywire: A 500-Year History* (New York: Random House, 2017). Anderson offers an even more hyperbolic version of Bercovitch's misreading of the Puritans. Incredibly, he *invents* a line and *adds it to Winthrop's sermon* to prove his point. Andersen tells us precisely that "three sentences" after Winthrop's "city on a hill line," his "end-is-near scenario isn't metaphorical at all. 'As the latter days begin to unfold,' Winthrop said, 'this may indeed be the city, the new Jerusalem that's unfolding'" (30). This line is itself a fantasy, a hoax of Andersen's own. Perhaps he meant to paraphrase Winthrop's sermon; but still it is a misreading of the text, and it certainly should not be put in quotation marks as though Winthrop actually said it. Even in a book

without footnotes aimed at a general readership, the invention of evidence and the creation of quotations out of thin air is highly questionable. Yet it is in keeping with a tradition of inventing facts to support the significance of Winthrop's sermon.

20. Jesse Byrnes, "Trump in 2015 on American Exceptionalism: 'I Never Liked the Term,'" *The Hill*, June 7, 2016, http://thehill.com/blogs/blog-briefing-room/news/282449-trump-on-american-exceptionalism-i-never-liked-the-term. It is important to remember that Trump did not invent the language of America First. That rhetoric has its own long history. See Sarah Churchwell, *Behold, America: The Entangled History of "America First" and "The American Dream"* (New York: Basic, 2018).

21. Reagan, "Farewell Address"; W. Clinton, "Remarks to the Democratic Leadership Council."

22. To demonstrate just how vague this sense of American history was, researchers went out and asked people to identify when America was great. Their answers varied, but most, regardless of age, identified a period when they were young. See Robbie Taylor, Cassandra Burton-Wood, and Maryanne Garry, "America Was Great When Nationally Relevant Events Occurred and When Americans Were Young," *Journal of Applied Research in Memory and Cognition* 6, no. 4 (2017): 425–433.

23. John O'Sullivan, "The Great Nation of Futurity," *United States Democratic Review* 6 (1839): 430.

24. Donald Trump, "Inaugural Address," January 20, 2017, accessed at https://www.whitehouse.gov/briefings-statements/the-inaugural-address/.

25. Donald Trump, "Transcript: Donald Trump's Foreign Policy Speech," *New York Times*, April 27, 2016, https://www.nytimes.com/2016/04/28/us/politics/transcript-trump-foreign-policy.html?mcubz=0&_r=0; George W. Bush, "Inaugural Address," January 20, 2005, accessed at the American Presidency Project, https://www.presidency.ucsb.edu/documents/inaugural-address-13; Byrnes, "Trump in 2015 on American Exceptionalism."

26. Donald Trump, "Remarks by President Trump to the 72nd Session of the United Nations General Assembly," September 19, 2017, accessed at https://www.whitehouse.gov/briefings-statements/remarks-president-trump-72nd-session-united-nations-general-assembly/; Trump, "Remarks by President Trump at APEC CEO Summit," November 10, 2017, accessed at https://www.whitehouse.gov/briefings-statements/remarks-president-trump-apec-ceo-summit-da-nang-vietnam/.

27. On the graph provided here, "Model" tracks how often an article uses the phrase primarily to argue that America *models* something as a "city on a hill." "Historical" tracks how often an article primarily makes some historical analysis of "city on a hill." "Critique" tracks how often the notion of America as a "city on a hill" is criticized. Our data fail to include a month of results from the campaign; it should be considered representative, not

comprehensive. Obviously, our categorizations require judgment calls, but however one parses the data, reading through 1100 articles makes it clear that "city on a hill" surfaced most often in opposition to Donald Trump on both the right and the left. To see the data and further graphs, visit The City on a Hill Archive: https://doi.org/10.7936/cityonahill.

Coda

1. The speeches and transcript can be found at "Ronald Reagan Funeral Service," C-SPAN, accessed May 21, 2019, https://www.c-span.org/video/?182165-1/ronald-reagan-funeral-service.

2. As Ann Uhry Abrams explains in her wonderful book on these rival paintings, both Chapman and Weir "embellished the Massachusetts and Virginia origin myths with suggestions that God willed the transportation of Protestantism to America." But in the case of Gadsby Chapman's *Baptism of Pocahontas*, a reporter for Washington's *Daily National Intelligencer* remarked that the "subject appears . . . to have been an unfortunate one for an historical painting, being more local and individual than national." Pocahontas was nothing but a *regional* tale; for this writer at least, only the Pilgrims were truly *national*. Abrams writes, "This was a revealing commentary on the differing degrees of acceptance accorded the Virginia and Massachusetts legends, for no such observations would be made about R.W. Weir's *Embarkation of the Pilgrims* when it was placed in the same hall four years later." Ann Uhry Abrams, *The Pilgrims and Pocahontas: Rival Myths of American Origins* (Boulder: Westview, 1999), 122 (quoting the *Daily National Intelligencer*). For Weir's painting, see Architect of the Capitol, "Embarkation of the Pilgrims," accessed May 30, 2019, https://www.aoc.gov/art/historic-rotunda-paintings/embarkation-pilgrims.

3. The rest of the artwork of the Capitol building begins to make up for these absences. For the art of the Capitol, see Architect of the Capitol, "Art," accessed May 30, 2019, https://www.aoc.gov/art.

Acknowledgments

THIS BOOK WOULD HAVE been impossible to write—and impossible to read—without the help of so many fellow readers and writers who took the time to make it better. First, I want to thank Washington University in St. Louis, where I have been consistently supported by the dean of Arts and Sciences (Barbara Schaal), the Center for the Humanities (led by Jean Allman), the John C. Danforth Center on Religion and Politics (directed by Marie Griffith), and especially by my excellent colleagues in the English department (chaired by Wolfram Schmidgen and Vince Sherry during the writing of this book). Others have also collaborated and enhanced this work, and I'm grateful to Jim Wertsch and Roddy Roediger, along with Jeremy Yamashiro and Andy Butler, for including me in a new group studying collective memory. Early in my time at Washington University in St. Louis, Joe Loewenstein introduced me to the Humanities Digital Workshop. Since then, I have spent many fun summers testing and expanding my ideas with the HDW, leading to an online archive and several related projects building out the story of John Winthrop's 1630 "city on a hill" sermon. I am deeply indebted to Joe, as well as to Douglas Knox and Stephen Pentecost of the HDW, and I want to thank all the students and staff through all the years who have worked on this project: Jacqueline Baik, Katie Collins, Karly Kessler, Katerina Klafka, John Ladd, Jonathan McGregor, Emily Murphy, Jennifer Padgett, Michael Schaefer,

Maya Schaer, and Tumaini Ussiri. I am also grateful to have been surrounded by excellent students and graduate students at Washington University in St. Louis. Thanks in particular go to Tim DeCelle, Kenyon Gradert, Paulo Loonin, and Hannah Wakefield.

Beyond my university, I want to thank the organizations and institutions that enabled this book to come about. I received a Faculty Fellowship from the National Endowment for the Humanities when I began this project and an NEH Public Scholars Award to finish it. I am enormously grateful to the NEH and all that it makes possible. The views, findings, conclusions, or recommendations expressed in this book do not necessarily represent those of the National Endowment for the Humanities. Other support for this book came from the Massachusetts Historical Society with a Benjamin F. Stevens Fellowship. The MHS was a marvelous place to work, thanks especially to Conrad Wright, Kate Viens, Anna Clusterbuck-Cook, and Dan Hinchen. My many weeks in Boston were made all the better by having found the best hosts in the world, Bob and Denise Meyer, who took me into their home and treated me with such kindness and care. This book involved travel to several archives. Thank you to Jamie Hicks-Furgang and Nancy Iannucci at the Emma Willard School (and to the wonderful Wendy Roberts for hosting); Marcella Flaherty and Rebecca Y. Martin at the Monroe C. Gutman Library; Tim Driscoll at Harvard University Archives; and Edward O'Reilly at the New-York Historical Society. In New York, I was most generously and delightfully hosted by Peter Thoresen.

Along the way, fellow readers and scholars have reshaped every single chapter of this book. I'd like to thank the participants at numerous conferences and colloquia, such as the John C. Danforth Center on Religion and Politics seminar series, the Missouri Regional Seminar of the Kinder Institute on Constitutional Democracy, the Colloquium on Religion and History at Notre Dame, the Rare Book School Symposium at the University of Arkansas, and the Society of Early Americanists. Thanks as well to those, like Jonathan Beecher Field, who have been so encouraging and supportive, in part by sending me a constant diet of "city on a hill" sightings. I'm grateful to the many folks who read various chapters of the manuscript or the whole of it: Francis Bremer, Jonathan Den Hartog, Michael Ditmore, Darren Dochuk, David Hall, David Holland,

Robert Milder, Mark Noll, Tom Scanlan, Leigh Schmidt, Scott Manning Stevens, and Gene Zubovich. Jennifer Banks has been a remarkable editor, carefully guiding this project into something much more enjoyable to read. Beyond these individuals, I am especially grateful to a set of friends who never fail to inspire and refresh me and who, in their great generosity, read and offered expert advice on the whole of this book: Greg Downs, Erik Gellman, Guy Ortolano, Gayle Rogers, and David Sellers Smith—thank you. Finally, I want to thank my two long-standing writing groups: the Early American Writing Group, consisting of Angie Calcaterra, Travis Foster, Greta LaFleur, Michele Navakas, Wendy Roberts, Kacy Tillman, and Caroline Wigginton; and the American Religions Writing Group of Anna F. Bialek, John Inazu, Laurie Maffly-Kipp, Katherine D. Moran, and Mark Valeri. These good people and extraordinary scholars suffered through the earliest drafts of everything I wrote and have read almost every word that has come to pass. No book is the creation of a single mind, and my own bears the imprint of too many minds and too much help to mention and thank in full.

During the course of finishing, Daniel T. Rodgers and I discovered that we were both completing books on similar topics. I want to thank him for his generosity and collegiality in the process, which enabled a lively engagement of ideas to develop into different stories about a single sermon and its rise to prominence in American culture.

Much of the work of my book has appeared previously in published form, and I want to acknowledge all those sources for letting me revise and reprint it here. Chapters 1 and 2, in an earlier version, appeared in the *New England Quarterly* as "Origins and Last Farewells: Bible Wars, Textual Form, and the Making of American History," vol. 86, no. 4 (2013): 543–592. Chapter 3 appeared in earlier form as "Claiming the High Ground: Puritans, Catholics, and the City on a Hill," in *American Literature and the New Puritan Studies* (New York: Cambridge University Press, 2017). I want to thank Bryce Traister for his excellent editorial work and feedback. Sections from part 2 have appeared in different form as "The Religious Pursuit of History: Jeremy Belknap and the Making of American Historical Societies," *Massachusetts Historical Review* 21 (2019). And finally, an earlier version of chapter 17 was published at *Religion and*

Politics, January 9, 2018, https://religionandpolitics.org/2018/01/09/american-exceptionalism-and-america-first/. Thank you to Tiffany Stanley for her editorial advice and suggestions.

Lastly, I want to thank those who supported this book by not reading it—my friends, who have sustained and endured me, taking care of me and my family and making life so much richer and fuller, even willing to listen as I talked endlessly into the night about the life of Perry Miller (here's looking at you, Jonathan Peelle). My family has also, as always, been wonderful: Hans and Pam, Stefan and Sharon, and Lucas; my mother, Suzanne; my father, John, and Kathryn; and my in-laws Barb and Bruce, Mara, Mark, Alyssa, and Jason. Thank you. This book is dedicated to my children, Simon, Grace, and Hendrik. Without you, the work of my hands would be a lifeless art. Above all, I want to thank Kristin, my best friend, closest companion, spouse, partner, and source of so much joy.

Index

Figures, notes, and tables are indicated by *f*, n, and *t* following the page number.